A Versatile
American Institution

A VERSATILE AMERICAN INSTITUTION

The Changing Ideals and Realities
of Philanthropic Foundations

DAVID C. HAMMACK
HELMUT K. ANHEIER

BROOKINGS INSTITUTION PRESS
Washington, D.C.

Copyright © 2013
THE BROOKINGS INSTITUTION
1775 Massachusetts Avenue, N.W., Washington, D.C. 20036
www.brookings.edu

Library of Congress Cataloging-in-Publication data

Hammack, David C.
    A versatile American institution : the changing ideals and realities of philanthropic foundations / David C. Hammack and Helmut K. Anheier.
        pages   cm
    Includes bibliographical references and index.
    ISBN 978-0-8157-2194-9 (pbk. : alk. paper)
    1. Endowments—United States—History. I. Anheier, Helmut K., 1954– II. Title.
    HV97.A3H36 2013
    361.7'6320973—dc23   2012042363

9 8 7 6 5 4 3 2 1

Printed on acid-free paper

Typeset in Adobe Garamond

Composition by Cynthia Stock
Silver Spring, Maryland

Printed by R. R. Donnelley
Harrisonburg, Virginia

Contents

Preface

Contentious debates about foundations continue in the United States and elsewhere. Americans argue about what foundations can do and how they should be regulated and taxed. Europeans express differing views about the possible uses of foundations to advance civil society and to encourage more flexible responses to public problems, opinions that resonate in regions as different as Australia, Latin America, or Japan. In Russia, parts of Asia, and throughout much of the Middle East, foundations are seen by some as a sign that a modernizing society is "coming of age," but are viewed by others as politically controlled islands of privilege. These debates are distinct, of course, yet they are also closely related, as they focus on a common ideal: a notion of the American foundation. Indeed, some leading American foundations promote the view that foundations can do much for civil society and the public good in any part of the world. European, Australian, and Japanese commentators refer to American foundations as they advance varying views about the current relevance of their own foundations.

With this book we hope to contribute to both American and international debates by examining what American foundations have actually accomplished and by considering what they might be able to do in the coming decades. The book is a double experiment. We have sought to combine the perspectives of an historian and a social scientist to identify facts and realities in ways that will be widely useful to policy debate. Facts and realities are always contested, but we think we have developed a fair and comprehensive account.

American and international discussions of foundations can be highly charged. Sharply focused advocates of effectiveness and of equality have energized the American debate in recent years as they compete for influence in legislatures, courts, board rooms, and in the minds of donors. Not infrequently they also engage with polemicists committed to other aims as well as with foundation defenders and apologists. The sometimes quieter European debate, often focused on the proposed European Foundation Statute, is taking place as Europeans confront continuing financial and political challenges to redefine their ideas about "state," "nation," and "private initiative." By contrast, the politically charged role of foundations in the Middle East or Russia reflects unsettled and divisive notions about what their place should be, in what kind of society. We seek to introduce a sense of proportion and reality into these debates. We also hope to show how history can add valuable dimensions to the policy discussions, and also how concern about an important current issue can lead historians to reconsider their understandings about the past.

This is one of several volumes commissioned by the Aspen Institute's Program on the Nonprofit Sector and Philanthropy. Our first book in the series, *American Foundations: Roles and Contributions,* an edited collection, brings together eighteen essays by twenty-six leading specialists on foundations in specific fields.[1] In this second volume, we offer a concise and synthetic historical discussion of what American foundations have done, as well as a distinctive assessment of the ways changing American contexts have changed foundations.

In *A Versatile American Institution* we consider foundations in a new way. Unlike previous general accounts we do not focus narrowly on foundations, their donors and their leaders, asking what they have intended to do, or whether we approve. Instead, to echo Waldemar Nielsen, we ask what sort of "strange or improbable creature" the foundation might be and how it fits into the "great jungle of American democracy and capitalism." We consider foundations as institutions in the contexts of their times and in the contexts of their communities. We focus on foundations as participants in the fields they address and we acknowledge from the outset that they may often be minor participants.

Society and policymakers will continually ask what foundations are good for and how we should regulate them. This book accordingly seeks to determine what foundations can actually do and what they have actually done with their independently controlled wealth. We propose that careful attention to historical context and to the many recent studies of foundation effectiveness can help us understand what foundations can contribute and to think realistically about how we can best evaluate them.

This volume differs from most accounts—and from most historical studies of the subject—by considering the full range of foundations. We have adopted this approach because the broad basic legal definition used by the Internal Revenue

Service necessarily shapes American policy debates. As the IRS puts it, a foundation has "a single major source of funding (usually gifts from one family or corporation rather than funding from many sources)" and engages primarily in "the making of grants to other charitable organizations and to individuals, rather than the direct operation of charitable programs." The IRS adds the general summary of U.S. law that charitable tax-exempt organizations pursue purposes that are "charitable, religious, educational, scientific, literary, testing for public safety, fostering national or international amateur sports competition, and preventing cruelty to children or animals." It goes on to state that "the term *charitable* is used in its generally accepted legal sense and includes relief of the poor, the distressed, or the underprivileged; advancement of religion; advancement of education or science; erecting or maintaining public buildings, monuments, or works; lessening the burdens of government; lessening neighborhood tensions; eliminating prejudice and discrimination; defending human and civil rights secured by law; and combating community deterioration and juvenile delinquency."[2] Elsewhere, the IRS makes clear that a foundation is an autonomous, nongovernmental organization controlled by its own board.

Because we start with this very broad legal definition, we avoid the usual undue focus on only the very largest, national, general-purpose foundations that date from the last decades of the nineteenth century and the first decades of the twentieth—a small group of foundations associated with such names as Peabody, Carnegie, Rockefeller, Rosenwald, Guggenheim, Ford, and Gates. We do not ignore these very large foundations; they have been most fully studied and their size and enterprise deserve attention. But they are not typical of the entire field. The work of many other foundations is poorly documented: we have looked hard for evidence about them and found a good deal of neglected material, but we are aware that in many cases we can only raise questions and suggest further study. Within the limits of available knowledge and of our resources we make a concerted effort to take a comprehensive view, to consider foundations of all kinds and foundations that pursue any of the purposes subsumed under the IRS definition.

Our concern with the American foundation as an institution—rather than as an instrument to serve ends that we approve—leads us to propose new ways to think about foundation history and about the foundation field today. Because we are concerned with the development of the American foundation as an institution, we pay much less attention to the personalities and intentions of donors that many other studies address. Our focus, instead, is on the rules and norms that govern private philanthropic foundations, on their practices, on their relations with other institutions, and on the increasingly independent institutional life they achieve once the role of founders and leaders fades.

In chapter one, we explore the characteristics and contexts of America's foundations, consider relevant definitions, and identify the actions and roles that foundations might conceivably play. We would emphasize that foundation grants amount to just a small fraction of all charitable giving. Yet foundations can give more than money—they also can contribute information and ideas, promote cooperation and collaboration, and seek to bestow legitimacy, honor, and prestige. But while such actions can advance an agenda, by themselves they cannot put any agenda into effect.

An introductory chapter that explores what an institution might or could possibly do is far from the usual way to begin a historical study. But such a start is essential both to our engagement with current debates about policy and to our approach to the historical development of the foundation. Because we take account of the law, we include foundations committed to religious purposes and to particular educational, social welfare, and arts purposes, as well as the more familiar secular, national, general-purpose foundations.

Focusing on foundations as separate from their contexts, several influential recent works have emphasized remarkable continuities. What stands out is that America's foundations have not changed greatly in what they can do, but that they have evolved to operate in varying and changing contexts—contexts that vary widely from field to field and from place to place; contexts that have changed sharply from each of four quite distinct periods to the next. As we show in this book, the periods can be described as the largely sectarian, particular-purpose era of the nineteenth century; the classic, institution-building era of the first half of the twentieth century; the postwar period of struggle for strategy and relevance that lasted into the 1990s; and if we are correct, a new period characterized by acceptance of variety and focus on results.

Hence in chapter two we emphasize that the history of the foundation as an American institution begins with the American Revolution. In contrast to the casual statements generally taken for "history," we note the rarity of endowed institutions of any sort in the American colonies and emphasize their rapid multiplication after the adoption of the Constitution. Foundations first appeared after the American Revolution, as a result, we think, of two of the Constitution's most fundamental qualities—emphasis on the rights of private property and on First Amendment freedoms of belief and action.

Foundations grew quite numerous over the course of the nineteenth century, long before the Peabody Fund or the writings and gifts of Andrew Carnegie and John D. Rockefeller. With their relatively modest resources, close engagement with an extraordinary variety of religious and cultural causes, and frequent engagement with local economic development, nineteenth-century foundations bore a surprising resemblance to the great majority of America's foundations today, whose assets, like those of their predecessors, are modest in relation to their stated aims.

Recognition of the variety of foundation purposes and of the persistence of smaller religious, local, and family foundations is one of the benefits of our approach to foundation history. The big foundations rightly attract a great deal of attention: since at least the 1920s, they have held by far the largest share of all foundation assets. But large, general-purpose foundations never replaced their much more numerous small siblings. The smaller funds have quite a continuous history from the early 1800s to the present day. Proposals to change the regulation of American foundations often reflect notions about small foundations: inevitably, such proposals also evoke responses from those concerned to defend them. From our perspective, policy discussions should include explicit consideration of these realities.

For more than a hundred years, American courts, regulators, and legislators have steadily agreed that foundations, including nonsectarian, general-purpose foundations, have a right to independent existence and indeed to favorable tax treatment, so long as they are not employed to increase the personal wealth of donors and their families, and so long as they avoid party politics and devote their resources to the very wide range of "charitable purposes" previously described. The core rationale is that so long as they accept these broad limits, foundations contribute valuably to American freedoms and American pluralism.

The acceptable range of charitable purposes has changed over time, reflecting the fortunes and misfortunes of American history, but it has followed a general trajectory. Like other charities, foundations encountered significant legal limits under slavery, during the Jim Crow era of racial segregation, and to some extent in times of war, including the cold war. Charities devoted to Catholic, Jewish, and other minority religious and cultural traditions long struggled against prejudice in public opinion as well as discrimination in law and legislation. But American charities have always enjoyed wide possibilities, possibilities that have expanded over the decades, even as federal regulation has largely supplanted control by the individual states. In the United States, foundations like other charities justify their existence, and their privileges—and indeed, establish their legitimacy—not so much by reducing poverty or by relieving taxpayers of the expense of public facilities and services, as by enriching and strengthening America's varieties of religious, cultural, educational, scientific, and policy analysis, and by increasing the possibilities for innovation. In our third chapter we turn to the few large, national, nonsectarian, general-purpose foundations that we certainly agree accomplished remarkable things in the decades that followed the end of the nineteenth century. We would add, however, that these foundations had more in common with a wider range of nineteenth-century funds than has been recognized. We observe that the general-purpose funds, from Russell Sage and the Rockefeller Foundation on, always faced limits to their ambitions, focused on a limited range of fields, and often encountered effective opposition.

Much writing about American foundations, whether intended to blame or praise, emphasizes the large national funds and takes for granted that they enjoy exceptional wealth and power. The historical record, we argue, does indicate that a few of the very large foundations did for a time enjoy great influence in some fields. But the historical record also shows that the influence of even the richest foundations was always limited and that it declined quite sharply by the 1940s. Even the biggest American foundations—similar to other social institutions— have always had to deal with their larger economic, political, and institutional environments. On reflection, it seems clear to us that the first twentieth-century foundation era started with the new century and ended in the 1940s, with the rise in general prosperity and the expansion of government ushered in by the New Deal and World War II.

We devote our fourth chapter to the struggle of foundations to retain their footing in the turbulent period that began in the 1940s, characterized by the cold war, the civil rights movement, and rising prosperity. In our view, this period continued into the 1980s. Drawing on the many excellent new studies of particular fields as well as on our own research, we show how foundations struggled in these years to live up to the reputations earned in earlier decades by a very few—and in relative terms much richer—foundations.

Our concluding chapter argues that foundations small and large may be reaching a new understanding, accepting their own variety and coming to terms with the limits of their resources. In some important ways, today's foundations resemble their nineteenth-century predecessors.

We are struck by the versatility of the foundation as an institution and by America's receptivity to foundation change and variation with time and place. The strongest case for the public acceptance and legal recognition of foundations has always been that there is a value in autonomous, endowed, and persisting charitable funds; that an array of established, funded, and self-guiding centers of initiative adds something valuable to society and to the body politic. But we are also struck by the reality that a foundation is one institution among many others. Foundations are intriguing beasts in the "jungle of American democracy and capitalism," but there are many other "beasts" in that "jungle"—business firms great and small, hundreds of federal and state executives, legislatures, and agencies; many thousands of municipal and county governments, local school boards and special districts and commissions—and a vast "nonprofit sector" that includes thousands of endowed charities, thousands of churches and other religious entities, and not a few organizations concerned with international affairs of one kind or another. It is useful to remind ourselves that as important as they seem, foundations are frequently less influential than other institutions. Nevertheless, America would be different—and poorer as a society and nation—without them.

On Foundations

Irrespective of the motives or the wisdom of testators, endowments are not likely to accomplish as much good work as is expected of them, because the character of boards of management is not all that could be desired. . . . Endowments should be somewhat regulated by law . . . there should be supervision—by the State Board of Charities where one exists . . . there should be authority for revising them . . . every donor [should be] persuaded not to impose any condition beyond a temporary period—and to take the advice of active charity workers. . . .

—Amos G. Warner, *American Charities,* 1894, 1908

In the great jungle of American democracy and capitalism, there is no more strange or improbable creature than the private foundation. Private foundations are virtually a denial of basic premises: aristocratic institutions living on the privileges and indulgence of an egalitarian society; aggregations of private wealth which, contrary to the proclaimed instincts of Economic Man, have been conveyed to public purposes. Like the giraffe, they could not possibly exist, but they do.

—Waldemar A. Nielsen, *The Big Foundations,* 1972

Philanthropy . . . dedicated itself to finding systemic solutions to underlying causes of poverty and other social ills, and over time, has become a recognized social process—in effect, a set of private legislatures defining public problems, setting goals and priorities, and allocating resources toward the general good. . . . Foundations are Society's Passing Gear.

—Paul Ylvisaker, 1989

Every organization that qualifies for tax exemption as an organization described in section 501(c)(3) is a private foundation unless it falls into one of the categories specifically excluded from the definition of that term (referred to in section 509[a]). In addition, certain nonexempt charitable trusts are also treated as private foundations. Organizations that fall into the excluded categories are institutions such as hospitals or universities and those that generally have broad public support or actively function in a supporting relationship to such organizations.

Private foundations, in contrast, typically have a single major source of funding (usually gifts from one family or corporation rather than funding from many sources) and most have as their primary activity the making of grants to other charitable organizations and to individuals, rather than the direct operation of charitable programs.

—Internal Revenue Service website, 2012

1

Foundations in the United States

As symbols and embodiments of private power, religious authority, modernism, and capitalism, America's philanthropic foundations have always attracted strong views. Critics object that foundations impose the arbitrary will of the "dead hand" on the pressing needs of the present; that they give unearned weight to religious orthodoxies—or that, by holding substantial assets, foundations violate a religious injunction to accept that "God will provide"; that they seek to remake social institutions in accord with a standardizing ambition that ignores tradition and popular preference; that they reinforce vested social and economic interests; that they provide cover for the secret, undemocratic ambitions of governments; and that they are the wasteful playgrounds of and for the rich.

Other critics reject such critiques and praise foundations for their potential to do great things—but complain that they do not do the things that a particular critic prefers. Or that they do approved things in ways that are ill-considered and ineffective.

American foundations live with controversy. Facing harsh and contradictory attacks, foundations often respond cautiously, blandly, and with copious amounts of information that is often vague and incomplete.

Whatever their overall view of American foundations, most writers work from a common but incomplete, and even mythic, understanding of foundation history. Philanthropic foundations, it is usually said, first appeared after the Civil War—anticipated by the Peabody Education Fund, modernized through writings by Andrew Carnegie and John D. Rockefeller, and made important by large monetary gifts from a number of foundation-creators between 1900 and 1920. Endowed with fabulous wealth and led by exceptionally well-connected administrators, American foundations did extraordinary things and can rightly point to remarkable achievements. Described as secular and committed to science, it is said that they launched whole classes of institutions, backed far-reaching social movements, and gave direction to government policy in many fields, and that they have continued to do all this. Much of this accepted story is a myth, however, as we will show in the following chapters when we examine the historical record of American foundations and look at the present.

America's foundations first appeared in the wake of the American Revolution and played important roles throughout the entire nineteenth century—including key roles in building the nation's "mainstream" Protestant denominations. Carnegie and Rockefeller did not invent the American foundation, though their funds did do remarkable things, especially in the first three decades of the twentieth century. And the relative position of the American foundation changed dramatically after World War II, as incomes rose to hitherto unimagined levels and as government spending on health, education, and welfare—the chief objects of foundation giving—soared. For several postwar decades, foundations struggled to understand what they could do as the rise of other forces reduced their leverage. From the 1990s, we venture to conclude, foundations have come to accept a new place for themselves.

With this book we set out to enrich the discussion of foundation policy with a historical perspective. We think it worthwhile to test the adequacy of the generalizations so often advanced to justify calls for change in American foundations. We also think that historical studies are more credible if they make their terms clear and explicit. A more accurate understanding of the development of American foundations will, we believe, provide a more reliable basis for policy. Specifically we ask, What have American foundations contributed to our country—and to our democracy? What have they contributed to particular fields? How have they changed, grown, and adapted as new circumstances have emerged over the decades? Where and in what fields have they been most active?

Historians and social scientists have answered some of these questions. Relying on their work and on both historical and current evidence that we have developed, we believe we can provide answers. And we hope to encourage other researchers to take current foundation realities seriously and to consider how they came to be. Most generally, we ask what difference has the foundation, as an institution, made to the United States?

Foundations Today: Diverse Purposes, Many Sizes

America's grantmaking foundations—numbering more than 76,600 in 2011 and worth $646 billion in assets—have grown rapidly over the last two decades despite the dot-com bust of 2000 and the Great Recession following the financial crisis of 2008. Grantmaking foundations differ considerably from state to state, and local foundations are quite active in most metropolitan regions across the United States. Foundations have grown so numerous, and so diverse in size and in purpose, that it has become impossible to describe their contributions in a single set of phrases or to provide a single set of numbers to measure their impact.[1]

While their promise makes them important, it is wealth that makes foundations possible and impressive. The funds they donate add up: according to the Foundation Center, in 2011 American foundations gave away nearly $47 billion.[2] Yet despite the attention their wealth attracts, American foundations are much smaller than is often assumed. In recent decades foundation gifts have run to about 8 percent of asset values. Assets first seem to have reached a level of at least 2 percent of the value of all outstanding U.S. common stocks in the 1920s, and since the 1950s assets have ranged from 3 percent to 4 percent. Because foundations have always held bonds, land, and other assets in addition to shares of corporate stock—and because foundations did not have to report their assets fully until the late 1960s, estimates for decades before the 1970s can only be suggestive.[3] Foundation wealth has never been sufficient to influence the entire U.S. economy, and in recent decades foundation assets have been surpassed by the funds held as endowment by universities, medical research institutes, hospitals, museums, and other charities.[4] Although their wealth has declined sharply in relation to the other resources engaged in their fields of work, grantmaking foundations continue to hold sums large enough to make a difference. Sums, we hasten to add, that are strongly concentrated in the largest foundations. In 2006 the 2 percent of all foundations whose assets topped $25 million employed essentially all of the professional foundation staff and held three-quarters of all foundation assets.[5] The 100 largest foundations, with assets in 2009 ranging from $564 million to $30 billion, held more than one-third of all foundation assets.[6] Many of the best studies of American foundations (like most of the best studies of universities, government agencies, or business firms) have understandably focused on the small group of very large cases.[7]

Size certainly matters. The 100 largest foundations whose 2011 assets exceeded $669.86 million (let alone the ten or twelve foundations whose assets exceeded $5 billion) clearly attract much more attention and arouse higher expectations than the 96 percent of foundations that give away less than $500,000 a year. More than half of all foundations have less than $1 million in assets and give away less than $80,000 a year; most of these operate more as the charitable checkbooks of generous families than as independent institutions. Altogether these smallest funds hold less than 3 percent of all foundation assets.[8] Community foundations—and related forms such as supporting foundations that take in numerous gifts of varying size—constitute the fastest-growing segment among

American foundations. Some community foundations and a few supporting foundations are among the largest of all grantmakers. But as "public charities" that continuously raise money as well as give it away, these entities operate under distinctive and somewhat less restrictive regulations. Even when they are very large, most community foundations operate more as charitable banking institutions for their donors than as unified civic actors on their own account.[9]

Foundations vary enormously in size. We focus primarily on larger foundations, though we also consider smaller foundations where possible. The definition of what constitutes a "larger" foundation has changed over time and depends on the field or topic, but we have typically focused on the 100, 500, or 1,000 largest foundations in existence at a given time or on the 100 or 500 largest grants. We are mostly concerned with the 3,000 U.S. grantmaking foundations that have paid staffs.[10]

Although a few foundations hold the bulk of foundation wealth and attract the most attention, compelling reasons exist to cast a wider net, particularly because a single set of laws and regulations applies to small and large foundations alike. Yet it is difficult to find good systematic information on smaller foundations; our own investigations have certainly lacked sufficient resources to undertake such a study. Every year, thousands of Americans create foundations or donor-advised funds or give money to community foundations. Most of these foundations and funds involve less than $1 million; each year only one or two of them exceed $500 million. Every day, regulators, judges, legislators, fund-seekers, journalists, and neighbors critique and evaluate foundations. But regulators have few resources and must focus their attention on egregious and controversial cases. When occasionally a foundation gets into publicized trouble, more often than not it is a smaller, more obscure one, but two of the most careful analysts in the field have concluded, "We really do not know the extent of abuse in small foundations."[11]

Foundations are neither unique to the United States nor uniquely American. Since ancient times, and across many cultures, substantial assets have been set aside for specific charitable and religious purposes.[12] Muslims preserve resources for religious and religiously prescribed social welfare and educational activity through traditional "vakif."[13] Foundations played major religious and charitable roles in medieval Europe and the Ottoman Empire. Foundations became, as elements of the ancien régime and as patrons separate from the national state, targets of the French Revolution.[14] In several European countries, foundations and trusts did emerge during the nineteenth century as significant underwriters of science, culture, and welfare. In Britain they helped define the need for reform in the fields of housing and social welfare; in Italy they helped advance the causes of literacy and science as the nation slowly became unified; in Germany they offered responses to social needs and did much to build great universities and cultural institutions. But in Europe and elsewhere during the early and middle decades of the twentieth century, many foundations saw their endowments erased by economic and political crises or by the hostility of some governments to independent centers of initiative. This was true not only in Germany and Poland but also in England, where governments redefined the purposes as well as the investment policies of foundations.[15]

New and revived foundations, such as Stephen Batory in Poland, Fritt Ord in Norway, Bosch and Mercator in Germany, the King Baudouin Foundation in Belgium, and the Compania di San Paolo in Italy have contributed to the cultural vibrancy of postwar Europe and also to the development of civil society and international engagement in postcommunist countries and throughout the expanded European Union. Today, notable groups of foundations exist in Australia, Canada, Germany, the United Kingdom, Scandinavia, Italy, the Netherlands, Spain, and Japan; recent policy developments encourage their proliferation in nations as diverse as France, Brazil, Qatar, Singapore, and even China.[16] Yet the United States stands out. In no other modern society are grantmaking foundations more numerous. Nowhere are they so prominent. Nowhere have foundations enjoyed such sustained autonomy for such a long period of time.

Defining Terms: "Charity" and "Philanthropy"

To determine what difference foundations have made to the United States we must begin by defining terms.[17] This is a more complicated task than we might assume, because key terms are used in different ways in different contexts. In legal contexts where some terms are of critical importance, meanings have emerged through a long history of judicial rulings, legislation, and regulation. Common parlance shapes the meanings of many terms in ever-changing ways. We treat some technical matters of definition in a note in appendix A, but some questions about the meanings of ordinary words call for some discussion here.

United States law defines the words "charity" and "charitable" in special ways; critics who rely on common understandings often employ these words in ways inconsistent with their American legal definitions. Current federal tax law defines "charity," as we noted in the preface, in broad ways to include religious, educational, scientific, literary, safety-testing, and cruelty-preventing purposes.[18] The Internal Revenue Service also notes, regarding "exempt purposes," that the "generally accepted legal sense" of "the term *charitable*" includes "relief of the poor, the distressed, or the underprivileged; advancement of religion, advancement of education or science; erecting or maintaining public buildings, monuments, or works; lessening the burdens of government; lessening neighborhood tensions; eliminating prejudice and discrimination; defending human and civil rights secured by law; and combating community deterioration and juvenile delinquency."[19] Congress, the courts, the U.S. Department of the Treasury, and the individual states use these broad definitions to determine whether a foundation or an organization enjoys exemption from income tax, property tax, or sales tax; whether donors to the organization can count their gifts as charitable in calculating their own taxes; whether an organization or its employees enjoy any form of "charitable immunity"; and whether a foundation's board has acted properly in approving grants, making investments, dealing with suppliers, acknowledging donors, or expressing views on questions relevant to politics.

Much commentary and criticism uses the word "charity" in ways shaped by nonlegal contexts. Most important are religious uses that continue to have a powerful influence, not only among professing Christians but also through common English-language phrases. Until the middle of the twentieth century, most writers on charity in the United States took for granted that a very large share of their readers had learned English in considerable part in Christian settings, so it is useful to take these historical contexts into account. One of the most frequently discussed passages in the King James version of the Bible, for example, is the translation of 1 Corinthians 13, in which the apostle Paul discusses "charity" in challenging terms as the greatest of "spiritual gifts." It says in part:

> And though I bestow all my goods to feed the poor, and though I give my body to be burned, and have not charity, it profiteth me nothing.
>
> Charity suffereth long, and is kind: charity envies not: charity vaunteth not itself, is not puffed up, Doth not behave itself unseemly, seeketh not her own, is not easily provoked, thinks no evil, Rejoyces not in iniquity, but rejoyces in the truth:
>
> Charity never fails: but whether there be prophesies, they shall fail; whether there be tongues, they shall cease; whether there be knowledge, it shall vanish away. For we know in part, and we prophesy in part. But when that which is perfect is come, then that which is in part, shall be done away.
>
> When I was a child, I spoke as a child, I understood as a child, I thought as a child: but when I became a man, I put away childish things. For now we see through a glass, darkly: but then face to face: now I know in part, but then shall I know even as also I am known. And now abideth faith, hope, charity, these three, but the greatest of these is charity.[20]

The Catholic Douay Bible uses almost the same English words: "And now there remain faith, hope, and charity, these three: but the greatest of these is charity."[21] More recent translations generally replace "charity" in this verse with "love," but these uses of "charity" are deeply embedded in English literature. Every year, many thousands of sermons and homilies quote these words about "charity" and reflect on their many meanings, which derive, at least in part, from the tradition restated by St. Augustine that love for God elevates Christians and leads them also toward true love for humankind—a tradition embraced by the Latin word "caritas." Adherents of other religious traditions have their own language for such discussions, and religious and nonreligious people alike debate the meanings.[22] Altogether, "charity" has meanings that are simultaneously technical, broad, and disparate in legal and religious contexts.

American, British, Australian, and Canadian notions of charity also owe much to the English Statute of Charitable Uses of 1601 (adopted just a decade before publication of the King James Bible), which served as a touchstone—often poorly understood—for legal reasoning about charity law into the twentieth century. The statute lists as examples of charitable purposes the following:

> Relief of aged, impotent and poor people . . . maintenance of sick and maimed soldiers and mariners, schools of learning, free schools, and scholars in universities . . . repair of bridges, ports, havens, causeways, churches, sea banks, and highways, education and preferment of orphans . . . relief, stock, or maintenance for houses of correction . . . marriages of poor maids . . . supportation, aid and help of young tradesmen, handicraftsmen . . . relief or redemption of prisoners or captives . . . aid or ease of any poor inhabitant concerning payments of fifteens, setting out of soldiers, and other taxes.[23]

What nineteenth-century and later commentators overlooked were the facts that the Statute of Charitable Uses gave the power to investigate alleged offenses to the bishops of the established Church of England and that most of these charitable activities were at the time carried out by the established church. Until the end of the nineteenth century, British courts invalidated as "superstitious" charitable bequests to religious charities affiliated with religious communities other than the Church of England. Throughout these centuries, other British laws defined the charitable status of religious entities. We agree with legal historian Stephen Diamond that there "never was . . . a beginning point, a moment when the social compact was created" on a "clean slate, unfettered by outmoded, Old World, and feudal—or monarchical—institutions and practices."[24] The Statute of Charitable Uses did not reflect such a beginning point, and neither did the American Revolution. But the revolution did bring a break with the British approach that established one religion—the Church of England—and to a greater or lesser extent "tolerated" other religions. After the revolution, the American legal environment granted greater deference to all religious traditions.

In short, notions of "charity" have been deeply shaped by religious belief and religious language, by religious conflict, and by efforts to create religious tolerance and even religious harmony. Notions of charity have also been shaped by the institutional structures that have held legal authority to oversee charitable activity, to protect charitable assets and direct them to socially approved purposes. And they also have been shaped by the idea that those who bestow charity are owed deference by those who receive—and by protest against such notions as implying falsely that inequality is divinely ordained. Further, they have been shaped by the idea that while giving can be a tool for establishing superiority and making clear who is a subordinate, it can also occur within a context of mutuality.

"Philanthropy" has an even broader range of meanings. It gained currency in the nineteenth century, in part because as a word based on the Greek word *philanthrōpos* ("loving people" or "love of humanity"), it seemed appropriate in nonsectarian and secular contexts and also in discussions of interfaith cooperation. Andrew Carnegie has been quoted often as saying that "indiscriminate charity" was "one of the serious obstacles to the improvement of our race" and that it would be "better for mankind that the millions of the rich were thrown into the sea than so spent as to encourage the slothful[,] the drunken[,] the unworthy."[25] Carnegie, John D. Rockefeller, and others urged that giving should be what has come to be called "philanthropic" in specific ways—supporting well-considered innovation to solve social problems, developing exceptional talent, encouraging more effective practices—rather than "charitable" in what is repeatedly asserted to be an old-fashioned sense of "relieving immediate needs." Yet no discussion of American foundations can avoid these highly contested terms, because they have long carried more-or-less specific meanings within the field. The contrast between relief-of-needs "charity" and well-considered "philanthropy" deserves serious critical scrutiny. However, it should be noted that this broad and simple distinction obscures another ancient and still-vital use of foundations and that is to control resources for highly valued activities intended to provide public benefit consistent with a donor's values and wishes and in keeping with the law.

Many, if not most, American foundations today insist that they are "philanthropic," in the sense that they thoughtfully seek important social change. When a foundation lives up to this standard, it might be acting as a social entrepreneur, an institution builder, a risk taker, or a conserver of values. Over time, have foundations become more entrepreneurial, more effective as institution builders, better at taking initiatives that are too risky for others? Because opinions differ widely as to what courses of action are ultimately "good" or are likely in a practical sense to produce desirable social change, we must also ask how foundations have changed their tactics as social entrepreneurs, institution builders, or risk takers. Additionally, have foundations proven significant as conservers of values, and if so, of whose? What values have donors sought to underwrite, and have they in fact made more efforts, or more effective efforts, to use foundations as instruments of control? Or have they contributed to changes in values—to the erosion of some values and to the protection, even the growth, of other values, religious or secular? Finally, what can be said of the use of foundations as instruments for forging local consensus, for promoting local priorities, and for developing local institutions in communities across the United States?

What Can Foundations Do? Law and Practice

Internal Revenue Service regulations make clear that a foundation is a legally established, autonomous, nongovernmental organization controlled by its own board. American foundations have acquired tax-exemption privileges if they adhere to changing restrictions. But it is important to recognize at the outset the importance of the basic right to exist. Most foundations are set up as corporations. As historian Pauline Maier reminds us, incorporation allows a group to create a lasting entity—to make binding rules for its self-government, to function in law as a single person with the right to hold property, and to sue and be sued in order to protect its assets—and to persist after the lifetimes of its founding members.[26]

Grantmaking foundations persist (at least for a certain time), but in an important sense they are incomplete institutions. Their activities are limited to holding, investing, and distributing money for purposes deemed charitable under U.S. law. They do not act themselves: they enable others to act. Foundations are charitable, but they themselves do not cure patients, conduct research, teach, reform, house the homeless, feed the poor, protect treasures, mount exhibitions or concerts, or conduct religious services.

So much is written telling foundations and the public what foundations ought to do that it becomes important to consider what foundations actually can do. This question can be looked at from two perspectives: that of a founder or donor and that of the larger community. Donors find in the foundation a legal instrument that expands their alternatives. Through a foundation a donor can reserve, protect, and invest funds and determine how and when they will be dispersed and for which charitable purposes. Foundations are not identical to philanthropy—they are not necessary to philanthropy, and only some philanthropic giving goes through a foundation. Instead of using a foundation, a donor could also make a gift to meet a crisis, to be spent immediately. Or a donor could give to an operating nonprofit organization (or its endowment) or to a government agency for a specific purpose, including use over time. Donors can also give to individuals. The availability of the foundation offers another possibility to the donor: to set funds aside to be held, invested, and given over time for specified or general charitable purposes.

The donor to an American foundation pledges that the gift will go to charity (and receives the associated tax benefits), but can become the dominant person in the group that later decides which particular charity will get the benefit and for what specific purposes. Whether the donor continues to be involved or not, he or she can determine in advance the foundation's purpose or range of purposes, define how it will invest (subject to certain limitations), and set the rate at which funds will flow over time (subject under current law to a minimum rate of 5 percent of a moving average of assets each year). If the donor wishes a foundation to last indefinitely, he or she must accept that control will eventually pass on to others and that, while the donor can set the initial purposes and select the initial directors or trustees, future foundation boards—and changing circumstances—will eventually exert their own influences.

Once created, a grantmaking foundation can accomplish charitable ends only through grants to other institutions—or, in some very specific cases, through grants to individuals. By virtue of their incompleteness as institutions, foundations are of necessity deeply enmeshed in the fields they address and in the wider contexts of their times. Much recent writing on foundations emphasizes foundation autonomy and ways of ensuring that foundations get the results they seek. We note that foundations must rely on others; hence any assessment of foundation work must focus on the ways in which foundations interact with others who share their objectives—or who are indifferent to them or oppose them.

To identify the specific actions foundations can take and have taken over the course of American history, we start from the observation that because foundations have very limited resources in relation to the fields they address, they always seek leverage. A foundation can take the following actions:

—Support religious activities through grants to pay for religious services, prayers, rituals, study, teaching, outreach, missions, buildings, libraries, or furnishings and equipment.

—Pay for direct aid for the poor, including food, clothing, and housing. No known foundation has had sufficient funds to relieve the poverty of large numbers of people; what foundations have been able to do is to call attention to poverty and encourage others to recognize need.

—Provide direct support to advance education, research, writing, and creative work through scholarships, fellowships, recruitment, and/or resettlement of researchers, scholars, writers, and artists, research grants, publication grants, conference funding, mid-career fellowships, and the like.

—Create an effective process that confers honor, prestige, or opportunity on people whose achievements, views, or qualities are held worthy of emulation, for instance, through scholarships for people with special qualities, fellowships that confer prestige, prizes for work completed, and prizes for notable actions.

—Help create communities of people committed to particular purposes—whether upholding particular traditions, advancing professions, or working for change—through grants for advanced substantive or leadership training, conferences, meetings, travel, writing, or publication.

—Seek to shape public opinion by supporting studies intended to call attention to particular problems and by conferring honor and prestige on those whose actions are believed worthy of emulation—through fellowships and research grants; convening specialists and officials to share information, identify best practices, and develop new knowledge; and by funding gatherings, conversations, and career development of people committed to a particular approach or agenda.

—Seek to help inform government policies that address specific problems through fellowships and research grants, support for explanatory materials, convening specialists and officials, supporting demonstration projects, subsidizing personnel and other costs of policy study, or making grants conditional on public support.

—Grant funds that enable nonprofit organizations or government agencies to provide activities deemed "charitable" under U.S. law (methods include scholarships, fellowships, and other subsidies for students; grants for direct provision of health care; grants for the construction or purchase of new buildings or equipment; and subsidies for performances and exhibitions).

—Subsidize the creation of new or the reorientation and reorganization of existing service providers through subsidies for consultants or employees with specific assignments or through substantial grants to endowment.

—Promote economic development through mission-related investments and loans, revolving loan funds, research grants, grants for education and training, and funding for consulting services.

—Promote changes in public behavior through exhortation, praise, or subsidy as well as through study and advocacy of policy. Past and present foundations variously encourage thrift, productive work, care for the environment, respect for women, and civility—and discourage indulgence in smoking, drinking, and out-of-wedlock sex.

Foundations are about the investment as well as the giving of money, although this key point is generally neglected. Some foundations have always sought to contribute to society through their investment policies, including what are now called "mission-related" loans and investments, as well as through grants. Some of the earliest mission-related investments by American foundations helped young craftsmen establish their businesses or subsidized buildings used for charity or education. Foundations have also sought to promote local economic growth through their investments as well as their gifts. Because they are about investment, control, and change, foundations necessarily engage with time.

Donors can give not only through grantmaking foundations but in many other ways—to operating foundations, supporting foundations, and active nonprofit organizations that enjoy somewhat greater tax advantages than foundations. Two questions arise: Do foundations have comparative advantages over other institutions? Have their advantages grown or declined over time?[27]

Concern with historical context and with the relation of foundations to time leads to additional questions. Foundations control the timing of grants. They have to consider when it makes most sense to start an initiative, how to support it as time passes, and whether to end support. Questions of timing arise whether a foundation is supporting an organization, a program within an organization, a specific action, or a continuing cause.

Because foundations always work through others, they also must consider the character of the fields they address and of the organizations they support, as well as relationships within fields and among organizations. Much can depend on the foundation's own relation with operating entities in its field, that is, on its reputation not only for wealth but also for understanding and judgment.

Foundation Roles, Advantages, Weaknesses

As noted in *American Foundations,*[28] the literature strongly emphasizes two roles for foundations: relief of immediate needs (sometimes denoted as "charity"—language that conflicts with the use of that term in U.S. law), and "philanthropy." Our studies have made it clear to us that both of these possible roles should be defined more precisely and that foundations very often play other roles that we designate as forms of "preservation and control." These are general terms, but the generality is necessary if we are to specify at the outset a basic framework for considering the work of foundations over a span of 200 years. As we show in this book, foundations have changed dramatically over the course of U.S. history, and they continue to change. We also agree that foundations can be discussed in terms of the values they espouse—religious, intellectual, cultural, social, or civic—and that the leading sets of values have changed over time.[29]

"Relief of need" occurs when foundations pay for services or goods that benefit others, characteristically the poor or the disabled, within an existing framework. Writers in the field sometimes suggest that foundation gifts of this sort might "complement" or supplement tax funds and individual gifts or might "substitute" or replace them.

Philanthropy describes foundation efforts to create something new in one of three ways: "innovation" in social perceptions, values, relationships, and ways of doing things; "original achievement" in the arts, philosophy and religion, science, and the study of society; and "social or policy change" intended to foster recognition of new needs, bring new perspectives to the table, and encourage efficiency, equity, peace, and social and moral virtues of all kinds, including law and order or economic growth.

Preservation and control also can be viewed as taking three forms. Perhaps most common but usually neglected are the "preservation of traditions and cultures" and "asset protection," whereby foundations hold and distribute funds intended to preserve and encourage valued beliefs and commitments. A variation of this last form of control might be described as the promotion of local infrastructure for education, the arts, and community services and recreational facilities—a role that can be described as "building out" the facilities of a community or region. Regional build-out emerges from our investigations as perhaps the most widely practiced role of American foundations. Critics of foundations, and some defenders, emphasize "redistribution," the voluntary redistribution of wealth from the rich to the poor—a use of the foundation that some critics would make mandatory.

A number of authors have suggested that foundations have significant comparative advantages over other institutions. Foundations can be "social entrepreneurs" that identify and respond to needs or problems that are beyond the reach or interest of market firms, government agencies, and existing nonprofit organizations. They can be "institution builders," using money and ideas to help establish sustainable organizations to meet unmet needs. They can serve as "honest brokers," mediating conflicts and convening coalitions of individuals and organizations capable of action across existing sectors, communities, regions, and borders. They can also be "risk absorbers," investing where there is great uncertainty and a return is doubtful. And they can act as "value conservers," supporting practices, virtues, and cultural patterns treasured by donors but unsupported by markets or legislative majorities.

The literature also attributes to foundations disadvantages that deserve notice. The most cursory consideration makes clear that insufficiency is standard: foundations very often lack resources adequate to their proclaimed goals and too frequently fail to recognize their own limitations. Particularism (the inappropriate favoring of one group of beneficiaries) is often alleged, perhaps because U.S. law forbids discrimination on the basis of race or gender—though it also allows foundations to require that beneficiaries meet religious, geographical, or ability tests. Paternalism (the primacy of a foundation's judgment over that of its beneficiaries), often combined with charges of elitism, is another complaint but also more difficult to identify. Critics object to foundation amateurism (the making of decisions by dilettantes who possess only a cursory understanding of the fields and issues they address); more than a few defenders of foundations instead celebrate amateurism as a useful counter to domination by an often narrow-minded technocracy.

Having identified these roles, advantages, and disadvantages, our study seeks to assess the degrees to which they describe American foundations over time and place.

Foundations as Institutions: Creating Patterns of Behavior

Foundations are important not only because they hold substantial funds, but also because as social institutions—even as incomplete institutions in the sense emphasized above—they can make ideas and practices regular, routine, and almost solid. In daily life, institutions define realities. Empowered by the political institutions that give them their autonomy and authority, social institutions focus and direct resources, enhance or restrict the power of those who work through them, and shape the social environment.[30] Foundations can make a difference not only through grants, but also by influencing beliefs and patterns of behavior. A goal of this study is to determine when, and how often, American foundations have made institutional contributions of this sort.

In pursuing their widely varied charitable purposes, American foundations try to do much more than give away money: they seek to confer legitimacy and worthiness. Working in conjunction with tax authorities, judges, legal writers, accountants, religious leaders, pundits, and many others, foundations can put into practice divergent and changing ideas as to what is "charitable," thereby giving ideas concrete expression. Foundations work to shape the actions of others both by granting money and by signaling that particular activities, purposes, and achievements are worthy of gifts and grants or of awards and prizes. Donors use foundations in these ways to pursue complex, sustained purposes.

In the ancient world, donors used foundations to memorialize their wealth and power and to win prestige by glorifying their cities, underwriting proper care for the dead, acknowledging some of the needs of poor girls and young women, and supporting temples and schools. Medieval foundations supported the saying of prayers, the study, copying, and preservation of sacred and ancient texts, rituals that symbolically represented the feeding of the poor, and the religious care of the sick and dying. Modern American foundations continue to do all those things, and they also reward heroism, good citizenship, writing on many topics, artistic endeavor, scientific and applied research, and innovation of many kinds. Modern foundations have also sought to encourage new social behavior; they have launched self-sustaining organizations and even reorganized entire fields of activity.

American foundations are often urged to make general contributions to society—to preserve religious and cultural beliefs and practices, to underwrite large programs of education and health care, and to redistribute wealth from the rich to the poor. But the most ambitious efforts require larger resources than even the largest foundations command.

Researchers have established some basic knowledge about the institutional achievements of American foundations. Foundation work does support religious traditions, extend educational opportunities, aid those who suffer from a rare disease, and advance particular artistic traditions. Foundations, like nonprofits in general, do redistribute wealth in these ways—but their direct reduction of inequality is limited by their small resources. Overall, foundations redistribute money from those who have a great deal to those who have less, but they do so chiefly by supporting activities that benefit the public in general.[31]

Through the influence of existence and example, some foundations have promoted the spread of the foundation as an institution by encouraging the creation of new foundations and by giving seed money to new community foundations.[32] That individuals are able to give money to a foundation, or if their means are sufficient, to set up a foundation of their own, may actually increase the total sum available for charitable purposes.[33] It is possible to imagine policy arrangements that would pull wealth into tax payments rather than allow it to be placed in foundations. Assessing the likely effects of such policies is not an easy task, given the complexity of the American taxation and finance systems. But the most persuasive analyses conclude that much of the money that flows through foundations "would not find its way into the tax stream,"[34] because wealthy people would find ways to avoid taxes, to pass wealth on to heirs, and to shape tax policies.

It is clear that foundations, like the endowment funds of nonprofit organizations and of their supporting organizations, do make it possible to set aside funds for the long term. A frequent objection is that foundations reduce the amount of money immediately available for charity at any given present moment.[35] We would note, however, that while federal tax law calls for foundations to pay out 5 percent of the value of their assets annually, a careful recent study found an "average payout percentage of about 8.7 percent." In practice, six of every seven foundations distributes more than the legal minimum.[36]

Some analysts argue for laws requiring higher payout rates and forbidding self-perpetuating foundations. Others stress the stability, diversity, and autonomy that foundations can provide for other institutions and for the ideas they promote.[37] Historically, foundations have been used to enhance the income security of those who devote themselves to valued but often less remunerative activities—religion, education, research, social service, nursing, and the arts. And they also enhance in a predictable and continuing way the opportunities available to students, children in foster care, the elderly, the sick, and those who seek access to the arts or to preserve the natural landscape. Large endowments also give foundations (and nonprofits) a degree of autonomy that allows them to contribute to the pluralism of American society.

Because they constitute independent sources of funds, foundations also complicate the direction of other institutions, especially nonprofit organizations and government agencies. A foundation's board can reconsider a given grant program and shift funds, sometimes on very short notice, from one activity, organization, or field to another, regardless of the concerns or plans of the organizations and communities they have supported in the past.[38] As the *Wall Street Journal* recently noted, donors can assure themselves that their gifts are used as they prefer in a variety of ways, by

> parceling smaller gifts out over a set time, rather than giving a larger sum to an endowment . . . set[ting] up a gift as an annuity within a trust, overseen by a third-party trustee, who can decide annually whether the gift's intent has been met. Instead of endowing a professor's chair in perpetuity, a donor might provide financial backing to a single professor only for his or her lifetime, guarding against a successor who might drift from the subject matter the donor wants taught.[39]

A foundation—unlike an individual donor—can impose and maintain conditions of these sorts indefinitely, so long as the university or other beneficiary organization is willing to cede the demanded degree of control over its appointments and other actions.

Barry Karl, Stanley Katz, and other influential writers have showed how certain foundations, at certain times, did much to invent and establish substantial new institutions—most notably public education in the American South, public libraries, the modern research university, and the academic medical center.[40] Foundations, working with other extra-governmental forces, did do much to give the United States strong university and research capacities in the early decades of the twentieth century, when the federal and state governments did not see this as an appropriate task.

America's constitutional, legal, and political traditions have generally created and encouraged religious freedom and, more generally, have made possible multiple bases for initiative. Foundations fit nicely into an American polity characterized by checks and balances in the federal and state governments, the assignment of important powers to state and local governments, the separation of church and state, an exceptionally long history of autonomy for business corporations and nongovernment, nonprofit organizations, and a widespread preference for expansive notions of private property.

Autonomy and variety in purpose have always been fundamental to American foundations. American political traditions insist that donors have the right to use their wealth to advance a wide range of beliefs, virtues, practices, and innovations. Donors have committed to a wide range of concerns, from religion, education, and culture to health, social justice, and the advancement of sports, hobbies, and collecting. Foundations (like other charities) can commit to a single purpose, such as reducing poverty or subsidizing government; however, since the late nineteenth century state laws have encouraged them to support increasingly varied causes and values.

Foundations constitute one among many institutional structures that shape concerted public action. American legal and political ideas and arrangements, including the arrangements that support foundations, reinforce what historians and political scientists variously describe as "polyarchy" and "pluralism."[41] This is a story that researchers in the American political development movement have ignored and that we think they should pursue. But there are reasons to think that it is a story from a specific and limited period in American history, and that is another question explored in this book.

For more than 100 years, American courts, regulators, and legislators have steadily agreed that foundations, including nonsectarian, general-purpose foundations, have a right to independent existence and indeed to favorable tax treatment, so long as they are not employed to increase the personal wealth of donors and their families and so long as they avoid party politics and devote their resources to the very wide range of "charitable purposes" described at the beginning of this chapter. The core rationale is that as long as foundations accept these broad limits, they contribute valuably to American freedoms and American pluralism.

In every era public opinion has limited the scope of initiative available to foundations. The acceptable range of views has changed over time, reflecting the fortunes and misfortunes of American history, yet it suggests a general trajectory. Like other charities, foundations encountered significant legal and political limits under slavery, during the Jim Crow era of racial segregation, and to some extent under wartime pressure to support the nation. Charities devoted to minority religious and cultural traditions long struggled against prejudice in public opinion as well as discrimination in law and legislation. But American charities have always enjoyed wide possibilities, possibilities that have expanded over the decades, even as federal regulation has to a considerable extent supplanted control by the individual states. In the United States, foundations like other charities justify their existence and their privileges—and, indeed, establish their legitimacy—not so much by reducing poverty or by relieving taxpayers of the expense of public facilities and services, as by enriching and strengthening America's varieties of religious, cultural, educational, scientific, and policy analysis and by increasing the possibilities for innovation.[42]

Our leading hypothesis is that it is flexibility—the ability to remove funding from one beneficiary or entire field to another—that makes foundations distinctive.[43] By their actions, foundations establish or help establish realities, such as the grant-seeking process itself, the worthiness of certain ideas or achievements, the legitimacy of certain professions and disciplines, and the very existence of new, self-sustaining organizations, or on rare occasions entire sets of interacting organizations that others come to take for granted.

Overall, this book asks whether American foundations have over time shifted away from meeting immediate needs—or whether meeting such needs was ever their focus. Have they changed their emphasis on control? Have they put emphasis on more ambitious forms of philanthropy? If so, are they acting as social entrepreneurs? As institution builders? As risk takers and risk absorbers for other institutions? As value conservers? What have been their understandings of the possibilities of fundamental change—and how have their understandings evolved?

2

Remarkable Nineteenth-Century Foundations

Americans developed the essential elements of the modern philanthropic foundation in the first half of the nineteenth century. In their modest wealth, creativity, local focus, engagement with national and international developments, and emphasis on religion, education, the arts, and local economic development, nineteenth-century American foundations had much in common with the foundations of our own day. They engaged with inescapable problems and established enduring patterns. Early in the century, every foundation was devoted to a specific purpose. By the middle of the century the best-endowed colleges were acting much like today's general-purpose foundations and so were the largest religious funds. In the next several decades a number of foundations that were specifically set up to be independent, nonsectarian, and general-purpose had joined them.

Misleading and often-repeated statements continue to confuse most discussions of nineteenth-century foundations and philanthropy. Continuing conventions of legal reasoning, in Britain as well as in the United States, have maintained fictions about the laws of charities and trusts. Religious passions shaped what was said in the past—and what was not said—with consequences that persist today. Battles over taxes continue to complicate discussion of religious and cultural freedom. Stories about the American Revolution, about the writing of the Constitution, and about the early presidents are brandished as trump cards in political debate; these useful but often mythic stories have also shaped what is said about early foundations.

Most nineteenth-century writers on charity and philanthropy sought not to describe realities but rather to instruct readers in their religious duties or to help

legal clients achieve their purposes; the same has been true of later commentators. Social critics condemn the wealthy and their works; reformers praise donors
for helping others to help themselves; celebrators of achievement dismiss criticism of the successful. In recent years, some critics have emphasized class above
all, insisting that we see all effective universities, colleges, hospitals, and arts
organizations as nothing more than devices for the dominance of elites. Others espouse a constitutional and early American legal history that would justify
radical changes in the relations of American governments and religion, in effect
moving the United States closer to an established church. The fogs of religious,
political, and social conflict continue to confuse discussions of foundations.

To work through the conflicting and often false assumptions and assertions
that dominate the literature and to find a history that helps account for today's
realities, it is important to start with a clear understanding of some of the key
political and religious issues of earlier times. It is also important to accept the
current legal definition of a foundation in the United States as simply a fund of
money held by a trust or corporation, with principal and income to be applied
over time to charitable purposes.[1] To say this is not to simplify: the notions of
"trust," "corporation," "charity," and "purpose" have always been subject to
debate. If we are to understand the history and development of foundations in
the United States, we have to grasp how these terms have been caught in (and
are still being caught in) conflicting ideas about the actual and proper relations
between church and state, between state and corporation, between the citizen
and the state, and between the nation and its parts.

Taking the large view, foundations began to appear in some states—notably
Massachusetts and Pennsylvania—almost as soon as the U.S. Constitution was
adopted. The famous Peabody Fund, the acclaimed essays by Andrew Carnegie
and John D. Rockefeller, and Carnegie's public library initiative contributed
notably when they appeared in the last decades of the nineteenth century. But
they did not invent the American foundation. Endowed charitable funds had
become significant participants in American life long before, especially in the
field of religion—where they did much to organize the main Protestant denominations—and in education, culture, and the arts. Indeed, funds and foundations
did a great deal to establish the American pattern of church-affiliated schools
and colleges—the pattern that the several very large new foundations created by
Carnegie, Rockefeller, and a few others would do much to challenge after 1900.[2]

Government, Religion, and Endowed Charities in Colonial America

To understand developments that followed the American Revolution, we need to
start with a brief look at the colonial period. The England that ruled the American colonies was neither unified nor unchanging, as indicated by the Puritan

Revolution of the mid-1600s, the Glorious Revolution of the 1680s, a century-long world war with France, the extraordinary growth of London into a world city, and the beginnings of the Industrial Revolution. Historians also increasingly agree that law developed differently in different American colonies, that "unrelated colonial ventures" recombined "English legal practices in different ways," producing "three new and distinct regional configurations—the Chesapeake and its southern neighbors, New England, and the Middle Colonies."[3] Yet in America as in England "the state relied on religious institutions for support in maintaining order," and English officials made strong efforts to employ an established church.[4]

In New York and the southern colonies, the Church of England worked closely with the English government. In New England during the 1720s, as historian A. G. Roeber reminds us, "Aggressive Anglicans pressured authorities in Britain to declare the de facto establishment of congregational churches illegal in favor of the Church of England."[5] In Pennsylvania, "Quaker replacement of oaths with affirmations did not satisfy suspicious Anglicans, who refused to honor them."[6] Baptists and Jews faced severe impediments and Presbyterians and Dutch Reformed were discouraged everywhere except in Rhode Island, Pennsylvania, New Jersey, and Delaware. Catholics were banned. In Virginia, Baptist preachers were jailed.[7] Throughout the colonies, churches and charities were generally understood to be parts of government.

England used its established church as an integral part of the government apparatus to the end of the eighteenth century, a reality that most popular accounts of charity and voluntarism in colonial America continue to ignore. Because the Church of England served the public interest as English officialdom defined it, the number of colonial corporations devoted to religious, educational, and other charitable purposes was severely limited. A comprehensive study of early American corporations noted that requests for charters from the British government often failed:

> Increase Mather sought one for Harvard by vigorous exertions extended over several years. . . . Samual Davies exerted himself on behalf of the New Jersey College at Princeton . . . Eleazar Wheelock for his Indian school later Dartmouth College and George Whitefield for the orphan school which he wished erected into Bethesda College. . . . [Also in 1762] an act incorporating . . . the Society for Propagating Christian Knowledge among the Indians of North America . . . was disallowed by the Privy Council.

Governments in several American colonies also refused local charters of incorporation to Presbyterians, French Protestants, and Lutherans in New Netherland.[8] London did grant a few corporate charters; colonial proprietors, governors, and assemblies issued more, but only under imperial supervision.[9]

Substantial religious or charitable enterprise required corporate status. A corporation could "make binding rules for its self-government" and "function in law as a single person with the right to hold property and to sue and be sued—and so to protect its assets." Corporate status also helped persuade courts to respect bequests.[10] Before Eleazar Wheelock obtained the charter for what became Dartmouth College from an English governor, his advocate wrote that incorporation "will not only acquire rights maintainable by law in the courts of justice" but would also "command the favor of the government who without that sanction may at such distance from the crown oppress the undertaking a thousand ways and utterly destroy it."[11]

Church of England domination in the southern colonies eased the way to corporate charters or the equivalent for many of its churches and, as early as 1693, to a rare royal charter for the College of William and Mary. Apart from the early trading companies that directed settlement in Virginia and Massachusetts, Church of England mission societies were the most important English corporations to focus on the American colonies; funds they administered offered key support to basic education as well as to religion.[12]

The American colonies also enforced English law regarding bequests, though they did so in different ways. In Virginia and other southern colonies, local variations on English courts of equity emphasized the property rights of widows and children, thus discouraging bequests to charity. In New England a "communal . . . religious commitment to Puritanism" encouraged men to consider the needs of community charities as well as the needs of their families.[13] The few charities that did accumulate endowments before the revolution built churches, schools, hospitals, and other institutions that provided facilities for local populations—facilities approved or at least tolerated by imperial authority. Chief among these were the mission societies of Britain's established churches, including the Corporation for the Relief of Widows and Children of Clergymen in the Communion of the Church of England in America, and the colleges that carried royal names—William and Mary and King's College (renamed Columbia after the revolution)—or that conceded key governing roles to the Church of England—including Harvard, Yale, Princeton, and the University of Pennsylvania.[14] Brown, Dartmouth, and Rutgers and a number of secondary schools also obtained corporate recognition. Other colonial corporations that had begun to accumulate resources before the revolution included the Pennsylvania Hospital, the Contributors to the Relief and Employment of the Poor in the City of Philadelphia, the Library Company of Philadelphia, the Hospital of the City of New York, the Redwood Library in Rhode Island, the Charlestown Library Society in South Carolina, and two library companies in New Jersey.[15]

It is sometimes said that America's voluntary organizations date from the earliest settlements; in reality, colonial policy strongly and effectively discouraged voluntary nongovernment activity. Discouragement was less than fully effective, and an excellent recent overview concludes, "Christendom's eighteenth-century Anglo-American periphery featured establishments imperfectly rendered according to European models, a Protestant pluralism, and numbers—how large is unclear—of unaffiliated individuals, many of them Africans."[16] Some colonists did seek to create effective non-Anglican institutions in the face of official discouragement, but their work was difficult. They did not create independent foundations.

Early Nineteenth-Century Foundations: Law and Regulation

In several states, the American Revolution and the adoption of the Constitution expanded the legal space for what we might now call concerted action for the public good, for donors, and for foundations. The revolution launched continuing change in the granting of corporate powers, the enforcement of bequests and trusts, the relation between church and state, and the flow of subsidies. State governments and state courts took charge of most aspects of these matters. Different economies, different religious histories, different notions of citizenship and community and state sovereignty, and occasional bouts of anti-incorporation or anti-tax enthusiasm led each state to set its own policies and procedures and then to change them from time to time. Within each state, legislation intended to regulate the real estate market or to accomplish another entirely separate purpose sometimes had profound although unintended consequences for charity or religion.[17] Distinct and complicated developments occurred in each state, and the overall story is still not well understood. We can offer here a few comments that suggest some of the concerns relevant to nineteenth-century foundations.

Immediately following the revolution, several states granted the power to incorporate much more liberally than colonial officials had ever done. But other states restricted incorporation. And "incorporation" had varied and changing meanings. For several decades legislators continued to view corporations as agents or indeed as agencies of state government and to insist that each corporation serve purposes deemed "public," such as improving transportation or otherwise promoting economic development, providing practical and moral education, or furthering a particular religious outlook. Prototypes for general incorporation laws—which could provide for tight state control of corporations or for broad autonomy—had already appeared in Massachusetts decades before the revolution. As early as 1784 New York adopted a general process, under a state entity called the "University of the State of New York," to provide standard terms for the incorporation and supervision of schools, libraries, and related organizations.[18] The University of the State of New York and the New York State legislature both continued to operate in a very general way, even during

the several decades after 1846, during which New York legislation and legal decisions sought to limit the granting of corporate charters and its judges moved to
limit donors' ability to leave property to charities.

While some states encouraged incorporation at some times, others discouraged it. Virginia's struggle to disestablish the Anglican Church went so far as
to leave "all religious organizations (including schools and philanthropic organizations) . . . without the ability to incorporate."[19] Key factors leading to this
outcome included memories of harsh Anglican domination; growing religious
diversity and conflict; concern for the security of widows and orphans in the face
of high mortality rates; and a strong desire to protect the rights of property owners. From the 1830s the desire to limit charitable and other actions that might
challenge slavery also reinforced support for tight state control over incorporation and bequests.[20]

The Church of England's loss of standing had important consequences for
charitable organization and giving in the United States. English courts continued
to favor the Anglican Church in establishing charities and approving bequests.
English courts even diverted bequests intended for Catholic, Jewish, or Unitar-
ian causes to the Anglican Church, because English law deemed those religions
"superstitious" or otherwise unacceptable. The First Amendment's clauses regarding "no law to establish" and "free exercise" applied only to the federal government, but most states quickly moved to allow all Protestant churches—and in
most cases Catholic and Jewish houses of worship as well—to form, to gain the
organizational continuity and asset security afforded by legal incorporation, and
to receive bequests.[21] As historian Irving G. Wylie argued, by the early nineteenth
century most American judges held the "whole concept of superstitious uses" to
be "obnoxious."[22] Every state came to host a diversity of religious communities
and associated schools and other nonprofit and voluntary organizations.[23]

The notion that "Christianity was part of a common law that should support religious and charitable trusts and incorporated societies for the common
welfare" was widely held, though legislatures and courts found it difficult to say
what that notion meant. Pennsylvania's Presbyterians, German Pietists, Episcopalians, Quakers, and others disagreed so much among themselves—and placed
so much emphasis on individual rights over private property—that the states'
courts "shied away from defining what the precise dimensions of that Christian
society should be."[24] Related controversies persisted in other states, and everywhere conflict became more intense as immigration introduced rising numbers
of Catholics. In some cases the religious disagreements underlay other debates,
including those that concerned the ownership and disposal of property and the
advantages or dangers posed by corporations.

One culmination came in 1844, when a unanimous opinion of the U.S.
Supreme Court in the case of *Vidal et al.* v. *Girard's Executors* held, "Although

Christianity be a part of the common law of the state, yet it is so in this qualified sense, that its divine origin and truth are admitted, and therefore it is not
to be maliciously and openly reviled and blasphemed against, to the annoyance
of believers or the injury of the public." Any effort to determine more precisely
"what is the public policy of a state, and what is contrary to it . . . will be found
to be one of great vagueness and uncertainty . . . above all, when that topic is
connected with religious polity in a country composed of such a variety of religious sects as our country."[25]

We should not exaggerate nineteenth-century America's liberalism with regard
to matters of religion and conscience: state legislatures and some state courts continued to favor preferred religions over others. As John Witte Jr. put it:

> Virginia . . . revoked the corporate charters of the Episcopal churches in
> the 1790s and 1800s and thereafter sought to confiscate or taxed large por-
> tions of their properties. . . . Massachusetts, New Hampshire, and Vermont
> adopted equally discriminatory policies towards the properties of Quakers,
> Baptists, and Episcopalians . . . and routinely denied or delayed delivery
> of corporate charters, tax exemptions, and educational licenses to non-
> Congregational bodies. New York and New Jersey dealt churlishly with Uni-
> tarians and Catholics throughout the nineteenth century. Few legislatures
> and courts showed respect for the religious rights of Jews and Mormons, let
> alone those of Native American Indians and African-American slaves.[26]

The separation of church and state created space for charities that expressed
differing ideas about religion and virtue; it also posed severe challenges for the
state's tax-based financial support of religious institutions and their dependent
schools and social care. The state of Virginia seized most of the lands that the
crown had granted to the Anglican parishes, but then debated for years what to
do with them.[27] In New York, Anglican churches and King's College retained
their lands but lost some subsidies—though New York City's Free School Society, a nonsectarian but broadly Protestant charitable corporation chartered by
the state legislature in 1805, continued to receive tax funds into the 1840s.[28]

Debates over taxation also persisted as the search for tax revenue brought pressure on property devoted to activities of all kinds, including religion and charity.
Precise policies varied, but the states generally did exempt charities and charitable endowments from taxation—simply on the basis of their intrinsic value. As
legal historian Stephen Diamond has shown, the "question asked" when exemption from taxes was granted to a charity in these decades "was not how much a
church or university was worth" or whether it relieved government of expensive
obligations, "but whether its continued existence was desirable." The reality was
that the "threat of tax liens was a potentially mortal one. . . . Taxation, when
there was no capacity to pay, was in a practical sense confiscation."[29]

The withdrawal of government funding and the threat of confiscatory taxation severely challenged churches and schools. Many Protestants placed great importance on a highly literate laity and highly educated clergy. The now-secure Catholic and Jewish communities also put great emphasis on education. All would now have to find funds for schools, colleges, seminaries, publications, new churches, domestic and foreign missions, elderly clergymen, and teachers and their dependents. They could turn to the states. But when they did, they encountered legislatures that had to deal with many pressing financial demands and that wished to keep taxes as low as possible.[30] Altogether, post-independence changes in law and regulation created both the desire for charitable endowments and foundations and increased opportunities to create them.

As A. G. Roeber recently observed, historians have still not fully explored "where property concerns and religious belief intersected or conflicted" with state laws relating to charities and trusts.[31] We might generalize that in the nineteenth century's first decades, most states required donors to name a specific purpose for each charitable endowment (often a purpose that carried religious implications), making it impossible for foundations to take an explicitly open-ended, general-purpose approach. In many states, at least for some part of the period, courts rejected certain purposes, discouraged charitable bequests, or governed the disposition of gifts and estates so as to assure that as many families as possible would have the land that made self-sufficiency possible. State law, legislation, and court decisions relevant to foundations varied widely throughout the nineteenth century, changed over time, and ultimately made possible a significant expansion in charitable and civic activity—an expansion that alarmed some just as it delighted others.[32]

Practical Realities

Nineteenth-century foundations operated in the practical contexts of their times. Through most of the century, the United States remained a nation of farmers and small proprietors. People held most of their wealth in land rather than in stocks and bonds—and, prior to the Civil War, in slaves. Although some slave plantations had as many as 100 slaves, most had only a handful, and the Civil War ended legal slavery and the "asset value" of slaves. In all fields, firms remained small: railroads began to employ considerable numbers only after the consolidations of the 1870s, and manufacturing plants expanded rapidly in many industries—though by no means in all—only from that decade on.[33]

In America's small, dispersed communities of the nineteenth century, the women and girls within families and households provided almost all care of the young, the sick, the disabled, and the elderly. County officials generally placed those who needed assistance but lacked family support as servants in the homes of those who could afford to keep them and put them to work. New England towns and many other northern communities provided public schools, but only for the few months when farm work did not demand child labor, and only for the half-dozen years required to teach the three Rs—reading, writing, and arithmetic. The southern states had no public schools before Reconstruction; New York City began to provide free public high schools for more than a few students only in 1900. Hospitals served largely to isolate and to pray for the souls of the sick and dying; by some measures, hospitals came to provide more help than harm to their patients' health only in the 1920s. Just 2 percent of young people were going to high school by the 1890s, and few of these, most of them males, went to college. Most colleges served the needs of particular religious denominations.[34]

Everywhere, communities levied taxes mostly to pay for roads, bridges, municipal water supplies and drainage, public order, and sometimes canal and railroad subsidies.[35] State support for higher education was limited and often took the form of encouragement and subsidy to institutions increasingly seen as "private." Northern communities that had relatively dense and affluent populations supported increasingly autonomous libraries; academies, colleges, and lyceums that provided adult education; "dispensaries" or clinics for the poor; pioneering institutions for the blind, the deaf, and the mentally ill; and orphanages and homes for unwed mothers, clergymen, and widows of clergymen. Most of these institutions remained small. Those who lived in rural areas or in the West or South had far less access to such facilities.[36]

Early Nineteenth-Century Endowments and Foundations

Devoted to distinctive approaches, determined to set their own courses, and forced to find their own resources, religious and educational institutions took new forms and pursued a wider array of purposes; they necessarily emphasized the collection and stewardship of funds.[37] Churches, schools, and other charities that had enjoyed government support through the Church of England reconstituted themselves as Episcopalian and looked for new private sources of funding. The churches and schools of New England, including Harvard, Yale, and Dartmouth, now identified themselves as Congregationalist or autonomous. They continued for some decades to receive government funding, but also faced rising opposition from taxpayers who did not share their religious commitments or their growing openness to inquiry.[38]

Working under their newly supportive legal regime, Americans created funds that managed resources for specified purposes—for religious missions at home and abroad, for students, for struggling colleges sponsored by religious denominations, for young men seeking to establish themselves as self-sufficient farmers and shopkeepers, for public school authorities, and for cultural institutions. By the middle of the nineteenth century, some of the most substantial funds and the endowments of the largest private universities already operated, in effect, as general-purpose foundations. By then the most adventurous colleges were offering instruction in fields ranging from ancient languages and religion to scientific research and music. They were maintaining museums and gardens and underwriting student athletics and community-service activities. A few cultural organizations were similarly building a growing range of libraries, art galleries, spaces for performance, and gardens.

Overall, foundations played important if not critical roles in creating and building the distinctive Protestant denominations of the United States and in building prominent educational and cultural institutions. Often, the early foundations worked to raise funds from year to year, in the style of today's community funds and supporting foundations.[39] Very few nineteenth-century American foundations were large, national, nonsectarian, and devoted to general purposes, although some did grow substantially in size and scope. Nineteenth-century funds were deeply involved in the conflicts of the time, supporting slavery as well as opposing it, resisting Catholicism as well as encouraging religious freedom.

The early foundations underwrote institutions that mobilized people to support transcendent objectives rather than to build individual fortunes for their own families. In 1710, in *Essays to Do Good*—possibly nineteenth-century America's most widely read book after the Bible—Cotton Mather put the case for giving to such institutions this way:

> He that supports the office of the evangelical ministry, supports good work; and performs one; yea, at the second hand performs what is done by the skillful, faithful, painful minister. . . . To take a poor child, especially an orphan, left in poverty, and bestow an education upon it, especially if it be a liberal education, is an admirable, and a complicated charity; yea, it may draw on a long train of good, and interest you in all the good that shall be done by those whom you have educated. . . . Hence also what is done for schools, and for colleges, and for hospitals, is done for a general good. The endowing of these, or the maintaining of them, is, at once to do good unto many. . . .
>
> Sometimes there may be got ready for the press, elaborate composures, of great bulk, and greater worth, by which the best interests of knowledge and virtue, may be considerably served in the world; they lie like the impotent man at the pool of Bethesda; and they are like to lie, till God inspire some wealthy persons, to subscribe nobly for their publication, and by this generous application of their wealth to bring them abroad.[40]

Mather and those who agreed with him wished to encourage highly capable people to commit to ill-paid religious, educational, scientific, medical, and cultural careers. Excellent people could not be expected to make such commitments unless the organizations that employed them enjoyed continuing support. Legislatures balked at imposing taxes for such purposes. Private giving was necessary. To provide support over time, new foundations were essential.

The separation of church and state and the end of tax support for churches and schools came with particular abruptness in Connecticut in 1818. Lyman Beecher, one of the chief leaders of Connecticut Congregationalism, described his response in dramatic terms: "It was as dark a day as ever I saw. The odium thrown upon the ministry was inconceivable. The injury done to the cause of Christ, as we then supposed, was. . . . For several days I suffered what no tongue can tell." But, Beecher continued, the end of state support turned out to be *"the best thing that ever happened to the State of Connecticut* [italics in original]. It cut the churches loose from dependence on state support. It threw them wholly on their own resources and on God." Beecher concluded that, contrary to popular belief, ministers had gained influence: "By voluntary efforts, societies, missions, and revivals, they [ministers] exert a deeper influence than ever they could by queues, and shoe-buckles, and cocked hats and gold-headed canes."[41]

Some of America's largest early funds and endowments devoted themselves to these religious denominations, their leaders, and their colleges.[42] In 1844 Robert Baird, a leader among Evangelical institution-builders, summed up the effort in this way:

> Funds are raised for the erection of church edifices, for the support of pastors, and for providing destitute places with the preaching of the gospel—this last involving the whole subject of our home missionary efforts. And as ministers must be provided for the settlements forming apace in the West, as well as for the constantly increasing population to be found in the villages, towns, and cities of the East . . . [and as education required institutions] from the primary schools up to the theological seminaries and faculties [funds had to be raised for those purposes as well].[43]

"Permanent funds" and foundations were important to these efforts. The Presbyterian retirement fund, for example, was incorporated in Pennsylvania in 1799; that denomination's Boudinot Book Fund for the support of "weak and feeble congregations" in 1821; Presbyterian mission, education, and publication "boards," designed to raise, invest, and dispense funds for these purposes, followed in the 1840s and 1850s.[44] In Connecticut, many Congregationalists set up "society funds" to support their churches.[45] The Methodists (who had separated from the Church of England and the Episcopalians) used their available resources more for the support of preachers than for their education, but their "chartered fund" of 1796, augmented by profits from the sale of Methodist books and the sale of annuities, also grew to substantial proportions.[46] The American

Bible Society (1816), the American Tract Society (1824), the American Sunday School Union (1825), and the American Education Society (1816) accumulated donations and bequests as well as sales income and encouraged broad-based cooperation as an alternative to narrower Protestant denominationalism.[47]

Broadly or narrowly conceived, most of these societies gathered funds continuously from many individuals, held and invested them, and distributed them over time—playing what today would be called a community foundation or federated fundraising role.[48] Jewish and Catholic institutions—both of which had long faced British restriction before the liberalizations of the nineteenth century—also obtained land, buildings, and funds to support schools, seminaries, homes for religious leaders, and social and medical institutions.

Although most early nineteenth-century American foundations supported particular institutions, they did not limit themselves to "tradition" or to "charity" rather than "philanthropy." Nor were they entirely particularistic, paternalistic, or amateurish. These funds controlled and preserved assets not just to maintain existing organizations, beliefs, and practices, but also to develop social capital and to build new activities better suited to their own times. The early religious funds helped create America's distinctive pattern of denominational Protestantism and a general tolerance of religious and cultural difference; they also underwrote much education. And although their overarching purposes were often narrow, the early foundations exhibited remarkable complexity and innovation in their own right. They engaged in fundraising and investment, sometimes in the forms of banking and insurance; and they also devised many kinds of scholarships, grants, and pensions.[49]

Early nonsectarian and secular foundations followed similar paths. In the years after the American Revolution, multiple "subscribers" came together in the more densely settled and prosperous parts of the Northeast to create hospitals, schools, libraries, lyceums, and facilities for the arts. From their early days the Pennsylvania Hospital (1751), the New York Hospital (founded in the 1770s and entirely rebuilt after the revolution), the Massachusetts General Hospital (1811), and most colleges raised and held endowed funds for specific purposes. Philadelphia's nondenominational Magdalen Society, established in 1800 to collect, hold, and distribute funds "to ameliorate the distressed condition of those unhappy females who have been seduced from the path of virtue and are desirous of returning to a life of rectitude," reorganized itself into a more general foundation only in 1918.[50]

Americans developed creative, innovative, and sometimes very complicated arrangements to support these institutions. Early "associations" often defy twenty-first century categories. As historian Robert F. Dalzell Jr. has emphasized, the Massachusetts Hospital Life Insurance Company (chartered in 1818, active after 1825) combined the functions of a trust company with those of an insurance company and a charitable endowment. Under a state charter that treated it as an agency for wide community benefit, it invested substantial sums for the benefit of many of its state's wealthiest families and nonprofit institutions, and it also donated a full third of its often considerable earnings to the Massachusetts General Hospital.[51]

Some of the nineteenth century's most remarkable funds bore a greater resemblance to the large general-purpose foundations of the twentieth century. Created by a single individual, these funds asked a small board to invest substantial capital for a range of purposes and gave the board the power to shift annual gifts among charitable and public purposes. Benjamin Franklin created the two earliest important funds of this kind in 1791, through bequests to benefit the people of Philadelphia and Boston. Following several English examples,[52] Franklin left for each city £1,000, to be loaned out by an unpaid board selected by Protestant and city council leaders, "at five per cent, per annum, to such young married artificers, under the age of twenty-five years, as have served an apprenticeship in the said town, and faithfully fulfilled the duties required in their indentures, so as to obtain a good moral character from at least two respectable citizens." Ten percent of each loan was to be repaid annually, so that the funds could respond to "fresh borrowers."

Franklin expected that the compounding of interest would, over 100 years, raise each fund to the equivalent of £131,000. He directed that £100,000 should then be given to each city for public works to be selected at the time, "such as fortifications, bridges, aqueducts, public buildings, baths, pavements." The remainder was again to be loaned at interest for another 100 years. At the end of the second period each fund would, he predicted, amount to £4,061,000: all the money would then go to public improvements. Franklin's elaborate wishes were carried out with more flexibility and success in Boston than in Philadelphia, but with remarkable effectiveness considering the time that elapsed and the challenges posed by economic transformation, depression, inflation, and war. In 1991 the two funds wound up their affairs with a total of $6.5 million.[53]

Franklin left his funds not to independent religious or charitable corporations, but—as befitted their entirely secular and civic purposes—to the municipal corporations of Philadelphia and Boston. The managers of Franklin's Philadelphia fund evolved into the City Trusts of Philadelphia, which might well be described as the nation's earliest approximation of a community foundation. The municipal corporation was also the appropriate trustee for the estate, worth several million dollars, that Philadelphia shipping magnate Stephen Girard famously left through his will of 1831 to support a number of charitable and municipal purposes and also to create a residential school for "poor white male orphans." This racial restriction provoked complaint and was invalidated during the civil rights era of the mid-twentieth century. Another clause proved more immediately controversial. Girard wrote, "I enjoin and require that no ecclesiastic, missionary, or minister of any sect whatsoever, shall ever hold or exercise any station or duty whatever in the said college; nor shall any such person ever be admitted for any purpose, or as a visitor, within the premises appropriated to the purposes of the said college." Girard immediately added that he did "not mean to cast any reflection upon any sect or person whatsoever."[54] His explanation is worth quoting as an influential response to religious conflict in the 1830s:

> But as there is such a multitude of sects and such a diversity of opinion amongst them I desire to keep the tender minds of the orphans who are to derive advantage from this bequest free from the excitement which clashing doctrines and sectarian controversy are so apt to produce. My desire is that all the instructors and teachers in the college shall take pains to instil [sic] into the minds of the scholars the purest principles of morality so that on their entrance into active life they may from inclination and habit evince benevolence towards their fellow creatures and a love of truth sobriety and industry adopting at the same time such religious tenets as their matured reason may enable them to prefer.[55]

Within a few decades the directors of the City Trusts of Philadelphia were investing and supervising the use of the income of the large assets of the Girard trust and of several other funds to support several schools, libraries, hospitals, and other charities and to improve substantial parts of the city's infrastructure. By the early years of the twentieth century, they were also handling the building fund for the massive Franklin Institute and, in general, encouraging local economic growth. For decades the Girard College orphanage won praise for its studies of child development, as well as for its work with the children assigned to its care.[56]

Several other substantial nineteenth-century charities also asked a board to invest a substantial fund both for growth—growth of the fund itself and growth also of prosperity for its home locality—and for a larger cause. The Smith Charities, created by a wealthy central Massachusetts bachelor's will of 1847, began with $200,000 (more than $5.6 million in 2011, measured in terms of the consumer price index) "as an accumulating fund" to be loaned at interest to young farmers and tradesmen until it doubled. At that point "$30,000 of the fund was to be set apart for the establishment of an agricultural school at Northampton," this sum to be further invested until a full sixty years after the donor's death. Meanwhile $360,000 was to be invested for the more immediate benefit of indigent boys, girls, young women, and widows, making "no distinction . . . [regarding] religious sect or political or other party." Half the income would provide small loans to enable apprentices to set themselves up as farmers or tradesmen; the other half would give "marriage portions" to girls who had successfully completed terms of service under the supervision of the trustees and other funds to poor married and widowed women. By the mid-1870s the Smith Charities had indeed helped scores of young people and contributed substantially to a state college; it still held more than $1 million in assets.[57]

In yet another complex arrangement, in 1855 cotton manufacturer Abbott Lawrence left a $50,000 endowment to provide model tenements in Boston through a plan intended to demonstrate that if investors would accept a limitation of dividends to 6 percent, it was possible to provide good housing in return for rents so low that people of very limited incomes could afford them. Half of the profit was to be reinvested in new model tenements; trustees were to give the other half "to organized public charities[,] not to individuals"—thus anticipating the charity organization movement by a generation.[58]

Other nineteenth-century funds allocated their resources from time to time to entire groups of organizations. The Lowell Institute, created by the will of John Lowell Jr. in 1836, was in some ways the earliest of all general-purpose foundations in the United States. Because it was required to return 10 percent of each year's earnings to its principal fund, the institute's assets grew to more than $1 million by the early twentieth century. The institute did far more than underwrite hundreds of popular lectures in the twenty-five years before the Civil War. Through its exceptionally well-paid Boston lectures, it gave important early support to science and scientists and also underwrote important educational activity. In the 1860s it provided critical early funding for MIT. Later, it also supported Northeastern University and the Harvard Extension School, both of which grew over the years to substantial proportions. In the mid-twentieth century, the Lowell Institute underwrote WGBH-TV, one of the most important originators of programming for American public television.[59] As their endowments grew, by the middle of the nineteenth century the trustees of Harvard, the Massachusetts Hospital Life Insurance Company, and the Lowell Institute together managed a notable portion of Boston's investment capital.[60]

Nineteenth-century institutions devoted to the arts and to literature also evolved into prototypes for the American foundation. By the 1850s both the Pennsylvania Academy of Fine Arts and the Boston Athenaeum, founded by a large number of "subscribers" in 1805 and 1807 and later aided by large gifts from wealthy citizens, had accumulated land, substantial buildings, and "permanent funds" of considerable size. They had built libraries, collections of sculpture and paintings, concert and lecture series, and, at the Philadelphia institution, an art school.[61] Access to these institutions was limited in various ways, but over time they became more freely open to the public. It can well be argued that the Boston Athenaeum served as a sort of foundation as it spawned efforts that produced the Boston Public Library, the Boston Museum of Fine Arts, and the Boston Symphony Orchestra.[62] Similarly the Wadsworth Athenaeum, launched in 1842, housed the Hartford Library Association, the Connecticut Historical Society, a public art gallery, and an art school. The Brooklyn Institute hosted a similar array of cultural institutions. The boards of these institutions encouraged donations and invested substantial capital for the support of multiple charitable purposes.

Several of America's largest private colleges also came to act much like foundations by the 1850s. By that decade several of these institutions had substantial endowments, invested by their trustees to support expanding arrays of activities. Earlier colleges had focused on undergraduate education, emphasizing classical and biblical languages and literatures and various approaches to mental discipline.[63] By the 1850s the more ambitious colleges were adding special facilities and endowments for the study of botany and science; gardens and arboreta; museums of natural history and art; research libraries; gymnasiums, swimming pools, and athletic fields. Chapels served as concert halls or as sites for public lectures. Many colleges offered short-term practical courses in surveying, bookkeeping, and other practical matters. In what was then the West, as historian Colin Burke points out, Oberlin had become by the 1850s "a huge educational complex with hundreds of students," women as well as men, in "departments ranging from the primary through a normal school to the regular college and a theological department."[64] After the Civil War, many colleges added special schools for graduate study and the professions. By the end of the century, a number of colleges had also added special facilities for the promotion of community service.[65]

As colleges transformed themselves into comprehensive universities, they lost their early identity as single-purpose charities. By the 1860s many college boards were, in effect, running multipurpose foundations. This reality surely helped capture the imagination of the exceptionally wealthy men who endowed complex new universities in this period—Cornell in 1865, Johns Hopkins in 1876, Clark in 1877, and Stanford in 1885.[66] The example of the college endowment also caught the attention of Andrew Carnegie and John D. Rockefeller.

As the purposes of universities multiplied—in similar fashion to literary and artistic "athenaeums" and medical centers—donors faced new challenges. Disputes over doctrine, social policy, and focus created notable disputes as early as the Dartmouth College Case of 1819. Conflicts over doctrine and slavery separated Congregationalists from Presbyterians, divided "Old Light" and "New Light" Presbyterians in the 1830s, and fueled the "Hicksite" split in the Society of Friends.[67] In more than a few instances these divisions also affected charitable funds. Caught up in these disputes, donors sometimes saw their gifts used for purposes they opposed. Multipurpose institutions created more opportunities for donor disappointment. In a series of notable cases, wealthy women found that even "coercive philanthropy" could fail to open opportunities for women to study in the new university-related schools of medicine.[68]

It was not surprising that donors who wanted to achieve specific ends looked increasingly to legal devices such as trusts and foundations to hold and dispense funds for the purposes they favored. Yet they could not ignore the possibility that their purposes might face scrutiny in court. Before his death in 1861, Francis Jackson created a trust "for the preparation and circulation of books, newspapers, the delivery of speeches, lectures and such other means as in their judgment will create a public sentiment that will put an end to negro slavery in this country" and also for "the benefit of fugitive slaves who may escape from the slaveholding states of this infamous Union, from time to time." When these trusts were challenged in the Massachusetts courts in 1867 the court ruled, "Before slavery was abolished in the United States this trust was valid and might be lawfully applied, consistently with the expressed intention of the testator, to the relief of fugitive slaves in distress, or the extinguishment by purchase of the claims of those alleging themselves to be their masters." Once slavery was ended, Massachusetts courts approved the use of these funds for related purposes: the education of freedmen in the South and the relief of impoverished African Americans in Boston.

But Jackson also created a third trust, which he intended "to become a permanent organization, until the rights of women shall be established equal with those of men." His hope was that this new organization would "receive the services and sympathy, the donations and bequests of the friends of human rights." He directed it to support "the preparation and circulation of books, the delivery of lectures," and other means to "secure the passage of laws granting women whether married or unmarried, the right to vote, to hold office, to hold, manage and devise property, and all other civil rights enjoyed by men." The courts ruled this trust invalid, because the state's laws did "not recognize the purpose of overthrowing or changing them" as the legitimate purpose of a charity.[69]

Late Nineteenth-Century Foundations:
From Particular to General Purpose

In many ways the general-purpose foundation was already coming into being in the 1850s. Diffuse, curiously complex investment-and-charitable entities like the Franklin Funds and the City Trusts of Philadelphia, the Massachusetts Hospital Life Insurance Company, the Lowell Institute, and the Smith Charities had characterized the century's early decades. By the 1860s large charitable endowments and funds held by Protestant groups and by colleges and art institutes were contributing to a widening range of charitable purposes. Several foundation-like efforts operated across state borders: Franklin placed his twin competing funds in Philadelphia and Boston; the Protestant denominational funds and interdenominational educational funds moved resources from East to West,

aiding schools and clergy wherever they located; colleges like Yale and Oberlin attracted students as well as funds from much of the nation.[70] By 1880 the
largest college and university endowments had surpassed $1 million; brand-new
Johns Hopkins had about $3 million, Harvard nearly $4 million, and Columbia
nearly $5 million.[71] Increasingly, state regulations separated what we now call
"charitable nonprofit organizations" from other institutions, leaving direct interventions into the local economy to savings banks and insurance companies. And
although New York continued to regulate charitable organizations more closely
than business corporations, Pennsylvania and states in New England were allowing greater scope and autonomy to charities and endowments.

Smaller funds devoted to local, religious, cultural, and educational purposes
continued to appear in the last decades of the nineteenth century and beyond;
their very numbers, during years in which some states were relaxing controls
over their activities, entitle them to more study than they have received. The
small numbers of large, new, and more general-purpose funds that appeared in
those decades, by contrast, have attracted considerable attention.

Having moved from New England to Baltimore to London, where he made
a great fortune in investment banking, George Peabody handled his philanthropy in the fashion of a foundation. Providing detailed, continuous advice
and instructions, he worked for years to create a remarkable group of institutions. Using a series of interrelated grants, he created self-sustaining enterprises:
the Peabody Institute libraries of Peabody and Danvers, Massachusetts; the Peabody Institute of Music in Baltimore; and the Peabody museums at Harvard,
Yale, and Salem, Massachusetts. He also created two pioneer and quite separate foundations, the Peabody Donation Fund of London (1862)—which built
and sustained substantial model housing projects—and the Peabody Education
Fund (1867).

Although large and expansive, all of Peabody's initiatives built on the examples of the Pennsylvania and New England funds under discussion. Launched
in 1867 with about $2 million, conservatively invested to produce an annual
income of about $80,000 and led by a carefully selected board chaired by a
former U.S. senator from Massachusetts but including southerners as well as
northerners, the Peabody Fund supported efforts to build local tax-supported
public school systems and state departments of public instruction across the
South. The fund pressed for policy innovation, but also for post–Civil War reconciliation between the white communities of the North and the South. It did
not seek racial equality. More than 80 percent of its money went to "white"
schools, and it directed funds for African Americans through white-controlled
local governments. The Peabody Fund did help institutionalize public schools
in the South. Under the conditions of the day, it could do this only by simultaneously helping to institutionalize racial segregation and the denial of equal

opportunity to African Americans. Once southern public schools were well established, the principal of the fund went to support the Peabody College for Teachers in Nashville.[72]

But the Peabody Fund was far from the only supporter of schooling in the post–Civil War South. Presbyterian, Congregationalist, Episcopalian, and Baptist denominational funds provided even larger total subsidies to southern church-related schools and colleges for African Americans. The American Missionary Association, created by antislavery Congregationalists, Methodists, and Presbyterians, applied the income from the exceptionally large Daniel Hand Fund ($1 million in 1888—the equivalent of $211 million in 2011 if measured in terms of gross domestic product per capita—later augmented by another half million), and much more besides, to the schools it sponsored.[73] We noted the repurposed Jackson fund above. The 1882 Slater Fund (launched with a $1 million gift) also significantly increased nondenominational support for the education of African American public school teachers in the region.

Like Peabody, Andrew Carnegie paid attention to the increasingly generous treatment that New England and Pennsylvania accorded to charities and endowments. And he well understood the special corporate powers Pennsylvania had granted to the Pennsylvania Railroad, which had launched and long served as a chief customer for his steel business, significantly contributing to his path to success. Pennsylvania law relating to corporations as well as to charities allowed his lawyers to create legal instruments to hold funds for the notable institutions he built in Pittsburgh: the Carnegie Institute, with its museums of art and natural history, and the Carnegie Institute of Technology.

Many states had discouraged the creation of multiple-purpose charitable corporations, limited the size of their endowments, and continued to look with disfavor on charitable bequests if estates could instead be assigned to living relatives; but by the 1890s pressures from donors, from institution builders, and ultimately from the public led to change. These pressures came to a head in New York. Despite that state's restrictive regulations, Columbia and Cornell had already grown into complex, multischool universities with endowments over $10 million.[74] The Metropolitan Museum of Art had a substantial, city-owned building and an already very valuable collection of art, held by a separate charitable corporation; Brooklyn had ambitious plans for cultural institutions. The Baron de Hirsch Fund, incorporated in New York in 1891 with $2.4 million from its Belgian donor, had a purpose that was simultaneously specific and general. It offered Jews fleeing religious persecution in Eastern Europe "protection . . . through port work, relief, temporary aid, promotion of suburban industrial enterprises, . . . land settlement, agricultural training, and trade and general education."[75]

Andrew Carnegie also launched his great public library project from New York during the 1890s. Through this initiative (run from a substantial New York office whose open call for applications gave it the character of a foundation without the legal framework), Carnegie gave over $60 million to more than 2,500 public libraries—an extraordinary number. To receive Carnegie library funds, a community had to agree to match the gift and to adopt a permanent library tax; Carnegie architects designed most of the library buildings and specified construction standards.[76] Carnegie managers in turn accepted local decisions regarding library location and sometimes discriminatory access policies. It has also been argued that the Carnegie designs included open, centrally placed structures for the supervision of all library visitors and imposed constricting roles on the overwhelmingly female library staffs.[77]

Through the Carnegie library initiative, as through the Lowell Institute and the Peabody initiatives, a very substantial fund was invested so as to yield a stream of income to be given over time to a set of institutions, though in this case the donor augmented the funds from time to time and did not establish a permanent fund. As with today's community foundations, money from such a fund was given in a flexible and well-advertised way intended to encourage other donors, paying students, and local governments to add their support to the cause and to permit the fund to respond to changing conditions.

This was the context when state courts invalidated former Governor Samuel J. Tilden's multimillion-dollar bequest, carefully designed to consolidate the outmoded and underfunded Astor and Lennox libraries into a prominent New York Public Library. In the eyes of the court, the bequest was flawed under the trust law of the time because the money was to go to an entity that had not yet been formally incorporated. At about the same time, New York courts also invalidated a major bequest to Cornell University on the ground that the university's endowment had already reached the total permitted by its initial state charter.[78] In each case, distant relatives won the substantial funds that had been intended to benefit the public. These court actions drew such strong protest that New York's legislature could not ignore pressure for change.[79] Bowing to the public outcry, the New York state legislature passed a new law declaring that no "gift, grant, bequest or devise to religious, educational, charitable or benevolent uses which shall, in other respects be valid under the laws of this state, shall or be deemed invalid by reason of the indefiniteness or uncertainty of the persons designated as the beneficiaries."[80] The legislature also relaxed its restrictive approach to institutional endowments. Acknowledging public preference for civic uplift rather than family enrichment, some of Tilden's relatives honored his vision by giving their portions to the library's promoters, who raised other funds and succeeded in creating the remarkable institution on Fifth Avenue and 42nd Street.

The "Tilden Act" is sometimes taken as encouraging the creation of philanthropic foundations with general powers. It did reverse the rules that, as Katz, Sullivan, and Beach note, "caused the failure of many testamentary gifts to charity during the 1870s and 1880s." But as they also emphasize, New York's laws were complex. They quote an 1888 decision of the New York Court of Appeals as emphasizing alternative ways to accomplish charitable purposes: "With us charity is found in our corporation laws, general and special, which have been extended so as to embrace the purposes heretofore known and recognized as charitable, and which are continually extending and improving, so as to meet the new wants which society in its progress may develop."[81] The Tilden Act attracted considerable attention and no doubt influenced other states. But state regulations remained diverse. Throughout the twentieth century the states continued to apply different rules to different kinds of charities and to limit the purposes and even the size of their endowments.[82] This is a vast, highly complex story and one that is still not well understood. Even today thousands of lawyers earn good livings helping donors and foundations understand what particular states permit them to do.

American Foundations before 1900

We have sought in this chapter to find our way through the thicket of religious and political dispute that usually obscures the early history of American foundations. If we take our cue from the law and include in our view the usually neglected religious funds and large, complex endowed charities, what can we conclude about the contributions of nineteenth-century funds and foundations? How did they shape the possibilities for Americans? To what extent do they deserve criticism for reinforcing division and subordination along lines of race, gender, and class? If foundations and closely related forms of private charity reflected inequality, what compensations did they offer in return?

Nineteenth-century funds, endowments, and foundations fell under laws relating to a number of topics—charities, bequests, trusts, corporations, the relation between church and state, the liberty of conscience, taxes and exemptions from taxes on property, as well as slavery, race, and the position of women. The relevant laws varied considerably from state to state and from time to time. In the current state of our knowledge, comprehensive, precise generalization is impossible. But it is clear that in some states—most notably those of New England as well as Pennsylvania and New York—foundations and foundation-like trusts and charitable organizations gained a distinct prominence by the 1850s. Most focused on a local community, but some of the largest religious and religious-education funds took much of the nation as their territory, and some of the most ambitious schools attracted students from many states. By mid-century some of the larger religious and secular funds and the best-endowed colleges and museum-library complexes had come, in effect, to play the role of the general-purpose foundation.

Critics have rightly noted that nineteenth-century charities of all kinds held limited funds. Taken together, the era's endowed charities, funds, and foundations lacked the resources to redistribute wealth in a significant way. They could not substitute for government. But they could and did complement government and, in a few cases, nudge governments toward new policies. And they could do and did do things that contemporaries thought entirely inappropriate for government. Nineteenth-century American governments relied heavily on families to cushion the impact of poverty; they counted on law and order, property rights, education in the "three Rs," and basic transportation facilities and postal services to encourage economic growth. Nineteenth-century funds and foundations complemented government support for families. Guided by religious impulses and possessing limited funds, however, they complemented government only in traditional and symbolic ways.

By the end of the century, religious communities, donors, and endowed funds had created literally hundreds of small charities for mothers, infants, foundlings, orphans, prostitutes, those who suffered from particular diseases, those who needed to learn a trade, those disabled by physical loss or age, those addicted to alcohol or drugs, and those discharged from prison.[83] A whole industry appeared, publishing guidebooks that explained how to find help for a blind Lutheran woman or a Catholic orphan. In the larger cities of the Northeast the resulting complex of small specialized charities offered a confusing and ill-funded response to need, but a few foundations were already seeking to bring a more rational organization to big-city charity.[84]

In the fields of organized religion, literature, the arts and sciences, and popular and collegiate education nineteenth-century endowed funds and early foundations played strongly innovative philanthropic roles as social entrepreneurs and institution builders. In all of these areas, foundations did things that governments did not begin to consider. The Lowell Institute lectures in Boston, the Protestant colleges of the West, and the Carnegie libraries significantly increased opportunities for many Americans. Colleges that admitted women and African Americans did appear, and some began to thrive in Massachusetts, Pennsylvania, Ohio, and New York—the states that most encouraged endowed charitable corporations. Foundations also provided valuable funds for schools and colleges for African Americans in the former slave states.

Yet overall the children of the poor received only a little training for a semi-skilled occupation (and instruction in accepting their "place"), while college remained available only to the few.[85] And only rarely did nineteenth-century funds challenge the discriminatory treatment of African Americans or women. Much nineteenth-century philanthropy was indeed particularistic, amateurish, paternalistic, and elitist. While the Peabody Fund, the Slater Fund, and others provided important support for the introduction and development of public schooling in the South after the Civil War, they also reinforced the racism of the era.[86] Eric Anderson and Alfred A. Moss Jr. rightly emphasize that the Peabody and Slater funds underwrote the color line; so did the Girard "college" orphanage of the City Trusts of Philadelphia. Anderson and Moss add, however, "In spite of their compromises and ulterior motives, the foundation philanthropists had a vision of race relations (and black potential) that was significantly different from that of the South's white majority." [87] The Boston Athenaeum, the Pennsylvania Academy of Fine Arts, the Oberlin Music Conservatory, even the individual Carnegie libraries, and the many multipurpose colleges and their like remained quite small by later standards. It is true that each of these, like the universities and even the Peabody and Slater funds, celebrated only selected forms of learning and art. But they did offer opportunities for learning, creativity, excellence, and independent thinking.

One of the greatest foundation achievements of the nineteenth century—and the most neglected—was to be found in the structures of America's Protestant denominations. As denominational funds grew, their very size served to preserve traditions and sometimes to encourage denominational factions to overcome conflicts and work together—though their riches also served on occasion as apples of discord. Arguably, the rough compromises Americans made over the relation between church and state, between permission to build religious communities and considerable reluctance (though never complete refusal) to use taxes to fund them, encouraged religious toleration during a century that saw harsh religious conflict in Ireland and many parts of Continental Europe.

Nineteenth-century endowments and funds did not, of course, escape criticism. Every denomination, every religious movement, indeed organized religion itself, had critics and detractors. Critics complained that religious funds wasted resources—or worse in some eyes promoted religious division and conflict. Every cultural and educational initiative evoked similar criticism.[88]

We can't say whether nineteenth-century funds and foundations increased the total given to all charitable purposes, including religion and direct relief of need.[89] We do know that American taxpayers of the day were not willing to spend funds for such purposes. Religious and other cultural divisions within the electorate reinforced the general resistance to taxes. American governments were not inclined to provide much support for religious, cultural, scientific, intellectual, or social activities. Foundations, trusts, and private donors did not substitute for nineteenth-century governments: they underwrote activities that would not otherwise have existed.

In Europe, royal, aristocratic, church, and state establishments underwrote religion, advanced education, and subsidized culture; such official funders had no counterparts in nineteenth-century America. (In addition to such official funders, nineteenth-century Britain, the German lands, and northern Italy also produced many private, merchant-family, and private association endowments that closely resembled America's.)[90] In Germany and Eastern Europe, as historian Timothy Snyder has written, "The pride of societies was the 'intelligentsia,' the educated classes who saw themselves as leading the nation . . . and preserving national culture." The intelligentsia was "the social embodiment of Enlightenment."[91]

Nineteenth-century America granted less prestige to a particular form of elite education and recognized no single "national culture." Close to universal literacy and citizenship rights for white men, as well as widespread property ownership, considerable economic opportunity, enthusiasm for many distinctive religions together with strictures against the establishment of religion, and the absence of a national university created a very different context for feelings about "national culture." We might argue that in the United States the "educated classes" took their ways of thinking not only from universities that celebrated the Enlightenment, but also from distinctive church communities and their colleges, from various cultural movements, and from their home regions. America's educated worked through a widely varied array of schools, arts organizations, religious institutions, charities, local governments, and professional and business firms. Toward the end of the nineteenth century James Bryce, the celebrated British interpreter of the United States, asked why America's "best men" did not go into politics. We might respond that the nation could have no single group of "best men," because its founding decisions in favor of federalism and a separation of church and state meant that it did not develop a unified culture that could define a single hierarchy of institutions and prestige. America's early foundations did not create this reality; rather, they took advantage of it to enable small numbers of donors the opportunity to advance, and to demonstrate commitment to, distinctive fragments of an extraordinarily plural nation.

3

The Classic Institution-Building Period, 1900–50

Three factors converged at the beginning of the twentieth century to create the classic period of American foundations: fortunes of unprecedented size, especially those of Andrew Carnegie and John D. Rockefeller; a dramatic shift from religious faith to science as the dominant basis for higher education, research, and the professions; and movements to create whole new classes of organizations—research universities, scientific and medical societies, high schools, county public health departments, and public libraries. The convergence of these factors allowed a small group of foundations to play outsized roles in American life for the entire first half of the twentieth century and to set a positive image of the role of the foundation in the public mind—an image that persists.[1]

The devotion of very large fortunes to new, science-based organizations brought other changes. Earlier foundation and foundation-like giving had come mostly from comparatively modest fortunes. Denominational funds and endowed universities had persuaded numerous donors to support educational and religious work through common efforts that anticipated both the general-purpose private foundation and the community foundation. Leadership in most of these early foundation activities usually came from professional managers educated under religious auspices, although there were conspicuous exceptions, such as the Lowell Institute and Stephen Girard's orphanage. The wealthiest new donors also sought professional managers, but increasingly turned to professionals educated in science or law rather than religion. Through the nineteenth century, religious communities, often supported in part by endowments, had dominated much discussion of state and local policy relating to education, family life, and social welfare. By the beginning of the twentieth century, the celebrated new foundations were underwriting policy-shaping work that was nonsectarian, secular, and science-based. And they were seeking to address national concerns in science, medicine, military defense, and international affairs as well as in education and social welfare.

The several Carnegie and Rockefeller foundations—the Carnegie Institution of Washington (1902), the Carnegie Foundation for the Advancement of Teaching (1906), the Carnegie Endowment for International Peace (1910), the Carnegie Corporation of New York (1911), Rockefeller's General Education Board (1902), the Rockefeller Foundation (1909), the Laura Spelman Rockefeller Memorial and the China Medical Board (both 1918)—along with the Commonwealth (1918) and Alfred P. Sloan (1934) funds and the A. W. Mellon Educational and Charitable Trust (1930)—held unprecedented wealth. These great foundations often collaborated with the Milbank Memorial Fund (1905), the Russell Sage Foundation (1907), the Rosenwald Fund (1913), the Twentieth Century Fund (1919), the Daniel and Florence Guggenheim Foundation (1924), the John Simon Guggenheim Memorial Foundation (1937), the John and Mary R. Markle Foundation (1927), and the John A. Hartford Foundation (1929)—and with smaller funds across the United States. The various donors of these funds have attracted criticism as well as praise, but whatever we think of the donors or however we evaluate their ultimate impact, these funds did pursue their objectives thoughtfully, creatively, and persistently. Through a series of targeted, sustained, often innovative interventions, they played critical roles in the dramatic transformations of several key areas of American life—especially in higher education and in scientific and medical research, but also in public education and public health. In these fields, foundations found strong partners. They had less success in the fields of social welfare, the arts, and international relations, where powerful forces struggled with one another and foundations could build fewer effective partnerships.

Any comprehensive effort to assess the contributions of foundations in these decades must pay attention not only to these ambitious new funds but also to many others. Many foundations and endowments continued nineteenth-century practices. They supported religious activity, formal and informal education, arts organizations, local economic development, and local social welfare. Some of the largest new foundations gave a modern twist to traditional purposes, deploying their resources with considerable creativity. For practical, business, or indeed religious reasons, several did not reveal their true assets or provide much information before the 1970s; as a result, it is still difficult to reconstruct their record. But they dominated the foundation field in numerical terms, some of them were among the nation's largest foundations, and they deserve close attention.

At least a dozen regional foundations, mostly located in the middle of the nation, did much to reinforce the appreciation of science and of national standards while also continuing quite traditional commitments to religion and their home regions. The W. K. Kellogg Foundation of Michigan (1930), which has always made available a good deal of information about its grants, promoted public health, public education, and economic development in the rural and small town communities that produced grains for Kellogg's cereals. The Lilly Endowment of Indianapolis (1937) devoted itself to higher education in Indiana and to religious activities and values. The Duke Endowment for the Carolinas (1924) held and dispensed very substantial funds for universities sponsored by Southern Methodists and Southern Baptists, for education, health, and community development, and for Methodist ministers. The Danforth Foundation (1927) sought to advance Protestant higher education and moral and religious values in general, especially in St. Louis but also in the South and beyond; the Kresge Foundation (1924) of Michigan implemented a similar set of foci, especially in the Midwest; the Charles Stewart Mott Foundation of Flint, Michigan (1926), long emphasized local causes, especially children's health and education. The Houston Endowment (1937) provided college scholarships and supported universities and other charities in its city, where the M. D. Anderson Foundation (1936) focused on health care. The Baptist Foundation of Texas (1930) discharged its "mission to manage endowment funds of Baptist institutions and agencies" (including Baylor University) with great effectiveness.[2] The Texas foundations emphasized direct funding of immediate needs, but they also worked effectively to create major institutions in their state, most notably Houston's Texas Medical Center. The Amherst H. Wilder charities in the Twin Cities (1910), like the Children's Fund of Michigan (1929), sought to create model clinics and other facilities for child welfare. The A. W. Mellon Charitable Trust (1930–80) directed a fortune into the National Gallery of Art; the Samuel H. Kress Foundation (1929) sponsored art exhibitions and art education across the nation; and the Juilliard Foundation built a great music school.[3]

Hundreds of smaller foundations supported local and religious charities in most parts of the nation—as their counterparts had done through the nineteenth century and continue to do today. Although some states closely limited the creation of foundations, no state paid much attention to what foundations did with their money once it had allowed them to be established. As we noted in chapter 2, the acceptance of general-purpose foundations by the state of New York in the 1890s did something to open the field, but in the Northeast the trend toward general purposes long predated 1890, while in the South state control over charities of all kinds became tighter as Jim Crow tightened its grip.

Exemption from federal income tax only became an issue when Congress created the income tax in 1914, and then the tax fell on such a small part of the population that the exemption of foundations and other charities evoked little public comment. In 1917 Congress included foundations among the wide range of charities that retained tax advantages even in the face of the dramatic tax increases occasioned by World War I. Critics justifiably complained that too many foundations paid out in grants only a paltry share of their incomes; that a number of foundations seemed designed chiefly for purposes of business or family control; and that most foundations provided no public accounting of their activities. From time to time majorities in Congress objected to foundation support for particular legislative or political purposes. A few critics also objected to some specific foundation actions.[4] All too many foundations lacked ambition or commitment.[5] None of these complaints attracted great congressional attention, although in the 1930s Congress did adopt a somewhat stricter distinction than the most permissive states had drawn between the "educational" activities that were appropriate to foundations and the "advocacy" or "political" activities that were not.[6] Quite apart from federal regulation, consideration of sensibilities within their states led foundations to approach controversial topics with care.[7]

Congress did not give special attention to the endowments of private colleges and universities and other charities, but these were also relevant to the larger foundation field. In 1910 several universities reported to the U.S. Office of Education endowments that far exceeded those of all but the very largest foundations. Columbia's endowment had surged to nearly $26 million, Stanford's had reached $24 million, and Harvard's was just under $22 million; those of Yale and Chicago were well over $10 million; Cornell's was slightly less.[8] These large endowments allowed the wealthiest university boards to act like foundations, using their own funds as they chose from time to time in particular fields, in specific research agendas, in the support of faculty, and in student scholarships.

During the first half of the twentieth century American foundations worked in a context that made it possible for them to build a remarkable set of new institutions. As Barry Karl and Stanley N. Katz have argued, at the beginning of the century every nation faced daunting economic, technological, health, social, and military challenges associated with industrialization, urbanization, and the greatly increased international movement of people, information, and goods. In responding to these challenges the United States enjoyed many advantages: the world's largest and most efficient internal market; exceptional access to raw materials; a population largely (though by no means universally) literate in English; the flexibility inherent in state (rather than national) regulation of most elements of economic action; the relative autonomy of American corporations and voluntary organizations; and a remarkably large number of ambitious private and state universities.

The most notable foundations of this classic era made their mark within this context, above all by helping to create new institutions to promote medical and scientific research and to strengthen colleges, universities, and secondary schools. In these decades foundations also created the earliest modern "think tanks," specialized secular agencies devoted to the study of particular sets of public problems. The United States lacked some of the problem-solving capabilities in these fields that the major Western European powers and Japan appeared to derive from the scientific, administrative, and educational systems of their national governments.[9] Foundations reinforced the more decentralized institutional pattern of the United States. They did this both by supporting new organizations directly and by helping many of them, especially in medicine, science, and higher education, to work cooperatively to set effective national standards.

Foundations were by no means the only important institutions that sought to solve the problems of modern society. Indeed, the United States derived important strengths from the diversity of its responders. Some of these constituted nonprofit organizations and voluntary associations: private universities, research bureaus associated with the charity organization and municipal reform movements, nascent professions in the natural and social sciences as well as in medicine and engineering, and the religious denominations. State, regional, and municipal governments—notably including state universities and some municipal public health bureaus—played significant roles, as did such parts of the federal government as the Interstate Commerce Commission, the Coast and Geodetic Survey, the Department of the Interior, the Army and the Navy, and—under Herbert Hoover—the Department of Commerce. Business corporations, like government agencies and the nonprofit and religious organizations, both created problems and sought to solve them. Some foundations also worked closely with private universities and other nongovernment, nonprofit organizations, and with leading state universities, the U.S. Office of Education, and other government agencies.

It was within this context of institutional variation and diversity that the largest early twentieth-century foundations made their contributions. In the first two decades of the twentieth century, foundations endowed by Andrew Carnegie and John D. Rockefeller held, according to Leonard P. Ayers of the Russell Sage Foundation, more wealth than all the nation's college endowments put together.[10] As exceptionally successful entrepreneurs, the wealthiest donors had gained great self-confidence and won considerable public deference. In New York, and then in Pennsylvania, Ohio, Illinois, California, and other states, a foundation could take the new legal form of a general-purpose charitable corporation. Freed from responsibility for a single field, a general-purpose fund could give flexibly, in ways its leaders judged strategic from time to time. It could pay for new hospitals or laboratories, or endow medical research chairs or professorships, or underwrite an entirely new department in a particular field of scientific research. To attract talent to new fields, it could create scholarships, fellowships, research grant programs, and retirement funds. It could subsidize conferences, publications, travel, and research. A foundation could make its own determination of a field's importance (medical research or Asian studies or Baptist outreach), and it could continue in that field as long as judged appropriate, leaving its once-favored laboratories, colleges, or religious missions to find new funds as it moved on to other concerns. A foundation could also make large renewable grants to governments that agreed to adopt a sustained course of action: whether to build public school systems, create public libraries, sustain campaigns to improve public health, improve the scientific capabilities of state universities, or add a great art museum to the Smithsonian Institution in Washington, D.C.

During the first half of the twentieth century foundations did all these things. Historians and other analysts have now published a small library of books on their successes and failures. Although many foundation efforts await close examination, we can build a rich and nuanced evaluation of foundation contributions in this extended half-century. Some foundations have been fairly criticized for such excessively broad and vague statements of purpose as advancing the "welfare of mankind"—though we do have to note the lawyer's very practical desire to provide language that a court would recognize as allowing the foundation to do what it chose, yet remain fully legal. Early twentieth-century foundations often worked at cross purposes, and they almost always worked in fields of great complexity. Their efforts led often to unintended consequences—as when foundations strengthened a profession only to see it oppose the foundation's priorities. Sometimes a good and desired result in one direction came with a negative consequence in another. Several key foundation initiatives provoked powerful opposition. In the contested and complex fields of health, education, and social welfare controversy was always present and the outcomes of any initiative were always difficult to measure. But during the early decades of the twentieth century the conditions of American life—the newness, modest size, and rapid development of universities, scientific research, high schools, and public health initiatives, as well as wide agreement about the importance of these fields and the value of science—created unusual opportunities.

The conditions that made such large contributions possible disappeared after the 1940s and are not likely to return. Many policy discussions ignore that reality and continue to assume that today's foundations could play roles as decisive as the roles played by a few foundations in the early decades of the last century. History can usefully identify the conditions that made such achievements possible then and show how those conditions no longer prevail.

Higher Education and Research

Many studies—not only of the foundations themselves, but of the development of the sciences, of research, and of higher education in the United States—have made it clear that during the first half of the twentieth century foundations made their most notable contributions to the growth of science, medicine, and higher education.[11] Able to focus resources on selected problems over a long period, foundations were uniquely positioned to provide stability to smaller, more fragile organizations in these rapidly developing fields (including the University of Chicago and MIT as well as public schools in the South) and also to give real substance to new coordinating, standard-setting institutions that did much to give shape to education and research as a whole.

At the beginning of the twentieth century a diverse, disjointed, competitive, far-flung collection of private colleges, private universities, state universities, and city colleges spread across the nation. In practical reality, many institutions that styled themselves as "colleges" were really high schools. A few private colleges whose endowments exceeded all but the very largest foundations mounted programs in fields ranging from science to athletics to art; in 1900 Stanford's endowment was $18 million, Harvard's and Yale's were above $12 million.[12] But most colleges relied on tuition from local students, who came, generally, from a narrow range of religious and cultural communities. Nineteenth-century foundations and fundraising operations supplemented tuition income, in ways that bound groups of colleges together within each of the major Protestant denominations. America's colleges and their faculties related to one another through distinctive religious traditions rather than through shared commitments to universal fields of knowledge and to the goal of educating the citizens of the nation as a whole.

The Carnegie, Rockefeller, Guggenheim, Rosenwald, and other best-known, early twentieth-century foundations added something quite new: money and institutions capable of supporting excellent scientific research and education on a national basis. Through strategic interventions the new foundations pushed decisively for the creation of a world-class system of university-based scientific research and professional education. As historian Steven Wheatley notes, the new foundation-shaped system simultaneously mixed "public and private institutions and resources" and reconciled "market mechanisms with fidelity to professional academic standards."[13]

Rich and clever as they were, the new foundations lacked the money and the knowledge to transform the American system of colleges and universities entirely by themselves. As noted earlier in this chapter, by the last third of the nineteenth century a number of American colleges were already growing into comprehensive universities. Some universities grew through the addition of new endowments, new schools, and new facilities. Others relied on state funding and land grants resulting from the Morrill Act. Like Cornell, Johns Hopkins, Stanford, Clark, Chicago, and Duke benefited from large founding or transformative individual gifts—just as Peabody's large gifts had provided museums for

Harvard and Yale and as Lowell funds aided MIT, Northeastern, and Harvard. As major national donors, the best-known American foundations saw that scientific researchers and university leaders were creating exceptional opportunities for strategic giving. They took notable advantage of these opportunities.[14]

As donors, Carnegie and Rockefeller initially created individual institutions in accord with nineteenth-century norms. Rockefeller's transformative support for the University of Chicago dated from 1890; Carnegie, having built hundreds of public libraries, launched what became the Carnegie Institute of Technology in 1900. Stand-alone research institutions followed: the Carnegie Institution of Washington and the Rockefeller Institute for Medical Research, both in 1902. But the research institutes produced mixed reviews,[15] and it was all too easy for critics to object that through their "own" institutions these two exceedingly rich men sought more to exert control than to contribute to the general welfare.[16] It became clear that if the aim was to build entire fields, or to advance science in general, individual universities and research centers—no matter how excellent— had to participate in larger systems.

Recognizing these realities, Carnegie and Rockefeller shifted much of their giving. Working closely with university and scientific leaders and enlisting other donors, they created sustained, targeted, and innovative campaigns to raise America's capabilities in science, medicine, and engineering. In 1900 Americans who wanted the best scientific and professional education had to travel abroad to Germany, Scotland, England, or France. The Carnegie and Rockefeller foundations undertook to create in the United States networks of universities, public as well as private, whose scientific research and professional education would rival the best institutions in Europe. They adopted three complementary approaches: reinforcing particular strengths in select research universities; enabling the best institutions to collaborate in defining national standards; and underwriting the research and travel that would connect the best American researchers with colleagues abroad.

These efforts had more in common than is usually acknowledged with nineteenth-century practices that continued long into the twentieth century: funding through denominational and interdenominational religious associations, through the Lowell, Peabody, and similar funds, and through the endowing of churches, colleges, and high culture. What was new was the commitment to science and to a scientific basis for the professions. The new foundation leaders believed that world-class science would lead to improved products and services. It would transform the professions of medicine, nursing, education, and even management and social service by providing professionals with principles for grounded and continuously improving practice. Expanded departments and research facilities in the scientific disciplines would educate many young people who would make useful contributions even if they did not find careers in scientific research.

At the century's start, only a few scattered physicists, biologists, and chemists worked at a world-class level within the United States; in medicine, research had little direct connection to the training of doctors. Basic sources of university support—tuition, gifts from local supporters, and appropriations of tax money by state legislatures—reliably underwrote education and supported scattered scientists. But modern world-class science had become too expensive and too demanding of sustained institutional commitment to be maintained in these ways. In Europe and Japan, national governments sponsored national systems for science. Single institutions could not accomplish that task on their own.

Historian Ellen Condliffe Lagemann has written that Henry Pritchett, the early leader of the Carnegie Foundation for the Advancement of Teaching, pressed his view that "progress" required "the training of talent in a hierarchically-organized system of institutions, admission to which would be more and more limited the higher one went."[17] Rockefeller Foundation leaders concluded that if the United States was to become internationally competitive in science, a small number of American universities would have to build exceptional departments in key fields. In the 1920s and 1930s Wickliffe Rose, director of the Rockefeller-funded International Education Board, emphasized his effort to "make the peaks higher" to provide the funds to create state-of-the-art laboratories, to gather clusters of exceptionally able graduate students, and to bring some of Europe's best scientists to centers of excellence in leading research universities.[18] The foundations also built notable facilities for the use of scientists from many universities. The Carnegie Institution and the Rockefeller Foundation built great telescopes on Mt. Wilson in 1908 and 1917, for example; Rockefeller's International Education Board funded the still more powerful telescope on Mt. Palomar near San Diego in 1948. After Louis Bamberger and his sister Caroline Bamberger Fuld created the Institute for Advanced Study in Princeton in 1930, foundations made significant contributions to its programs, including those in physics and mathematics. And in 1930 the Rockefeller Foundation launched the Woods Hole Oceanographic Institution near the marine biological laboratories already established on Cape Cod.[19] The Rockefeller Foundation also made grants in many places and to many individual researchers. As Gábor Palló insists, writing of support for scientific work in provincial Szeged, Hungary, some Rockefeller grants produced valuable results—even though they went to "places that had not much hope to become peaks."[20]

Altogether, investments from the Rockefeller Foundation, the General Education Board, the Alfred P. Sloan Foundation, the Daniel and Florence Guggenheim Foundation, and the Josiah Macy Jr. Foundation, augmented by the venerable Lowell Institute and local foundations in many places, brought remarkable results in physics, aerodynamics, biology, and other fields. Four very different foundations—the Chemical Foundation created by the U.S.

government from assets seized from German chemical companies during World War I; the Research Corporation that managed patents for many researchers and their universities; the Wisconsin Alumni Research Foundation, which also managed patent assets; and the Engineering Foundation supported by many makers of sophisticated instruments and by professional engineers—also helped build research capabilities in several fields of science and research.[21] The contributions of foundation-supported physicists, chemists, aeronautical engineers, and medical researchers to the American military effort during World War II and the postwar creation of the National Science Foundation provide just two dramatic measures of foundation effectiveness and influence in this field.

Critics have argued that these foundation interventions pushed American universities too far toward narrowly scientific approaches to knowledge.[22] Like the American public at large, the foundations certainly did favor investments in science and the science-based professions. Despite the notable support of individual work in the arts and humanities by the John Simon Guggenheim Foundation, the humanities funding of Paul Mellon's Bollingen Foundation, and some notable foundation investments in libraries and art museums, the most comprehensive early review of the field noted, "The humanities have surely not fared too well."[23] The largest foundations rarely gave priority to the arts and humanities. They may have assumed that well-established religious, arts, and cultural philanthropy supported these fields; they certainly sought to focus their limited resources on matters of immediate practical concern.

The Rockefeller, Carnegie, Russell Sage, Rosenwald, and other foundations did make influential investments in social science research in these decades. Between 1907 and the late 1930s, the Russell Sage Foundation supported rigorous studies of housing, work, child labor, consumer lending, and school achievement and provided editorial support for the *Encyclopedia of the Social Sciences*.[24] The Laura Spelman Rockefeller Memorial and the Rockefeller Foundation together invested about $26 million in social science during the 1920s and 1930s,[25] partly in "centers of excellence," concentrating many grants at the University of Chicago, the University of North Carolina at Chapel Hill, the London School of Economics, and a few other very strong programs—but also in the form of grants to individuals, often through the Social Science Research Council or the National Bureau of Economic Research.[26] The Spelman and Josiah Macy Jr. foundations put significant assets into the social, psychological, and physical development of children. The Carnegie Corporation invested hundreds of thousands of dollars in *An American Dilemma,* the major study of race relations in America. Smaller foundations supported social science research in many directions: the Viking Fund (later the Wenner-Gren Foundation), for example, became very important to anthropology.

The humanities and especially the social sciences attracted far more controversy than science, and the new foundations understood that support for social science would evoke criticism. Because social science deals with questions of economic organization, inequality, race, crime, family relations, child development, and gender, it cannot avoid questions at the center of religious and political conflict. Controversy—over labor relations, over race, over "vice," over birth control, over religion, over the appropriate role of government—led foundations to move cautiously in these areas and to focus much of their support on careful empirical studies, rather than on theory or on questions of values and ethics. To this day, different observers evaluate the impact of foundation-supported social science in widely different ways.

Limited resources force foundations to make choices, and the emphasis on "excellence" in this period certainly brought results and increased foundation influence, despite the reservations of those who objected that much of the best work in a field comes from less-regarded departments, that "pluralism" can "foster iconoclastic ideas."[27] It was also true that grants often produced results quite different from those a foundation intended. The Payne Fund's investments in studies on the influence of movies on adolescent behavior, for example, had much less impact than hoped on morals, but had an enduring effect on methods for studying communications.[28] Yet it is clear that foundations made a real difference to the expansion as well as to the "empirical bent" of the social sciences.

In addition to building individual centers of research excellence, the new foundations provided critical support for "the intermediary mechanisms that could reinforce standards, measure achievement and signal new directions" in the natural and social sciences. More broadly, the foundations strongly reinforced what historian Ellis Hawley has described as the "associative state," a nation that worked through more or less voluntary associations to strengthen national authority.[29] The Rockefeller, Carnegie, Rosenwald, Russell Sage, and other new foundations gave fresh energy to the National Academy of Sciences by funding its new National Research Council. They provided substantial funding to the American Council of Learned Societies and the Social Science Research Council, and, along with G.E. and some other large business firms, they helped set up the National Bureau of Economic Research.

Russell Sage itself—like the Milbank Memorial Fund, some of the offices assembled by the Rockefeller and Carnegie funds, and the Twentieth Century Fund—became a pioneer think tank. With funds from the Rockefeller, Rosenwald, and other foundations, Russell Sage organized *Recent Social Trends* for use by President Hoover and the state-of-the-art *Encyclopedia of the Social Sciences*.[30] And foundations underwrote the Association of American Universities "in its efforts to rank institutions 'in the general interest of education,'" as

Steven Wheatley has put it.[31] Ellen Condliffe Lagemann and others have shown how the Carnegie Foundation for the Advancement of Teaching further helped connect American universities with secondary schools and with one another by underwriting the College Board (an association of colleges and universities) and its development of nationally standardized admissions testing for college and for graduate and professional schools.[32]

By launching what became the Teachers Insurance and Annuity Association (TIAA)—a pension program for professors that has grown into one of America's largest retirement systems, serving employees of many nonprofit organizations— the Carnegie Foundation did a great deal to improve the economic position of professors and researchers. The TIAA also accomplished something much more fundamental: it provided colleges with an alternative to the retirement funds of the Protestant denominations. So long as professors and colleges had to rely on the mostly Protestant retirement funds, they had to accept the terms and conditions those funds imposed. Carnegie's new fund allowed an entire set of colleges and universities to shift faculty evaluation from conformity to religious orthodoxy to the new academic standard of significant achievement in research, as judged through peer-reviewed publication, as well as teaching and service as evaluated by the colleges themselves. The Carnegie fund also had the unintended effect of reinforcing distinctions between northern and southern states when southern colleges and universities—in contrast to those in the North and West—almost universally refused to separate from their sponsoring denominations so that their professors could qualify for TIAA pensions.[33]

The large new foundations added to existing complications in the funding of American higher education. American colleges and universities had always had to take account of the preferences of donors, both local and distant. In the colonial period, most colleges had depended on subsidies voted by provincial assemblies; charities of the established churches in England and Scotland provided important supplemental aid.[34] After the revolution, denominational and interdenominational bodies of American Protestants channeled much private support; after the Civil War federal land grants and state subsidies provided large additions, especially for utilitarian purposes. Relying as they did on these substantial sources of funds, American colleges had never enjoyed the autonomy that some commentators have wished or have attributed to their English counterparts.[35]

The new foundations did not create the environment for college and university fundraising, but by backing distinctive and often new ideas with a lot of money they did add to its complexity. Foundation research funds clearly improved the quality and flexibility of the American research system as a whole, helping it meet changing public priorities. Like private donors, religious bodies, and state governments, the big foundations accomplished these goals at some cost to the autonomy and power of individual colleges and universities. When external funders invested in "individuals rather than in institutions," [36] they challenged the authority of university leaders and the influence of donors who gave higher priority to local or religious concerns. When the College Board helped colleges and universities create an academic channel for evaluating applicants for admission it weakened to some degree the long-dominant networks of families, schools, and churches.[37] When the new secular, national foundations underwrote the new institutions of peer review they challenged the previously dominant ecclesiastical and local frameworks for student recruitment and advancement in academic careers—even as the more traditional foundations continued to support those frameworks.

Medicine and Health Care

The large new national foundations had a distinctive impact on medicine and health care. It was in this field that science most immediately transformed professional education and professional practice. Scientific medicine set unprecedented standards for university medical schools as well as for the medical profession—standards that other fields rarely found the resources to emulate. Foundations did much to move medicine in this direction, but by the early 1930s the medical enterprise as a whole was already so large that foundations could affect it only at the margins.

Foundations shaped America's approach to medicine and health care in several ways. As Steven Wheatley has documented in detail, the Rockefeller Foundation's emphasis on "centers of international excellence" proved particularly effective in medical research and education. Early in the century Abraham Flexner, working for the Carnegie Foundation for the Advancement of Teaching, praised Johns Hopkins University for organizing its medical school around a full-time medical faculty responsible for education, research, and advanced patient care and for providing that faculty with up-to-date laboratories and a state-of-the-art hospital. The Rockefeller Foundation's 1910 endorsement gave national prominence to the Johns Hopkins approach; Rockefeller then set out to replicate that approach in a dozen private and state universities across the nation. The Rockefeller Foundation provided the essential core funding for this campaign; substantial additions came from the General Education Board, the Markle Foundation, the Josiah Macy Jr. Foundation, the International Cancer Research Foundation, the Mayo Association, and other funds, including many smaller funds in each region that built a new-model school. Notable research-based medical schools thus emerged quickly, in more than a dozen private and state universities across the nation. They transformed medical research and education in the United States.[38]

Foundations also did much both to project the new medical knowledge to places where it could be useful and to promote the prestige of scientific medicine.

Commonwealth Fund grants allowed hundreds of doctors and medical researchers to enhance their specialist knowledge. Rockefeller's General Education Board
brought modern medical and public health practices to its effective and highly
praised campaign against hookworm in the American South. Rockefeller's China
Medical Board almost single-handedly built the most important center for medical education and research in China during the 1920s, creating a key Asian
outpost for American medicine. Rockefeller-funded efforts launched in 1915 led
to an effective vaccine against yellow fever and to the saving of tens of thousands
of lives during World War II and after.

Foundations also sought to redesign the systems through which Americans
receive health care, but this task proved far more difficult. Daniel Fox shows that
the Rockefeller, Carnegie, and Russell Sage foundations, the Milbank Memorial Fund, the Commonwealth Fund, and others committed millions of dollars
between 1900 and the 1930s to advance "hierarchical regionalism." The idea
was to move knowledge out from the great research centers to doctors in general
practice across the nation and the world and to bring to those centers patients
who suffered from rare or difficult illnesses. University-based research specialists
would diagnose difficult cases and prescribe the most effective treatment. "Clinical prevention and treatment of low-income patients . . . would be carried out
in regional hierarchies of hospitals, clinics and private medical offices," while
"population-based disease control, notably surveillance, quarantine or isolation,
mass inoculation, and health education, would be the responsibility of government."[39] All this would follow the model of the Rockefeller Foundation's campaign against hookworm.[40] Foundation grants for such purposes amounted to
less than 5 percent of all the money spent on health care at the time, but did help
persuade local and state governments, the early health insurance movement, and
during the 1940s the federal government to provide much larger funding for
hierarchical regionalism.[41]

Yet hierarchical regionalism failed. In 1932 the Carnegie Foundation for the
Advancement of Teaching, the Commonwealth Fund, the Josiah Macy Jr. Foundation, the Milbank Memorial Fund, the Rockefeller Foundation, the Rosenwald Fund, and the Russell Sage Foundation jointly backed *Medical Care for
the American People*, a report that recommended hierarchical regionalism as the
basis for medical care and insurance.[42] Local physicians responded with a fire-
storm of protest.[43] State and local medical societies, working with key American
Medical Association officials, arranged for critical coverage in the medical and
general press. Some called for a boycott of Borden condensed milk because that
company was the source of the funds that Elizabeth Milbank Anderson had used
to endow the Milbank Memorial Fund. According to Fox, "Most of the foundations that had sponsored the [report] reacted to vilification in the medical and
general press by ceasing to support discussion or even analysis of controversial

issues of organizing and financing health services." Despite their increasing respect for science, "Most physicians resisted the organizational logic of hierarchical regionalism." Insisting that doctors and their professional associations govern "clinical decision-making, licensure, professional discipline, and the setting of fees for their services, [they] adamantly refuse[d] to cede control of these activities to colleagues with better training and more knowledge."[44]

Retreating from health care delivery reform, the big foundations turned toward narrowly focused research grants. Some grants for research into the causes, prevention, control, and cure of diseases produced dramatic results. Working in the new hospitals and medical research laboratories, foundation-supported scientists fought hookworm, developed the Pap smear, identified insulin as a treatment for diabetes, and made other advances. Foundation grants also led to influence on federal funding for medical research, especially when in 1942 the Albert and Mary Lasker Foundation focused much of its giving on discussions of that topic. The Lasker Foundation became a leading voice among those seeking greatly increased federal appropriations for research and for channeling the money through the National Institutes of Health. Boosted by the apparent effectiveness of federal mobilization to produce the atom bomb and radar and to deliver greatly improved medical care to U.S. troops during World War II, federal funding for medical research rose rapidly. By the late 1940s, NIH grants far surpassed those from foundations. By the 1960s, the Lasker Foundation was supporting efforts to have Congress increase its direct influence on the uses of research funds. In this case, foundation philanthropy not only supported innovation: it sought to persuade government to shift much larger funds to the priorities and approaches it favored.[45]

Elementary and Secondary Education

Several of the biggest national foundations did much to shape American ways of organizing and managing elementary and secondary education in the first half of the twentieth century. Their most noted interventions may be described in four ways.

First, the Peabody Education Fund, the very large Rockefeller-funded General Education Board, and the Rosenwald Fund, along with a number of smaller funds, did a great deal through strategic grants to school districts and state departments of education to encourage and enable the post–Civil War and early twentieth-century South to build a system of public education that increasingly resembled the systems of the rest of the nation.

Second, until the civil rights movement successfully challenged the laws and the politics that imposed racial segregation, southern public school systems built with foundation aid remained segregated by law, despite the devotion of some of the smaller foundations to racial justice and despite the preferences of more than a few foundation leaders. Educational segregation reflected southern racial politics, but it also was consistent with the assumptions about racial inequality and national priorities held by some key foundation leaders.[46]

Third, the Carnegie Foundation for the Advancement of Teaching, the Russell Sage Foundation,[47] and other funds did much—together with the demands of government and the practical and legal pressures faced by school authorities—to define the organization of the American high school, to promote "age-grading" in elementary schools, and to encourage the application of statistics to educational tests and measurements.

Finally, the Carnegie Foundation for the Advancement of Teaching and other funds worked with private and public colleges, universities, and schools to standardize the relation between secondary schools and colleges by defining the standard college-preparatory curriculum and by creating the Scholastic Aptitude Test, the Advanced Placement program, and the Educational Testing Service. Whereas in other nations it was the national government that accomplished these tasks, in the United States they were fulfilled by private associations, led in considerable part by private universities and significantly funded by private foundations. Foundation-supported development work related to high schools won praise for expanding the pools of college applicants and for opening opportunity to students who lacked the advantages accorded by private schools and elite academies that had close ties with prestigious colleges and universities. The foundation-supported high school curriculum could best be taught by graduates of colleges and universities that endorsed and supported high standards in English, history, foreign languages, mathematics, and science.

Critics complained that these innovations reinforced the high school's tendency to overemphasize college-bound students, who often came from advantaged families, and that the tests unfairly discriminated against students who were female, members of racial minorities, or poor. On the other hand, as noted above, the promotion of high academic standards to larger numbers of high schools and the creation of standardized college-admission tests did something to dilute the privileges enjoyed by the children of affluent, well-educated parents.

Foundation influence on public education peaked in the early 1930s. Influenced by foundation initiatives as well as by other forces, all states had by then created public school systems through high school. They had defined the core high school curriculum. They had regularized many of the terms on which teachers and administrators would be hired, promoted, compensated, evaluated, and retired. They also had established the local property tax as their fiscal basis and developed state schools of education to prepare teachers and administrators.

After the early 1930s, foundations faced a very difficult environment for new initiatives in elementary and secondary education. Major change now required the action of state governments, state universities, and thousands of self-funding local school districts. Elected school boards led the school districts, and most public school funds came from property tax levies that had to be reauthorized through a public election every few years. Major change would now also require attention to Catholic schools, which had become, after World War II, by far the largest and most influential system of nonpublic schools. Foundations had had very little to do with Catholic schools.[48]

These new circumstances, as sociologist Pamela Walters shows, assured the failure of the General Education Board (GEB) to change public school curricula between 1933 and 1940. The GEB argued that America's schools bore some responsibility for the Great Depression, because they had failed to prepare most students for "immediate practical" work. It mobilized prominent consultants, conducted national surveys, and engaged leading associations of educational leaders and public officials as it pressed for a curriculum more "responsive" to contemporary realities.[49] The GEB had, in part, adopted a "structural" explanation for Depression-era unemployment, an explanation that was highly controversial then and remains controversial today.[50] Many critics objected to its proposals. Foundations had done a good deal to develop public schools throughout the nation and to align their curricula with college admissions. But in the 1930s foundations found it next to impossible to overcome disagreement about curricula and to promote change in the nation's radically decentralized public school systems.[51]

Social Welfare

During the first half of the twentieth century, foundations played central roles in building new institutions of higher education, science, and medical research. Because social welfare is such an all-embracing concept, foundation contributions in this field, though sometimes notable, are difficult to evaluate. Social welfare concerns family life—marriage, single parenting, child protection, foster care, and adoption. It concerns work—job training, job availability and placement, health and safety, and compensation. It concerns income security—hence access to health care, disability, and retirement. One way or another it concerns personal behavior—eating, drinking, and exercise habits and substance use and abuse. It concerns personal safety at home and away. To many, it also has to do with religious commitment.

Early twentieth-century foundations large and small gave to each of these aspects of "social welfare." But in this complex and contradictory field, foundations often adopted conflicting approaches, spent far less than government and other private actors, and faced challenging conditions. As Rockefeller Foundation trustee Harry Pratt Judson observed, health, long life, and prosperity for all were universally desired if apparently unattainable; but religion and moral reform always provoked controversy and opposition.[52] Americans disagreed profoundly over the control and use of tobacco, alcohol, and other drugs. They differed over questions related to sex and reproduction as well as the role of government in guaranteeing the rights of women and children within the family. Yet many foundations viewed their campaigns in those fields as "social welfare." Inevitably, the outcomes of their campaigns "almost always confounded prediction," as historian Judith Sealander observed.[53]

Unlike education, scientific research, and medicine, the field of social welfare saw no single dominant transformation of key institutions in the first half of the twentieth century. Many states assumed increased powers to regulate the education, living conditions, and work of children and their families and of orphans. Sometimes adjacent states adopted similar approaches; often they did not. In some ways government increased its role. The Social Security Act of 1935 gave the federal government a critical new role in providing a minimum level of financial support for the elderly, for poor children, and for the blind and physically disabled. Using federal as well as state and local funds, county and municipal as well as state welfare departments expanded greatly during the 1930s.

But government did not come close to displacing the private, nongovernment social efforts of religious groups. The gradual decline of mainline Protestant hegemony in America only increased the fragmentation of social service organizations. Catholics, many evangelical Protestants, and Orthodox Jews maintained their own approaches and increasingly created foundations to support them.[54] Their child-care organizations, hospitals, and homes for the elderly had not infrequently benefited from state or local funding; during the New Deal years and after, some federal funding followed.[55] Despite their aspiration to serve all, welfare organizations sponsored by religious groups mainly served members of their own religious (and cultural, social, and economic) communities. The foundations that underwrote religious schools, hospitals, and social service organizations thus had a clear impact not only on the teaching of ideas about charity but also on the organization of social welfare in the United States. Arguably, one result was the reinforcement of institutional arrangements that make it so difficult for the United States to develop and maintain a comprehensive "safety net."

Competing changes relating to gender, race, and class also reshaped social welfare in the first half of the twentieth century. With very little aid from foundations, women gained more equal rights to property, more legal rights and better access to the law, and more personal autonomy during the first four decades of the century. For African Americans conditions got worse or at best only marginally better. Urbanization pulled millions from the countryside, in Europe as well as in the United States, to America's rapidly growing cities. The nation's industrial districts offered real opportunity in the 1900s, the 1920s, the

1940s, and the 1950s, with wages much higher than those available in farming, fishing, logging, or mining. They also offered unfamiliar social settings, uncertainty, and sometimes dire misery. During the deeply depressed 1930s unemployment rates remained above 25 percent for nearly ten years. Organized labor won federal protection with the Wagner Act of 1936, but faced powerful opposition in many states.

In the social welfare field no counterpart to the universities and medical centers appeared to help advance a foundation's agenda. Indeed, as they built up partners in other fields, foundations complicated social welfare work. Medical schools and universities attracted donations away from social service agencies; as doctors and nurses gained authority, social workers found it increasingly difficult to raise their own standing. Foundations also found it difficult to work with state governments that commanded the power to tax and the power to enter and inspect homes and institutions. States—through their legislation and their courts—wielded the power to enact and enforce rules for marriage and adoption (including the miscegenation laws that forbade marriage and adoption across racial lines), divorce, and the removal of abused or delinquent children.[56] States also held the power to insist that a child care for a parent. Foundations sometimes found it easier to influence the cities and counties that actually implemented much welfare policy, but as "minor civil subdivisions" of their states, local governments could not make policy.

Despite much disagreement among themselves, a number of foundations did engage in joint efforts to improve social welfare. They encouraged private charities to cooperate and worked to establish social work as a profession with high and consistent standards. They sought to bring care for orphaned, abandoned, and delinquent children into line with evolving standards of medical, mental health, and educational practice. They invested in empirical research on the sources of poverty and economic opportunity. They successfully promoted national and state park systems dedicated to public recreation. Sealander shows that foundations tried but failed to win public funding for vocational education, parent education, juvenile courts, and public education about sexually transmitted diseases.[57] With a few exceptions, foundations did not push for Social Security, for the right of labor to organize, or for the rights of women or African Americans.[58] Extraordinary efforts to understand the business cycle launched after World War I and partially funded by foundations eventually contributed greatly to economic analysis, but not in time to prevent the Great Depression.

From its creation in 1907 to its transformation into a notable funder of social science research after World War II, the Russell Sage Foundation led many of these cooperative efforts. Working largely as an "operating" foundation with its own staff, Russell Sage built its own substantial headquarters near the United Charities Building in New York City. From that strategic location it organized the Pittsburgh Survey and promoted both the "social survey" and the "educational survey" as devices to build consensus and encourage civic action. The Russell Sage headquarters housed the New York School of Social Work, national associations of social workers in various fields, and the nation's most complete library of works on social welfare and social reform. For many years the Russell Sage Foundation subsidized both the *Social Work Yearbook* and *Survey* magazine, widely read by the executives and trustees of charities in the fields of health and welfare. Russell Sage also produced widely used social work textbooks and manuals and underwrote the work and annual meetings of social work associations. When founder Margaret Olivia Sage left additional money after her death in 1918, the foundation added additional floors to its building for the use of the Regional Plan Association of New York and Environs. Over the nearly thirty years of Russell Sage sponsorship, the Regional Plan published extensive studies of housing, community services, and urban development in the three-state region that extends from New Haven, Connecticut, to Princeton, New Jersey, and includes Long Island as well as New York City. Eventually, the Regional Plan Association spun off as a freestanding entity.

Allying itself with leaders of the charity organization movement, with professional social workers, and with many community leaders and public officials across the nation, the Russell Sage Foundation encouraged private social service organizations to publicize their work, cooperate with one another and with government agencies, and employ professionally trained people. It encouraged legislation to improve public health and building codes, to regulate pawnshops, and to ensure better working conditions for women and children and greater protection of the rights of working girls, married women, and children. Through the publication of directories and technical handbooks, the foundation promoted good foundation practice, encouraged foundations to emphasize social welfare, and increased public access to basic information about foundations.[59]

Russell Sage Foundation initiatives sought to professionalize social work and comprehensive city planning, and a Russell Sage librarian went on to be the influential initial director of the Foundation Center. But while Russell Sage worked well with leaders of a wide range of Protestant and Jewish organizations, it encountered resistance from Catholics[60] and was ignored by many evangelical Protestants and Orthodox Jews. It also failed to persuade New Deal administrators and Congress to preserve the private social service system. Although its Regional Plan Association of New York and Environs set a standard for studies of the physical infrastructure of metropolitan regions, its effort to promote regional planning as the basis for housing reform and community development fell short. Discouraged by these experiences, in 1947 the Russell Sage board took advantage of its power to change course as it ended support for social work and social service agencies and committed itself to social science.[61]

Russell Sage was by no means the only foundation that sought to build new institutions in the field of social welfare. The Laura Spelman Rockefeller Memorial invested heavily in the study of child development and in parent education. John D. Rockefeller Jr.'s Bureau of Social Hygiene undertook pioneering work in the study of sexuality, campaigned against prostitution, and supported public provision of accurate information about sex and reproduction. The Commonwealth Fund put substantial resources into the child guidance movement. The Children's Fund of Michigan, the Amherst H. Wilder Charity of St. Paul, the Buhl Foundation of Pittsburgh, the Samuel N. and Mary Castle Foundation in Hawaii, and other foundations joined these projects in their own locales. Buhl, in particular, underwrote pioneering statistical studies of social problems. The Carnegie Corporation organized the great study of race relations that eventually yielded Gunnar Myrdal's famous *An American Dilemma*—though the corporation allowed long delays in that project, despite its strong potential for social welfare.[62] Many foundations also supported campaigns to promote collaboration among private charities and to create community chests (predecessors to the United Way) and community foundations.[63]

The W. K. Kellogg Foundation did many of these things, but it also made a commitment to promoting self-help and self-sufficiency in the farming communities that produced the grains Kellogg made into cereal. Rather than work chiefly with private social welfare agencies, the Kellogg Foundation made strategic investments in public agencies dedicated to helping people understand how to earn a living and maintain healthy homes. Through building grants, scholarship funds, and demonstration projects, Kellogg supported and encouraged taxfunded county extension and public health services, community hospitals, public schools, and university-based continuing education. Like the Smith Charities of mid-nineteenth-century Massachusetts or Andrew Carnegie's public library initiative, Kellogg worked to help people acquire the knowledge and understanding that would—if all went well with the economy at large—enable them to earn their own living and avoid poverty.[64] In the same spirit were the General Education Board's substantial investments in southern agriculture, public education, and African American colleges and the Rosenwald Fund's investments in education for African Americans in the South and in YMCA and other community facilities for African Americans in the North.

In more general terms, during the first half of the twentieth century a good number of foundations enjoyed significant success in the field of social welfare as philanthropic innovators, social entrepreneurs, institution builders, and advocates of policy change. Before the New Deal, the Russell Sage Foundation played a substantial national role as convener, mediator, and policy advocate in many fields of welfare service. At the same time, not a few foundations emphasized the application of traditional and religious values in social welfare.

Yet it is also true that taken as a whole, foundations complicated the tasks of those who sought to advance social welfare. To the extent that foundations succeeded in building the new institutions of medicine and higher education, they created competitors for authority and for money. To the extent that certain religious and other local foundations succeeded in protecting assets, absorbing risks, and defending particular traditions, foundations complicated efforts to promote collaboration toward social welfare goals. To some extent foundations reinforced the powerful racial, religious, regional, and gender conflicts that continued to divide the nation. But the biggest challenges to social welfare came not from foundation actions but from the severe dislocations associated with inequality, war, depression, and the sheer magnitude of the problem; Franklin D. Roosevelt famously asserted that he saw "one-third of a nation ill-housed, ill-clad, and ill-nourished." From the perspective of many social workers, foundations seemed wonderfully rich and powerful. But from a foundation's perspective, the social welfare field presented daunting challenges. In the face of such daunting challenges, foundation resources were certainly insufficient, and foundation initiatives were all too often criticized as paternalistic, amateurish, and ineffective—sometimes unfairly, but often with justice.

International Affairs

The nineteenth-century "boards" that gathered, held, and distributed funds for foreign as well as domestic Protestant missions helped establish the foundation as an American institution. Foundations continued through the twentieth century to underwrite much American missionary activity, including the building of influential colleges, universities, and medical schools in several nations. Early in the twentieth century, new foundations, including the Carnegie Corporation, the Carnegie Endowment for International Peace, and the Rockefeller Foundation, responded to rising international tensions in new ways that set a persisting pattern of private American engagement with world affairs. Steven Heydemann and Rebecca Kinsey identify the elements of this pattern as "an explicit focus on public policy, elite opinion, and public education as domains in which . . . knowledge" might bring constructive change and "a hybrid pattern of state-foundation relations that combined an uneasy mix of partnership, autonomy, conflict, and constraint." To pursue these aims, the leading foundations promoted "norms that legitimated non-state participation" in international affairs.[65]

Heydemann and Kinsey show that in pursuing this new approach, American foundations have sought to play several distinctive international roles, seeking to legitimate favored activities, to gain influence as evaluators and gatekeepers for programs and people, to amplify the credibility of their grantees, and to import and export ideas and practices among nations and their officials, civil society, and various publics. To these ends foundations built institutions for international cooperation and encouraged international coalitions to represent positive visions of international understanding and cooperation. Given the overwhelming immediate role of national and military power in international affairs, foundations necessarily paid especially close attention to government policy as they pursued these goals.

Even before World War I, the Carnegie Endowment for International Peace aimed to provide "the organization and the means for a sustained and systematic effort to reach and convince the public opinion of the world by scientific argument."[66] Following the failure of the United States to join the League of Nations, the Carnegie Corporation, the Rockefeller Foundation, the World Peace Foundation, the Woodrow Wilson Foundation, the American Foundation, the World Unity Foundation, and others provided considerable support for the League of Nations and within the United States for an international, as opposed to an isolationist, approach to America's relations with foreign nations. They helped build facilities for the league and its staffs in Geneva, then subsidized league research and publications. In the 1920s and 1930s the Rockefeller Foundation alone gave over $2.5 million to support activities of the league and its associated agencies—a substantial level of support, considering that the total combined annual budgets of the League of Nations and its two most important associated entities, the International Labor Organization and the Permanent Court of International Justice, never exceeded $8 million. The Rockefeller Foundation also gave more than $1 million to the Geneva Graduate Institute of International Studies.[67] When Germany invaded the Low Countries and France in 1940 and seemed likely to gain control of Switzerland, the Rockefeller Foundation transplanted the league's entire Economic, Financial, and Transit Department to Princeton, New Jersey. After World War II these interventions facilitated the creation of the United Nations.

In the 1920s, 1930s, and 1940s several national foundations also joined with local funds to encourage "councils on world affairs" and similar study groups in many cities. As Heydemann and Kinsey put it, American foundations promoted "a liberal internationalist sensibility that became, and remains, a defining element of American foreign policy and of broader public conceptions of what Tony Smith calls America's Mission."[68]

Another group of foundations emphasized relations between the United States and another nation. The American and Chinese governments created one of the largest foundations of this kind. In 1924 the U.S. Congress agreed to put the more than $12 million remaining in a fund given by China to indemnify Americans for losses in the Boxer Rebellion, into a new China Foundation for the Promotion of Education and Culture, with the money to be spent for educational and cultural purposes in China.[69] At this time, only about a dozen

American foundations held more assets. Nongovernment donors created many smaller, U.S.-based foundations devoted to improving relations between the United States and another nation. The American Committee for Syrian and Armenian Relief, founded in 1915 to aid minority communities during the violent upheavals that accompanied the dissolution of the Ottoman Empire and renamed Near East Relief in 1919 and then the Near East Foundation in 1930, raised scores of millions to aid and resettle refugees and later to encourage economic and social development in the region.[70] Near East Relief emphasized its continuing fundraising work, but all of these foundations also protected assets, celebrated ideals, preserved and promoted traditions, and absorbed risks.

Other foundation efforts advanced international relations, although that was not their explicit purpose. The several Rockefeller foundations in many ways constituted a special case: because Rockefeller-controlled firms did a great deal of business within many nations (in 1900, Standard Oil dominated China's market for kerosene, for example), they often donated funds where they had earned them. Rockefeller Foundation funds supported public health movements in several nations,[71] created in the Peking Union Medical College a replica of the Johns Hopkins School of Medicine complete with up-to-date hospital and research laboratories,[72] gave critical aid to the London School of Economics,[73] underwrote the rebuilding of Oxford's Bodleian Library, and paid for business-cycle studies at half a dozen European universities. Altogether the Rockefeller Foundation invested more than $40 million in universities in Europe and China alone between the wars.

New funds for the support of international missions also supplemented the old mission boards. In the 1940s the Luce Foundation became an important supporter of Christian colleges in China and throughout Asia.[74] American supporters of Canton Christian College (later Lingnan University) set up a foundation in the United States to hold assets for that institution; when the communist revolution cut that institution's ties with its American supporters, the foundation redirected its support to related projects in the United States and Asia.[75] Other foundations supported Catholic and Jewish causes overseas.

All of this advanced American relations with foreign governments and with the citizens of other nations. The Rockefeller-funded International Education Board, whose funds paid for hundreds of foreign students to study at American universities, like the Commonwealth Fund's underwriting of exchanges for American and British medical researchers, had similar effects. The same could be said of the Rockefeller Foundation's actions in helping some of Europe's most distinguished scholars and scientists escape the Holocaust and enrich the faculties of American colleges and universities.[76]

These international efforts were ambitious and enjoyed broad public support, although their purposes were not always shared by all Americans. In pursuing these goals, the foundations paid close attention to the official policies of the United States. No doubt foundation resources were far from adequate to achieve peace or to establish international norms in any field. Often a foundation could do little. But it would be difficult to argue that foundations did not have a good deal of success in these decades—in establishing new institutions for international affairs, in improving American understanding of much of the rest of the world, and in supporting the larger movements for international standards in science, medicine, public health, and even in the study of society.

The Arts

In the first half of the twentieth century, the most important foundation contribution to the arts was the holding, and in many cases the careful management, of funds for the support of particular museums and musical organizations. Often the foundation-supported institutions were new; gradually, they contributed to the creation of a national collection of museums and orchestras that in some ways paralleled America's growing networks of universities, hospitals, and research institutes. Perhaps most notable of all was Andrew W. Mellon's use of a trust to hold the scores of millions he set aside for the National Gallery of Art. By disbursing the money only as the National Gallery was approved, designed, built, and filled with works of art, Mellon assured that even as Congress and the administration changed, his gift would build the national art museum he sought.[77] Similar stories, much like those of such nineteenth-century arts centers as the Boston Athenaeum and the Philadelphia Academy of Fine Arts, could be told about the funds devoted to the Juilliard School and the Solomon R. Guggenheim Museum in New York City, the Barnes Foundation museum and the Longwood Gardens in Pennsylvania, the Cleveland Museum of Art, the Cranbrook School in Michigan, the Amon G. Carter Museum in Fort Worth, the Nelson-Atkins Museum in Kansas City, the Huntington Library Art Collections, and Botanical Gardens in San Marino, California, and many other institutions.

Foundations also supported individual artists and promoted the teaching of art. The John Simon Guggenheim Memorial Foundation and several smaller foundations made individual grants to many artists and writers. The Samuel H. Kress Foundation supported research in art history; it also held a notable collection of works of art that it made available to colleges and other venues.[78] The Carnegie Corporation of New York also made notable contributions to the teaching of art as a college subject.

Apart from commissioning public buildings, including some art and music classes in public schools, and undertaking several short-lived Depression-era initiatives of the Works Projects Administration for writers and artists, American governments continued to have little to do with the arts in these decades. So, it cannot be said that foundations of the first half of the twentieth century supplemented government work in this field or that they played a role in the reconsideration of government arts policy. In sharp contrast to the European pattern of continuing national, provincial, and municipal government arts patronage, American governments simply had no arts policy, except to leave the arts to the private sphere.

Foundations did build institutions in the arts, sometimes innovative ones. Upon occasion they also encouraged arts organizations to collaborate with one another. In the cases of the Kress Foundation (and similar regional funds such as the Kulas Foundation of Cleveland),[79] foundations supported arts activity, rather than the creation of a single arts organization. No one doubts that foundation initiatives in the arts could be amateurish and patronizing or that they could occasionally reinforce the tendency of elite arts organizations to ratify social inequality.[80] But arts organizations also served (and continue to serve) educational, religious, and even local economic-development purposes, as well as the cause of beauty for its own sake.[81] Foundations sought to advance all of these purposes as their funds granted time, opportunity, and occasionally authority and prestige to artists, to researchers in the arts, and to those who studied and taught about the leadership of arts organizations. And they did make arts experiences available to the public. As museums, orchestras, and other arts organizations grew, they also found that, similar to universities, they had to work not only with their own boards, donors, students, and audiences, but also with the foundations that controlled sometimes vital resources.

Religion

The long-standing and too often ignored commitment of American foundations to religious activities continued through the first half of the twentieth century. In 1950, for example, half of the foundations in Texas and more than one-third in California emphasized their religious commitments. In this same period the Rockefeller Foundation and its sister Davison and Sealantic foundations in New York, the Lilly Endowment in Indianapolis, the Danforth Foundation in St. Louis, and others among the nation's largest foundations made very substantial grants for religious purposes. Some foundations also underwrote Jewish causes. In the nineteenth century, some Catholic funds based in Europe had educated priests and nuns or aided fledgling Catholic efforts in the United States: now, a few Catholic foundations began to appear within American borders.

In the first chapter of this book we noted the implications of religious disagreement for understanding American law relevant to foundations and other endowments. Religious texts have also been used to support widely differing foundation policies. Sayings of Jesus, for example, can be quoted as authority for devoting resources to immediate need, as in Matthew 6:28–29: "Why take ye thought for raiment? Consider the lilies of the field, how they grow; they toil not, neither do they spin: And yet I say unto you, that even Solomon in all his glory was not arrayed like one of these." But another passage in the same New Testament book can also be read to urge the intelligent, sustainable investment of resources. According to Matthew 25:20–21, Jesus spoke favorably of the praise a master bestowed on a steward who has profitably invested assets entrusted to him. "Well done, thou good and faithful servant: thou hast been faithful over a few things, I will make thee ruler over many things: enter thou into the joy of thy lord." Despite its importance and complexity, the relationship between religion and foundations in the United States has attracted little attention.

Economist Henry J. Aaron identified one of the key places to start: the favored tax treatment of all foundations and nonprofit organizations is based on the American approach to religious freedom. As Aaron put it:

> The real function of the tax advantages to religious institutions is to provide encouragement free of direct administrative or political control to an institution that an overwhelming social consensus has long regarded and still regards, rightly or wrongly, as essential to the formation of the bedrock values of our society and political system. . . . By connecting such subsidies to a legal form that excludes the explicit pursuit of profit by the owners, legislators have tried to enable those controlling such organizations to pursue objectives other than those enforced by the profit motive. Much the same is true of foundations, social service organizations, and educational institutions, as well as cultural and artistic organizations.[82]

Given the American practice of separating church and state, foundation grants for religious purposes have generally worked to create a separate sphere of activity, not to complement or substitute for government programs. In a democracy government programs necessarily seek to serve everyone and to avoid imposing religious observance on any citizen. Religious foundations, Robert Wuthnow and Michael Lindsay note, emphasize their distinctiveness, their particularism. "Shared religious tradition . . . serves as an important bonding agent," they observe, creating a "silo effect" in which religious foundations tend to concentrate their giving on institutions within their own religious community. Often, religious foundations are very closely tied to a particular religious organization or group of religious organizations. More generally, "much foundation funding for religion" is "countercyclical," designed to "maintain, revitalize, or renew religious traditions" in the context of the forces of secularism or a rising religious pluralism. Thus foundations serve not only to control and protect assets for the preservation of religious traditions, but also to build new institutions and to engage in religious forms of social entrepreneurship.[83]

Foundations engaged with American religious life in many ways during the first half of the twentieth century. Often they maintained the long-established patterns we noted earlier in this chapter. The distinctive Congregationalist, Episcopalian, Reformed, Lutheran, Presbyterian, Southern Presbyterian, Methodist, Southern Methodist, Baptist, and Southern Baptist "funds," foundations, and "boards" remained independent of one another. Some of these continued to rank among the nation's very largest foundations. On occasion, some of these funds crossed regional lines: African American churches and church-related schools, colleges, and seminaries in the South relied most heavily on gifts and tuition from within their own African American communities, but support also came through Protestant boards and funds from New England, upstate New York, Ohio, and Illinois.[84]

Wealthy individuals created several important new denominational foundations in the first decades of the century. Scottish-American investment banker John S. Kennedy added a Building Aid Fund to the array of Presbyterian funds in 1911. From 1924 the Duke Endowment for the Carolinas held funds for the support of Protestant-affiliated Duke, Furman, and Johnson C. Smith universities and Davidson College, as well as for rural United Methodist churches in North Carolina and their retired pastors. The Oldham Little Church Fund in Texas (1949) underwrote the costs of church buildings for Southern Baptist congregations, which were often too small and too poor to maintain their own buildings. Groups of donors joined to create state foundations for Baptists and Presbyterians in several southern states. An early leader of the Baptist Foundation of Texas recalled that in the 1920s his denomination's colleges in the state "had no money; . . . they had no assets, or if they did, no one who knew how to handle them." The new foundation hired investors and stewards capable of earning the confidence of Baptist donors, some of whom had struck oil.[85] The notable growth of Baylor University and the Baylor Medical School was one result.

The Baron de Hirsch Fund and many other Jewish funds supported Jewish education, Jewish social services, and Jewish refugees, both in the United States and abroad. The Holocaust posed devastating challenges, religious as well as practical,[86] and spurred the addition of many other such funds after 1945. American Catholics had long put most of their resources into building churches, orphanages, schools, colleges, and hospitals rather than foundations, but by the mid-twentieth century a few Catholic groups were creating foundations alongside those established by Protestants and Jews. The largest included the Raskob Foundation for Catholic Activities (1945) on the East Coast, the De Rance Foundation (1946) in the Midwest, and the Doheny Foundation (1949) in California.

Some foundations encouraged cooperation among Protestants and across the divisions among Protestants, Catholics, and Jews. John D. Rockefeller, his son John D. Rockefeller Jr., the Rockefeller Foundation, and their Davison and Sealantic funds devoted much care and energy as well as money to the support of liberal Protestantism, the alignment of Protestant theology with science, and the exchange of views between distinct religious communities. The Danforth Foundation built twenty-four chapels to serve the rapidly growing numbers of students at state universities;[87] through graduate and postgraduate fellowship, research, and publication programs the Danforth and Hazen foundations worked with the National Council on Religion and Higher Education and the Faculty Christian Fellowship to encourage Christian values among professors.[88] The Henry Luce Foundation's China program supported a unified Protestant network of Christian colleges.[89] All of these efforts sought to inculcate potential leaders with particular ideas about culture as well as faith.

Whatever tradition they supported, foundations provided not only income security for religious entities and their clergy, but also support for groups of religious workers committed to particular religious ideas and practices. Like all foundations, those devoted to religious work had to make choices that earned the same sorts of credit and detractions that came to their secular counterparts. As in other fields, foundation investments in religion built institutions and created spaces where professionals could gain training, find mentors, form networks, consider options, study and write, and develop plans for action.

Social Movements

Myriad difficulties confront any attempt to assess the contributions of foundations to social movements in the first half of the twentieth century, or indeed in any period. Observers disagree sharply over what qualifies as a social movement, what actions advance a movement, and how different movements relate to one another. The authoritative *Blackwell Companion to Social Movements* includes separate chapters on labor, women's, environmental, peace, ethnic, and religious movements.[90] By some definitions social movements must be led "from below"; by other definitions, supporters must feel that they are part of a "movement." Yesterday's progressive movement can become, in the eyes of some, today's entrenched special interest.

As Alice O'Connor points out, while the Garland Fund and a small number of other progressive foundations funded such indisputably "progressive" social movement initiatives as the NAACP's legal defense fund as early as the 1920s, nearly all foundations at that time had other priorities. Foundations did little if anything to help African Americans win "equal access to jobs and wages, integrated housing and schools, elimination of racially-motivated restrictions in Social Security, Fair Labor Standards, collective bargaining, [or] other pillars of the New Deal welfare state." Just a few foundations came gradually to "embrace movement goals"; fewer still "dedicated themselves to an explicit and more overtly politicized movement-building agenda."[91] Social movements for the poor—efforts to advance the rights of organized labor, of African Americans, of immigrants, of poor women—depended far more on self-help than on gifts from foundations.

Yet the religious and moral reform initiatives of the first half of the twentieth century might also qualify as "social movements," and some of these, including effective campaigns to improve access to basic education, received important support from foundations. The historically black colleges in the South provided employment for many of the African American ministers, professors, and others who pushed for rights and respect through the most difficult years of lynching and Jim Crow. "Peace" can also be described as the object (admittedly an object difficult to define and inchoate) of an important social movement; several foundations put considerable resources in this general direction, especially between the creation of the Carnegie Institute for Peace in 1910 and the outbreak of World War II. In a different set of fields, from the 1920s on the Rockefeller, Milbank Memorial, Markle, Scripps, Brush, and other foundations made substantial investments in the study of reproductive physiology, women's health, family planning, and related matters. Some of this work supported notions of eugenics that are now widely condemned; some of it supported aspects of the birth control movement that is now very widely accepted even as it remains controversial in some quarters. Surely the campaigns for eugenics and for the control of fertility, as well as the much wider campaign for women's rights, meet the definition of a "social movement." Foundations did not support activist campaigns such as those of Margaret Sanger, but by the 1960s the fruits of foundation-supported research into reproduction and women's health were certainly advancing the women's movement in important ways.[92]

Foundations as Institution Builders

During their classic period, general-purpose foundations certainly added to the pluralistic quality of American life and to the pluralistic character of the nation's institutions. Taken one at a time, the foundation efforts emphasized in this chapter were intended to be philanthropic, to support innovation and social entrepreneurship, to build institutions, to reinforce values, and to promote policy change. Even efforts to relieve immediate need were intended to lead through example. Recognizing the limits of their resources, foundations rarely set out to substitute for government. Rather foundations complemented government, most often by demonstrating the value of particular activities. Thus foundations invested in campaigns for public libraries, public schools, state universities, and systematic and scientifically based programs of public health.

Foundations also, on occasion, supported specialized, unusual, misunderstood, or controversial activities (often religious, cultural, or intellectual) unlikely to win government support.

In the fields of education, social welfare, religion, the arts, civil liberties, and the search for international peace, foundations controlled, protected, and invested resources for the preservation, renewal, and advancement of valued traditions and activities, helping to manage financial risks. They also reinforced America's pluralistic, divided, sometimes contentious array of religious communities, with their distinctive approaches to health, education, and welfare. American foundations continued the nineteenth-century approach of helping people learn to help themselves, rather than redistributing wealth directly from the rich to the poor. Foundation resources were insufficient to bring peace, to spread Christianity around the globe, to equalize access to education, to persuade the nation to adopt a system of universal access to health care. Foundations, like business corporations, lacked the resources to control everything that happened in the programs they supported. But they were able—in collaboration with others—to play major roles in the creation of America's system of research universities, in the development of the sciences, and in the reorganization of the medical, academic, and social work professions. Together with wealthy individual donors like Robert Brookings and Edward A. Filene and the early municipal bureaus, foundations played an even larger role in inventing the American think tank.

It is sometimes assumed that early twentieth-century foundations worked above all to expand the role of government. The evidence reviewed in this chapter makes it clear that the reality was much more complicated. Foundations did reinforce the national, indeed, the international, movements toward government provision of elementary and secondary education, of libraries, of more individualized treatment of orphans and others in need of social assistance, and of some elements of sanitation and public health. By mid-century, foundations had helped persuade the federal government to accept a large share of the responsibility for funding research in the fields of science, medicine, and public health. But American foundations never abandoned their commitment to individual initiative and self-help. In comparison with their European counterparts, American students and their families, as well as private donors, continued to bear large shares of the costs of college and professional education. American audiences, congregations, campaigners, as well as the donors who supported them, continued to bear nearly all the costs of the arts, of religion, and of social advocacy. Foundations reinforced those tendencies.

Foundations often embraced elitism as a necessary strategy. If they were to make a significant impact with their limited resources, they had to deploy them strategically, intervening to increase the capacities of the best and most influential researchers, institutions, and policy innovators. As the Rosenwald Fund put it, many celebrated their "investment in people." Given the limits to their resources and their commitments to specific values and priorities, foundations were necessarily particularistic. Under American law and consistent with America's political culture—and with the limitations of their financial and intellectual resources—they exercised their First Amendment right to be narrow, often passionate, sometimes heedless. In a more general sense, the most notable secular general-purpose foundations joined America's long-established religious and local foundations both in advancing professionalism (now science-based) and in further diversifying the pluralism of the nation's religious, intellectual, scientific, and artistic life.

4

After World War II: Readjustment and Redefinition

The moment when American foundations could reshape entire fields had largely ended by the 1930s. Foundation interventions in medicine, science, research universities, public schools, and public libraries had by then done much to create new self-sustaining enterprises and professions that could now set their own course, without regard to foundation preferences. The exceptional advantages in wealth and focus—advantages in relation to the resources of other American institutions and governments—that the biggest foundations had held during the first decades of the century had faded. Government activity had expanded greatly in the face of depression and war. Americans had entered a period of rising incomes and declining economic inequality that would last for three decades, greatly increasing people's ability to pay with fees and taxes for education, health care, and other classically foundation-supported services. The movements for equal rights for African Americans, Hispanics, Native Americans, and women confronted foundations, like other institutions, with articulate and urgent demands. Disruptions of war and cold war, decolonization, fear that rapid population growth would bring famine and unrest, and a vast increase in the resources available to international agencies all changed the international landscape.

Yet at the time neither foundation advocates nor foundation critics recognized the implications of these changes. To all appearances, American foundations remained exceptionally wealthy and influential. The Rockefeller, Rosenwald, Carnegie, and Guggenheim funds, with others, had proven their value in war by investing in technological research that underpinned both American air and atomic power and greatly improved medical care for soldiers and sailors. Foundations (and endowments) had won considerable credit for building research universities as well as regional and faith-based colleges. Foundations were playing key parts in creating such centers for the arts and for patriotic celebration as the National Gallery in Washington, Colonial Williamsburg in Virginia, and national parks across the United States.

Critics also reinforced the sense that foundations continued to wield great power. Some objected to the (rare) foundation support for the expansion of government. Ignoring earlier complaints that secular foundations undermined denominational authority, some insisted that they actually worked to maintain Protestant domination. Some liberals blamed the defeat of New Deal congressmen on propaganda issuing from a few conservative foundations and organizations that used the "foundation" name. Assuming that foundations had the ability to shape events, some insisted they should do more for the poor, for education, for the environment, for the arts and humanities, and for other causes.

Accounts that focus exclusively on foundations often see the hostile political scrutiny that culminated in the Tax Reform Act of 1969 as responsible for restricting foundation activity. It is true that abuse of the foundation as a legal instrument for family aggrandizement and for blatantly political causes provoked the rewriting of laws and regulations and that regulation had an impact. But the decisive challenges were economic and institutional.

The Ford Foundation's *Gaither Report* of 1950 embodied a sense, born of the great achievements of the first decades of the century, that foundations could decisively shape events. A comprehensive discussion of priorities for what had just become the wealthiest foundation in the world, the Gaither Report attracted great attention both because the Ford Foundation held billions of dollars and because so many prominent people sat on its board. The authors of the report used language appropriate for a summit meeting between heads of state. As the United States and Soviet Union built hydrogen bombs and waged war by proxy in Korea, the report opened portentously: "Fundamental to any consideration of human welfare is human survival." In language that echoed the wartime Atlantic Charter—a statement of war aims issued by Franklin Roosevelt and Winston Churchill in early 1942—it called for economic growth to eliminate from the entire world "undue anxiety over the physical conditions of survival." Beyond peace and prosperity, the report urged respect for "the dignity of man," which it described as resting "on the conviction that man is endowed with certain unalienable rights and must be regarded as an end in himself." Society everywhere, it proclaimed, "must accord all men equal rights and equal opportunity," tolerate "individual social, religious, and cultural differences," and assure "freedom of speech, freedom of the press, freedom of worship, and freedom of association."[1]

The Ford Foundation was the very largest new postwar foundation, but it was not alone. Depression and war had limited the creation of new foundations in the 1930s and early 1940s, yet new foundations joined Ford in the late 1940s and through the 1950s and 1960s. Ford made notable efforts to advance its extraordinary agenda; most other foundations also worked to advance the causes they had chosen. But all had to work within a transformed and rapidly changing context. They quickly came up against limits. Unable to transform entire fields, foundations—even the largest—found themselves working within complex systems that they could not control but that they could hope to encourage toward excellence and sustainability. After discussing how the growth of the institutions of science, medicine, and education, the expanding role of government, and sustained national prosperity all combined to reduce foundation influence, this chapter will review the ways American foundations worked in the postwar years to promote excellence, sustain distinctiveness, reform lagging fields and unproductive behavior, and advance international ambitions.

Foundations, Government, and the Market

It is easy to forget how extensively Americans transformed their governments in the 1930s and 1940s. Before the New Deal, state and local governments had taken the lead in domestic policy. The federal government had little to do with health, education, or welfare. Prior to World War II, the federal government provided scant support for scientific research (apart from the venerable Coast and Geodetic Survey), for higher education (apart from the one-time grants to the land-grant universities), for health and medicine (apart from the small Food and Drug Administration and Public Health Service), or for elementary and secondary education (except for the limited information-collecting work of the U.S. Office of Education). Before World War II, the U.S. government had no comprehensive program of foreign aid. It had been precisely in these fields that American foundations had made their most notable contributions.

Depression and war had brought great changes in many fields:

—In science: the Manhattan Project and other wartime federal research initiatives led to the Atomic Energy Commission (1947) and the military's Office of Technical and Scientific Services (1947, a predecessor to the Defense Advanced Research Projects Administration of 1958); the National Science Foundation (1950); and the National Aeronautics and Space Administration (NASA, 1958).[2]

—In higher education: the educational and job-training benefits of the G.I. Bill (1944) and the National Defense Education Act (1958).[3]

—In health and medicine: the creation and expansion of the National Institutes of Health (launched with modest funding in 1937, then expanded); the expansion of wartime hospital-support programs into the Hill-Burton Hospital Construction Act (1946); and the rapid growth of employer-provided health insurance, spurred by federal tax policy in the late 1940s.

—In social welfare and family policy: Social Security and federal aid to the blind and the disabled, unemployment insurance, Federal Housing Administration insurance for home loans (while most of these date from 1936, they became effective only during the 1940s and were significantly expanded only during the 1950s).

Additionally, World War II, the Marshall Plan, and the cold war transformed the U.S. government's approaches to international relations, foreign aid, military research, and defense. Instead of its formerly "limited and even negative role in foreign aid," the United States contributed $3 billion of the $4.3 billion spent by the United Nations Relief and Rehabilitation Administration. Between 1944 and 1949, it appropriated $400 million for Greece and Turkey, launched what became the $22 billion Marshall Plan to rebuild Western Europe's economy, and started the Point Four program of aid to developing nations.[4]

By the early 1950s, the U.S. federal government was spending vastly more than the foundations in each of these fields. By that time, too, local public school, public library, and public health districts had firmly established themselves across the nation. Beyond the federal government, states and localities had added sales and income taxes to their traditional property-tax revenue bases during the Depression and now raised more money, more steadily than ever before for health, education, welfare, and recreation.

But the growth of government we associate with the New Deal had only modest influence on the fields in which foundations had been most notably active—health care, scientific and medical research, and higher education— and little influence on religion or the arts. That would change in the 1960s. The success of the civil rights movement and the consequent passage of Great Society legislation in that decade directly changed the context for foundation work. In just two years, 1965 and 1966, Congress passed historic civil rights and voting rights acts, created Medicare and Medicaid and a national program of grants and loans for college students, greatly expanded federal support for job training and other antipoverty and economic development initiatives, and launched the National Endowment for the Arts and the National Endowment for the Humanities. Congress also greatly increased funding for the National Science Foundation and the National Institutes of Health and expanded payments under Social Security and aid to the disabled. These large increases in federal funding enabled most of the important foundation-aided fields to grow rapidly, at a time when foundation assets were growing slowly. Several decisions of the U.S. Supreme Court from the 1950s through the 1970s further affirmed federal guarantees of individual rights against trespass by state and local government—or by private institutions, whether business or nonprofits.

Together, newly confirmed rights and newly sustained government funding imposed novel constraints and uncertainties on foundations. As federal funding

rose, schools, colleges, hospitals, social service organizations, public school districts, local governments, and other providers of services grew rapidly, but now in
ways defined by government. Because federal and state priorities changed from
year to year, often shifting or cutting funds, service providers struggled to cover
expenses and increasingly turned to their traditional supporters among foundations and other private donors.[5] But foundations argued, reasonably enough,
that if they allowed themselves to be coerced into filling gaps created by government inconstancy, they would be giving up control of their own funds.

Changes in the ways that government funded service providers brought new
pressures. In the 1940s, 1950s, and 1960s, large portions of the funds appropriated under the G.I. Bill, the Hill-Burton Hospital Construction Act, the
National Defense Education Act, and the Great Society had gone, in the form
of grants, directly to existing nonprofit organizations and government agencies.
Sometimes, especially where, as with Head Start, local governments would not
serve those populations, federal funds went to nonprofit organizations newly
created to provide services to previously underserved populations.[6]

Then in the 1970s and 1980s, Congress dramatically shifted the bulk of
direct funding to voucher, voucherlike, and loan programs, such as the student
grant programs of the G.I. Bill and the Great Society's Pell Grants and Medicare
and Medicaid programs. This change enabled patients, students, the disabled,
the elderly, and increasing numbers of the poor to act more like consumers in
a marketplace. Vouchers allowed consumers to select, if they preferred, church-
affiliated schools, hospitals, and other facilities, without violating constitutional
constraints on direct government support of religious institutions. Medicaid
and Medicare left it to patients (and those who advised them and sometimes
to state regulators) to select hospitals, clinics, doctors, and treatments and then
paid (substantially if not completely) for the services rendered. Federal college
and graduate student-aid programs increasingly offered loans and loan guarantees rather than grants, leaving it to students to select schools. This was a big
change from granting funds to schools that could then seek to attract the students they wished to admit. Vouchers decreased the autonomy of schools and
other service-providing organizations, even as they increased public support for
federal funding.[7]

Because vouchers come with federal strings—with rules about the licensing
and management of those who provide a service, about health and safety, about
program design and provider accreditation—vouchers did not decrease federal
regulation. But vouchers did reinforce market forces created by rising incomes.
Disposable (after tax) income, measured in constant 2000 dollars per capita, rose
steadily from about $10,000 in 1960 to $17,000 in 1980 to more than $25,000
in 2000.[8] Although incomes became increasingly unequal after 1980, the general
rise from the 1940s into the 1970s allowed Americans to buy more and more

services from nonprofits and governments—from schools and colleges, from clinics and hospitals, from agencies that serve children and the elderly, and from providers of recreation and the arts. As market forces grew stronger, nonprofit and government agencies became less responsive to foundation influence. As late as 1973 memories of earlier times still led some observers to say that foundations served as "the institutional core of the private philanthropic sector."[9] But if this had ever been true, its time was already in the past.

By 1973, foundation grants amounted to less than 1 percent of all U.S. expenditures on health, education, or social welfare. In that year the federal government alone spent seven times as much as foundations on higher education, more than thirty times as much on international assistance grants, forty-two times as much on health, fifty-six times as much on science, seventy-seven times as much on social welfare, and eighty-three times as much on elementary and secondary education.[10] It was not that the federal government had simply "crowded out" the foundations: federal funds, combined with unprecedented private purchasing power, were transforming every field. Massive federal funding allowed services to reach far more people, more quickly and more effectively, than had ever been possible. And it allowed scientific and medical research to be organized on a far more systematic and sustained basis, through institutions located in almost every part of the nation.[11]

Facing new material and regulatory environments after World War II, foundations also had to deal with increasingly stringent regulations. Congress had raised personal and corporate income taxes to unprecedented levels during World War II. When financial advisers helped many taxpayers to use foundations to shelter some of their wealth and to control their businesses—and some charities claimed tax exemption for the income of businesses that had been given to them, as New York University Law School did with the Mueller Spaghetti Company—President Truman proposed, and Congress agreed, to tighten regulations.[12] By insisting that foundations not be used to enrich donors, leaders, or their families, by imposing a tax on the income that foundations and other charities derived from "unrelated businesses," by requiring increased disclosure of information about investments and expenditures, and by drawing a clearer distinction between what would come to be known as "private foundations" and "operating foundations" or "public charities," the Revenue Act of 1950 significantly increased regulation.[13]

But officials found it difficult to make the regulations effective. When the Shubert family set up the Sam S. Shubert Foundation in 1945 to control its empire of Broadway theaters, New York and federal officials struggled for more than twenty years to clarify the foundation's tax and charitable obligations. When in 1954 Texas oilmen Clint Murchison and Sid Richardson creatively formed the "Boys Inc. Foundation" to purchase, operate, and receive the declared profits of California's Del Mar and other racetracks, they avoided taxes as well as close government scrutiny of some business practices.[14] Despite the new regulations, some financial advisers continued to advertise their skill in using foundations to shelter wealth.[15] Former Treasury staffer Thomas Troyer quotes *Business Week* as having asserted in 1960 that the "real motive behind most private foundations is keeping control of wealth (even while the wealth itself is given away)."[16]

Most foundations did give to charity and did follow the law. In a notable 1958 case, the board of the Kress Foundation actually took legal action to force the family member who was still in control to create more value for charity.[17] In 1964 the Securities and Exchange Commission found no evidence that foundations speculated in the stock market.[18] Yet a careful 1965 Treasury Department report, which included all foundations whose reported assets exceeded $10 million, found that some had invested 20 percent or more of their assets in a single business and that half of these reported no income at all from such investments. In this way income that had been pledged to charity went instead to enrich donors and their families and friends.[19] Such abuses were real but seem to have affected only a small share of foundation assets. In 1972 foundation critic Waldemar A. Nielsen found a few "heavily conflicted boards" among the largest foundations, but (with two or three exceptions) "no evidence" that most trustees had "indulged in the cruder forms of self-aggrandizement."[20]

Foundations received criticism, and increasing regulation, not only for financial misdeeds, but also on political grounds. Some of the harshest critics of the welfare state and of internationalism in foreign relations applied powerful rhetoric about "subversion" by "hidden hands" to foundations as well as to political leaders and other institutions. Defenders of segregation and states' rights did not appreciate the Carnegie Corporation of New York's support for *An American Dilemma* or a few foundations' later support for the registration of African American voters.[21] Those who thought the U.S. State Department had failed to recognize the Soviet threat at Yalta and had opposed the creation of the United Nations noted that Alger Hiss (who was later convicted of spying for the Soviet Union) headed the Carnegie Endowment for International Peace after he left government service. During the 1950s the Cox and Reece committees of the House of Representatives attracted considerable publicity with their hearings into such "subversive" influence in the large foundations.

A few very wealthy conservatives thought it only appropriate to use the foundation idea not to pioneer new government services but to divert money from taxes to agitation against government spending. H. L. Hunt's Facts Forum Foundation, formed in 1952, was not legally a foundation; it was an operating charity that Hunt personally financed at the rate of a million dollars a year. Through broadcasts on several hundred radio stations across Texas and beyond and through widely distributed pamphlets, Facts Forum supported Dixiecrats and attacked national Democrats as "the instrument of socialism and communism."[22] The Gannett Foundation of New York really was a foundation; it used profits from the Gannett newspapers to underwrite Frank Gannett's campaign against big government.

Political leaders did not make careful distinctions between "foundations" and other kinds of tax-exempt organizations. Offended by H. L. Hunt's broadcasts against him, in 1954 Senator Lyndon B. Johnson proposed on the Senate floor that tax-exempt funds should not be used in election campaigns. Republicans joined Democrats in agreeing without debate to Johnson's proposal to deny "tax-exempt status to not only those people who influence legislation but also to those who intervene in any political campaign on behalf of any candidate for any public office." Faced with this legislation and with challenges from Congress and the possibility of questions from the IRS, Hunt closed Facts Forum in 1956.[23]

But Hunt's renewed LIFE LINE Foundation and related efforts by other conservative funds attracted renewed criticism in the next few years. And on the conservative side, the *New York Daily News* complained that Mobilization for Youth, a prominent antipoverty organization funded in part by the Ford Foundation, employed radical troublemakers and that Ford and other foundations were underwriting campaigns to register African American voters in northern cities like New York and Cleveland as well as in the South.[24]

Then over several years in the mid-1960s Johnson's Texas colleague, Congressman Wright Patman, who had long fought Hunt and other free-spending conservatives who opposed New Deal Democrats, launched an ambitious series of hearings into what he held to be financial misbehavior by many foundations. Phrasing his complaints in general terms, he objected that the "rapidly increasing economic power in foundations . . . is far more dangerous than anything which has happened in the past in the way of the concentration of economic power." He complained, "Foundation-controlled enterprises possess the money and the competitive advantages to eliminate the small businessman." Fundamentally, he insisted, in terms relevant to tax-exempt organizations of all kinds, "When any taxpayer reduces his tax by a deduction for contribution to a foundation it means that all other taxpayers must make up for the tax reduction."[25]

Patman ignored the differences between foundations of different types and between foundations and religious, cultural, or service-providing nonprofits; he exaggerated foundation wealth and the frequency of bad foundation behavior, and he issued reports before giving those he criticized a chance to respond.[26] But he had a reputation as a dogged investigator, and his investigations struck a chord in Congress. And as Richard Magat, who for several years handled public relations for the Ford Foundation, has written, "social and political issues" lay under "the visible surface of concerns over financial manipulation."[27]

Congressional criticism culminated in the Tax Reform Act of 1969, which singled out foundations from other kinds of charitable nonprofits and imposed much more onerous regulations on them. Foundations now faced tightened prohibitions against "self-dealing" and "self-inurement." Foundation donors had to observe stricter rules to qualify for charitable deductions. Sharpening the distinction between foundations and other nonprofits, the law also imposed a 4 percent federal "audit fee" on independent foundation income (reduced a few years later to 2 percent or under certain conditions to 1 percent). Unlike other nonprofits, foundations also had to "pay out" annually, in grants and certain grant-related expenses, a proportion of their assets that foundation leaders feared was so high that it would render continuing endowments unsustainable. And foundations had to meet more stringent annual public reporting requirements, though all nonprofits had now to reveal more detailed and accurate financial and investment information. After 1969, for the first time, all nonprofits, including foundations, had to make audited annual financial reports public. The 1969 law affirmed the limitations on direct political activity. And it introduced a wider array of penalties for foundations and foundation officials who violated its provisions.[28]

Because it confirmed their treatment as "public charities" exempt from the new tax on foundation assets and from some other restrictions and reporting requirements, the Tax Reform Act of 1969 encouraged community foundations, which over the next twenty-five years grew much faster than independent foundations.[29] It also encouraged the creation of new "supporting foundations" attached to individual religious and secular nonprofit organizations or to state universities and other government entities.

Following the passage of the 1969 Tax Reform Act, independent foundations grew at a slower rate. Smaller foundations raised their payout rate.[30] Community foundations—which emphasized transparency and accountability—proliferated. So did supporting funds closely tied to operating charities—and these now attracted criticism formerly directed to independent and family foundations for allowing donors to control charitable funds for narrow or selfish purposes.[31] The Tax Reform Act deserves some responsibility for these changes, but other forces also imposed new limits on foundations. Stock market reverses and very high inflation reduced the value of foundation assets during the 1970s.[32] The nonprofit world grew both more regulated and more diverse as government funding and private spending fueled its growth.

Because reporting requirements were minimal until the Tax Reform Act of 1969 took full effect, we don't have good measures of the numbers or assets of foundations until the late 1970s and must base general judgments on information regarding larger and better-known foundations. In 1960, the still very incomplete data collected by the Foundation Center indicated that twenty foundations held 51 percent of all reported foundation assets, and the next 110 largest held another 25 percent.[33] With its assets newly enlarged to $3.3 billion—fully half the reported assets of the twenty largest American foundations—the Ford Foundation dominated public discussion.[34] As a group, foundations were not static. Most of the largest dated from the 1920s and 1930s, but new or expanded foundations joined the top group in the two decades following the war.[35] Some of the most notable older foundations consolidated with other funds, spent out their assets, shifted focus, or converted themselves into operating charities.[36] In other cases, operating charities became grantmakers.[37]

Because they differed greatly in size, purpose, locality, and outlook, foundations responded to change in widely different ways. Their postwar activity cannot be summed up in a phrase like "supported the creation of American denominationalism" or "built major institutions in public education, higher education, medicine, international relations, and research." In the wake of the congressional investigations, the Treasury Report, and the Tax Reform Act of 1969, much contemporary debate among foundation leaders focused on the question of activism: how should foundations engage with public affairs?[38] They continued to launch new institutions, help build new facilities, and train new cadres of experts and activists. But postwar foundations more often worked to fill out existing sets of institutions. Many worked to bring excellent facilities to their own part of the nation. Some underwrote what they hoped would be strategically influential pilot programs or research within already-established fields of activity. Some encouraged governments to provide continuing funding for effective innovations. Often foundations sought to enable people and organizations to help themselves, subsidizing church construction, community development, job training, and the opening of jobs and civic opportunities to formerly excluded groups. Across fields both traditional and new—science, education, health care, social welfare, international aid, religion, and social movements that aimed to integrate the formerly excluded—foundations looked for ways to maximize their influence, perhaps most often in efforts to encourage exceptional achievement.

Large Gifts, Established Patterns

Seeking to raise universities, medical centers, and arts organizations in every region of the United States to world-class standing and to expand access to the best in medicine, science, general knowledge, and the arts, American foundations made a number of extraordinary gifts to endowments and building funds during the three or four decades after World War II. In these years, universities and medical centers relied more and more on federal and state funding and on tuition and patient fees. Medical centers, in particular, looked increasingly to federal funding for capital purposes; the Hill-Burton program alone provided $3.7 billion for hospital construction between 1946 and 1971. Gifts from individuals and support from local governments were also important, though foundations did make supplementary investments in medical research facilities.[39] Joining with other private donors, foundations now focused on facilities for key universities and arts institutions. The aim was not to create new kinds of institutions, but to raise quality, increase accessibility, and bring world-class institutions to every part of the nation.

These general observations apply even to the Ford Foundation, which in 1950 was by far the largest of all foundations. Ford's 1956 distribution of vast sums—the equivalent of about $4 billion in 2010 dollars—constitutes the single most striking foundation effort to reinforce existing institutional patterns across the nation. In a single grand gesture that took account only of the institutions' current sizes, Ford gave $210 million to 617 private colleges and universities (Catholic, Protestant, and Jewish), $200 million to 3,100 not-for-profit hospitals, and $90 million to forty-two privately supported medical schools.[40] It also put considerable shares of its initial assets into two separate and independent funds, for the Advancement of Education and for Adult Education. Some of Ford's other exceptionally large early gift programs focused on exemplary institutions rather than on entire fields. One program sent scores of millions in direct and matching grants to each of twenty-two leading private research universities. In 1971 Ford added a $100 million fund to support minority fellowships and historically black colleges.[41]

The Howard Hughes Medical Institute invested more specifically in excellence at existing institutions. Although it is not technically a foundation, the Hughes Institute in many ways acts as one, holding a large amount of capital for application to charitable research and educational purposes and distributing substantial grants. It operates its own very large research programs, but it also provides large grants to researchers in universities across the United States. Founded by Howard Hughes in 1953 and already active in the 1950s and 1960s, the Howard Hughes Medical Institute's resources grew rapidly after the founder's death in 1976. In 2009 it reported that its endowment was $17.5 billion (larger than any foundation except Gates) and that over the past twenty years it had devoted over $8.3 billion to science "support, training, and education," much of it through the support of substantial "Hughes laboratories" at seventy-one U.S. universities and research centers.[42]

Taken together, gifts from Ford, Danforth, Hughes, and other foundations strongly reinforced the leadership of a select group of institutions. These grants did not change existing patterns, but they did help confirm a national standard. Henceforth, American universities would increasingly be evaluated in the same terms, emphasizing, as historian Roger Geiger puts it, science, "striving for academic distinction . . . increasing emphasis on graduate education . . . [and] an abundance of research activity."[43] Establishing the standard was more important than the relatively modest funding foundations could provide. Going forward, university success would require large, continuing support from individual donors and from the federal government.

Seeking to give the best possible opportunities to local students and to build the intellectual and technological capital for the development of their home regions, many foundations further reinforced the new national university standard by giving on a continuous basis to nearby universities. The Duke Endowment for the Carolinas and the Wisconsin Alumni fund continued their work. The Houston Endowment and the M. D. Anderson Foundation provided critical support for their city's impressive and rapidly growing Texas Medical Center.[44] The Lilly Endowment funded many initiatives for Indiana colleges and universities, just as the Northwest Area Foundation (before 1960 the Louis W. and Maud Hill Foundation) supported the University of Minnesota and other colleges and universities in what the foundation takes to be the greater Northwest, and the Weingard Foundation underwrote student aid programs at fourteen Los Angeles institutions. Many smaller foundations also gave mostly to one or a few nearby schools. In Cleveland, for example, the Elizabeth Severance Prentiss Foundation, together with special funds held by the Cleveland Foundation, underwrote exceptional research initiatives at Case Western Reserve University's School of Medicine, while the Case Alumni Fund made certain that its funds went to support engineering and related scientific work at that university.

Several of the largest individual foundation grants of the next few decades also went to established research universities: Brown, Columbia, Pennsylvania, Johns Hopkins, Wisconsin, Indiana, Rockefeller University, Stanford, and the California Institute of Technology. More went to raise the standing of ambitious regional institutions. The Danforth Foundation transferred the greater part of its endowment to Washington University of St. Louis; Atlanta's Woodruff Foundation gave much of its endowment to Emory University. Other exceptionally large foundation gifts helped build up public as well as private universities and colleges across the United States, including Stony Brook University on Long Island, the University of Southern California, the Claremont Colleges, Vanderbilt, and the universities of Arkansas, Mississippi, Texas, Arizona, Oregon, and Washington. More than a score of the foundation grants of $50 million or more made during the 1970s, 1980s, and 1990s went to individual research universities, usually to support scientific research.[45]

Nearly 100 U.S. research universities had achieved world-class standards by the 1970s, thanks in good part to foundation aid. American researchers became more concerned with one another than with foreign competitors, and many observers credited their strength to competition among the American institutions. After the 1970s, as historian Steven Wheatley has concluded, the ties that bound most large foundations closely to universities quickly eroded.[46] University leaders feared that foundations were shifting to other priorities; however, the universities' great growth helped distance them from foundations. Foundations continued to support universities in their home regions, but they could do little to change the direction of university development as a whole.

Leading arts organizations also benefited from the postwar foundation emphasis on excellence in the four or five decades after World War II. Large foundation gifts filled out America's scattered collections of arts organizations. The Ford Foundation again took the lead, a few foundations underwrote campaigns to establish national standards for giving to the arts, and many foundations focused their efforts on the arts in their home regions.

In their contributions to the American public television system, postwar foundations played the institution-building role that had been so much more common during the classic decades of the first third of the twentieth century. Ford provided about $300 million for public television projects (including the national public television system and the Children's Television Workshop [CTW]) between 1951 and 1976.[47] The Markle Foundation also made crucial gifts to the CTW's *Sesame Street* project.[48] And it was in this period that the Lowell Institute (which dated from the early nineteenth century) committed itself to WGBH-TV in Boston.[49]

Between 1962 and 1972, the Ford Foundation also gave nearly $200 million to campaigns to increase the numbers of symphony orchestras, dance companies, and theaters across the United States. Ford insisted that local groups develop "community sources of support," and its funding helped persuade many local foundations to contribute to the nearby arts institutions.[50] Also nationally notable was the J. Paul Getty Trust, which created not only the Getty museums in southern California, but also important national centers for education, research, and the conservation of works of art.

Foundations made substantial contributions to new or expanded arts activity in New York City and also in Atlanta, Washington, D.C., Houston, Los Angeles, Las Vegas, and indeed nearly every American city, as well as to key regional centers for the arts such as the Shakespeare Festival in Ashland, Oregon, and Colorado's Aspen Music Festival. In Cleveland during the 1950s and 1960s, the Leonard C. Hanna Jr. Fund made major gifts to the Cleveland Playhouse and the Cleveland Museum of Art, while the Reinberger and Kulas foundations steadily contributed to classical music through the Cleveland Orchestra, the Cleveland Institute of Music, the Oberlin Conservatory, and other institutions. In Minnesota, local foundations joined individual donors and corporations in underwriting an array of arts organizations, including the Guthrie Theater, the Walker Art Center, and the St. Paul Chamber Orchestra.

Foundation funds also played a role in bringing minority communities into the national arts fields. The Ford Foundation again set the example by funding the creation of the Dance Theater of Harlem, the Negro Ensemble Company, and initiatives designed to expand opportunities for Hispanics, women, and others who had not been well served in the arts. Some regional funds followed suit, as when Cleveland's Hanna Fund contributed to Karamu House, a nationally prominent regional theater long committed to racial integration. These were new departures for foundations. Yet arts funding directed toward minority communities remained very limited.

A recent analysis argues that these newer organizations "diversify the regional arts offerings away from an older, monopolistic model in which a city would have one major fine arts museum, one symphony orchestra, and one repertory theatre company," generating more competition for arts organizations and more public attention to their work.[51] Overall, in television and the arts, government spending complemented foundation funding, rather than the other way around.

As foundations shifted without acknowledging the change from creating new classes of institutions to strengthening those they had already created, they did sometimes launch new institutions. A number of the most celebrated of these appeared in policy-related areas. Following the Rockefeller Foundation's pioneering creation of the International Education Board and the Spelman Memorial and subsidies for the Social Science Research Council and, after World War II, the Population Council,[52] the Ford Foundation created Resources for the Future (1952) and the Fund for the Republic (1953)[53] and put the Vera Institute for Justice, among other organizations, on a sustainable basis (1966).[54] Ford also provided substantial start-up funding for the Mexican-American Legal Defense and Education Fund (1968). These were new organizations, but in many ways they followed the pattern of the foundation-supported think tank that dated back to the beginning of the century with the Milbank Memorial Fund, the Russell Sage Foundation, and the Twentieth Century Fund.

Sustaining Exceptional Achievement

Lacking sufficient resources to invent and build new fields or whole institutions, most postwar foundations sought to encourage exceptional achievement within those that were already established. The most notable examples can be found in higher education and the arts.

As Steven Wheatley, Peter Frumkin, and Gabriel Kaplan argue, scientific and medical research in the American research university had become such a large enterprise by the 1950s, so dependent on federal funding and so institutionalized, that most foundation grants could only support the application of established practices to selected problems.[55] At the same time, however, some of the most important supporters of scientific collaboration funded themselves through fees, patent income, and corporate contributions and did not rely on foundations.[56] The most notable foundation research initiatives of the postwar decades achieved strategic impact, often with relatively modest budgets, on practical, applied topics to which government research agencies gave low priority.

The Rockefeller Foundation's "green revolution" investment in agricultural innovations intended to raise living standards among the world's poor constituted perhaps the most-cited example and one of the most debated. The Lasker Foundation's cancer initiatives have also been celebrated and debated. Also notable were studies of population, reproduction, and related health matters. The Robert Wood Johnson, Ford, and later the Aaron Diamond foundations early responded to the need for research on HIV/AIDS. Through such initiatives, foundations sometimes underwrote work that lacked political support; on other occasions they encouraged more federal funding for the budget of the National Institutes of Health (NIH). As Richard Rettig and others have shown, foundations in these ways helped shape the NIH by provoking the "proliferation of new institutes, centers, and program offices attached to the Office of the Director."[57]

Other foundation gifts reinforced the success of the small number of large gifts in expanding the research capabilities of American universities far beyond the dozen early leaders in the Northeast, the Great Lakes, and California. The Getty, Packard, and Hewlett funds invested substantially in several new California institutions. The Robert A. Welch Foundation supported chemical research in Texas, the Castle Foundation underwrote child study at the University of Hawaii, and the M. J. Murdock Charitable Trust invested in scientific research in the Pacific Northwest.[58] The Samuel Roberts Noble Foundation underwrote studies of the biology of plants; the McKnight Foundation supported work on agricultural and neurological science. The Burroughs Welcome Fund (large and independent after 1993), based in North Carolina, funded medical research on a national basis. Continuing its established focus on opportunities for adult education, especially in grain-belt areas, the W. K. Kellogg Foundation added its support to the large federal, state, and county government financing of continuing education programs at many universities.[59] Other very large foundation grants went to university-related research centers including the Olin Engineering College, the Keck Graduate Institute of Applied Life Sciences, the Donald Danforth Plant Science Center, and the Monterey Bay Aquarium Research Institute.

Foundations also helped build fields outside science and medicine that received little or no federal funding. During the 1940s and 1950s the Josiah Macy Jr. Foundation of New York did much to create the field of "cybernetics" by bringing together a remarkable group of social scientists and medical researchers, especially in a series of "Macy Conferences" between 1946 and 1953.[60] Many of the Kresge Foundation's challenge grants for buildings went to research institutions far beyond science—and also far beyond its home in Michigan. The Samuel H. Kress Foundation continued its well-established support for art history by adding works to many collections, underwriting the preservation of paintings and sculptures in the United States and in Europe, and offering research fellowships. In the early 1960s, Kress gave large numbers of art works to the National Gallery of Art and to universities, as well as to independent museums across the United States.[61] By the 1990s the William R. Kenan Jr. Charitable Trust had endowed as many as ninety-two professorships, often in the humanities, especially in many southern research universities.[62] On an even more national basis, the Luce Foundation invested several million dollars in Henry R. Luce Professorships emphasizing interdisciplinary work in the humanities as well as the social sciences at many universities between 1968 and 2009.[63] The David and Lucile Packard Foundation supported substantial work in the humanities and then in 1987 endowed the Packard Humanities Institute.

Given the limited size of foundation resources and the small number of foundations involved in the humanities, efforts in those fields were welcome. Nevertheless, those concerned about the humanities and social sciences continued to worry that foundation and other private giving remained far too low to offset the federal emphasis on science and technology. The Ford Foundation put less than 2 percent of its grants into the humanities; by the early 1970s "the freewheeling days when the Rockefeller Foundation was funding translation projects, indigenous drama in Nigeria, [and] creative writing in Mexico" had come to an end.[64] The Andrew W. Mellon Foundation, which emerged with a $500 million endowment in 1969, did something to restore the balance when it launched a major new set of research fellowship programs in the humanities.[65]

Applied research on practical problems attracted more foundation support. Ford now joined Rockefeller, the reorganized Russell Sage, and others in making substantial postwar investments in what these foundations called the "behavioral sciences," notably at Harvard, Columbia, and the universities of Michigan, Chicago, and Wisconsin. Ford also launched the Center for Advanced Study in the Behavioral Sciences in Palo Alto, next to Stanford's campus. The social and behavioral sciences did not rely on foundations alone: federal science and military research programs provided far more money.[66] But Ford took a clear lead in underwriting new departures in law and social science, business education, and clinical research. Ford, Rockefeller, and a number of smaller foundations invested large sums in the scientific study of poverty.[67] There is some evidence that economists have preferred to seek funds from sources specifically targeted to their own field, such as those provided by the Alfred P. Sloan Foundation as well as by the U.S. Department of Commerce and the Federal Reserve, and have often ignored requests for interdisciplinary proposals.[68] Late in this period the Ford, Mott, Kellogg, Packard, and Mandel foundations and the Atlantic

Philanthropies invested several million dollars in the academic study of non-profit organizations and civil society. As noted below, large Ford, Rockefeller, Luce, and Freeman foundation investments complemented federal support for area studies relevant to the cold war, decolonization, and globalization.

In the multifaceted field of social welfare, the growth of government and family incomes, as well as the influence of organized labor, constituted the most powerful postwar forces. Yet a quiet and little-noticed campaign by many foundations did much to increase the sustainability of community chests as key fundraisers for private social welfare—and as influential local voices in this field. Even as the Russell Sage Foundation withdrew from the field, the Rockefeller Foundation commissioned a study of the community chest payroll-deduction movement. And for two decades after World War II, continuing annual gifts from many local foundations helped community chests, which had found it difficult to survive the Great Depression, World War II, and the rise of health charities, to create a more stable place for themselves. By the 1960s the community chest (and the successor United Way) campaigns organized by local business leaders were raising tens of millions of dollars annually for the most widely supported social service organizations in most of the larger cities, especially, but not only, in the Midwest, Northeast, and West Coast.[69]

Similarly, from the 1970s on, the Lilly, Mott, Ford, and other foundations provided technical assistance and seed money to many new community foundations. The Tax Reform Act of 1969 sparked these efforts, but foundations did much to advance them. Local funds such as these, similar to independent foundations, raise, hold, and distribute resources for charitable purposes. And like other foundations, they also complicate control of the organizations they fund. Community foundations, like the supporting foundations attached to increasing numbers of operating charities and government agencies, have sometimes attracted the criticism that they reinforce inequality (those that serve wealthier populations attract more money) and particularism (by allowing donors to determine where their money goes). Community foundations have responded that they seek to increase voluntary giving to sustain charities that serve needs of all kinds.[70]

Postwar foundations also encouraged sustainable excellence in the arts. In addition to new arts organizations, foundations underwrote projects in museums, art studios, and facilities for the performing arts in colleges and universities. Ford and other foundations not only provided endowment and challenge grant funds for arts organizations, they also helped stabilize the funding of arts associations. Stefan Toepler notes in this connection the American Symphony Orchestra League's Americanizing the American Symphony initiative and the Excellence and Equity and Museums and Communities initiatives of the American Association of Museums.[71] In the arts, foundations increasingly preferred to support core organizations that helped nonprofit arts groups confer and coordinate, but that did not employ significant numbers of expensive experts. The federal National Endowment for the Arts (NEA) briefly gathered, summarized, and evaluated information on a national scale. When the NEA abandoned this role in the 1980s, foundations and other donors tried to take up the work, but could not mobilize sufficient resources.[72]

Certainly it was true in this period, as Paul DiMaggio found in a very careful study of the mid-1980s, that "few of the hundreds of independent foundations that give to the arts have lived up to the promise of the sector to make a difference for enterprises that other patrons will not support."[73] It was also true that foundations lacked the resources to underwrite arts activity on a large scale. The foundation contribution had more to do with the overall structure of arts activity in the United States. James A. Smith observes that the possibility of foundation support—and even more, of direct gifts from private donors—encouraged arts organizations to adopt the nonprofit organization form in this period, so that the number of arts nonprofits grew from a few thousand in the 1960s to some 50,000 in 2009.[74] Throughout these decades, as before, American arts organizations have had to earn much of their revenue and could expect little from government. Individual donors, who can act quickly and flexibly, provide them with substantially more money than foundations. Postwar foundations underwrote facilities and provided seed money, but they asked arts organizations, like other grantees, to sustain themselves.

A related set of foundation initiatives in these decades provided new support for individual achievement and creative work—again, generally within established institutions. Among advanced fellowship programs, most attention has gone to the MacArthur Foundation. MacArthur expanded on the continuing practice of the John Simon Guggenheim Foundation and the Commonwealth Fund, relying on nominations rather than applications and emphasizing community service as well as academic or artistic qualifications. Exceptionally, MacArthur fellowships also enabled recipients to devote as many as five years to creative work, allowing great independence. These initiatives did not create new fields or institutions. But they did help universities, academic fields, and certain social and artistic initiatives expand, sometimes dramatically, in areas that received little government funding. They thereby modestly increased the numbers of people who could pursue their ambitions in these fields.[75]

Other foundation initiatives launched after 1945 strengthened the new research universities by subsidizing highly capable people who were admitted to work at them. Between 1952 and 1979 the Danforth Foundation gave nearly 3,500 fellowships to "bright and motivated" young people who hoped to earn Ph.D.s in the humanities and social sciences. Although the foundation emphasized moral values and commitment to teaching as well as motivation, its carefully designed competition rewarded outstanding academic achievement above all. Those who won its graduate fellowships were concentrated in the highest-rated universities.[76] A Ford gift of the late 1950s enabled the Woodrow Wilson Foundation to quintuple to 1,000 the number of fellowships it offered to first-year graduate students annually. Following its long-established tradition of working with governments, in 1955 the Carnegie Corporation of New York joined the Ford Foundation to initiate the Merit Scholar program for exceptionally promising college applicants, administered through the Educational Testing Service.[77] The Hertz (1963), Thomas J. Watson (1968), and Sperry funds (this last under the name Beineke) also underwrote significant postwar graduate fellowship programs.[78]

As the federal government and individual colleges and universities took over the provision of financial aid, foundation attention shifted to students from formerly excluded communities. The Danforth Foundation, under the very active leadership of Merrimon Cuninggim, former dean of the Perkins School of Theology at Southern Methodist University, provided substantial support to historically black southern colleges during the 1960s and 1970s.[79] The Ford Foundation joined this effort in 1970, launching a graduate fellowship program for African Americans and other people of color, and soon gave it $100 million. In 1990 the Annenberg Foundation gave $50 million to the United Negro College Fund. The billion-dollar Gates Millennium Scholars program, launched in 1999, funded academic "opportunity for outstanding minority students with significant financial need." When federal policy shifted student aid strongly from grants to loans in the 1980s, the Starr Foundation moved to create scholarship funds at more than 100 universities and colleges, joining many other foundations and individual donors in enabling promising students to minimize their tuition debt.[80]

By encouraging all universities to build resources for scholarships, demonstrating the need to individual and corporate donors, and helping persuade the federal and state governments to increase funding for scholarships, foundations worked effectively to institutionalize the "search for talent" in a way that sought both to encourage achievement and to expand opportunity. Hundreds of smaller foundations also made substantial scholarship-fund contributions.[81]

Every effort to promote excellence is subject to the criticism of elitism. The systems of excellence supported by postwar American foundations collectively sought to meet that criticism in several ways. Raising institutions in every region to world-class standards appealed to local pride, met wide public approval, and expanded opportunity.

The postwar foundation emphasis on sustainability, including charging for services, reinforced trends that had strong momentum. In these decades popular demand, local pride, private donors, the new availability of federal research funds, and the rising public ability to pay for tuition and for the arts would have led to new and improved universities, medical research centers, religious schools, and arts organizations whether foundations existed or not. Yet foundations did help particular organizations appear and grow, become more impressive in some details, add innovations or currently out-of-favor initiatives, and become more inclusive even as they celebrated "world-class" standards.

Reform

On occasion, postwar foundations sought more to reorient or reform existing systems than to sustain or expand them. Following the earlier examples of Carnegie with libraries and schools, Russell Sage with social services, and the Rockefeller, Commonwealth, and Milbank Memorial funds and others in health, some postwar foundations supported campaigns to reform standards set by nongovernment professional associations and trade groups. No doubt because the Ford Foundation came onto the scene only after the federal government had greatly expanded its role, Ford leaders sometimes sought big changes by working directly with federal agencies.[82] Overall, foundations pursued limited purposes with limited resources. They provided only limited support for the civil rights movement until after it had achieved legislative success and had little to do with Medicare and Medicaid, the most important achievements of the Great Society. Historian Linda Eisenmann has added, "Philanthropic foundations in the 1950s were not attuned to . . . women's issues."[83]

For many American foundations, to reform an institution meant in practice to promote particular religious or secular values. In other cases, foundations sought general results—effectiveness, excellence, and inclusiveness. Different foundations had different, and not infrequently conflicting, priorities. Whatever their approach, many foundation-supported reform campaigns encountered formidable resistance—sometimes from other foundations.

In the health field, as Daniel Fox has shown, foundations had largely withdrawn from national system building and standard setting by the mid-1930s. The W. K. Kellogg Foundation supported nursing education and the John A. Hartford Foundation funded work in nursing the elderly but not for medical research or education.[84] And when in the 1980s Robert Wood Johnson became the largest foundation in the health care field, it accorded highest priority to access for underserved populations. Initially it emphasized reform at the edges of medicine: emergency response systems, new mid-level health professions for primary care (in collaboration with the Commonwealth Fund), and health services in schools. It also experimented with subsidies for the expansion of health insurance coverage in selected locales. Gradually it turned toward the encouragement of healthier day-to-day living. Only in the 1990s would Robert Wood Johnson and other foundations take on more ambitious questions relating to the nation's health care system as a whole.

Steven Wheatley concludes that in many ways foundations also withdrew from higher education reform in the postwar period. Peter Frumkin and Gabriel Kaplan add that for many foundations, universities became interesting only when they could be diverted from teaching and research to focus on community service. To the extent that leading universities emphasized outreach to formerly excluded minority groups and to women in these decades, they relied more on their own funds, on the associations they had built in earlier decades, and on federal subsidies than on foundations. Foundations were much more likely to fund research on the effects of such activities.[85] The Knight Foundation's continuing support for a commission on intercollegiate sports sought to limit glaring abuses in spectator entertainments and not to promote a comprehensive reformation of undergraduate social life.[86]

Several foundations sought to transform the religious life of American colleges and universities through private rather than government action. Danforth built chapels at a score of state universities and regional colleges across the central states and provided considerable funding for campus ministries. It also cooperated with Connecticut's Hazen Foundation in encouraging faculty to pay attention to religious questions in their teaching and research. In the mid-1960s Danforth invested in a striking self-study evaluation of its campus ministry work, then, disappointed with its achievements, abruptly ended its work in that field.[87] But as Danforth withdrew, the Lilly Endowment increased its support for more academic religious studies. Many other foundations, especially in the South, continued to underwrite religious activity on campus. The Baptist Foundation of Texas maintained its support of Baylor and other Baptist colleges in the state, and the Houston Endowment supported an Institute of Religion at the Texas Medical Center.[88] The most generous among the numerous recent examples include 1995 trusts totaling $110 million from Atlanta's J. Bulow Campbell Foundation for Columbia Theological Seminary and for Berry College in Georgia and trusts adding to $166 million established by the Pitts family for the Emory University School of Theology and Young Harris College in Georgia.[89]

Foundations made other notable postwar efforts to add programs, departments, and schools to colleges and universities, most notably in area studies and the behavioral sciences. Area studies—the interdisciplinary study of the politics, economic conditions, histories, languages, literatures, cultures, and social lives of large regions of the world—dated from the 1930s. It was strongly advanced by the federal government during World War II and the cold war but it also received parallel funding, first from the Rockefeller Foundation and the Carnegie Corporation, then at a much higher level ($100 million over one five-year period) from the Ford Foundation.[90] The vaguely defined behavioral science approach had won substantial Rockefeller Foundation funding, notably for human relations at Yale, in the 1920s and 1930s.[91] In five years between 1951 and 1956 Ford concentrated $40 million on a small number of programs in the field—creating the Center for Advanced Study in the Behavioral Sciences in Palo Alto, substantially underwriting the Institute for Social Research and the Research Center for Group Dynamics at the University of Michigan, the Laboratory of Social Relations at Harvard, and the Bureau of Applied Social Research at Columbia.

Similar foundation initiatives were judged less successful at the time. Writing of other foundation efforts in the social sciences in 1984, a somewhat gloomy Marshall Robinson—a highly respected vice president of the Ford Foundation—asserted, "In other fields, using the same amount of money, they changed nothing."[92] Yet that seems too pessimistic a conclusion. From the 1940s through the 1960s, several foundations, small and large, underwrote important studies of the law, politics, and history of religious toleration, the reduction of religious, ethnic, and racial conflict, and civil rights and civil liberties in the United States. Cumulatively, these studies developed support for arguments, and eventually for court decisions and legislation, respecting the rights to speak, assemble, petition, and organize in support of the causes of labor, of African Americans and other racial minorities, of Jews, Catholics, and dissenters, of women, and of advocates for controversial causes of all kinds. Foundations were not indispensable to these efforts, but they did contribute to them. The Phelps Stokes Fund and the Rosenwald Fund were early contributors, as were the Rockefeller Foundation, the Ford Foundation, and the Ford-created Fund for the Republic. A few small foundations—notably Field, Taconic, and New World, but also less celebrated funds such as the Moses Kimball Fund of Boston—did contribute modest but sometimes strategically timed funds to the civil rights movement. Field also contributed to the work of developmental psychologist Erik Erikson. These funds helped advance larger efforts to create space for social movements and their leaders by promoting the idea that a healthy adult necessarily engaged in independent, autonomous thought.[93] In this way these foundations aimed to stiffen resistance to pressures toward conformity.

The legislative successes of the movements for African American, Mexican American, and women's civil rights had much to do with the addition of related departments of study at American universities in the 1970s and 1980s. Yet the Ford Foundation did play a creative role in launching and underwriting such programs, as historian Noliwe Rooks has recently shown in detail for African American studies.[94] Linda Eisenmann has shown that the women's studies movement followed a different pattern. The Russell Sage Foundation had underwritten important studies of women's work and family lives early in the twentieth century, and the Carnegie Corporation supported continuing education for women after World War II. The creation of library resources and then of the Radcliffe Institute at Harvard through faculty efforts and grants from the Carnegie Corporation, the Rockefeller Brothers Fund, and others in the 1940s and 1950s helped expand opportunities for women; then, during the 1970s and 1980s, the Ford Foundation substantially funded key centers of women's studies. Yet Eisenmann persuasively concluded, "Foundation money tells only part of the story." More critical were "contributions by local women's groups, alumnae, and individual benefactors."[95]

In a movement consistent with the emphasis on the active agency of ordinary people emphasized by African American and women's studies alike, some of the most acute current historians of the social and behavioral sciences are now arguing that social scientists in all fields adapted creatively after World War II "to a system that provided unprecedented levels of funding with any number of apparent strings attached."[96] Researchers did take account of foundation and government priorities, but they also had their own quite independent agendas. Foundations provided small amounts of money, but by diversifying the sources on which researchers could draw they made possible work that they knew nothing about.[97] Yet this field, like others, had grown far beyond the resources held by foundations. In the early 1980s Marshall Robinson estimated that the federal government was spending about $500 million annually on social science research and that university salary and sabbatical support for research by social science faculty amounted in 1983 to $305 million.[98] To these numbers we should add university and federal funding for graduate students in social science fields, because work on Ph.D. dissertations constitutes a very large share of all academic research. Total yearly social science funding from the ten foundations most active in the field at that time came to only about $25 million.

By the 1940s elementary education had become so universal and so subject to locally elected public school boards and locally voted school taxes that it was almost impervious to foundation influence.[99] Historians David Tyack and Larry Cuban have shown that by mid-century a widely accepted "grammar of schooling"—a set of assumptions earlier shaped in important ways by the Peabody, Carnegie, and Russell Sage foundations as well as by the practical exigencies facing school administrators—made it difficult for teachers, parents, voters, or school leaders even to conceive of significant change.[100] But foundations undertook so many ambitious (and conflicting) initiatives in education that the topic deserves exploration in more detail.

Some foundation initiatives, especially in secondary education, achieved considerable success because they aligned well with established standard-setting institutions. The Carnegie-supported Educational Testing Service (ETS) now played a central role. Critics complained that by certifying certain kinds of achievement ETS reinforced inequality,[101] but it also served as a neutral, nongovernmental center for debating what sorts of achievement were important and how to measure them—relieving individual colleges and universities of the responsibility for setting all aspects of their admissions standards. To its already established Scholastic Aptitude Test, it added the Advanced Placement (AP) program in the 1950s (an initiative launched by the Ford Foundation's Fund for the Advancement of Education). Through the AP program of defining courses, supporting teachers, and requiring rigorous national examinations, colleges and schools, professors and teachers worked together to develop college-level courses taught in public as well as private high schools.[102] Once the AP system was established, fees charged to test-takers sustained the entire operation, providing funds to promote the tests to new schools, to update the tests, to bring active teachers into a high-quality test-grading system, and to underwrite research on testing, learning, and fairness.[103] Thirty years later Carnegie funds also provided essential initial underwriting for the National Board for Professional Teaching Standards, designed to encourage and certify professional advancement for classroom teachers—and also intended to become self-sustaining through fees paid by aspiring teachers and their employers.[104]

Hoping to achieve more, the Carnegie Corporation of New York made a "generous grant . . . administered by the Educational Testing Service" to Harvard's former president, James B. Conant, to undertake a series of studies of American education in the 1950s and 1960s. Conant's work, as Diane Ravitch has pointed out, promoted a "skillful blend" of "academic excellence and democratic values."[105] Recognizing that their limited resources could never, by themselves, achieve Conant's ambitious agenda, the Carnegie, Ford, Rockefeller, Sloan, Kettering, and other foundations undertook what they hoped would be strategic interventions in teacher recruitment, education, and career development. But these efforts had limited success. Ford and others invested $70 million or more in the master of arts in teaching (MAT) degree designed to bring graduates of liberal arts colleges into high schools. The MAT failed to gain anything like the acceptance won by the College Board, and the initiative could not overcome state licensing rules, persuade principals to hire well-educated teachers, or persuade college and university liberal arts departments to emphasize the education of teachers.[106]

Foundations also devoted considerable support to high school curricular reform efforts. But state education departments and school districts, under local pressure to continue established practices, uphold traditional values, and restrain expenditures, continued to shape the textbook market. Despite notable funding in the mid-1960s from the National Science Foundation and the new Department of Education, the "new math," "new physics," and "new social studies" efforts achieved only modest success, and that came much more through the Advanced Placement exams than through changes in the standard curriculum.[107] After a very few years in the 1960s, both the federal government and the foundations largely abandoned their efforts to improve the quality of teachers and curricula.

Influential writers, including Francis Keppel and Harold Howe II (who served as U.S. commissioners of education under Kennedy and Johnson), Theodore Sizer, and David Tyack did continue to promote efforts to enhance the professional effectiveness and morale of teachers and the quality of learning materials, despite the shift in the priorities of the big foundations.[108] Local and specialized funds continued to support minor aspects of the effort, such as brief, inexpensive summer "institutes" and workshops and in-school staff collaborations that sometimes brought teachers together with college and university experts. Such activities did not bring transforming change, but they did win continuing support from school districts and from state and federal governments, and they did contribute positively to teacher competency and morale. The Lynde and Harry Bradley Foundation's support for excellence in the study of American history constituted a notable example of such foundation investment in a particular field; several other foundations supported continuing education for teachers in the sciences.[109] In the 1990s Sizer and others had considerable influence on the $500 million Annenberg Foundation Challenge effort to remake many aspects of America's schools. Detractors, however, criticized the Annenberg Challenge as excessively broad and unfocused, inadequately funded in relation to its ambitions, and out of step with conflicting (and often foundation-supported) movements for inclusion, for uniform national standards, for charter schools, and for school vouchers.[110]

More radical prescriptions for school reform won a good deal of journalistic attention in the postwar years; with few exceptions, foundations gave them little support. Responding more to the demands for equality for African Americans than to the radical critics of schooling, Ford and some other foundations did shift focus from the drive for excellence to the effort to promote inclusion and equality.[111] Ford's best-known intervention—strong initial support for the "local control" of such New York City schools as Intermediate School 201 in Harlem and Ocean Hill-Brownsville in Brooklyn—pushed the movement for the decentralization of New York City's public schools in the late 1960s. Opposition from teachers, administrators, and many others who feared that "community control" would mean "a politicized, racist, parochial, and inefficient system" soon minimized and after some time forced an end to decentralization.[112]

Working from a different direction, from the 1990s the Gates, Walton, Thomas B. Fordham, Lynde and Harry Bradley, and other foundations, including several community foundations, put more emphasis on the structure and overall size of the school, on its funding, and on "student outcomes," rather than on the education, ethos, and motivation of the teachers or the quality of the curriculum. In fact, the Annenberg Challenge grants went largely to coalitions outside of formal school governance systems that developed their own local models and measures for success. Annenberg also worked with the Hewlett and other foundations to support local coalitions such as the Bay Area School Reform Collaborative. Through the Small Schools project, the Texas High School project, the Partnership for Regional Education Preparation in Kansas City, and other collaborations with local foundations and school districts, the Gates Foundation specifically targeted low-performing school districts and supported approaches too untried for elected officials. Walton supported "charter schools" that enjoyed some school-level autonomy as well as vouchers that shifted tax money to nonpublic schools; Fordham and other foundations emphasized the voucher movement.

As Elisabeth Clemens and Linda Chyi show, the voucher and small school movements focused as much on public policy as on private standards and practices. Whereas the Peabody, Carnegie, and Rosenwald foundations had "worked with local and state school authorities," Ford, operating after passage of the civil rights and Great Society legislation, "sometimes worked with the Federal government." The Gates Foundation, they add, "likes to work alone and calls small schools its 'national champions,'" while Thomas B. Fordham, Walton, and others cooperated closely with activists in the voucher and charter school movements.[113] A desire to obtain public funding for religious-sponsored schools drove much of the voucher movement, but the foundations in this field emphasized questions of effectiveness rather than faith.[114]

Overall, in elementary and secondary education, postwar foundations generally took philanthropic approaches, though they also often worked to advance particular values ranging from "excellence" to inclusion to faith. They funded curricular innovations, sought to improve the quality and morale of the teaching force, invested in demonstration projects, and supported several kinds of policy innovation. Because foundation resources lagged further and further behind the overall cost of elementary and secondary education, foundations necessarily aimed to persuade others—consumers and school leaders as well as legislatures—to take up their ideas. As they shifted focus from pedagogy to content to inclusion to structure, foundations disappointed the teachers and others they no longer championed. Many who worked in the field believed that campaigns to improve education required persistent commitment as well as money and publicity, if they were to have a chance to succeed. In reality, foundations had less wealth than educators hoped.[115] Because foundations pursued competing agendas, one sometimes limited another. Critics charged that some foundation initiatives were elitist, paternalistic, or impractical or that they insulted parents, teachers, women, or particular communities. Acknowledging that their resources were limited, many foundation leaders concluded that in education, foundations could only call attention to difficult problems, clarify complex issues, and perhaps ease conflict among stakeholders. Others determined to push as hard as they could for their distinctive agendas of policy reform.[116]

Similar assessments can be made of postwar foundation work related to social welfare. As in the past, foundations continued to promote individual and family self-sufficiency and self-reliance, to encourage cooperation among private and public social service organizations, and to reduce need. They reexamined practices relating to the care of the young, those in troubled families, the disabled, and the elderly, often seeking to advance favored values of family, religious, and racial continuity. During the 1940s and 1950s some continued to invest in psychiatric services for children, juvenile courts, and child study, before deciding in later decades to retreat in the face of significant, though inconsistent and varying, federal spending in these fields.[117]

Religious foundations maintained their historic concern for the care, as well as the religious education, of children. Chicago's Chapin Hall, like almost all other orphanages, eventually closed its residential programs; unusually, it shifted to studies of child care designed to enlighten the federal regulation that increasingly shaped children's lives.[118] By the 1980s the Annie E. Casey Foundation, together with the Ford, Mott, Rockefeller, Chapin Hall, and other foundations, had taken up much of the earlier Russell Sage role of seeking consensus and effective national standards in key areas of social care, especially in the care of children, because Medicare, Social Security, and federal disability programs had done much to relieve distress in old age.[119]

Entering the field just as the federal government was rapidly expanding its role in health, education, and welfare, Ford Foundation leaders sought to capitalize on what they took to be one of their chief differences from the Rockefeller, Commonwealth, Carnegie, and Russell Sage funds—their lack of "connections to old charitable philanthropy." Free of such ties, they joined federal "change agents" to create new relationships with populations that had suffered discrimination and exclusion.[120]

In 1963 Paul Ylvisaker, one of Ford's leading program officers at the time, described the foundation's approach as inspired by "a social application of the art of jujitsu: of exerting smaller forces at points of maximum leverage to capture larger forces otherwise working against us."[121] Some of Ford's first efforts in these directions became among the most controversial foundation initiatives of the postwar decades. Ford grants helped several leaders of Mobilization for Youth focus angry pressure on New York's City Hall—which had helped create their organization. Ford grants to New York City's Ocean-Hill-Brownsville and Intermediate School 201 school decentralization experiments empowered advocates of "community control" who threatened the autonomy of teachers and principals and challenged the authority of the central board of education. Other grants supported voter registration drives in New York and Cleveland,

and the "Gray Areas" initiative in general. A considerable shelf of books debates these initiatives.

Emphasis on controversial grants such as these has led many observers to ignore larger Ford Foundation initiatives that were more consistent with the long foundation tradition of supporting job training, savings plans, and other efforts to promote self-sufficiency. Particularly notable in this way has been Ford's substantial contribution to the Local Initiatives Support Corporation.[122]

More generally still, in social welfare as in elementary and secondary education, foundations struggled in the postwar years to find an appropriate role for themselves. Federal programs operated at levels far above anything foundations could consider; foundations disagreed among themselves. Some withdrew from the field they had occupied; some tried new approaches that proved ineffective—or deeply controversial; many smaller funds quietly continued their established commitment to religious or community traditions.

Responding to the complaints that led to the Tax Reform Act of 1969, foundation leaders emphasized innovation and positive action. Postwar foundations did innovate. But most often they acted in familiar ways and within already-established systems. They strengthened and added features to existing institutions. They continued to sustain religious communities—increasingly Jewish and Catholic as well as Protestant. They worked to replicate the research university, the academic medical center, and the large arts complex in most large metropolitan regions across the nation. Working generally in long-established ways, they sought to encourage individual achievement.

International Initiatives

Difficulties multiply when one attempts to assess foundation contributions in the international arena. International purposes are necessarily vast, complex, and remote. Relatively few foundations provide the great bulk of the funds for international giving. Outcomes are determined by local political and cultural factors that outsiders struggle to comprehend and have little ability to control.[123] In the wake of the Second World War, many international efforts long supported by foundations seemed to have failed entirely. Millions of foundation dollars had not enabled the League of Nations and related institutions to maintain peace. Foundation-supported networks of church missions, schools, colleges, clinics, and hospitals in Asia, the Near East, and Africa had fallen to war and invasion.

Yet foundation efforts had also succeeded in many ways, survived the war, and emerged stronger than ever. This was perhaps especially true of foundation support for specialized international organizations (ranging from the International Court at the Hague to cooperative efforts in health and labor) and for advanced education in international affairs. Foundation-funded organizations and experts proved invaluable to the United Nations and related organizations, to international scientific and commercial exchange, and to channels for continuing flows of students. Those channels did much to advance the postwar commitment of the United States (and Great Britain) to engage the rising generation of Europeans in the project to create a strong, peaceful Europe tied firmly to the "Atlantic community." Supplementing the much greater efforts of the U.S. Army, of many British institutions, and of international commerce, foundations religious as well as secular supported educational and exchange initiatives. And foundation funding contributed to the increased international use of English and to international scientific and religious exchanges that are still vital and active.

Although foundations are commonly described as remarkably independent, in the field of international philanthropy they have necessarily subordinated their work to national policy. As Steven Heydemann notes, "The state is always present, and it bears heavily both on what foundations are able to do internationally and how they conduct themselves." Historically, foundation activities were not only "scrutinized and regulated" by the U.S. government, but sometimes controlled, co-opted and sanctioned. At times, Heydemann shows, foundations have been "vulnerable" to state influence. While some foundations followed agendas independent of U.S. foreign policies, most "exhibit self-censorship," avoiding risk rather than serving as risk-absorbers. Yet even during the height of the cold war, government did not entirely crowd foundations out of the international field.[124]

Postwar foundation leaders recognized that the United States was spending far more than ever on military activity, on the stabilization of the international financial system, on postwar reconstruction, on refugees, on disaster and famine assistance, and on international organizations and that other nations also contributed to these ends. Seeking to make the best use of their very limited funds, most large foundations turned away from international organizations and from most religious missions and toward support for "development."[125] They emphasized economic development, but also the building of administrative capabilities in nations that had emerged from colonialism. And they increased their emphasis on human rights, conflict resolution, and the international education of Americans.[126]

Most celebrated, and most similar to its own earlier efforts in medicine, public health, and the social sciences, were the Rockefeller Foundation's investments, dating from 1943, in research and technical training for agricultural productivity. In the 1950s and 1960s the Ford Foundation and several national governments in Latin America, Asia, and Africa increased resources, using new strains of rice, wheat, and corn, to forge a "green revolution" of increased agricultural productivity. This effort won much praise, including award of the 1970 Nobel Peace Prize to Rockefeller-supported plant scientist Norman Borlaug.[127]

The Ford Foundation's "Gaither Report" proposed objectives so much more ambitious that no one has yet attempted to assess its overall success in reaching them.[128] The foundation began with a grand political affirmation that reflected themes made prominent by the cold war: "Man must choose between two opposed courses. One is democratic, dedicated to the freedom and dignity of the individual. The other is authoritarian, where freedom and justice do not exist, and human rights and truth are subordinated wholly to the state." The Ford Foundation proposed to "assist in the analysis of fundamental issues or policies" relating to "world peace," to "freedom and democracy," and to "the economic well-being of people everywhere"; to improving "the organizations and administrative procedures by which government affairs are conducted"; and to strengthening "the adjudication of private rights and the interpretation and enforcement of law." As historian Merle Curti wrote, in the 1950s the Ford Foundation "went beyond anything hitherto done in supporting social and economic research, in cooperating with governments in developing and implementing over-all economic and social planning." He added, "The programs in Asia, the Near East, and Africa designed to increase the effectiveness of government operations were rightly deemed crucial."[129] Acknowledging that it is governments that take general responsibility for law and order, for the implementation of policy, and in general for peace and prosperity, the Ford Foundation proposed to intervene only "where such private aid is proper and officially welcomed."[130]

The Ford Foundation needed official welcome from the U.S. State Department and other nations in order to implement its agenda. During the 1950s and 1960s the Ford Foundation invested nearly $125 million in new universities in Latin America, Asia, the Middle East, and Africa and an additional $61 million in the 1970s and 1980s.[131] It devoted millions more to national scientific and medical research laboratories in Asia and Latin America, to the Free University of Berlin, and to entities such as the Indian Institute of Public Administration in New Delhi and the Institute for Comparative Economic Studies in Vienna. The governments of the host nations had vital interests in these institutions. The Ford and Rockefeller foundations necessarily thought carefully about their relations with the U.S. federal government and with the governments in which the new institutions were located.[132] And they devoted resources to staff and facilities that would win credibility with those governments.

No discussion of the international activities of U.S. foundations in the 1950s and 1960s would be complete if it omitted the uses made of the foundation form by the federal government itself, through the U.S. Central Intelligence Agency (CIA). The CIA set up at least two substantial foundations in the 1950s, the Asia Foundation (later reestablished on a forthright and independent basis) and the Farfield Foundation, and channeled money through several others. These funds were used largely to support cultural and literary activities, often on the "noncommunist left." One recent reviewer notes that in the 1950s the making of grants to many of their beneficiaries "would have . . . ruined other foundations by association."[133] The most debated activities involved underwriting the expenses of the Congress for Cultural Freedom and *Encounter* and other magazines and also sponsoring tours by American orchestras, abstract expressionist artists, editors, and writers, who were then asked for information about the views and actions of people they had met. Federal money also underwrote the expenses of cultural centers, conferences, and the travel of writers, scholars, and public figures in several European, African, and Asian nations as well as of many Americans. The money was explicitly intended both to enhance America's international reputation for excellence in the arts and for openness to a wide range of political views and to support those who revealed the repressions enforced by the Soviet Union.

These initiatives did not meet the definition of foundation activity used in this book, because they were directed by government rather than by autonomous donors. But they did make use of the foundation form. And although in many cases those who received the money pursued their own purposes, refusing to follow a predetermined ideological line, they may have advanced U.S. objectives in the early years of the cold war. They also damaged the international reputation of American foundations and other institutions. Yet when much of the story became public in the late 1960s, all American foundations found themselves denounced as mere "fronts" for the CIA.[134]

Critical accounts of CIA uses of "foundations" often fail to note Americans' long-standing practice of using foundations, as well as other fundraising and fund-distribution practices, to safeguard and dispense funds for the support of overseas causes. Postwar conditions created many needs and opportunities. We noted above the responses of the Henry Luce Foundation and the China Medical Board to the defeat of the nationalist government in China. Private American donors also rallied, through the Christian Children's Fund and similar agencies, to the support of orphans in Europe and Asia; to Catholic causes in postwar and post–Iron Curtain Europe; to Robert College in Istanbul, the American University of Beirut, the American University in Cairo, and similar institutions; and to the challenges and opportunities created by the establishment of the state of Israel. Most of these efforts long predated the cold war.[135]

Historian David Oshinsky commented that leaders of the Congress for Cultural Freedom "had been fighting totalitarianism for most of their lives" and that the congress would have acted the same way "had it been bankrolled by a private foundation."[136] Since the congress was not funded privately, we cannot know for certain. Edward Shils, himself a participant in the congress, later wrote of his own confidence in "the ramshackle obduracy of such countries as Great Britain, France, the Netherlands, and the United States, in their tenacious devotion to liberal democratic institutions."[137]

Several foundations did contribute significantly to broader efforts to build, both in the United States and in other countries, medical, educational, and cultural institutions that explicitly sought to promote good causes and to impress peoples and leaders abroad.[138] When Rockefeller and other philanthropies restored the temples at Delphi, supported American schools of classical studies in Athens and Rome, or built centers for scholarly study and international exchange at Bellagio on Italy's Lake Como, they were both advancing the cause of learning and demonstrating America's cultural sophistication to international audiences.

As national governments took on the support of universities and research centers after the 1960s, the biggest foundations increasingly moved to strengthen new organizations, to engage people from "neglected groups," and to enhance "national capabilities of developing countries in educational planning, administration, governance, and research." But these were also the kinds "of assistance that governments find it hard to accept from other governments."[139] To do this work well, the foundations continued to emphasize credibility, diplomacy, and discretion.

In addition to direct assistance, the Ford, Rockefeller, and other foundations (notably Kellogg, Carnegie, Lilly, and Clark) also funded much research on economic and political development.[140] In this area especially, government played by far the most active role, in action as well as analysis. This research has been exceptionally complex and interesting; it has had to do with alleged differences between markets and central planning, between "capitalism" and "socialism," between "west" and "east." In practice, both government and private donors must work through multiple agents who have their own purposes and engage widely diverse governments, business firms, NGOs, and individuals across borders—each, again, with distinctive, often multiple, intentions.[141] Especially in the 1970s and later, Ford, MacArthur, and other foundations also supported efforts to expand civil liberties, efforts that were perhaps especially important in South Africa under the apartheid regime and in Latin America during the period of the dictatorships.[142] The several funds and institutions launched by George Soros in the 1980s and 1990s undertook related efforts in Central and Eastern Europe, in addition to funding the new Central European University.

Like all development-assistance efforts, whether mounted by national governments, by intergovernmental organizations, by business firms, by religious communities, or by foundations themselves, this funding has attracted critics as well as enthusiasts. Effectiveness in promoting open societies and civil liberties required credibility and political seriousness.[143] As Heydemann has put it, "A close, complex, and often unsettled association" arose "between the U.S. state and foundations." Foundations "struggle to carve out and consolidate domains of autonomy and influence," but they necessarily remained generally "subordinate to and reactive toward the evolving configuration of state institutions, roles, and authorities."[144]

With the end of the cold war, many opportunities opened up, and foundations supported social innovations of many kinds in the transition economies of Eastern Europe and Asia by helping to build civil society institutions. Since the 1990s many U.S. foundations have encouraged nongovernmental and technical assistance organizations in Eastern Europe, Central Asia, South Asia, Africa, and Latin America. Foundation Center data indicate that foundation grantmaking has moved in these directions. Lehn Benjamin and Kevin Quigley show that although foundations still direct a majority of international grants through U.S.-based nonprofit organizations, grants made directly to overseas recipients almost tripled between 1990 and 2002. Among the international intermediaries that received notably increased funding were community foundations, the Environmental Partnership for Central Europe (supported by a collaboration between the German Marshall Fund and the Mott, Pew, and Rockefeller foundations), and the Ford Foundation's Trust Africa, which seeks to strengthen a network of NGOs concerned with governance and accountability.

Overall, it is just as difficult to define which efforts of American foundations are international as to define which American activities are international. When American foundations invest in "orphan" drugs to treat conditions that afflict small numbers of people, the successful drugs that result can be used abroad—just as the developers of those drugs may be tempted to try them out on populations outside the United States. American foundations played key roles in creating *Sesame Street* for the United States; later it inspired similar preliteracy television programming in many other parts of the world. *Sesame Street* clearly constitutes an important aspect of the United States' engagement with other parts of the world, but studies of the international impact of American foundations usually ignore it. It should be added to the account.[145]

Public Policy

As this chapter's previous sections have made clear, postwar U.S. foundations took many actions to support public policy adopted by the federal government and the states. They worked to advance national foreign policy goals, often by taking on tasks of advising, convening, and institution building that the government itself could not effectively perform. At critical points foundations provided important capital for the completion of the nation's system of research universities—a system increasingly shaped by federal and state policy and funding. Foundations contributed to major medical centers and sometimes took the lead in addressing neglected health concerns, as in the cases of cancer and AIDS. Foundations sought repeatedly, even if in competing and disappointing ways, to improve the quality, effectiveness, and accessibility of elementary and especially secondary education. Accepting the separation of church and state, foundations continued to underwrite religious education, religious reflection and observance, religious outreach, and religious careers. Recognizing the difficulty of winning substantial taxpayer support for the arts and for public broadcasting, foundations increasingly played important roles in building arts centers and in underwriting the creation and distribution of content.

As political scientist and former senior Rockefeller Foundation official Kenneth Prewitt has argued, foundations generally "accommodate prevailing . . . practice."[146] Or as Ford Foundation President McGeorge Bundy put it in 1974, in many cases "the foundation and the government [often] engaged jointly in funding an activity that is of accepted importance to both."[147] By supporting existing public policy, foundations advanced their own purposes while earning public support—except from those who objected to particular policies.

Yet postwar foundations also pursued improvement and change in public policy. The Tax Reform Act of 1969 did impose some restrictions on foundation activity related to involvement in election campaigns, lobbying for specific pieces of legislation, and the use of grant funds by recipient organizations.[148] The restrictions on both "direct lobbying" of legislators and "grassroots lobbying" intended to sway public opinion on pending legislation have created real concern for both foundations and their nonprofit grantees. But the act, the regulations created to enforce it, and subsequent legislation actually allowed foundations to address public policy in many ways. If immediate legislation is not at stake, foundations can discuss regulation, administration, enforcement, executive orders, and litigation; they can raise broad issues of social policy and priority for public consideration; they can publish nonpartisan analysis and research; they can give technical advice to legislative and executive officials who ask for it; and they can advocate in defense of their own interests.[149] Several foundations took advantage of these opportunities.

Foundations moved into new policy areas after the 1940s. Sometimes this involved seeking new approaches to long-standing problems. Sometimes, as the Ford Foundation's McGeorge Bundy emphasized, it involved efforts to strengthen "the American democratic process itself." For the Ford Foundation, it often meant supporting the cause of "equal opportunity" for women, African Americans, and other minorities.[150] By 1980 Congress, the Internal Revenue Service, and the courts were all holding that it was "charitable" for nonprofit organizations to defend "human and civil rights" as defined in constitutional or statutory law or to protect and restore environmental quality through litigation that served "a public rather than a private interest"—and that it was appropriate for foundations to fund such activity.[151] Increasingly, however, foundations also looked for ways to support public officials as they searched for their own policy solutions.

The environment posed the most important new policy field taken up by postwar American foundations. Just as they had created museums for the preservation of beautiful works of art, foundations (notably those created by the Rockefeller family) had long emphasized the preservation of beautiful land-scapes.[152] In the 1950s Rockefeller, Ford, and other funds launched Resources for the Future and the Population Council, both of which paid great attention to environmental questions. By the 1970s foundations were pursuing a wide range of new environmental initiatives. Some of these emphasized the popularization of better or best private practices—as, for example, in the case of the W. K. Kellogg Foundation's systematic campaign to engage farmers and others in collaborative action to improve the ecological welfare of entire watersheds.[153] Others focused on the impact of population growth and industry on the environment, promoted awareness of environmental threats, underwrote movements to save land from development by creating parks, reservations, and easements (approaches emphasized by the Richard King Mellon Foundation), or worked to reduce land, air, and water pollution.[154] These efforts called for changes in the behavior of industries, farmers, and consumers, but they also called for extensive changes in public policy. And each of them provoked questions about which interests were truly being served.

Foundations took up other new policy areas as well. Several foundations invested in studies of nuclear arms and disarmament.[155] In response to the Great Society's remarkable expansion of federal activity in the fields of health, education, and social welfare, the Kellogg, Mott, Atlantic, Rockefeller Brothers, Ford, Packard, and other funds invested substantially in the study of philanthropy and voluntarism—and in the study of policy initiatives that would encourage the "nonprofit sector."[156] In response to the end of the cold war, the Ford, MacArthur, Mott, Kellogg, Open Society, and other funds put quite large resources into the encouragement of American and international policies that would support civil society in many parts of Central and Eastern Europe and East Asia.[157]

Regarding domestic policy, it has become a sort of conventional wisdom that foundations moved into "liberal" policy work in the 1960s, then from the 1970s shifted toward "conservative" ideas.[158] The truth is much more complex, and what strikes us is the increasing variety of foundation engagement with public policy in these decades. As we've noted, over the previous 100 years some foundations had supported causes that might be described as "liberal"—public education, public libraries, public health, international peace, various reforms in housing, workplace safety, and consumer relations. Yet the ways in which foundations usually supported such causes, seeking to stimulate individual effort, family responsibility, and religious continuity, could equally be characterized as "conservative," as cautious and designed to reinforce existing social arrangements. America's religious communities had always debated questions of public policy; religious leaders had from time to time specialized in the analysis of public questions. From the 1870s Americans mostly educated in religious schools organized serious discussions of ways and means to reduce poverty and crime, to improve public health and reduce disease, to care for the sick and the mentally disabled, and to rehabilitate delinquents, criminals, and alcoholics.

As we've seen, from the beginning of the century a few foundations had helped invent policy think tanks and had undertaken policy analytic work themselves.[159] More frequently, foundations had supported the consideration of public policy within religious communities, most notably those of the nation's Protestant denominations—whose mutual disagreements, it is too often forgotten, can put them into conflict with one another. Postwar foundations continued to do all this, through new action agencies as well as think tanks.

In the 1960s particular attention went to "action" initiatives. During this period the Ford Foundation's Gray Areas program, designed to bring poor people directly into efforts to reduce poverty, had a direct influence on some of the most controversial aspects of the War on Poverty waged by the Kennedy and Johnson administrations. Seeing economic development, social inclusion, and political participation as inextricably interlinked and as equally essential to the reduction of poverty and the overcoming of racism and paternalism, Ford's approach encouraged extraordinarily ambitious policy initiatives. However, government never provided War on Poverty initiatives with anything close to sufficient funds and never adequately clarified the initiatives' details.[160] Civil rights leaders and advocates for the poor objected that in practice most of these foundation efforts, certainly as implemented, worked chiefly to channel protest and co-opt protest leaders. Data presented by Alice O'Connor, Debra Minkoff, and Jon Agnone show that these complaints are difficult to deny.[161] Defenders of vested interests, meanwhile, complained of unfair treatment.

Very few foundations supported programs anything like Ford's Gray Areas. The small Taconic and the temporary Cleveland Associated Foundation both supported voter registration, community-organizing drives, and other activities of the civil rights movement. But that movement depended almost entirely on self-help and contributions from individuals, chiefly individuals in the African American community. Not all aspects of the War on Poverty failed; as historian Maris Vinovskis has recently shown, the Ford Foundation's Great City Schools and Gray Areas projects were important sources for the long-running federal Head Start program.[162] "Progressive" policy work continued, not least through such strongly foundation-backed organizations as the Institute for Policy Studies (1963), the Joint Center for Political and Budget Priorities (1970), the Southern Poverty Law Center (1971), the Center on Budget and Policy Priorities (1982), and the Progressive Policy Institute (1989).[163] Yet it is clear that while a few foundations supported some of the ideas that animated aspects of the War on Poverty, political forces did much more to shape it.[164]

Overall, foundations did continue to broaden their engagement with public policy. Ford and other foundations provided substantial funding to new organizations designed to give voice to the formerly excluded and, as McGeorge Bundy put it, to support "groups working to make sure that the law itself stands on the side of equal opportunity."[165] The small American Fund for Public Service, the Field Foundation, and a very few other small foundations had earlier supported the NAACP and its Legal Defense Fund (LDF). But from the late 1960s Ford led a new departure—*after* passage of the key civil rights legislation and *after* federal and state courts had greatly expanded the effective civil rights of minorities of all kinds. At that point Ford and other large foundations came in with additional funds for the NAACP-LDF and also for the Mexican-American Legal Defense and Education Fund, the Native American Rights Fund, the Puerto Rican Legal Defense and Education Fund, the National Committee Against Discrimination in Housing, and the Lawyers Committee for Civil Rights Under Law. Most foundations had withheld funds from efforts to study women's education in the 1950s, but by the late 1960s Ford and others were underwriting legal work for women's rights and supporting other women's causes, including the Berkshire Conference on Women's History.[166]

More generally, the Internal Revenue Service recognized the charitable status of "human and civil rights organizations" in very general terms; a 1984 summary statement, citing a 1973 ruling, put it this way: "Organizations, whose purpose is to provide representation to others (or to institute litigation as a party plaintiff) in cases involving the defense of human and civil rights, may be considered charitable organizations for purposes of IRC 501(c)(3). An example of this type of organization . . . provides funds to defend members of a religious sect in legal actions involving substantial constitutional issues of state abridgement of religious freedom."[167]

"The defense of human and civil rights"—to quote the legal language—can be defined in many ways. One foundation or another has underwritten work in the service of many of the possible definitions. In the context of the expansion of legal protections for civil rights and civil liberties during the 1960s and 1970s, the Tax Reform Act of 1969—followed by the active and often foundation-led response—eventuated in a clarification and codification of the rules applying to advocacy and almost certainly in an increase in the numbers of advocacy organizations.[168]

Foundations also invested in organizations that sought the economic development of disadvantaged communities. Such work was not new; antecedents can be traced to Benjamin Franklin's Philadelphia and Boston funds of the 1790s, to the Smith Charities of nineteenth-century Massachusetts, and to the subsidized housing programs of limited-dividend 5 percent philanthropy. From the 1970s Ford and a growing number of other foundations did much to sustain community development corporations, subsidizing their overhead, promoting their income-earning loan and investment activities, and underwriting policy work designed to help them become eligible for government funds. Ford also created the Local Initiatives Support Corporation (LISC) and similar intermediaries. Launched in 1979, LISC had by 1992 raised nearly $900 million from 1,100 business firms and foundations to support community development activities from offices in thirty-eight cities. By 2006 LISC was raising $1 billion each year.[169] In the 1970s the Ford Foundation launched the Police Foundation, which pioneered effective approaches to community policing, and invested in the Vera Institute for Justice, which studies ways to improve the fairness and efficiency of the courts and the criminal justice system.

Like the movement for equal rights, the "public choice" and "law and economics" movements did not owe their origins or their successful development to American foundations. Their inspiration can be found in Adam Smith, in the Austrian school of economics, and in critics of fascism, state communism, and imperialism. But several foundations provided important support to the conservative policy movements. The William Volker Fund, probably one of the nation's fifty largest foundations in 1946, was one of the first in the field. During the 1940s it provided substantial funds to the Foundation for Economic Education (which, like H. L. Hunt's Facts Forum Foundation, was a charitable organization devoted to conservative education, not a foundation in the legal sense). A few years later the Volker Fund's last several million dollars went to the Hoover Institution at Stanford.[170] From the early 1960s the John M. Olin Foundation, the J. Howard Pew Freedom Trust, the Sarah Mellon Scaife Foundation, and the Koch, Smith Richardson, Lynde and Harry Bradley, and Walton Family foundations did much to create an effective movement for conservative policy advocacy.[171] Among the key institutions they supported were such new think tanks as the Hudson Institute (1961), the Institute for Contemporary Studies (1972), the Heritage Foundation (also a charity rather than a foundation, 1973), the Cato Institute (1977), the Manhattan Institute for Policy Research (1978), and the Thomas B. Fordham Institute (1997) and its school-standards-and-choice predecessors. Together these organizations provided an increasingly influential conservative response to the government programs of the Great Society and to the environmental and national economy management initiatives of the Nixon administration.

Altogether, as Alice O'Connor argues, conservative foundations built "a different kind of rights-based, social movement philanthropy that has proved far more radically alternative than any challenge from the left." The alternative infrastructure they built embraced "conservative thought, jurisprudence, private interest law, legal defense funds, policy advocacy, and public policy think tanks."[172] Perhaps paradoxically, when the element of "choice" was combined with government funding—as with Medicare, college student grants and loans, food stamps, housing subsidies, and school voucher programs—this movement seems to have had the effect of greatly increasing public support for Great Society initiatives and of making it that much more difficult to cut government spending.[173] As in the case of the Ford Foundation's Gray Areas initiative, the "conservative" or "pro-market" approaches championed by foundations sometimes had unintended effects.

The contest between "liberal" and "conservative" initiatives by no means exhausts the field. As international and domestic pressures led the federal government to take on more and more responsibilities, Americans organized ever more think tanks and other instrumentalities to assist, support, monitor, critique, and influence federal action. While arguably the Russell Sage Foundation, Milbank Memorial, Carnegie Endowment for International Peace, and other early twentieth-century foundations had created the secular think tank, it was the work of government, associations, and business corporations that caused them to proliferate. Yet many of the new organizations qualified for tax exemption and tax-advantaged gifts. Foundation grants sometimes provided critical aid. The Committee for Economic Development, launched in 1942 to advance what might be described as corporate Keynesianism, received perhaps $2 million from the Ford Foundation in the 1950s. The RAND Corporation, initially established to undertake technical and operational research for the U.S. Air Force, relied on Ford Foundation grants and loan guarantees to transform itself into a freestanding think tank in 1948.[174] In the 1950s the Carnegie Corporation enabled the Foundation Center to continue and expand the data-gathering efforts of the Russell Sage Foundation's library, which had closed. Other new think tanks depended heavily on federal, state, and local government funding: the Urban Institute and Mathematica Policy Research, Inc. (both 1968), Manpower Demonstration Research Corporation (1974), Child Trends, Inc. (1979), and many others. Designed to carry out specific applied research for demanding clients, the new policy research institutes competed successfully with university social science research operations for foundation funding.

Meanwhile foundations expanded the precedents of the 1920s in working directly with government agencies and even with state legislatures to define and gather information relevant to particular policy goals.[175] Russell Sage (operating both as a funder and as a think tank with funds from other foundations) did much to support a movement led by government administrators in the 1960s and 1970s to create an annual report of "social indicators" comparable to the economic indicators studied by the federal Council of Economic Advisers.[176] This episode demonstrates the difficulty of evaluating foundation impact, for while Congress refused to create a Council of Social Advisers, efforts by government and private groups to measure aspects of the quality of life, health, the environment, learning, and aging proliferated. In the 1960s the Carnegie Corporation of New York did much to launch the rigorous and influential National Assessment of Educational Progress, which did win continuing federal funding. Through its Kids Count and other activities, the Annie E. Casey Foundation sought to do the same for children's welfare. Resources for the Future and the Population Council play the same role in their fields. In the same spirit, foundations made possible the creation of the substantial data collection and categorization scheme for the nonprofit field currently maintained by the National Center for Charitable Statistics, as well as the more narrowly focused work of the Foundation Center and the GuideStar website.

Because data are never truly neutral and because every policy engages complex fields of action, foundations have also found increasing opportunities to help government officials make sense of the available information and evaluate the likely impact of alternative policies. Daniel Fox has reported the success of the Milbank Memorial Fund in helping state legislators secure reliable, expert information relevant to health policy. In the early 1990s the Robert Wood Johnson Foundation risked censure from public officials and the media in order to promote national discussion and more informed debate of the Clinton health plan. The Kaiser Family Foundation joined the effort by creating and making available key data relating to health. With regard to the health field, Fox concludes that foundations "influenced the resolution of significant health problems in health affairs when their goals were congruent with the goals of key decisionmakers and when these decisionmakers judged foundation staff to be trustworthy and their cash to be helpful. Foundations have sometimes helped to make history, but they have rarely made it themselves."[177] Jennifer Mosley and Joe Galaskiewicz add that the Annie E. Casey, Charles Stewart Mott, Ford, Rockefeller Brothers, and other foundations have similarly come to fund research on economic development, persistent poverty, the unequal opportunities open to women and people of color, and the changing makeup and functions of the American family.[178] In many cases, foundations have supported policy research directed to legislators and other decisionmakers. In other cases, they have funded documentaries intended to expand public understanding of complex policy issues—and, inevitably, to emphasize one approach or another.

Multiple Roles in Complex Systems

Altogether, foundations moved in many directions, often competing directions, to define their postwar roles. In marginal but well-publicized cases, self-regarding individuals and government officials used a foundation in an unfortunate way, and public opinion and federal legislation strongly denounced these aberrations and imposed some limits on foundations. But the changing context imposed greater limits. Government expanded to a scale unimaginable in the 1920s, the American population became more and more prosperous through the 1970s, and foundation-launched universities, hospitals, the medical profession, and public schools grew far beyond foundation control. Foundations responded to their increasingly complex environments in many ways.

Most commonly, foundations continued their usual work, relying on resources that were growing at a slower rate than the fields in which they wished to engage to improve the quality of regional or local institutions. Foundations continued to support the religious causes that had dominated their activity in the nineteenth century. New donors now used foundations to provide Jewish, Catholic, and evangelical Protestant activities with some of the kinds of support previously concentrated on "mainstream" Protestants. Some of the larger foundations continued to promote community foundations, community chests, and other funds designed to bolster the resources and prestige of private charity.[179] Foundations generally reinforced accepted government policy—but American state and local governments were seldom unified. In a few instances, foundations introduced—or more often studied—new policy departures.

Postwar foundations certainly played philanthropic roles, underwrote institutions, and sought to encourage excellence in innovative ways—yet their uses of scholarships, fellowships, think tanks, and other devices were quite traditional. Because government was growing in so many fields, foundations usually complemented government. Because government funds and private fees overwhelmed foundation capacities, it made less sense than ever to think of foundations, even the Ford Foundation in the 1950s, as substituting for government. Because foundation assets were so limited, they simply could not constitute a significant direct redistribution of wealth.

Foundations had many reasons to seek new definitions of their roles after the 1980s. The myth continues to be repeated that foundations can do great things, that they can substitute for government, and that they can create self-sustaining organizations that can solve major social problems, but the reality is quite different. Contrary to the widespread misconception, foundations—indeed charities of all kinds—have never come close to providing anything like an adequate response to immediate material need. Foundations have never had the resources to play central roles in economic development—and certainly not in the postwar era. Foundations have provided a small portion of the funds needed to sustain key groups of clergy, teachers, and providers of social care; on occasion they have provided very useful support to students and artists. Through such means, they have played definite parts in the creation of the structures that sustain America's Protestant denominations and its colleges and universities. At an exceptional and critical juncture at the turn of the twentieth century, a distinctive group of foundations was able to step in with remarkable effect in building a national system of tax-supported public libraries. They were instrumental in the reorganizing of secondary education, the creation of the research university, and the founding of the modern academic medical center. That juncture lasted just a few decades and is now long past. In the postwar decades, foundations tried many new departures. By the end of the twentieth century they may have come to terms with their new realities.

5

Variety and Relevance: American Foundations at the Start of the Twenty-First Century

Realities—legal, economic, political, institutional—define what foundations can do. This has always been true in the past, and it is true today. American foundations have repeatedly reinvented themselves. But as argued in this book, foundations have been shaped not only by their own visions and choices, but also by their times, by law and regulation, and by the institutions and actualities of American society at large.

In the early twentieth century, the actions of a few foundations accelerated the development of science, medicine, and education in the United States. For many, the legacy of that great achievement sets the standard for today's most ambitious foundations. Yet conditions have changed and, in order to be effective, foundations and policymakers concerned about foundations must take current realities into account. At present American foundations resemble their nineteenth-century predecessors: they are diverse, capable of interesting work, deeply committed to self-help and individual achievement, and strong proponents for a growing range of cultural and religious initiatives. They seek to stimulate professional work, encourage excellence, foster recognition of new needs, and sometimes empower people who have been shunted to the margins. They find creative ways to control, protect, and enhance financial and other resources devoted to a wide range of charitable purposes. All but a tiny number of the very largest lack the resources to undertake anything like transformative change.

Today, foundations can encourage people and organizations to help themselves; enable selected individuals to engage in research, writing, art, or religious work; underwrite limited initiatives; join with others to align their home regions with national and international standards; and call attention to specific problems.

Many more foundations than usually recognized have redoubled their emphasis on religion, the arts, valued traditions and beliefs, the search for useful knowledge, and social justice in a particular sphere. Increasing numbers work hard to provide reliable, useful information about current issues. Working with many others, foundations can encourage the self-organization of society, inviting a plurality of actors to care about and contribute to the common good. On their own, foundations cannot begin to meet social needs, create social or cultural unity, or bring harmony out of conflict. But they can underwrite the work of small groups of participants in national debates.

More numerous and more varied than ever, American foundations respond in individual and idiosyncratic ways to the challenges, opportunities, and constraints posed by today's realities. Foundation wealth has grown, yet the wealth of government, nonprofit organizations, private individuals and families, business, and finance has grown faster. Newly influential religious and cultural movements reject nonsectarian foundations and the sciences they support. Secular ideas, popular culture, and persistent mainstream religions confront new funds devoted to revived notions of cultural purity. Some foundations seek to eliminate poverty around the world; some hope to usher in their view of a heavenly future. Yet for all their variety and their disagreements, foundations increasingly recognize their differences and limitations.

Recognizing their limits, many foundations now focus on impact and influence, as well as on visions and goals. In sometimes innovative but more often traditional ways, foundations seek leverage within current systems. Existing funds look for ways to do more with less; new donors try out "hybrid" forms that emphasize investment as well as donation and that push against long-established legal boundaries. Encouraged by stricter regulation, many foundations have come to see transparency as a means to greater influence. Strategic initiatives and philanthropic ventures attract attention, though they are less common and more difficult to distinguish from traditional foundation work than the publicity that surrounds them might suggest. Foundations have always engaged with public affairs; increasing numbers seem to be adopting explicit approaches in this direction. Foundations have always encouraged social innovation; that, too, seems to be attracting more frank discussion.

America's 75,000 or more active foundations defy precise evaluation. Drawing on our own extensive research, on the explorations of basic data from the Foundation Center, and on the increasingly extensive array of studies by other serious students of American foundations, we conclude with an analysis of these current initiatives among foundations, the roles foundations currently play, and the contributions they are making to American society. Foundations and their regulators alike should, in our view, be careful to look below the surface of popular portraits and accounts of their achievements, keep in mind the intrinsic value of large numbers and diverse purposes of foundations, and take thoughtful account of current realities.

Challenges

The growth of foundations over the last few decades reflects several aspects of American history: opportunity to amass great fortunes; the persistence of many religious, social, and national traditions and distinctive secular perspectives; the rise of the West and the South; continuing commitment to communities defined by locality and culture; and the American struggle to balance commerce with lasting values and with expanded rights to individual autonomy and freedom of expression.

The largest foundations continue to hold the greatest share of all foundation wealth and to receive the most attention. But much has changed. At the end of World War II thirty-three of the fifty largest foundations were based on the East Coast, mainly in New York, while a dozen more clustered in the big cities around the Great Lakes and the upper Mississippi. Only two of the top fifty were then located in the West—Irvine (not yet very active) in California and Bishop (which supports a school) in Hawaii. Three foundations were in the South: Duke in the Carolinas, and Moody (like Irvine, not yet very active) and M. D. Anderson in Texas. Industrial leaders (Rockefeller, Carnegie, Mellon, Ford, Sloan, Mott, Guggenheim, Hill, Kettering, Olin, duPont, Sage, and Penrose) and mass marketers (Kellogg, Duke, Kresge, Luce, and Field) had been prominent among foundation donors. Health care had already produced three of the top fifty (the Lilly Endowment, the Wisconsin Alumni Fund, and the Mayo Clinic). Three of the largest foundations devoted themselves exclusively to religious purposes: Presbyterian and Congregationalist funds that dated from before the Civil War, and the Catholic De Rance fund. Among others in the "top fifty," Lilly, Duke, Danforth, the China Medical Board, and Luce all emphasized Protestant activities. The Carnegie Institute, Hawaii's Bishop Estate, Minnesota's Wilder Charity, the Wisconsin Alumni Fund, the Longwood Foundation, the Mayo Properties Association, and the Juilliard Musical Foundation each supported a single institution; the Duke Endowment and the City Trusts of Philadelphia supported just a few.[1]

By 2010 only thirteen of the fifty largest foundations of 1945 remained in the top group.[2] The foundation had truly become a national institution, with assets more evenly distributed across the nation, though still somewhat concentrated in the Northeast and on the Pacific Coast (see figure 5-1). The largest located themselves somewhat evenly across the United States in 2012, with a dozen on the West Coast, seven in the South, eleven in the Midwestern and Great Lakes states, and twenty on the East Coast. Electronic technology had produced at

Figure 5-1. *Share of U.S. Foundation Assets by Region, 1979–2009*

Percent

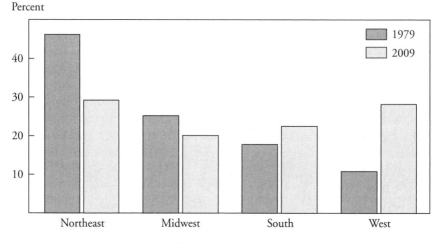

Source: Foundation Center data 1979, 2009.

least four (Gates, Hewlett, Packard, and Moore); pharmaceuticals accounted for two, and the conversion of a nonprofit health insurance company accounted for another. Overall, insurance, finance, publishing, and home building had joined manufacturing and mass distribution as ways to great wealth. Five of the largest were community foundations in Tulsa, Cleveland, New York, Chicago, and California (in order of decreasing assets).[3]

Expanding on rarely used precedents, decisions by regulators, judges, and corporate leaders created several notable new foundations.[4] Corporate decisions driven by the tax laws created several very big foundations, including a notable group in the pharmaceutical field. State attorneys general and state courts required nonprofit health insurance companies and nonprofit hospitals to put their substantial charitable assets into "conversion foundations" before moving to profit-seeking status. Other new foundations owed their origin to the settlement of lawsuits over environmental matters or consumer safety. The great denominational funds (which had continued to grow and to underwrite scholarship and other activities in addition to maintaining insurance and retirement funds for clergy and sometimes for adherents) were no longer counted as "grantmaking" foundations, but among the top fifty of those that did make grants, Lilly, Weinberg, Templeton, Walton, and Anschutz put notable, though certainly not exclusive, emphasis on religious causes.

Altogether, America's large foundations now pursue widely varied purposes. Although the international financial crisis of 2008–09 reduced the financial assets of foundations by a striking 22 percent, earnings from earlier years allowed

Figure 5-2. *U.S. Foundation Assets as Share of Total Financial Assets, Households and Nonprofit Organizations, 1980–2010*

Percent

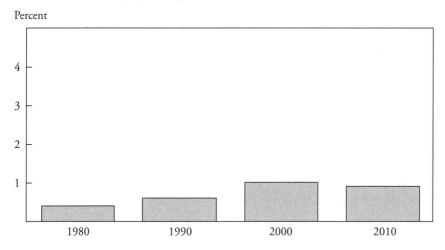

Source: Calculated from data on assets of households and nonprofit organizations from the U.S. Federal Reserve, EconStats website (www.econstats.com/fof/fof_BB__1e.htm) and the Foundation Center (http://foundationcenter.org/findfunders/statistics).

grant totals to hold steady at about $46 billion annually between 2008 and 2011.[5] Following "best practices" and Internal Revue Service (IRS) regulations, foundations had typically diversified their investments, minimizing losses and positioning investments for recovery. Foundation wealth, income, and gifts had become so large—and attracted so much attention from critics who saw foundations as enormous—that it makes sense to consider them in terms of the overall gross domestic product (GDP). Foundation grants per capita for the United States as a whole, in constant 2000 dollars, rose from $28.73 in 1975 to $117.00 in 2010. Assets were perhaps above 4 percent of GDP in 2000, somewhat lower in 2010. However, foundation wealth remained under 1 percent of the value of all wealth held by households and nonprofit organizations (see figure 5-2).

For all their size and variety, American foundations at the beginning of the twenty-first century found their ability to shape events in decline, especially in their customary fields of health, education, and social welfare. These fields had continued to grow ever larger and more complex. By the early 2000s, when medical charges for a healthy, normal birth generally exceeded $8,000, public schools spent on average more than $9,000 annually per pupil, and a year at a state university cost over $15,000 (and could easily cost twice that or more), foundation grants at the rate of less than $120 per person could have only very limited impact.[6] Total grants from foundations of all kinds amounted only to about a third of 1 percent of GDP in 2010.[7]

American incomes and government spending had been growing much more rapidly. Per capita income almost doubled between 1967 and 2000 before leveling off. Through the 1970s gains were widely distributed, and incomes became less unequal. The increasing inequality of the next three decades reversed that trend,[8] but many people continued to enjoy rising incomes, and most held on to postwar gains. Health care illustrates the steady growth of spending: from 1960 to 2009 private and public expenditures on health care rose from under 5 percent of GDP to over 15 percent.[9] Wealthier people spend larger shares of their incomes on services, especially on health care and education, but also on recreation, the arts, and personal interests of all kinds. Greater spending evoked rapid growth in supply. Medical facilities, schools, arts centers, and many other organizations became larger and offered more and more services. Wealthier people could and did ask for more expensive services, raising everyone's expectations. Hospitals provided more private rooms; colleges expanded their academic offerings and upgraded their facilities for research and student life; arts centers added programs for wider ranges of ages and tastes. The activities and organizations that foundations had classically supported grew in scale, complexity, and cost.

The substantial and continuing increases in government spending, especially at the federal level, dwarfed foundation resources. Many discussions of foundations assume or imply that federal funding declined sharply after 1980 and never recovered. Some federal spending certainly did decline, especially in the field of job training and aid to organizations that serve the poor. But the story of federal spending is complicated: the cuts of the 1980s followed even larger increases in the 1960s and 1970s, and spending never returned to the low share of GDP that had prevailed during the Kennedy administration and before. Income security spending—Social Security, aid to the disabled, unemployment insurance, support for the poorest families—rose a great deal. Some of the "cuts," moreover, actually reflect the shifting of costs from "social services" to the "mental health" and "disability" categories. Even the abrupt ending early in the Reagan administration of the Comprehensive Employment and Training Act program, which had expanded rapidly during the Carter presidency, did not return federal spending for social services, job training, and related purposes to pre–Great Society levels (see figure 5-3).

In short, private and government spending allowed the classic fields of foundation interest to grow more rapidly than the economy as a whole, even as foundations themselves grew little in relative terms. Health care spending in the United States tripled from about 5 percent of GDP in 1960 to more than 17 percent in 2009.[10] Higher education revenue more than doubled as a GDP share.[11]

The fact that so much private and government money flowed into the fields of foundation interest had great practical consequences. Hospital administrators saw the overall share of donated funds—from all sources, not just

Figure 5-3. *Federal Spending for Social Services, Job Training,*
and Disaster Relief, 1962–2010

Percent share of GDP

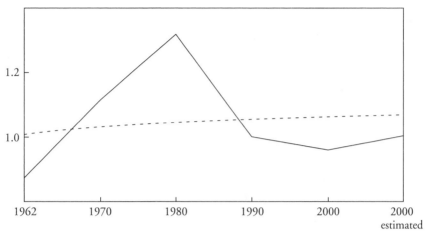

Source: Calculated from the U.S. federal budget for fiscal year 2010 (U.S. Office of Management and the Budget 2009).

foundations—fall from more than 33 percent in the 1960s to 2 percent or less from the 1980s. School superintendents held responsibility for budgets that dwarfed foundations: by the late 1980s the Cleveland, Ohio, public school budget was about $600 million, while the Cleveland Foundation, by far the region's largest, was giving just $60 million for all purposes. The local Cuyahoga County budget for welfare in all forms, including the prevention of child abuse, job training, and other vital services, was well past $1 billion. Foundations found it increasingly difficult to exert influence in any of these fields.

Greatly enlarged streams of private and government funding brought new uncertainties and new dynamics. Private income, and hence private ability to pay for nonprofit services, rises and falls with the general economy. As the Great Recession of 2007–12 is making clear, a sudden drop in family income can push students to drop out of nonpublic schools, leave patients unable to maintain health insurance, and force donors to abandon promised gifts. On the public side, policy shifts as well as tax receipts can change significantly from year to year, from administration to administration. Such changes affect different fields at different times—spending on elementary and secondary education grew most strongly (relative to GDP) in the 1950s, on higher education in the 1960s and 1970s, on research in the 1950s and 1960s, and on social services in the 1960s and 1970s. Health care spending grew continuously, but its sheer size brought repeated efforts to reorganize and limit it, culminating in the ambitious health care reforms passed in March 2010. Every effort to reshape America's health care system must thus take account of complexity, instability, and change as well as growth. In all fields, governments and consumers alike seek more services at lower cost, squeezing providers. As their sources of funding change and diversify, providers of health, education, and social welfare services increasingly encounter financial challenges that foundations cannot begin to address.

The extraordinary proliferation of religious, cultural, and social impulses in the wake of the civil rights movement and the immigration reforms of the 1960s also challenged America's foundations. In the 1830s, de Tocqueville had thought that a common culture of mild evangelical Protestantism, characterized by rivalry but also by cooperation among denominations and by a broad tolerance for dissenting views, provided the essential basis for voluntarism in American society. One hundred and fifty years later efforts to maintain a common American culture are under considerable strain. The "mainline" Protestants (Episcopalians, Presbyterians, Congregationalists, Methodists, some Baptist denominations) that had once dominated public expressions of religion (and foundations) had dwindled to the status of small minorities as Southern Baptists, Catholics, and assertive evangelical movements grew dominant.[12] New guarantees for individual rights extended to religious and cultural expression as well as to race, gender, sexual orientation, national origin, and language. New federal regulation, as well as a new social consensus, countered social pressure to conform to a single cultural standard.

Religion, the arts, initiatives to advance values of all sorts, and creative activities of all kinds relied heavily on private giving. Even as they proliferated, such activities attracted little in the way of increased government funding. This was consistent with the American commitment to separating church and state and also with the persistence of deep political, cultural, and ideological disagreements. Federal funding for community organizing, legal aid to the poor, and similar work did grow briefly during the War on Poverty, but quickly declined. The 1965 creation of the National Endowment for the Arts, and its subsequent endorsement by the Nixon administration, stimulated federal funding hopes— hopes that were mostly disappointed after controversies over NEA policy in the 1980s and later. The potential for earned income is also famously inadequate in religion, social movements, and the arts.

Despite a lack of funds, religious and other expressions of cultural and social commitment multiplied rapidly. Religious activity flourished; according to one of the most careful analyses, more people have actively engaged with religious organizations in recent decades than ever before in the nation's history.[13] While some older religious groups struggled to maintain accustomed levels of activity, others grew rapidly. Arts organizations proliferated. So did legal defense funds, think tanks, and other organizations devoted to the advancement of social movements.[14] As ever, Americans sought to project their values abroad, even as the world's population doubled and the entire globe seemed to come together in an economic expansion that rapidly outran the resources available to foundations.

Private giving for culture and the arts did increase. Nonprofit arts organization revenues exceeded one-fifth of 1 percent of GDP by 1997 and reached one-quarter of 1 percent in 2007, equal to all foundation grants for all purposes.[15] Fifty million people went to art museums in 1979, 225 million in 1993. Dance companies numbered twenty-eight in 1958 and more than 400 by 2000; the twenty-nine opera companies in 1964 had multiplied to 209 by 1989. In the two decades before 2000, most large American cities built at least one substantial mixed-purpose arts center.[16]

Yet growth brought challenges. A 1998 study of symphony orchestras, for example, noted that large grants from the Ford and other foundations in the 1960s and 1970s "inspired rapid expansion for which many orchestras were unprepared, and some were unable to . . . raise [or earn] the funds necessary to continue it."[17] Foundations could fill only part of the gap. Foundation grants accounted for just over 7 percent of the income of nonprofit arts organizations in 1998 and for somewhat less in 2007, before encountering the crisis of the deep recession that followed 2008.[18]

Continuity and Leverage

Because their resources are so limited, most foundations have always relied on long-established impact-maximizing practices. They have focused their giving on particular organizations or fields, supported limited arrays of projects, emphasized scholarships, fellowships, partial funding for expansion, or other subsidies to activities largely funded by others. Foundations continue to control, invest, and parse out funds for religious and charitable purposes and valued causes. They continue to launch new organizations that are intended to become independent and, more often, to help existing organizations grow, along well-established pathways, into greater self-sufficiency. They manage risk for causes dear to their donors by holding and investing funds for small, poorly financed churches, social agencies, and arts organizations. Foundations advance particular understandings of certain religious or cultural matters, promote specific virtues, and underwrite favored purposes within large institutions, just as they have done for 200 years.

Although their resources are too limited to do much, some foundations maintain the tradition of addressing immediate need. Recognizing their inability to substitute for private and government funding in the broad fields of health, education, welfare, and disaster relief, foundations occasionally complement government in these areas. More often, foundations continue traditional efforts to promote and celebrate private as well as government efforts.

Headline contributions to emergency relief are often impressive. Foundations quickly provided over $330 million in response to the 9/11 attacks on New York City's World Trade Center in 2001.[19] Four years later many foundations joined in another great outpouring of aid in response to Hurricane Katrina's devastating destruction in New Orleans and the central gulf coast.[20] Foundations responded creatively to the Midwestern floods of 2008: Chicago's McCormick Foundation quickly underwrote the work of local agencies in assessing community and individual need, while within individual states initiatives such as "Embrace Iowa" distributed foundation, corporate, and other gifts through community foundations.[21]

Yet resource constraints force foundations to limit themselves largely to publicizing need and helping to coordinate relief. Embrace Iowa's $30 million (from corporate and individual donors as well as foundations) could not repair the $3 billion in property damage: that sum could only begin to identify priorities.[22] A careful analysis by the Indiana University Center on Philanthropy concluded that over the entire period since 1978, foundation giving as a whole has shown "little association with crisis or other events." Foundations did absorb some of the risk to activities they valued by maintaining quite steady spending levels during severe economic downturns.[23] But overall, while their giving sometimes supplemented government disaster relief, it could not begin to replace it.

Foundations also continue to look for opportunities to build new organizations, but in recent decades they have found it almost as difficult to launch new organizations as to substitute for government or private funding. The Indiana University Center on Philanthropy systematically tracks large gifts. Only a few such grants in recent years went to start new institutions, mostly schools and arts centers, located chiefly in underserved western and southern locations.[24] Most of the 100 biggest foundation grants made since 1990 went to expand the capacity and improve the facilities of existing hospitals and universities.[25] Seeking to increase local giving, the Lilly, Mott, Ford, W. K. Kellogg, Knight, Rockefeller Brothers Fund, Packard, Irvine, Claude Worthington Benedum, and other foundations created new community foundations in many places; other foundation initiatives have supported related efforts to channel surplus supplies through food banks or to encourage investment in loan funds for community redevelopment and housing.[26] Strongly stimulated by foundation grants, community foundations—which largely support existing local charities—grew more than twice as fast as independent foundations between 1990 and 2008, when the recession stopped their growth.[27]

Even as secular tendencies often have seemed to overshadow faith traditions, religion has remained a central focus for many foundations. Moving beyond their earlier focus on the "mainstream" Protestant denominations and Reform

Judaism, foundations increasingly supported evangelical Protestantism, Catholicism, and Orthodox Judaism.[28] Two of the biggest foundation gifts of recent decades—the 1992 transfer of the De Rance Foundation to the Catholic Diocese of Milwaukee and a $100 million gift of the Robert Wood Johnson Foundation in 2001 for Catholic health initiatives—went to religious and faith-based efforts. As immigration brings to the United States increasing numbers of Buddhists, Hindus, Muslims, and adherents of other faiths, some of them, too, are coming to use foundations. As a result, many foundations, including among the largest the Danforth Foundation, the Pew Charitable Trusts, the John Templeton Foundation, and the Arthur S. DeMoss Foundation, have been supporting a growing variety of approaches to underwriting religious life. The Lilly Endowment steadily funds consultations and conferences to develop effective leaders within American congregations; in recent decades it devoted a remarkable $500 million in grants to the recruitment, training, and sustaining of ministry professionals. Classic examples of foundations that continue to underwrite religious activity include the Oldham Little Church Foundation of Texas, the Texas Baptist Foundation, and Tennessee's Maclellan Family Foundations and Trusts, dedicated to "furthering the Kingdom of Christ."[29]

Other foundations have funded Campus Crusade for Christ, Prison Fellowship Ministries, Habitat for Humanity, Samaritan's Purse, and the Salvation Army—organizations, sometimes described as "parachurches," that echo and seek to update the nineteenth-century Sunday school, religious outreach, and YMCA movements. The available data are limited; though intended to encourage religious belief and behavior, foundation grants to such organizations are often recorded as for "social welfare" and described as providing direct relief for families, for children in foster care, and for the homeless.[30] Many smaller religious foundations join their larger counterparts in supporting such religious-social services and in complementing government-provided material relief with religious education.[31] In another effort to change behavior, the DeMoss Foundation devoted over $100 million to national campaigns against abortion and to promoting *Power for Living* (a book that profiles prominent Christians); the Anschutz Foundation engaged in similar efforts.[32] A number of foundations also continued to support similar religious activities overseas. Sociologists Robert Wuthnow and Michael Lindsay note that foundations go well beyond traditional congregations and staffs to support new organizational forms and new means for religious expression, playing important roles as institution builders. They conclude that foundations "are disproportionately influential," although they "provide a small proportion of the total funding to religious causes."[33]

Implicitly acknowledging that their limited resources could not begin to substitute for direct government spending to relieve poverty,[34] foundations also continue the tradition launched by the Russell Sage Foundation and its allies

at the beginning of the twentieth century, underwriting studies and demonstrations intended to maintain traditional values within secular social welfare
institutions. Examining foundations during the welfare reform discussions
of the Clinton era, Jennifer Mosley and Joseph Galaskiewicz found the Mott,
Ford, Casey, McKnight, and other foundations appropriating funds for planning, coordination, or demonstration projects to agencies that worked directly
with the poor.[35] Foundations overwhelmingly continued to promote traditional
values in the style of the turn-of-the-century charity organization movement,
encouraging individuals to take initiative and accept personal responsibility, urging families to stay together, pressing social service organizations to be efficient,
and asking the public to offer social acceptance and opportunity. Thus the Lilly
Endowment reinforced the new welfare policies with large grants for "workforce
development." And in 2003, the Harry and Jeanette Weinberg Foundation—the
nation's second largest funder of human services as measured by the Foundation
Center—shifted its emphasis from direct services to improving the capabilities
of organizations, funding workshops on nonprofit management, and promoting
partnerships among foundations, government agencies, established nonprofits,
and grassroots organizations.[36]

Foundations have also intensified their long-standing approaches to the arts.
Some of the largest recent foundation grants went to the creation or expansion
of established museums and performing arts centers in such cities as Atlanta,
Chicago, Cleveland, Washington, D.C., New York, and Boston. Foundations
also helped build new institutions in accepted modes, both in areas that have
lacked such facilities, such as northwestern Arkansas and Las Vegas, and in
many places determined to add to their array of cultural facilities, including Los
Angeles, Pittsburgh, and Tulsa. Often foundations provided substantial support
through a series of smaller grants, releasing funds only as others added funds
and projects moved ahead.[37] But in the arts as in religion and the social services,
smaller grants, often from small foundations, also flowed into small organizations. Stefan Toepler, who has focused on arts funding, concludes that because
foundations consistently outspend all three levels of government combined, government appropriations for the arts "complement" private funding, rather than
the other way around.[38]

Foundations have also continued their long-standing practice of underwriting
the international projection of secular as well as religious values and social practices. As Lehn Benjamin and Kenneth Quigley note in their analysis of international grantmaking, several of the largest—notably Ford, MacArthur, Mott,
the Rockefeller Brothers Fund, and Soros—moved quickly during the transition
decade following the dissolution of the Soviet Union to encourage the revival of
civil society in Central and Eastern Europe and Central Asia. These and other
foundations undertook similar work in South Africa and elsewhere in Africa,

Asia, and Latin America. They contributed to efforts to make laws more hospi-
table to independent organizations, to provide technical advice and new sources
of funding for nascent civil society agencies, and to help potential NGO leaders.[39] Also, following the examples of the Carnegie Foundation for International
Peace and the Peace Foundation of the interwar years, they did what they could
to encourage peaceful resolution of conflicts.[40] Foundations have also continued
their persistent efforts to advance economic development. Ford and others have
strongly encouraged microlending. The Ewing Marion Kauffman Foundation
has worked with the International Trade Administration of the U.S. Department
of Commerce to export "best practices in entrepreneurial leadership" as a way to
promote economic growth. Other foundations directed attention to the needs
and concerns of people outside the United States who shared their own national,
ethnic, or religious identities.

As emphasized in this analysis, foundations have continued to support major
American institutions. Almost half of the 100 largest foundation gifts in the
twenty years after 1990 went to colleges, universities, and medical schools and to
such allied institutions as the Library of Congress, the Monterey Bay Aquarium,
and the Packard Humanities Institute. Yet as Steven Wheatley shows, universities are no longer the dominant focus of foundation attention.[41] Tacitly moving
away from their former efforts to transform the entire fields of higher education
and medicine, foundations have focused their largest grants on leading universities in their home regions, on work in specific fields, and on the promotion of
particular values. The creation of entirely new schools by the Ave Maria Foundation and the F. W. Olin Foundation are rare exceptions.[42] But many foundations do maintain close, continuing relationships with universities and colleges,
state-assisted as well as private: Keck and recently the Gordon and Betty Moore
Foundation with Caltech, Danforth with Washington University, Woodruff and
Lettie Pate Evans with Emory, Hewlett and Packard with Stanford, Hewlett with
the University of California, the Duke Endowment with its favored schools in
the Carolinas, Lilly in Indiana, Gates in Washington, and the Walton Family
Foundation in Arkansas with a group of private colleges devoted to shared religious commitments. In the mid-2000s, the Mellon, Mott, and Ford foundations, the Atlantic Philanthropies, and others joined the corporate foundations
of Coca-Cola and the Southern Company to underwrite the Center to Serve
Historically Black Colleges and Universities within the Southern Education
Foundation.[43] More generally, as Peter Frumkin and Gabriel Kaplan conclude in
their analysis of recent higher education grantmaking, almost one-quarter of all
2001 grants in that field went to institutional support or capital improvements.[44]

Foundations also continue to hold funds for the support of specific, and
already established, fields of scientific or academic study. The Mellon Foundation and the Packard Humanities Institute have been especially notable in

the humanities, the Arthur M. Sackler Foundation in art and archeology, the Wenner-Gren Foundation in anthropology, the Lilly Endowment in religious studies, the Bill and Melinda Gates Foundation in public health, the Welch Foundation in chemistry, the Alfred P. Sloan Foundation in economics. In recent decades the Atlantic Philanthropies, Lilly, W. K. Kellogg, Mott, and Ford foundations have invested several million dollars in the study of nonprofit organizations and civil society.[45]

A notable proportion of the foundation funding relevant to elementary and secondary education has gone to college scholarship funds, rewarding students whose lower schools have taught them effectively. Among the very largest recent foundation gifts, the John and Mary Cain Foundation's 2007 contribution of $100 million to the John Motley Morehead fund at the University of North Carolina at Chapel Hill was strikingly large. Its four-year undergraduate scholarships aim both to reward achievement in high school and to create a cadre of leaders willing and able to "accept rigorous challenges that may intimidate others."[46] The W. K. Kellogg Foundation had similar purposes for its 1990 International Youth Fund, as did the Bill and Melinda Gates Foundation in funding leadership development opportunities for school administrators in 2000, the Ford Foundation in its International Fellowships funds of the early 2000s, and the AT&T Foundation in its One Economy Corporation of 2006.[47] Smaller and family foundations continued, as always, to provide a certain level of support to enable elementary and secondary school teachers to attend retreats, to participate in summer institutes, and to meet some of the immediate needs of students.[48] Much foundation support also continued, as it had for more than 100 years, to go to private schools, both religious and nonsectarian, and to religious schools, retreat centers, camps, and after-school activities.

In view of the shift of so much federal support for higher education from institutional grants to student loans, the failure of federal funding for university-based research to keep pace with inflation, and significant cuts in state funding per student, state universities increasingly describe themselves as "state-assisted." Like private universities, they look to foundations. But foundations can at best play only complementary roles. As in religion, the arts, and culture—and also in health care, social welfare, and even international affairs—foundations have been most notable in sustaining the diversity, the devotion to excellence, and the growth of programs committed to deeply held cultural, religious, and scientific values that are among the most notable features of American colleges and universities.

While we think it is appropriate to describe the work summarized in the preceding few pages as following long-established patterns, nearly all the foundations involved would describe their grantmaking as innovative, creative, and effective action to solve important problems, encourage excellence, and develop leaders. Most would reject the suggestion that they merely subsidize existing traditions, values, and institutions.

Consider a recent case. In March 2010, Cleveland's Milton and Tamar Maltz Foundation made a $12 million grant to Case Western Reserve University to create a performing arts center. Rather than build an entirely new structure, the grant led a campaign to raise $30 million to renovate the landmark buildings of the Temple, for several decades the home of Tifereth Israel, one of Cleveland's oldest Jewish congregations. The renewed complex will preserve historic facilities while housing theaters, practice spaces, offices, and classrooms for the university's departments of music, theater, and dance. Tifereth Israel has moved its daily operations to the suburbs, but will continue to use its landmark building for the high holy days and for celebrations. Emphasizing that his congregation would not limit the artistic freedom of the university's faculty or students, Rabbi Richard Block said, "We understand a range of expression will be there. The arts and education are very important Jewish values."[49] Milton Maltz also presented the grant as reaffirming the Jewish community's engagement with the city of Cleveland; although Case Western Reserve is private and receives no municipal funds, Cleveland Mayor Frank Jackson acknowledged the gesture and offered the city's appreciation.[50] How should we characterize this grant? It simultaneously supports higher education, the arts, religion, and civic life; it advances a regional institution that can be described as elite and private but also provides a very high level of financial aid; it encourages—indeed success will ultimately require—philanthropic giving by others. Above all, it celebrates deeply held values in creative and quite substantial ways.

Overall, compared to earlier periods in American history, the most recent decades have seen larger numbers of foundations committed to a wider array of values. Catholic foundations have become more prominent; the number of Jewish foundations has increased; Protestant foundations both continue to support the "mainline" denominations and, more and more, to underwrite evangelical impulses of many sorts. Other religious traditions, including Islam, use foundations[51] and may well produce American versions if their numbers continue to grow. Secular foundations have also proliferated. The greater public and legal recognition of individual rights has led to more foundation support for minority interests and values of all kinds. Causes that draw significant foundation funding now embrace many aspects of race, ethnicity, and gender, as well as cultural commitments, religious and secular. In general the larger institutions that draw foundation support are ever more likely to embrace both women and men, from every conceivable social and cultural background. At the same time, thousands of foundations do their best to advance very particular causes, sometimes in small, narrowly focused organizations.

Innovations in Form

Even as most foundations maintained established practices, many have responded innovatively to their relative decline in resources. Because foundations have become somewhat more transparent, releasing more information about their work, we can know more about them—and more foundations can seek to lead by example. Finding their activities increasingly regulated, some foundations—as well as some donors and even some regulators—have created or proposed new legal forms. Finding their resources increasingly limited in relation to their fields of interest, foundations seek ways to do more with less—to help their grantees find outside resources, to employ leverage, and to find strategic ways to intervene. And more foundations seek impact through policy innovation, social innovation, and social entrepreneurship.

Across almost all fields, foundations continue to emphasize self-help, sweat equity, and earned income. They encourage grant-seekers to search for hitherto-untapped sources of private donations by any effective means, including new social and web-based media as well as all the well-established fundraising techniques. The Edna McConnell Clark Foundation's Growth Capital Aggregation Pilot program, for example, finds other donors to match its grants to youth-serving organizations on a two-for-one basis and also provides investment management services.[52]

Many foundations continue to urge their grantees to be prudent with resources and to keep a clear focus on their missions. Robert Wuthnow and Michael Lindsay quote one evangelical executive as saying, "Very few of the [evangelical] foundations are willing to take a risk . . . Some of the big ones like DeMoss and Ahmanson might try something new, but most of us are too nervous that smaller [projects and] groups won't deliver what they promise."[53]

Some donors and foundations have sought new legal forms to increase their financial leverage. Community foundations date to World War I and won financially advantageous status as "public charities" rather than "private foundations" under the 1969 revisions to the federal tax code, and since about 1980, they have grown more rapidly than other kinds of foundations. Yet by 2009 they held only about 8 percent of the wealth of private foundations.[54] Community foundations have always catered to donors, but with increasing donor-advised and designated or field-of-interest funds, they have found new ways to give donors influence if not full control over the flow of foundation and foundation-like funds. In part, commercial gift funds pressed them to move in this direction after winning important endorsement in the U.S. Claims Court decision in the case of *National Foundation, Inc.* v. *United States* in 1987. Tax-exempt entities that hold and invest charitable funds and make gifts from them in accordance with the advice of their donors—developed in the 1990s by commercial and investment banks and by investment firms such as Fidelity Investments, Vanguard, and Charles Schwab—have grown to hold as much money as the biggest community foundations.[55]

The supporting organization, another alternative to the independent foundation, also resembles community foundations in seeking contributions from many donors, paying close attention to donors' wishes, and enjoying the "public charity" advantages of the organizations they support.[56] Section 509(a)(3) of the Tax Code divides supporting organizations into three classes, depending on the degree of control held by the sponsoring organization and by the donor. Supporting organizations include both the "foundations" linked to many state universities and increasing numbers of public schools and libraries and also a wide range of public charities, including fundraising organizations linked to nonsectarian, Protestant, Catholic, and Jewish causes. Like donor-advised funds in community foundations and commercial gift funds, supporting organizations have helped bring more money for charity. Rapid growth of such donor-advised funds, together with allegations of abuses such as inappropriate degrees of donor control and self-dealing, led Congress to include tighter rules in the 2006 Pension Reform Act; the process of creating federal regulations, which entailed extensive consultation with those affected, was still in process in 2012.[57]

Specialized foundation-like entities, and entities designed to make it easier for foundations to work through mission-related loans, have also appeared. Mission- or program-related loans and investments long predated World War II, continuing the nineteenth-century approach known as "5 percent philanthropy"—limited dividend investments intended to subsidize housing for students, nurses, or ambitious young craftsmen and tradesmen or to provide office and work space for charities.[58] The reforms of the 1950s and 1960s that required foundations to avoid risky investments made it difficult to maintain this practice. In the mid-1960s John Simon of the Taconic Foundation began to explore ways around these limitations; Lou Winnick of the Ford Foundation joined the effort. Together, Taconic and Ford successfully promoted a limited revival of program-related investments.[59] This initiative led perhaps most notably to the Local Initiatives Support Corporation (LISC), launched by the Ford Foundation in 1979. LISC in turn created subordinate foundation-supported initiatives, including Living Cities, which offers low-interest loans. LISC's claim to have "raised $11.1 billion to build or rehab 277,000 affordable homes and develop 44 million square feet of retail, community and educational space nationwide" is impressive. These funds were surely welcome and useful. But they were small in the context of housing and urban development as a whole: the initial investment in Disney's Celebration, a town for just 20,000 people built in the 1990s, was on the order of $2.5 billion. Recognizing the limits to its own ability to provide funds, LISC argues that it has leveraged nearly $33.9 billion in total development activity over the 30 years since its first loan in 1980.[60]

The decision of the National Endowment for the Arts to eliminate individual fellowships led to several efforts by the Ford Foundation and others to help individual artists raise their incomes—and to enable foundations to help this cause, which was also complicated by limitations on individual fellowships as well as on risky investments in the Tax Reform Act of 1969. One result was the Andy Warhol Foundation's launch of Creative Capital, a sort of community foundation for the arts, in the mid-1990s. Creative Capital has also received major support from the Rockefeller Foundation and the Doris Duke Charitable Foundation. At the end of the decade, Ford, Rockefeller, and Prudential joined Alaska's Rasmuson Foundation to launch United States Artists, hoping it would come to resemble even more a special-purpose community foundation, sustainably building an endowment to support fellowships for artists.[61] As James A. Smith has noted, a number of individual artists—or their estates—have also set up foundations designed to promote the artist's particular vision, as well as to preserve and promote his or her work.[62] Like program-related investments and the charitable gift funds, such artists' funds can raise questions about charitable purpose (most artists are, after all, hoping to earn their living—ideally a very good living—and leave something to their families, by selling their works) and have attracted continuing attention from the Internal Revenue Service.

Some new foundations have further challenged established notions about the foundation form by emphasizing a special relationship between philanthropy and profit-seeking. Newly wealthy technology entrepreneurs have created most of the best-known examples, including the Omidyar Network, started in 2004 by eBay founder Pierre Omidyar, and Google.org, a for-profit philanthropic arm of the popular search engine launched with what was said to be nearly $1 billion. Both Omidyar and Google proposed to combine for-profit funding mechanisms with private activities appropriate to nonprofit foundations. They also emphasized socially responsible investing and environmentally and socially "sustainable" approaches to business.[63] Omidyar Network donations and investments have gone to microfinance and "participatory media," to transparency in government, and, as through Common Sense Media, to help families influence the media they consume. Omidyar's early investments in socially focused, profit-seeking enterprises included Meetup.com and Socialtext (vehicles for building social capital) as well as Prosper (an online person-to-person lending business) and the Enthusiast Group (which proposes to assemble online communities of fans of sports and other activities).[64]

Jeff Skoll, the first president of eBay, created his own foundation, devoted to "social entrepreneurship," in 1999. The Skoll Foundation says it seeks the rare people who will be "change agents for society, seizing opportunities that others miss, and improving systems, inventing new approaches, and creating sustainable solutions to change society for the better." It also underwrites the Skoll Centre for Social Entrepreneurship at Oxford and the wide-ranging Skoll Awards for Social Entrepreneurship.[65]

Established in 2005 with an announced commitment of about $1 billion, Google.org proposed to combine philanthropic grantmaking with business investments to address issues such as global warming, renewable energy, global health, poverty, and citizen empowerment. Its early investments went to energy and power companies to promote research on solar and wind power and also the development of hybrid vehicles. Further, it made philanthropic grants intended to advance policy debate and government accountability in India and Africa. More recently, however, Google has moved to a more conventional approach, moderating its claims and separating its philanthropic giving from its efforts to address social problems through creative, and hopefully profitable, engineering.[66]

The Omidyar, Skoll, and Google efforts have yet to receive large permanent funds, so they have operated on a year-to-year basis, in the style of company foundations. Unless federal and state laws governing charitable and exempt activity are changed, the new hybrid of profit-seeking foundations will have to devote great care to assuring that philanthropic donations are not working chiefly to enhance commercial profits. This new foundation form is attracting attention, but only time will tell whether it develops into a significant part of the foundation world.

In recent years the older Ewing Marion Kauffman Foundation has also undertaken distinctive entrepreneurship initiatives, including Advancing Innovation and its trademarked "FastTrac" process intended to help entrepreneurs. Its Advancing Innovation initiative underwrites academic research into ways to remove barriers to economic productivity and entrepreneurship and into ways to commercialize university-based research. Like several of the other venturesome initiatives in the foundation world, the Advancing Innovation initiative challenges the long-established legal separation of "charity" and "philanthropy" from economic development.

To encourage the wider use of program-related investments, some foundations have recently encouraged changes in the legal form of nonfoundation organizations, including enterprises that are usually thought of as "businesses." Robert Lang of the Mary Elizabeth and Gordon B. Mannweiler Foundation proposes the creation of low-profit limited liability—"L3C"—corporations, explicitly devoted to "charitable or educational purposes" rather than to profitmaking, although they may still make and distribute "limited" profits.[67] By 2010, a few state legislatures had approved legislation intended to authorize this new form, or the related "B corporation," businesses certified by B Lab, a Philadelphia-area nonprofit launched in 2006, as following sustainable, beneficial practices. Under the current U.S. tax code, however, L3Cs and B corporations do not enjoy tax advantages or priority in relationship to government programs; a number of experts have criticized them on several legal grounds.[68]

The rising cost of drugs led to the creation of another specialized form of foundation. From the mid-1990s the largest American pharmaceutical corporations moved to establish operating foundations—rather than corporate giving offices—"for the purpose of distributing medications to patients" who could not afford to pay for them and for providing public information about diseases and medications. The pharmaceutical foundations were designed in part to implement new laws and regulations governing the sale and promotion of drugs, and they will inevitably continue to attract attention as the United States seeks to contain the costs of health care.[69]

State courts and attorneys general have in recent years occasionally resolved disputes by directing that corporations place money into new foundations. Most prominently, this approach produced a number of "health conversion foundations," funded by the transfer of legally "charitable" assets, as a condition for the transformation of a nonprofit health insurance company or hospital into a profit-seeking business. Courts have also directed that class-action lawsuits in such industries as electronics, managed care, and tobacco be resolved by the payment of funds into new foundations charged to address the issues in dispute. Suits concerning the privacy of Facebook accounts and the violation of environmental regulations are among those resolved in this way.[70] Reflecting the role of government in their creation, these court-directed foundations—unlike the corporate-directed foundations of the big pharmaceutical corporations—have included on their boards "community" representatives who sometimes give their funds a distinctively populist quality.

A number of funds also engage in shareholder advocacy, pressing the corporations in which they invest, as the Rockefeller Foundation puts it, to adopt policies that support the foundation's "program and values" and "barring holdings in companies deemed particularly problematic."[71] Shareholder advocacy can also raise challenging questions: will it reduce income, have the intended effect, split the board? But this approach offers yet another way for foundations to maximize the impact of the funds they control, even as they recognize that those funds are very limited in relation to their ambitions.

Transparency

Continuing a trend that dates to the 1940s and in some ways to the big national foundations of the 1910s, many of today's U.S. foundations are providing more information about selected aspects of their grantmaking, both to discharge their obligation to the public and to enhance their influence.[72] Much of the most important work is accomplished not by individual foundations, but through specialized websites. Beyond providing a valuable interface between foundations and grant-seekers, the Foundation Center, for instance, collects official information about the financial assets and grants of foundations of all kinds—private, corporate, and community. Its website provides useful information about patterns and trends in foundation giving. Since the late 1990s GuideStar.org has made freely available the annual "990" forms that all nonprofit organizations, including foundations, must file annually with the Internal Revenue Service. The Urban Institute's Center on Nonprofits and Philanthropy offers many studies of current topics; its National Center for Charitable Statistics (which joined the Urban Institute in 1996) posts on the web a wide range of data aggregated from the forms nonprofits and foundations file with the IRS. Studies made available by the Indiana University Center on Philanthropy, the Johns Hopkins University Center for Civil Society Studies, and the International Center for Nonprofit Law complement this work.[73] The growing collections of the Rockefeller Archive Center (which now holds the records of the Ford Foundation as well as those of the several Rockefeller funds, the Russell Sage Foundation, the Commonwealth Fund, and the Markle Foundation), the Philanthropy Archives of the library at Indiana University–Purdue University at Indianapolis, and other archival collections also make information about foundations increasingly available to the public.

More and more foundations produce annual reports and post them, together with their 990 forms, on their websites. Some go further, providing brief but substantive, and sometimes evaluative, accounts of their grant initiatives.[74] As more national measures of foundation activity have become available, reports from individual foundations have become more informative. The Commonfund, the large nonprofit investment management organization launched by the Ford Foundation in 1971, carries out an annual "Benchmarks Study" of foundation investment performance. It showed, for example, that on average foundation endowments lost 3.1 percent over the three years 2006–08 and gained just 2.2 percent for the five years 2004–08. It also reports results for foundations of different sizes and for the most widely used types of investments.[75] The Foundation Strategy Group, working with the Columbus Foundation and the Council on Foundations, recently began an annual report on broad measures of community foundation investment returns, operating expenses, and grantmaking.[76]

With regard to grantmaking, in addition to the basic information offered by the Foundation Center, the Center for Effective Philanthropy (CEP) began in the early 2000s to create "Grantee Perception Reports," systematic surveys of the opinions of people associated with the organizations that receive grants, for scores of foundations. Many foundations not only discuss these reports with their boards and staffs, but also make them available on their websites. In addition, the CEP aggregates findings for individual foundations into studies of overall trends and concerns.[77] A few foundations go significantly further. Minnesota's McKnight Foundation, for example, commissions substantial studies of the fields with which it engages and of the effectiveness of its programs and posts summaries on its website. The Wallace Foundation maintains its own highly capable analytic team and posts on its website extensive and rigorous evaluations of its grantmaking programs. The Robert Wood Johnson Foundation houses an even larger team that has published a series of rigorous book-length evaluations of its activities.[78]

Also across most fields, foundations seeking to maximize impact have gone far beyond reporting on their own grants to collecting and publishing reliable data and authoritative analysis for the fields they address. They can afford to collect and analyze information. Through gathering information they find appropriate ways to work with other organizations and specialists in their fields. By providing excellent data and information, foundations can win the valuable prestige of credibility. Far from new, this work extends the early twentieth-century example set by the Milbank Memorial Fund, the Russell Sage Foundation, the Twentieth Century Fund, some early Carnegie and Rockefeller funds, and such regional foundations as Haynes in Los Angeles, Old Dominion in Virginia, and the Cleveland, Chicago, and other community foundations in the Midwest. But information analysis has flourished in recent years. In health care, for example, the Robert Wood Johnson, Kaiser Family, and other foundations did much by the 1990s to develop methods, produce research, and make available on their websites essential evaluations of professionals and institutional providers.[79] In 2007 the Robert Wood Johnson Foundation moved to extend its work by launching *Pioneering Ideas*, a blog for innovators to share "breakthrough ideas" for health and health care. In some cases, as with the foundations that support the National Center for Charitable Statistics or the Lilly Endowment's underwriting of facilities for information about religion in the United States,[80] the actual work appears under another organization's name.

Researchers based in schools of education and public policy have done much of the recent analysis of K–12 education (often with foundation support), but the Wallace Foundation sets a high standard with its studies of school leadership and arts education. In the face of intense policy conflict, the Thomas B. Fortune Foundation (an operating rather than grantmaking fund) has won attention for its rigorous analyses.[81] The Annie E. Casey Foundation's Kids Count program is perhaps the most notable example of universally praised, foundation-led research in the social welfare field, but the Edna McConnell Clark Foundation's studies of programs for low-income youth and Chicago's Chapin Hall are also very impressive.[82] Several foundations also underwrote studies related to the "End of Welfare as We Know It" campaigns of the 1980s and 1990s, with "conservative" funds pushing new approaches and demonstrations, while "mainstream" foundations underwrote rigorous studies of specific problems and evaluations of programs.[83] Similar foundation efforts in the arts have been noted above.[84] The Jessie Ball duPont Fund limits its grants to a list of about 350 organizations, mostly in Florida, Virginia, and Delaware, supported by the foundation's donor during her lifetime. To guide and extend the impact of its grantmaking, it makes public substantial studies of philanthropy and the nonprofit sector, health care, and related topics in those states.[85]

Strategic Initiatives, Venture Philanthropy

Doing more with less means finding leverage that will increase the impact of the grants a foundation is able to make. In addition to seeking resources and mobilizing knowledge, foundations bring people together, commit early to promising projects, and encourage strategic action. The same approaches do not work in every field or for every initiative in any field. In the vast, complex fields of health care, education, economic development, environmental reform, and social services, foundation initiatives must take account of enormous flows of private demand and government subsidy. Private participants in the relevant markets—whether or not they are profit-seeking—and governments all claim to pursue not only advantage and mission but also the best outcomes for society as a whole. Responding to the challenges of complexity and scale, many foundations have asked grantees in these fields to employ explicit models of strategic action.

Most writers agree that strategy models are most difficult to apply to religion, the arts, social movements, or any effort to promote distinctive values or to encourage excellent, exceptional achievement. These fields advance the public good by encouraging and providing space for strongly held values, for surprising ideas, for new thoughts, and for dissent. They do not seek to produce standardized "public goods." They do seek to create opportunities for innovators, artists, and teachers—for those who must respond creatively to individual situations and problems. Foundations can support the institutions that provide such opportunities, but despite the remarkable examples of the Guggenheim, MacArthur, W. K. Kellogg, and Templeton fellowships, foundations often find it impossible to channel significant resources to creative people.[86] Toepler recently found relatively few foundation grants for creative work in the arts, for example, and Minkoff and Agnone observe that while foundations have increased their support of social movements, in almost every case they leave it to others to take the first steps.[87]

Health care and education have grown into such vast enterprises that foundations have confined themselves almost entirely to study and analysis or to very narrowly targeted initiatives, urging attention to little-studied diseases, to favored topics for study, to neglected populations, or to policy. The same is largely true of federal expenditures for the direct relief of poverty and emergency need. Foundations remain very active in these fields, but their initiatives must focus on details of practice; even their policy work rarely engages large-scale systems. In California, the relatively large foundations created by the conversion of charitable hospitals and health insurance organizations to profit status emphasize not the core provision of medical care, but prevention and community-based health care. Knickman and Isaacs celebrate the Robert Wood Johnson Foundation's success in promoting the improvement of systems for handling medical emergencies and in treating end-of-life care as a special health care field. They note that the foundation found it much more difficult to increase the number of doctors in "generalist practice" or to advance the cause of expanding health insurance coverage.[88] The Kaiser Family Foundation, like Robert Wood Johnson, focused exclusively on the provision of expert general information during the health insurance reform debate that culminated in substantial new legislation in March 2010. Similarly, the David and Lucile Packard Foundation's "Insuring America's Children: States Leading the Way" initiative of 2007 aimed to advance the cause of health insurance for all of America's children—and ultimately to inform federal policy—by underwriting advocacy, policy analysis, communications, and training.[89]

In the international field foundations have also created new organizations and sought to enable local actors to develop consensus about community problems. In the immediate aftermath of the dissolution of the Soviet Union, the Carnegie, Ford, MacArthur, and other funds convened meetings of private and corporate donors as well as representatives of the World Bank and the U.S. government to encourage support for civil society. These gatherings speeded action and, Benjamin and Quigley argue, "leverage[d] the foundations' investments by attracting significant other resources." Similarly, the Rockefeller Brothers Fund, the Mott Foundation, and the Mellon Foundation brought together local nongovernmental organizations (NGOs) in various countries to identify key local questions. Mellon, for example, helped universities in the Czech Republic, Slovakia, Hungary, and Poland organize to address library needs.[90] Overall, as Benjamin and Quigley show, between 1990 and 2001 this sort of foundation support for civil society and democracy building increased from $3.57 million to $33.36 million. Among the widely noted initiatives were the Soros Foundation's creation of the Central European University in Budapest and the much more narrowly targeted Ford Foundation grants to the University of Witwatersrand in South Africa to examine post-apartheid governance.[91] But these efforts were designed to start self-sustaining initiatives in places that have not always welcomed them—the repeated actions to control nascent civil society organizations in Putin's Russia offer a prominent case in point. They succeeded in attracting attention and provoking thought, but institutionalization has proven to be a challenge.[92]

Elementary and secondary education is also a vast field, but as Clemens and Lee argue it is another in which a few foundations—Annenberg, Gates, Walton Family, Bradley, and several others—are hoping to achieve "transformational philanthropy." In such cases foundations act "neither as charities nor as partners with established elites, but as catalysts for change—organizational, institutional," and policy-related.[93] Defenders of the massive Annenberg Challenge program also saw it as attempting to transform by building stronger relationships with local communities. A thoughtful evaluation of its New York City work concluded, "The largest impact is likely to be seen not in the schools, but in the nonprofit organizations that were recipients of the funds."[94]

Because school systems are so large and so strongly shaped by reliance on local property taxes, parental concerns, deeply established law, and long-standing organizations of school board members, teachers' colleges, state officials, and teachers, even Gates and Walton are finding transformation elusive. No foundation has sufficient resources to displace public funding and provide its own model of an ideal school on the scale of even a moderately large public school district. Major demonstration projects can "concentrate the mind." Yet the Annenberg Challenge, the Gates Small Schools grants, and the campaign for school vouchers have all gone in different directions and produced results that are at best controversial. The Gates Foundation began on its own, calling its small schools "national champions." But local school authorities retain great authority; in Kansas City, Missouri, for example, Gates joined local corporate and family foundations in a Partnership for Regional Education Preparation that sought consensus among local stakeholders. The Walton, Lynde and Harry Bradley, and other foundations have done a great deal to promote another school reform: the public funding of charter and private schools. Diane Ravitch and others have viewed this initiative, as well as the great national emphasis on the continuous testing of students and the ranking of schools, as an example of the excessive influence of foundations. But these initiatives, too, continue to face daunting obstacles.[95]

Continuing the pattern of the postwar decades, so many foundations have recently entered the K–12 debates, with so many different priorities, that their initiatives mirror the conflicts of national debate and sometimes cancel one another out. What these foundations have often shared is an approach that starts with a demonstration project or program and then adjusts it according to a rigorous system of monitoring and evaluation. Much the same is true of foundation social welfare initiatives. The Joyce Foundation, for example, brought together state officials and others to develop and evaluate welfare-to-work and other responses to welfare reform; it also funded outside advocacy groups to evaluate those responses.[96]

American colleges and universities have always been highly entrepreneurial and competitive, aggressively and creatively expanding their fields of study, their services to students and others, and their efforts to recruit students and attract financial support. Frumkin and Kaplan note that foundation giving to higher education tends to support ongoing partnerships with well-established institutions, rather than efforts to divert universities from research and teaching into engines of direct social transformation, as some critics would prefer. Foundation efforts to equalize access also generally underwrite the traditional university functions. Foundations also often rely on the most prominent universities to model new approaches. Thus in 1999 the Bill and Melinda Gates Foundation granted $50 million to enable Columbia University's School of Public Health to improve the medical capacities of local governments in Africa, Asia, and Latin America. As an indirect consequence, foundation efforts to reach the dispossessed sometimes reinforce the standing of the most elite institutions.

Seeking a single measure for "innovative" foundation funding in the arts, Stefan Toepler examined Foundation Center reports of support for program development and seed money. He found that during the 1990s funding for these purposes increased both in terms of total dollars and in terms of share of total arts support. Although both the funding in terms of absolute dollars and share of total arts support declined after 2001, support for program development (15.3 percent of total arts support) ranked third behind capital support (33.9 percent) and general operating support (20.3 percent) in 2004. Toepler concludes that most foundations try to avoid the "liability of newness."[97] No doubt many foundations would argue that capital and operating grants allow arts organizations to grow and to make their own decisions about how to "innovate" in their programming, their employment practices, and their commissioning of new works.

In the fields dominated by large nonprofit and government providers of public goods—health, education, economic development, environmental reform, and social services—many foundations increasingly ask grantees to employ an explicit strategy, including "logic models."[98] These aim to show how a proposed project should be expected to produce desired results. The W. K. Kellogg Foundation has devoted particular attention to logic models, though it has also continued to champion broad improvements in American social life and culture.[99]

The logic model can have the virtue of encouraging clear thinking and a good understanding of the relation between resources and aims. But the logic model approach can also impose expense, delay, and rigidity on efforts to intervene in complex, uncertain, and very human affairs. It can encourage naïve efforts to find easy ways to measure complex phenomena and promote the application of inappropriate or poorly understood social theory. As Bruce Sievers has noted, "Nonprofit activity has a complex and intangible range of aims that often elude simple classification and measurement." Whereas a venture capitalist seeks only one result—profit—"an organization dedicated to the creation and performance of new music" might be measured in terms of "positive reviews . . . performances

... audience satisfaction ... audience numbers ... or earned income" or in terms of opportunities given to young performers. Yet, Sievers concludes, "What may be most important is the transformative impact of the organization's work on the field of modern composition, and that is a highly subjective judgment call." As he notes, the notion of a "double bottom line" does not apply, because the nonprofit's purpose is not to make money, eliminating that element as one of the measures of its effectiveness; moreover, any nonprofit is simultaneously pursuing not one but several charitable purposes, few of which are easily measured.[100]

Clearly, some foundation aims are as difficult to realize today as they were sixty or seventy years ago.[101] Knickman and Isaacs, for example, leave the impression that the Robert Wood Johnson Foundation found it especially difficult to discourage drug abuse, promote physical exercise, and reduce obesity. The W. K. Kellogg Foundation's 2007 approach to child poverty acknowledged that there can be no simple, single solution and that the layered influences of work, home, school, and community that make up the fabric of people's daily lives make it imperative to develop a complex program whose several elements are designed to work together. Kellogg also acknowledged the importance of engaging the people it aims to help; one part of its response was to launch an online public dialogue, but it understands that computer-based outreach will be relevant to very few poor families. Nevertheless the current emphasis on strategy reflects increasing awareness of the limits to foundation resources, the concomitant need for thoughtful strategic action, and the desirability of efforts to specify intended outcomes and to engage in continuous self-evaluation.

Policy Engagement

As government policy and government funding have become more and more important to American health, education, and social welfare, foundations have increasingly sought leverage by focusing on public policy. Foundations cannot engage in electioneering, in campaigning for particular candidates, or in advocating for particular pieces of legislation. But they can, and increasingly do, serve as mediators, facilitators, analysts, and policy entrepreneurs while remaining quite neutral in relation to party politics. As we've seen, this role has a long history, going back to the Peabody Fund post–Civil War work for southern education, Carnegie support for public libraries and for improving the college preparation work of American high schools, and the Milbank Memorial Fund and Russell Sage Foundation efforts in public health, city planning, and social welfare.

Foundation policy work is substantial and increasingly varied. Clemens and Lee conclude that 23 percent of 2007's total grant dollars in the field of elementary and secondary education went toward school reform efforts. Different foundations emphasize different, sometimes conflicting, policy approaches. The

Annenberg Challenge sought to reconcile professional expertise with community concerns, the Gates Small Schools grants named their own objective, campaigns for school vouchers have sometimes emphasized public charter schools, sometimes nonpublic schools. The W. K. Kellogg, Edna McConnell Clark, Surdna, Mott, Danforth, and other foundations have reinforced government and court pressure toward inclusiveness.

In the field of higher education, foundations play much more modest policy-related roles now than in the past. At the beginning of the twentieth century, relatively munificent resources allowed the Carnegie and Rockefeller funds to set agendas for research universities and for college student recruitment; in the 1930s and 1940s the W. K. Kellogg Foundation did the same for the professionalization of nursing and the expansion of university-based continuing education, or "university extension." Such ambitions seem beyond the reach of today's foundations. But foundations do continue to support studies of policy relating to particular aspects of higher education and occasionally underwrite trials of specific innovations. The Carnegie Foundation for the Advancement of Teaching continues to commission important studies of higher education policy.[102] The Knight Foundation's studies of intercollegiate athletics attract attention. Several of the newer foundations based in high technology have supported studies of science and engineering education and research in American universities. Other foundations have supported investigations into the implications of U.S. education policy for the education of scientists in liberal arts colleges. Foundations have also supported studies of college costs and of policies relating to student aid as well as of ways to increase college, university, and professional opportunities for women and people of color.[103]

The Robert Wood Johnson Foundation, one of the very largest, took a leading part in making foundations more relevant to key national health care issues with its reorganization and the enlargement of its resources in the 1980s. It accorded highest priority to increasing access for underserved populations to medical care. Early programs helped to spread 911 emergency response systems, to support new mid-level health professions in order to improve access to primary care (in collaboration with the Commonwealth Fund), and to subsidize health services in schools. In the early 1990s it risked censure from public officials and the media in order to promote national discussion and more informed debate of the Clinton health plan.[104] The Kaiser Family Foundation joined the effort by creating and making available key data relating to health. Meanwhile the Milbank Memorial Fund found creative ways to help state legislators secure useful, expert information relevant to health policy.[105]

The opposing foundation interventions in the debate over social welfare policy have been previously noted. Foundations helped several influential think

tanks in the Washington, D.C., area play important roles as welfare policy entrepreneurs.[106] The Olin Foundation, to take a prominent example, funded Charles
Murray's widely influential book *Losing Ground*. John Miller describes the Olin
Foundation and its companion conservative foundations as representing a "full-
fledged movement" to shape welfare reform.[107] Alice O'Connor agrees that the
"different kind of rights-based, social movement philanthropy" created an effective "alternative infrastructure" for conservative causes.[108]

At the same time, as Mosley and Galaskiewicz show, more than a dozen large
foundations supported related studies by the Urban Institute, the Brookings
Institution, the Center on Budget and Policy Priorities, and others on economic
development, persistent poverty, the unequal opportunities open to women
and people of color, and the changing makeup and functions of the American family. Meanwhile the Russell Sage Foundation used its research initiatives
to expand the dialogue surrounding welfare reform. That foundation's research
focus on the "future of work" in the mid-1990s may have pushed the welfare
reform debate in a new direction. The Lilly Endowment also acted entrepre-
neurially in its early and influential efforts to support faith-based organizations
and promote faith-based initiatives. Working in yet another direction, the Annie
E. Casey Foundation sought to address the increasing gap between government
funding for foster care, which universally ends when a child has his or her eighteenth birthday, and the support that most families continue to provide their
children through their mid-twenties and beyond. Casey's work has effectively
called attention to the reality that foster care forces many young people into the
labor force before they have the education and training that American society
now takes to be the norm.

Mosley and Galaskiewicz show that in general, foundation giving for research
and for start-up and demonstration projects in welfare-related areas—workforce
development, child day care, family services to adolescent parents and pregnancy
prevention, safety net, and research on welfare reform policies and poverty—
increased during the late 1990s, then tailed off as the pace of legislative change
slowed in the latter part of the decade.

"Religion and policy" is a large and complex topic. Foundations have not
been notably involved in direct efforts to challenge American traditions of the
separation of religious belief, worship, and practice from government support
and regulation. In some cases, foundations have also supported religious institutions in developing arguments to retain their exemptions from state and local as
well as federal taxes and from federal reporting obligations. The Bradley, Olin,
Walton, and other foundations have also contributed in various ways to efforts
to obtain government funds for "faith-based" social and rehabilitative services
and for private elementary and secondary schools sponsored by religious groups.

Foundations also join with others to develop arguments for easing, or not easing, the regulations that govern the flow of large streams of government money into colleges, hospitals, and clinics under religious sponsorship.

Although the United States has lacked a robust and effective national arts policy, foundations have sometimes taken an interest in what government does. As Toepler notes, cultural policy debate shifted in the mid-1990s to such issues as intellectual property rights, cultural heritage preservation, media concentration and regulation, the role of creativity within workforce and economic development, cultural diplomacy, and cultural diversity in an increasingly interconnected world. The Center for Arts and Culture, an independent think tank founded by a consortium of small and mid-size foundations in 1994, continued its effort to move the arts policy debate beyond the traditional narrow focus on government support. Using a mostly research-based network, the center focused its policy agenda around seven major issues: law, access, education, investment, community, international relations, and preservation. The center created a public information and outreach program. But it too ceased operations in 2005 when foundations seemingly lost interest in building a stable cultural research infrastructure. Other individual foundations, notably, but in different ways, the James Irvine Foundation and the Wallace Foundation, have maintained their own approaches to arts support. But cultural research, with all its potential for policy innovation, has been a "fitful pursuit."[109]

Social Innovation

American foundations increasingly seek leverage through social entrepreneurship, broadly conceived. Lacking their earlier ability to provide crucial support to entire groups of new institutions, foundations continue to support new ways of defining challenges and responding to them. Some define success as changing behavior, of organizations as well as of families and individuals.

For Peter Frumkin and Gabriel Kaplan, private foundation grants to higher education can be seen as "philanthropic" most clearly when they push universities and colleges to focus on underserved populations and community building, especially for the poor and for people of color. Reviewing Foundation Center data for 2001, they emphasize grants for college preparatory programs for disadvantaged youth living in areas adjacent to the campus, for a minority MBA program, and for a law clinic for elderly citizens living in the nearby community. In the same vein, the MacArthur Foundation underwrote a study of the effectiveness of community college "learning communities" and other programs intended to help underprepared college-age students extend their education.[110]

During the 1990s debates over welfare reform, the Open Society Institute and the Smith Richardson Foundation responded to the argument that single mothers must accept work outside their homes by supporting new approaches to day care. In the wake of severe cuts in federal support for the arts, some foundations have pushed private initiatives to engage diverse communities with cultural institutions. Examples include the American Symphony Orchestra League's Americanizing the American Symphony initiative and the Excellence and Equity and the Museums and Communities programs of the American Association of Museums. In religion, some foundations have given less aid to established congregations and existing practices than to the encouragement of parachurch organizations and faith-based social service.

With regard to social movements, Debra Minkoff and Jon Agnone concluded, on the basis of their study of funding for 395 civil rights organizations of various types, that foundations encourage professionalization. Foundation support went by preference to civil and women's rights organizations that had paid staff and that did not rely on volunteers or members and did not strongly underwrite social entrepreneurship. Elite foundations tended to support organizations whose efforts advanced civil or women's rights in ways the foundations preferred; women's organizations that engaged in advocacy, for example, received grants that at about $200,000 were nearly three times as large as the grants to women's or minority rights organizations that provided education or service but did not advocate. For reasons that are not entirely clear, minority rights organizations that engaged in protest activities obtained more than twice as much support as women's rights organizations that did the same.

In the international field since the late 1980s, foundations have sought to encourage cooperation among civil society institutions and to strengthen nonstate actors such as NGOs and advocacy coalitions. Foundations have supported and initiated large transnational networks. They played a major role, for example, in helping to establish the Global Fund to Fight AIDS and Tuberculosis. A diverse set of foundations (including Ford, Tinker, and the United Nations Foundation) provided critical funding for Transparency International.

Since the 1990s many U.S. foundations have encouraged nongovernmental and technical assistance organizations in Eastern Europe, Central Asia, South Asia, Africa, and Latin America. Foundation Center data indicate that foundation grantmaking has moved in these directions. Lehn Benjamin and Kevin Quigley show that, although foundations still direct a majority of international grants through U.S.-based nonprofit organizations, grants made directly to overseas recipients almost tripled between 1990 and 2002. The international intermediaries that received increased funding emphasized nongovernmental and transnational activity: community foundations, the Environmental Partnership for Central Europe, and the Ford Foundation's Trust Africa, which seeks to strengthen a network of NGOs concerned with governance and accountability. Among other activities, the Ford, Soros, Mellon and Pew foundations helped

create think tanks and other elements of policy infrastructure throughout Eastern Europe.[111]

Foundations have sought social innovation by seeking to stimulate change in
individuals and families as well as in organizations. Indeed, foundation innovations in the fragmented, variegated social welfare field are so numerous that they
defy measurement. One notable example suggests the scope. In the late 1990s
and early 2000s, sixteen major foundations funded a series of Urban Institute
studies of "kinship care policies" ranging from foster care and adoption to nursing homes for the elderly. These studies sought to inform efforts to identify and
meet challenges that are emerging as the American population changes, public
concerns shift, and governments revise their policies.[112]

Limitations

What does the newfound emphasis on transparency and achievable results suggest about the weaknesses or limitations foundations face? Their virtues, argued
in this book, have largely to do with control and innovation, with providing
reliable, continuing support for sustaining cherished values and institutions
and for promoting change. Foundations have sometimes been effective entrepreneurial institution builders, especially at the local level, bringing local efforts
to world-class standards. The relative decline in foundation resources, together
with their independence from the institutions and causes they support, has inevitably meant that, as they pursued their vital purposes, foundations have also on
occasion acted in ways that can fairly be described as insufficient, particularistic,
paternalistic, and amateur.

Our associates in the Contributions of Foundations project agree that the
chief limitations of American foundations in recent decades have been insufficiency and particularism. The theme of insufficiency does not need elaboration here. Foundation resources are clearly limited, especially in relation to the
vast enterprises that now dominate elementary, secondary, and higher education, health care, the relief of basic need within the United States, and international affairs.

As fields of activity, religion, culture, and the arts are only a fraction of the
size of higher education or health care. And yet even in these fields foundation
resources are much too limited to dominate or even to achieve many foundation goals. In 1998 foundation funding accounted for just 9 percent of total
revenue for arts and culture nonprofit organizations. Arts organizations earned
more than half of their income, relied on endowment and investment income
for 16 percent, on individual and other private giving for another 16 percent, on
government for 9 percent, and on corporate philanthropy and sponsorships for
5 percent.[113] As James A. Smith notes, individual donors give arts organizations

substantially more money than foundations, and individuals can act with speed and flexibility. Although foundations now rival the federal government as direct patrons of the arts, state universities and community colleges, with their programs of arts education and performance, must exceed foundations as funders for the arts.

A local emphasis is necessary to the efforts of most foundations, even when their intentions are universal. This is obviously true of community foundations. The concentration of recent large foundation gifts on particular universities—Caltech, Columbia, Emory, Indiana University, Johns Hopkins, New York University, Stanford, the University of Arkansas, the University of Southern California, the University of Washington, Washington University in St. Louis—is clear.[114] Many other institutions have received equally large gifts from individuals rather than foundations or larger numbers of just slightly smaller foundation gifts or have already built up substantial endowments. But the list points up, in contrast to the field-defining ambitions of the classic period, the narrower focus of recent foundation giving. Many even of the biggest foundations give chiefly near home: the Duke Endowment is "for the Carolinas," the Lilly Endowment focuses on Indiana, the George Kaiser Family Foundation concentrates on Tulsa, and most foundations in Texas look solely to their own state. The Alfred I. duPont Testamentary Trust is so closely tied to hospitals in Delaware and Florida that it qualifies as an active charitable nonprofit rather than a foundation.

Alice O'Connor suggests that foundations are also quite particularistic in "channeling" social movements into the mainstream. Recently, foundations have funded Washington, D.C.-based women's organizations with a national focus and more locally based minority organizations with a local or a community focus. As Debra Minkoff and Jon Agnone observe, "Grantees in the area of women's rights fit closely to the image of D.C.-based professional advocates." By funding them, foundations support effective work in a strategic location, yet at the same time reward professionalism rather than experience at the grassroots.

Foundation aid to religion is almost by definition particular, because even religious movements that proselytize must focus on existing members.[115] The Jewish tradition of support for interfaith and secular efforts is so strong that Jewish analysts conclude that the great majority of Jewish foundation grants go to causes that are not specifically Jewish, although a few very substantial Jewish funds do now focus on Jewish religious life.[116] Such Catholic philanthropies as the Koch Foundation and the Dan Murphy Foundation fund only Catholic projects; the same is true of many evangelical foundations and also of those that support Islam. Wuthnow and Lindsay describe this as a "silo effect," in which religious grants flow within, rather than among, religious communities. They emphasize that, consistent with American traditions of religious freedom, this effect has "bonding" and "unification" consequences more significant than the tendency to reinforce exclusion. Yet to focus on a specific faith tradition is particularistic in an important sense.

In education, no foundation can avoid particularism. Even the largest fund can support demonstration projects in only a few places. If a demonstration succeeds, the funder must then hope that governments provide tax money or that families or others change their private spending. Seeking to shape national practice and public policy in the field of education, the large national foundations have focused their grants on big cities and state capitals. In our study of foundation grants for 2001, the top ten cities funded were New York, Indianapolis, the District of Columbia, Chicago, Atlanta, Los Angeles, Houston, Sacramento, Boise, and Boston.[117] Mosley and Galaskiewicz found a similar pattern of foundation engagement with social welfare during the 1990s: employing limited funds while seeking to change the flow of large government expenditures in a contentious and competitive field, foundations supported initiatives in states with stronger welfare reform efforts. Because opposition to state action and other reforms was usually greater in the states where poverty was most severe, foundations directed less funding to them. In all these cases, to be strategic was to emphasize the particular. With much greater resources in very different conditions of an earlier century, the Peabody southern education, Carnegie library, and Rockefeller medical center and research university campaigns could engage much or all of the nation.

This criticism perhaps applies least to health care, a field in which private donors of all kinds, including foundations, have long been overwhelmed by government and government-regulated private insurance funds. Foundation (or other private) claims of great significance in the support of hospitals or medical research would be subject to criticism on the grounds of insufficiency. But many foundations have responded creatively. The Kaiser Family Foundation, the Robert Wood Johnson Foundation, and the Milbank Memorial Fund, to name just three of the most prominent, have supported comprehensive approaches to the analysis of health care practice and policy, as well as to public awareness. Meanwhile the foundation-like Howard Hughes Medical Institute has added notably to the research capacities of many medical schools. A number of foundations have won acclaim for innovative, approaches to research on neglected diseases, and the Ford and several community foundations developed and coordinated responses to AIDS.

Since the early 1990s American foundations have directed great attention to civil society development abroad, but they could rarely provide sufficient resources. It is unclear whether foundations realistically understand what it would take to achieve their ambitious objectives; whether they reached a judgment that the "grants economy" they were helping to create was separating civil society leaders from their neighbors and threatening their legitimacy; or whether they simply lost patience and interest. In any case, many local observers came to view the response of many U.S. foundations as insufficient as well as amateurish.

Paternalism, like insufficiency, is inherently part of a private institution that seeks to address public issues. Although casual conversation with grant-seekers can leave the impression that foundations are often offensively paternalistic, research reveals less paternalism than particularism. However, the complaint has more credence in such fields as elementary and secondary education, social welfare, and social movements, where foundations refuse to offer to specialists and professionals the recognition and deference they accord to doctors, scientists, university presidents, religious leaders, and even artists and performers. Such complaints have some validity because foundations operate on the underlying assumption that schools, for example, will be open to foundation "expertise" and to foundation ideas about "best practice." It is often true, as well, that foundations can use their wealth to push "reforms" without considering the desires of those who have to make such initiatives work. Foundations counter that their efforts to improve access to quality education for all is fundamentally philanthropic and responsible and that the beneficiaries are children who cannot judge for themselves. Foundations claim that while the critics are often self-interested, the foundations play legitimate roles when they persuade people to pay attention to difficult problems, when they frame complex issues so people can comprehend the opportunities and challenges they face, and when they ease conflict among stakeholders.[118]

The complaint of paternalism also appears in the international field. Benjamin and Quigley write, "While [the] democratic model works relatively well in the U.S. context, it is not easily exportable. There was an implicit sense that U.S. foundations were involved in helping to make Eastern Europe more like us."[119]

Finally, amateurism is inherent in foundation work as well; almost by definition, it is generalist foundation boards that set foundation policies and approve grantmaking programs and large individual grants. Our colleagues found few situations in which this struck them as problematic. In part this may have reflected a sometimes unavoidable focus on the direction and purposes of grants rather than on their quality or effectiveness. It also may have reflected their emphasis on the larger, more professionally staffed foundations.

Amateurism in both the historical and contemporary contexts occurs when foundations lack relevant expertise or fail to recognize the "big picture." As Clemens and Lee note, "In elaborating theories of change, each of these models" recently employed by foundations "directs attention to the design of the intervention rather than the character of the object, the schools or school systems that are to be changed." With the foundations acting as outsiders emphasizing interventions rather than the situations of the schools, they too often fail to anticipate potential difficulties that can "easily flare into local conflicts." In all fields, they write, amateurism can connote a failure to take work seriously and to understand basic realities—usually not a good thing—or a useful lack of preconceptions and professional prejudices.[120]

Towards a New Realism: Repositioning for Achievable Results

In the face of continuing challenges, the United States' foundations have achieved nationwide acceptance and presence. It is always speculative to forecast the future; changes in the "enabling state" or in the character of civil society could well upset current calculations.[121] But the wide range of evidence reviewed in this chapter suggests that American foundations and their leaders may well be in the process of accepting their own diversity, emphasizing their strong commitments to core values, acknowledging their roles as supporters of regional institutions, and making realistic yet creative efforts to achieve significant results with the usually quite limited resources at their command.

Encouraged no doubt by the law as well as by tradition, most foundations continue above all to celebrate values and underwrite institutions. They hold and distribute funds for a wide and expanding range of religious, cultural, and charitable causes—globally as well as at home. More often sustaining than building in the current era, foundations seek to help local and regional organizations—in health care, education, the arts, social care, religion—manage risk, expand, thrive, meet both national and global standards, and respond to new challenges. Foundations often make certain that the organizations they support continue to uphold key values and beliefs, especially, as several state legal systems have insisted, values, beliefs, and priorities that can be ascribed to their initial donors.[122] They continue to underwrite professionalization. Notably, though uncommonly, foundations encourage the recognition of unmet needs and seek to engage and occasionally even to empower people who have been marginalized.

Recognizing that their resources cannot begin to match the scale of commercial, governmental, and nonprofit activity in fields that concern them, American foundations increasingly emphasize efforts that go far beyond grantmaking. They try to focus their efforts and find niches in which they can be particularly effective. They work to invest their own funds more productively, to make creative use of program-related loans and investments, and to persuade legislatures and regulators to update the rules that control foundation and charitable investing. They give more publicity to at least some of their work, to their grantees, and to the collection and effective presentation of information about their fields. They help their grantees find ways to increase income through more effective fundraising, through smarter pricing for the services they sell, through shrewd approaches to investment and to income "related" and "unrelated" to their mission. They insist that grantees seek better control of costs and consider mergers in the interest of efficiency. They seek effective strategy and leverage for themselves and for their grantees. Many of these efforts are as old as the American foundation and the American nonprofit school, museum, or clinic.

American foundations have never put more emphasis than they do today on the proactive and imaginative search for resources and effectiveness. The social impact bond initiatives are an example of this search. Social impact bonds or pay-by-success bonds are based on financial models for funding public goods by shifting risks of failures from governments to private investors, including foundations. Social investors, not governments, would pay for risks and receive rewards, depending on performance of public programs, be it reductions of recidivism rates among ex-prisoners or health care outcomes. The basic model, spearheaded by the London-based Young Foundation in 2010, is being tested in a variety of fields and locales in the United States.

As government and many nonprofits have grown larger and as government regulation has grown more pervasive, American foundations have also placed greater emphasis on policy innovation and social entrepreneurship. Different foundations support different policies and different social initiatives. Which policy innovations and social changes will take hold depends on a range of factors, including the broader political context.

In health care, education, the arts, and even some aspects of social welfare, complex "social markets" are already developing, with nonprofit, profit-seeking, and government organizations competing for the resources to provide public, quasi-public, and merit services. Some foundations are actively encouraging this development by underwriting policy development and program innovation.

Many foundations do continue to devote much of their giving to religious causes, to many aspects of the humanities, to cultural activities, and to the arts. Other foundations have strong commitments to particular communities, to the promotion of deeply held religious values and practices, to civil and religious liberties in the United States and abroad, to the rights of women, to equality for racial and ethnic minorities, to the preservation of endangered languages and human communities. Some foundations commit to particular environmental causes or to providing relief for people who suffer from diseases that afflict thousands rather than millions and are thus unable to attract commercial producers of drugs or medical devices. A foundation may embrace almost any minority cause, almost any approach to grantmaking. Cause and approach seem to observers to be at odds, as when the rhetoric associated with social entrepreneurship appears to fit poorly with the advocacy of foundation-preferred approaches rather than engagement with efforts to identify "best practices" or to meet very particular needs rather than pursue work that can "go to scale." Often, foundations seek multiple outcomes simultaneously and do not see a way to set a single priority.

Over the decades, some foundation initiatives have meshed well with other sources of support and achieved considerable success—in the building of denominational colleges, in the promotion of public libraries and public schools, in the creation of research universities and advanced centers for medical research and education, and in the building in most big cities of the United States of remarkable complexes devoted to the visual and performing arts. Other initiatives, especially those that have sought to persuade large segments of the population to adopt personal behaviors and values that are by one standard or another more moral, ethical, or healthy, have found it difficult to identify plausible theories of change or "logic models" appropriate to the ambition.

We might ask whether current debates about "strategic," "venture," "high impact" foundations and philanthropy might be viewed as the first indications of a profound reorganization of the foundation world—one that could lead to greater diversity in form. Could it be that we are at the beginning of a period of differentiation, when one organizational form splits into more specialized forms that can achieve greater overall efficiency and effectiveness? Or do these assertive terms reflect foundation efforts to compensate with brave language, or simple shrewdness, for the relative decline in their resources? Are foundation leaders ready to acknowledge and celebrate the great diversity of foundation values, purposes, and commitments?

Concluding Comment

What does the story of American foundations mean, especially for current advocacy of greater roles for, even reliance on, private institutions serving the public good? What implications and lessons can be drawn, for the United States and for other countries? Five essential elements suggest themselves, based on the evidence covering more than 200 years of United States history and the four distinct periods of foundation development.

A first element refers to what the French historian Ferdinand Braudel called the *longue durée*: long-term continuity in constitutional arrangements that provide favorable conditions for foundations to emerge and persist. Although the United States has amended its constitution and reinterpreted portions of it (for example, with regard to judicial review, slavery, women's suffrage, and the relative importance of the federal government), the document has continuously maintained legal protections for private property and individual freedom. The country's political culture supported and continues to support these aspects of constitutional continuity with a culturally embedded code that both encourages the acquisition of wealth and expects broadly defined responsibilities of stewardship for the public good. The long-term outcome has been a mutually reinforcing pattern of individual rights and obligations.

A second element is the general acceptance in the United States of the notion that the nation's institutions should have an "open systems architecture," with government constituting only one of many sets of institutions. This creates opportunities and possibilities for self-organization within a political culture comfortable with self-directing centers of independent wealth. Foundations came to constitute one such center of wealth, but wealthy families, business corporations, and endowed religious and secular operating nonprofit organizations have always greatly outnumbered them. While the role of foundations has been tested at various times in U.S. history, and serious political charges have on occasion been brought against them, they have not been challenged in ways that would contest their legitimacy. As a result, the story of American foundations is one of exceptional continuity as well as change.

A third element of the history and current positioning of American foundations is that government regulation enabled foundations to grow but also restrained them. It was important that regulation set foundations apart, legally and fiscally, from government agencies and other institutions, especially nonprofit entities, and that state as well as federal authorities have been charged with policing the border between foundations and the business world, on the one hand, and between foundations and politics, on the other.[123] It has also been important for the current period of foundation development that foundations have responded to regulation by giving some emphasis to self-regulation through greater transparency.

A fourth element is that the contributions of foundations are by no means constant. They have varied over time, and, as demonstrated in this book, they continue to change and evolve. At the most general level of generalization, foundations today assume complementary roles—they act alongside nonprofits, government agencies, and businesses to help society address public problems. Their "incompleteness" as institutions forces foundations to seek partners, usually grantees. No longer able to serve as dominant financial actors, they have had to become adept at seeking leverage to enhance both their role and their impact.

Related to complementarity, the dominant foundation role is pluralism, created over time by a multiplicity of private actors pursuing distinctive agendas, uncontrolled by any centralized political authority. In the United States, each search for a solution to a public problem can easily fall into a cacophony of different ideas, proposals, and models. Recent debates about social welfare, education, and health care illustrate the point. While cacophony may ultimately increase the capacity of society to find good and sustainable solutions, it requires a political culture comfortable with complex, multiple agendas serving conflicting purposes.

Finally, for the most part throughout United States history and especially in the current period, foundations and the interests they represent have avoided capture by a single dominant elite and have not served first and foremost the preferences of a single elite. Foundations have clearly advanced many elite projects, yet because they have pursued diverse objectives, using different approaches and addressing a variety of population groups, they have also contributed to the openness of American society. Their funds have underwritten both the persistence and the proliferation of diverse value patterns in the United States— in terms of religion, culture, regional distinctiveness, and preferences in public affairs. The outcome so far has been to discourage the emergence of a single, unitary national elite culture.

Foundations are curious institutions—they are, as Waldemar Nielsen said, the "strange creatures in the great jungle of American democracy."[124] Yet irrespective of the achievements or failures of individual foundations, their greatest and lasting contribution may well have been to reinforce the notion of self-organization of American society. Foundations have promoted the idea that society can be greatly enriched by endowed private agencies devoted to broad conceptions of the public good—private agencies based not on association and collective action, but rather on independent private wealth dedicated to a common cause. This notion seems to be more widely accepted in the United States than elsewhere. As presented in this study, American foundations are far from providing a universal basis for the nation's social organization, and in important ways they have been losing ground to larger forces. Yet the annual formation of thousands of new foundations, small though most of them are, reflects the continuing power of the self-actualizing ideal.

The foundation as an institution has become generalized and deeply embedded in the American social landscape. But in its specific form, the grantmaking foundation is increasingly one among many institutions seeking to contribute to public benefit and is by no means the most important. Foundations increasingly face the competition of well-endowed nonprofit hospitals, private colleges and universities, and arts and religious organizations; of community foundations, donor-advised funds, supporting organizations, and commercial gift funds; and of corporate social responsibility programs, social investment models, and related efforts—as well as the competition of business organizations aiming purely for profit. Despite much political agitation, the role of government—in maintaining security and policing borders but also in relation to economic growth, welfare, education, and health—has if anything been growing. The competition, interaction, and cooperation of many forces promise many benefits to society. Perhaps the United States will maintain the sort of environment that encourages foundations to find new ways to make positive, sustainable contributions to the nation.

Appendix A: What Is a Foundation?

F. Emerson Andrews, the Foundation Center's first director, employed a broadly positive definition that emphasized foundation autonomy. His definition has been very widely repeated: "A nongovernmental, nonprofit organization having a principal fund of its own, managed by its own trustees or directors and established to maintain or aid social, educational, charitable, religious, or other activities serving the common welfare."[1]

Private Foundations

This book about American foundations starts with the U.S. Internal Revenue Service's definition of foundations, because the IRS is the most important foundation regulator in the United States. The individual states issue corporate charters for almost all American foundations, and the state attorneys general have an important role in supervising foundations. State definitions and regulations vary somewhat, and the state attorneys general are the key regulators under state laws and state court decisions. But all states take account of the IRS. The law enforced by the Internal Revenue Service takes an indirect approach described below:

> Every exempt charitable organization is classified as either a *public charity* or a *private foundation*. Generally, organizations that are classified as public charities are those that (i) are churches, hospitals, qualified medical research organizations affiliated with hospitals, schools, colleges and universities, (ii) have an active program of fundraising and receive contributions from

many sources, including the general public, governmental agencies, corporations, private foundations or other public charities, (iii) receive income from the conduct of activities in furtherance of the organization's exempt purposes, or (iv) actively function in a supporting relationship to one or more existing public charities. Private foundations, in contrast, typically have a single major source of funding (usually gifts from one family or corporation rather than funding from many sources) and most have as their primary activity the making of grants to other charitable organizations and to individuals, rather than the direct operation of charitable programs.[2]

General Characteristics of American Foundations

Because the term "foundation" is used in many ways—not only within the United States, but also internationally—and because there is much debate about what a foundation ought to be and to do, our study focuses on foundations that are:

1. *Legally defined, non-membership organizations.* Our study concerns foundations that are nonprofit corporations (or, rarely, legal trusts) that possess significant assets from one or more donors who intend that the resulting income, and sometimes the assets themselves, will be given away for purposes deemed "charitable" under U.S. law. Like other corporations, a foundation is usually set up to continue indefinitely, but sometimes a foundation is designed to give away all of its assets within a specified period, such as twenty-five years after the donor's death.

2. *Private.* Foundations are institutionally separate from government and are "non-governmental" in the sense of being structurally separate from public agencies. A foundation cannot be an instrument of government whether federal, state, or local. Therefore, foundations do not exercise governmental authority and are outside direct government control. The National Science Foundation and the National Endowments for the Arts and for the Humanities are government agencies, not private foundations, in our sense, and we do not include them in our analysis—although they have certainly built on the examples and practices of private foundations and constitute important parts of the larger worlds in which foundations operate today.

3. *Self-governing.* Foundations control their own activities. They have their own internal governance procedures, enjoy a meaningful degree of autonomy, and control their own finances. They have their own separate accounts; their assets, expenditures, and other disbursements are not part of the balance sheets of either a government agency or a corporate organization.

4. *Non-distributing.* Like other nonprofit organizations, foundations do not return any profits or surpluses (from investments or from commercial activities) to their founders, family members, trustees, or directors. A foundation may

accumulate a surplus in a given year, but the surplus must be applied to its basic mission (depending on payout requirements stipulated in the relevant tax laws). Beyond this, under U.S. law a foundation may not be used for the "private inurement" (financial advantage) of a donor or members of a donor's family. A foundation may pay a fee to its directors and may cover the expenses that directors incur in attending board meetings, but a foundation cannot employ a donor or director (except for a director ex officio) or allow a director or a director's firm to benefit from foundation activities.

5. *Grant making*. A foundation generally serves its purposes primarily through grant making, that is, making available financial and other resources free of charge to either organizations (typically nonprofits) or individuals (prizes, stipends, and the like), though some foundations also operate their own programs. In economic terms, grants are transfers and do not involve a direct quid pro quo.

6. *Serve a public purpose*. Legally, a U.S. foundation must do more than serve the needs of a narrowly defined social group or category, such as members of a family or a closed circle of beneficiaries. A foundation may contribute to any tax-exempt purpose.

7. *Understand and identify itself as such*. While there is great diversity in foundation forms, names, and foundation-like institutions, in this study we focus on foundations that have an organizational identity or self-understanding as a "foundation," that is, as distinct from an operating nonprofit, a fund-raising organization, or another kind of fund-distributing organization.

Foundations vary enormously in size. This study focuses primarily on larger foundations, though it also considers smaller foundations where possible. The definition of what constitutes a "larger" foundation depends, to some extent, on the field or topic, but we have typically focused on the 100, 500, or 1,000 largest foundations in existence at a given time, or on the 100 or 500 largest grants. Most foundations receive all of their donated assets at the time they are created, but some receive additional assets over time, and some grow through successful investment of their assets. This book examines mainly the 3,000 U.S. grant-making foundations that have paid staffs today, together with earlier foundations that were comparably large.[3]

Community Foundations

Some of the largest American foundations are "community foundations." Under rules set under the Tax Reform Act of 1969 community foundations enjoy the special status of "public charities," exempt from some of the federal regulations and fees that are applied to private foundations, if they meet the tests for continuing "public support" that in general require them to receive a substantial amount of money in new gifts each year from a substantial number of separate donors, none of whom gives more than 2 percent of a measure of the community foundation's total income.[4] The Council on Foundations recently defined community foundations in this way: "A community foundation is a tax-exempt, nonprofit, autonomous, publicly supported, nonsectarian philanthropic institution with a long term goal of building permanent, named component funds established by many separate donors to carry out their charitable interests and for the broad-based charitable interest of and for the benefit of residents of a defined geographic area, typically no larger than a state."[5]

To meet the council's standards, a community foundation should retain the "variance power" to modify restrictions that donors place on the distribution of funds "if circumstances warrant"; focus its grantmaking "within a defined local geographic area"; and maintain "a broad grant program to multiple grantees that is neither limited by field of interest nor limited to serving only parts of the population." Religious groups and other donors concerned with particular causes both within the United States and internationally have created similar collective foundations that do not meet the narrower definitions of giving adopted by the council, but that do in many cases meet the legal requirements for "public charities."

Other Types of Foundations

Discussions of foundations sometimes embrace corporate, operating, and supporting foundations. This book gives less attention to these kinds of foundations. Corporate foundations are generally not really autonomous, but are closely tied to and controlled by the business firms that fund them. Their business-firm donors rarely endow them with substantial funds for investment. Instead, the sponsoring corporation invests in its own business and then uses its foundation to manage certain of its gifts for charitable purposes.

Operating foundations are often well endowed and autonomous, but they do not make grants—or if they do make grants, grantmaking is only a sideline to a larger commitment to providing services. Because they provide services, operating foundations not infrequently derive significant income from their sale.

Like corporate foundations, supporting foundations are not fully autonomous, but serve the purposes of the organization they support. "University foundations" and similar financial support entities established to raise and hold funds for state universities, school districts, and other public entities fit our definitions awkwardly because in many cases they are not truly independent of government control.

This study also excludes annual fundraising entities (such as the March of Dimes Birth Defects Foundation) in its discussion of foundations after 1900. But we note that these distinctions were less clear in the nineteenth century, when some institutions combined the characteristics of a foundation and an operating charity, and others combined some of the functions of a charitable foundation with those of insurance and trust companies.

Finally, we note that in the United States some government agencies, including the National Science Foundation, and some operating nonprofit organizations, such as the "Cleveland Clinic Foundation," use the term "foundation" in their titles but are far from meeting the legal definition of a private foundation. Such organizations seem to seek the credibility that they believe attaches to the term "foundation." We leave for another study the question as to how valuable any such credibility might be.

Appendix B: On Sources

Because *A Versatile American Institution* considers foundations in a way that takes account of how "charitable purpose" is defined in current American law, and focuses on the foundation as an institution among institutions, we offer a broad approach to the definition of sources. We do, of course, take account of statements by and about foundations, their donors, and their leaders, as previous general studies have done. But we also take account of sources that help place both evidence and comment about foundation intentions in their larger contexts.

Because American law allows foundations to pursue purposes that include "relief of the poor, the distressed, or the underprivileged; advancement of religion; advancement of education or science; erecting or maintaining public buildings, monuments, or works; lessening the burdens of government; lessening neighborhood tensions; eliminating prejudice and discrimination; defending human and civil rights secured by law; and combating community deterioration and juvenile delinquency,"[1] we consider a wide range of foundation aims. Because the law applies to foundations of all sizes, we have sought sources on small foundations as well as large ones—though we also take account of the reality that the large foundations have long controlled the bulk of foundation assets. The large general-purpose foundations that have attracted most attention entered the scene only at the end of the nineteenth century, but their arrival did not disrupt the work of smaller, local, educational, arts, and religious foundations. So we take account of the latter, even as we acknowledge the work of the larger general-purpose funds.

Concerned with the American foundation as an institution—rather than as an instrument to serve critic-approved ends—we emphasize sources relevant to the evaluation of the impact of foundation action. As we noted in the preface, our institutional emphasis also means much less emphasis on founders or donors than in many other studies of foundations. Our focus is on the contributions— negative as well as positive—that foundations make once they have been created and are operating.

Documents, First-Hand Accounts, Advocacy

Writings about the development of foundations have relied heavily on works by foundation leaders and foundation critics. We pay attention to such works, but we have done our best to treat them as primary sources, providing evidence of intent and angles of evaluation, not as definitive estimates of achievement.

Only a very few foundations issued annual reports before the 1960s. Perhaps the longest series is that of the Board of Directors of City Trusts of Philadelphia, which began in 1870 and still continues today; the Peabody Education Fund published the *Proceedings* of its directors and the *Report* of its general agent for about fifty years from its first meeting in 1868. Andrew Carnegie (1889), John D. Rockefeller (1909), and Julius Rosenwald (1929) published statements of intent successfully designed to be widely read and imitated. Seeking to leverage the influence of their grants, a few foundations have issued detailed annual reports over long spans of time—notably the Carnegie Foundation for the Advancement of Teaching (from 1906), the Rockefeller Foundation (from 1913), the Carnegie Corporation of New York (from 1916), and the John Simon Guggenheim Foundation.[2]

A desire to claim originality and distinctiveness also shaped much-cited early works by the Russell Sage Foundation's Leonard Ayres (1911) and the Carnegie Corporation's Frederick P. Keppel (1930). A spate of works published between World War II and the 1960s consisted, in effect, of self-advertisements for the great general-purpose foundations even as the era of their greatest prominence came to a close. Authors included Russell Sage's John Glenn, Lillian Brandt, and F. Emerson Andrews (1947), the Rosenwald Fund's Edwin Embree (1949), and several Rockefeller fund leaders: Abraham Flexner (1952), Raymond D. Fosdick (1952), Dean Rusk (1961), and Warren Weaver (1967). People closely associated with the Chicago Community Trust (Loomis 1962), the Cleveland Foundation (Howard 1963), some of the Guggenheim foundations (Lomask 1964), and the Twentieth Century Fund (Johnson 1948; Berle 1969) also wrote in this vein. From the 1960s more foundations have published annual reports; increasingly they are available on the web.

With a few exceptions, the foundations celebrated in these works were large, nonsectarian, and broadly ambitious; by the 1910s they were explicitly devoted to general rather than particular purposes. Several of their leaders wrote, consciously or unconsciously, to obscure memories of the much older church-related funds with whose aims they were now competing, and to downplay the endowments of the universities and medical and arts centers they were now trying to shape. Contemporary defenders of church-related schools objected (Candler 1909; Byran 1911). Other pre-war critics objected to what they saw as the uses of foundations for labor-control (Walsh 1915), conservative-political (Laski 1930; Coon 1938), dynastic (Lundberg 1937), or cultural (Lindeman 1936) purposes. After World War II, critics on the right expanded earlier objections to foundation secularism into complaints about what they perceived as the "leftist" tendencies of the big foundations (Josephson 1952; Wormser 1958).

Responding to these various political critiques, foundation leaders emphasized foundation contributions to American pluralism and, in some cases, the virtues of activism. Pluralist arguments are prominent in Commission on Foundations and Private Philanthropy (1970, the "Peterson Commission" report); Cuninggim (1972); Andrews (1973); Heimann (1973); CIBA (1973); Commission on Private Philanthropy and Public Needs (1975, the "Filer Commission" report). Also in this vein are Smart (1970) on the Baptist Foundation of Texas, James Douglas and Aaron Wildavsky on "The Knowledgeable Foundations" (1978), Kenneth Prewitt (1999), Bruce R. Sievers (2010) on foundations in general, and Kathleen McCarthy on civil society (2003). The activist emphasis on innovation and action is by no means missing from writings by Cuninggim and Prewitt, Wildavsky, and others listed above. But activism comes to the fore in many writings and speeches of Paul N. Ylvisaker, as noted in Marris and Rein (1973, pp. 42–53); Simon (1973); Waldemar A. Nielsen (1972 and 1985); Richard Magat (1979); Barry D. Karl and Stanley N. Katz (1981, published 1983); Emmett D. Carson (1993); Gilbert M. Gaul and Neill A. Borowski (1993); Susan Ostrander (1995); Stanley N. Katz (2001); Mark Dowie (2001); Peter Frumkin (2006); Carl J. Schramm, (2006); and Paul Brest and Hal Harvey (2008). McCarthy (2003) and Zunz (2011) introduce some of the recent concerns about race, gender, ethnicity, and civil society into works that largely accept the claims of early advocates for the transformative power of philanthropy and foundations.

Seeking to counter the pluralist and activist arguments are conservative responses by, for example, Hart (1973); Kristol and others (1980); DiLorenzo and others (1990); Olasky and others (1991); National Commission on Philanthropy and Civic Renewal (1997); and Holcombe (2000). These are united more by their objections to what they take as the unfortunate policy preferences of some foundations than by commitment to a notion that foundations ought to devote themselves above all to immediate needs.

Foundation leaders necessarily favor particular approaches to foundation work and write in ways intended to persuade other foundation decisionmakers to adopt their favored approaches. Among the most influential have been Keppel, Flexner, and Weaver, noted above, as well as Robert M. Hutchins (1956); Simon (1973); James Douglas and Aaron Wildavsky (1978); Emmett D. Carson (1993); John J. Schwartz (1993); Reynold Levy (1999); Kenneth Prewitt (1999); Schramm (2006); Fleishman (2007); Brest and Harvey (2008); and Sievers (2010).

Legal conceptions of what constitutes "history," and legal understandings of facts, matter greatly when foundations find themselves in the courts. And although they are deeply infused with normative assumptions and assertions that historians find dubious or simply wrong, legal writings contain general statements about what foundations do and have done that have also entered into general discussions of foundations. The most important milestone works on the law of American foundations include Marion R. Fremont-Smith (1965) and John G. Simon (1987). Other influential studies of the law of foundations include M. M. Chambers (1948); Irving G. Wyllie (1959); Albert M. Sacks (1960); Howard Smith Miller (1961); Congressional Research Service (1983); Katz and others (1985), and Silber (2001). As noted in chapter 2, there is no single "American law of charity" or philanthropy or foundations. Rather, as Katz (1987), Silber (2001), Diamond (2002), Roeber (2001, 2006) and others have shown, while federal tax law has much to do with tax exemption for foundations and tax deduction for donors, the federal courts also have much to say about the First Amendment rights relating to church and state and to freedom of speech. And federal law rests on top of state law relating to property, bequests and inheritance, corporations and trusts, state and local taxation, the relation of church and state, and state and local taxes.

Notable examples of liberal critiques include Robert F. Arnove (1980); Edward H. Berman (1983); James Anderson (1988); Mary Anna Culleton Colwell (1993); Peter Dobkin Hall (1992); Sara Diamond (1995); and Joan Roelofs (2003). For celebrations of activist liberal foundations, see, for example, Rabinowitz (1990) and Ostrander (1995).

Lester M. Salamon's works (1989 and 2002) have been most influential among the students of public affairs who have advanced the view that foundations should be seen—or can best be defended—as the partner of government in providing services—or, from the perspective of government officials, among the larger inventory of "tools of government."

There is much of value in all these works. We see them as primary sources because they either derive from such immediate engagements with foundations or take the very general approach that is appropriate to advancing a general stance relevant to the public perception—and the government and legal regulation—of the foundation field.

Foundations in Their Contexts

We have made extensive use of many published books and articles about foundations, including not only the standard works on individual foundations and on foundations in general, but also the increasing numbers of excellent studies of the varied fields that American foundations address. It is sometimes said that there is little honest writing about foundations, that researchers inevitably seek to avoid giving offense to potential funders. However that may be in particular cases, we've been impressed by the high quality of published evaluations of change in key fields, and by the many evaluations that make clear where foundations have played important roles —and where they have not.

In the past two decades or so, historians and other social scientists have made sustained efforts to focus on specific, manageable topics, and to examine foundations in the contexts of the fields they address. This more detailed work has been crucial to our own study of the contributions of foundations. It also provides a hitherto underappreciated body of work that is deeply relevant to the current enthusiasm for the evaluation of foundation work and for the analysis of the outcomes of foundation grants. Serious evaluation is rare because it is very expensive. As products of well-supported research efforts and of dissertation research in excellent departments, these studies constitute some of the most impressive evaluations yet completed.

Some of the earliest scholarly works on foundations did focus on "foundations in their fields" rather than on individual funds or on foundations in general. Many of these works were simply directories, but the most notable examined foundations and the fields of higher education (Sears 1922; Ogg 1928; Hollis 1938; Weaver 1967), or child welfare (Coffman 1936). Louis R. Harlan's pioneering *Separate and Unequal: Public School Campaigns and Racism in the Southern Seaboard States, 1901–1915* (1958) also paid close attention to foundation work in its immediate context. Rockefeller Foundation leader Warren Weaver (1967) wrote as an insider who put foundations at the center of the story, but he and the other contributors to his book had strong academic credentials and did write about foundations in relation to particular academic fields. In the 1960s several researchers (many encouraged and funded by the Russell Sage and Ford foundations) examined foundations and public policy (Dickinson 1962; Karl 1968); higher education (Curti and Nash 1965), the arts (Fox 1963), and international aid (Curti 1965).

Some of the best studies of the 1970s, especially in the history of science, paid even more attention to field context of foundation work (Coben 1976; Kevles 1977); Barry Karl also brought especially thoughtful attention to political context in his writings on foundations and government, notably in his study of academic entrepreneur and foundation adviser Charles E. Merriam (1974). In the 1980s researchers paid still more attention to the relations of foundations and their fields, especially their academic fields. These include Hanle (1982) on aerodynamics, Bulmer (1984) and Stanfield (1985) on sociology, McCaughey (1984) on international studies, and Sontz (1989) and Achenbaum (1995) on gerontology.

Some studies now broadened their focus to larger fields of action: Ettling (1981) on public health in the South, Karl and Katz on public policy (1981), Lagemann (1983, 1989) on elementary and secondary education in the United States as a whole, Anderson (1988) on education and segregation, Geiger (1986) on research universities, Wheatley (1988) on academic medical centers, Kohler on science as a whole (1991), Hall on elites and the "nonprofit sector" (1992), Kay (1993) on molecular biology, Siegmund-Schultze on mathematics (2001). Some studies took on larger fields in which foundation impact can be still more difficult to isolate: Alchon (1985) on "planning," J. A. Smith on think tanks (1991), Hammack and Wheeler (1994) on social work and social science, Sealander (1997) on aspects of social policy and moral reform, and Anderson and Moss (1999) on segregation in Southern schools. The substantial collections edited by Clotfelter and Ehrlich and by Lagemann (both 1999) include several essays that consider foundations in their fields.

As they took the larger context more fully into account, many researchers found reason to be skeptical about what foundations had accomplished. This was especially true in such broad fields as social reform, where clear-cut conclusions were elusive. Notable examples include the works noted above by Sealander and by Anderson and Moss; as well as Jenkins (1985) on aid to farm workers, Magat (1999) on the labor movement, O'Connor on antipoverty work (2001), Hess (2005) and many others on elementary and secondary education, Shiao on affirmative action (2005), and Brown and others (2003) on community change. Following the embarassments that attended the Watergate-era revelations of the use of ostensibly independent foundations by the U.S. government, students of foundations and international relations also gave more attention to the larger context of foundation work and to the difficulty of determining just what foundations had accomplished. Notable studies include Weindling (1995), Kuehl and Dunn (1997) on the League of Nations, Quigley (1997) on democracy in Central Europe, Sharpless (1997), and Korey (2007). Even as they acknowledged the difficulties, many researchers became more sophisticated in approach, and some grew bold enough to take on ever-more elusive topics. Ilchman and others on scholarship competitions (2004), Szanton on academic disciplines, (2004), English on "the economy of prestige" (2005), Shiao on race and diversity (2005), McCarthy (1982), Ginzberg (1990), and Walton and her contributors (2005) on women. Many others have recently brought sharper analytic tools to bear.

The national capacity-building concerns of the very large national foundations emphasized by Karl and Katz and others have, curiously, usually been ignored in recent writings in the "Organizational Synthesis" and "American Political Development" schools. To some extent, this may reflect the fact that neither of those schools has focused on elementary, secondary, or university education; it seems also to reflect a sense that in many fields, foundations were minor players, a view that we share. An exception is Brian Balogh's assertion that foundations and foundation-supported research organizations constituted "crucial bridges between professionals and the national government and that thrived precisely because of professional, public, and political reticence about the fusion of these two powerful sources" (Balogh 1991, p. 6). Theda Skocpol briefly notes some of the work of the Russell Sage Foundation, Milbank Memorial Fund, and Carnegie Corporation in aspects of the social welfare field (Skocpol, 1992). And Stephen Teles (2008) gives considerable attention to foundation support for both liberal and conservative legal movements since the 1950s. Foundations are relevant to the arguments in key works by Richard Bensel (1984), Daniel Carpenter (2001), Jacob Hacker (2002), Julian Zelizer (2004, 2010), and Jill Quadagno (2005), but receive almost no attention in these works.

Data

To evaluate foundation activity in context, it is essential to have information about contexts as well as about foundations. The studies noted above take a variety of approaches to the study of contexts; we've had our own experience with evaluating foundation work in such fields as elementary and secondary education, city and regional planning, human services, regional economic development, and international political development: Hammack (1982, 1988, 1994, 2003), Hammack and Heydemann (2009), Anheier and Toepler (1999), Anheier and Leat (2006), Anheier and Daly (2007).

The best comprehensive effort to assemble data showing long-term trends in American philanthropy in general is Peter Dobkin Hall and Colin B. Burke's chapter in *Historical Statistics of the United States* (2006). But this offers limited help to our inquiry into long-term trends, because comprehensive and consistent data on foundations are available only since the Tax Reform Act of 1969 went into effect in the late 1970s. Russell Sage Foundation and Twentieth Century Fund publications are often cited as definitive lists of known American foundations between 1915 and 1960. But these early lists were not intended to be comprehensive or definitive; they focused only on a particular group of foundations —secular or nonsectarian funds concerned in a broad way with "social welfare." *American Foundations for Social Welfare* (Harrison and Andrews, 1946) was the first directory of foundations based on a well-funded effort to contact and gather information about a large number of foundations. Yet its authors limited themselves to currently active foundations that held capital assets of at least $50,000 in 1945, as well as a few that were "recently formed" and "expected to grow." Like its predecessors, the 1945 list explicitly omitted "ecclesiastical and educational foundations" as well as others that were "not functioning independently" because their boards were closely associated with outside associations or operating charities (Hammack 2006, 2012).

The much broader common practice at the time, consistent with federal tax and state charity law, treated any charity (including those affiliated with religious groups or with one or more nonprofit schools, museums, or other organizations) that possessed an endowment, or indeed substantial assets of any kind, as a "foundation" (Jenkins 1950; Fremont-Smith 1965). An indication of the narrowness of Harrison and Andrews' definition of "foundation" is the fact that for their 1946 volume they first identified "some 5,000 presumptive foundations," then set aside more than 80 percent that they concluded were "defunct," smaller, or not "independent" (Andrews 1973, pp. 85–86). A 1903 U.S. Census survey of "benevolent institutions" found that more than a third of all active charities had "ecclesiastical" sponsorship; in 1910, the proportion recorded—in a way inconsistent with the 1903 survey—was more than 40 percent (U.S. Bureau of the Census 1905, p. 16; 1913, p. 69); "benevolent institutions" were mostly operating charities, not foundations, but many relied in part on endowments or foundation aid. Religious foundations, and foundations that supported religious charities, remained important in the 1940s—as they do today. But many of them have redefined much of their work as "insurance," "annuity," or more generally "investment," and have spun off much of their activity, and their capital, into new entities regulated under the laws relevant to those fields rather than to foundations.

Although he worked as an insider committed to the advancement of the foundation field, Andrews wrote repeatedly about the difficulties of obtaining information about foundations. Merrimon Cuninggim, an important leader of the Danforth Foundation and a founder of the Center for Effective Philanthropy, similarly complained in 1972 that "because of the long-time myth that philanthropy is a personal and private thing many foundations grew up practicing silence rather than communication" (Cuninggim, 1972, p. 239).

Since its creation in 1955, the Foundation Center has continually improved its collection of information about foundation assets, grants, and programs both from the foundations themselves and from the Form 990 or 990PF filed annually by each foundation with the U.S. Internal Revenue Service. In the early years, the federal government refused to permit the photographing of the forms, but it gradually provided better access, until in the late 1990s the government agreed that such forms could be made available in digital form on the web. As a result it has gradually become possible to identify trends in the data about foundations with some confidence. In preparing this volume, we have drawn on studies of recent trends by the Foundation Center and also by the Urban Institute's National Center for Charitable Statistics.

Particularly important to this book and to the Contributions of Foundations project overall has been the Foundation Center's carefully constructed sample of grants made by foundations in 2001. Created to aid grant-seekers, this database includes basic information about 124,844 grants of $10,000 or more awarded to nonprofit organizations and government agencies by a sample of the 1,007 largest private and community foundations. For community foundations, only discretionary and donor-advised grants were included. The sample omits grants to individuals. Each record contains fields for foundation name, foundation state, recipient name, recipient city, recipient state or country (for non-U.S. recipients), recipient unit (for example, the medical school of a university), country of benefit (for international grants to domestic U.S. recipients), and type of recipient. Each record also includes fields for recipient population group, grant amount, grant duration, year authorized, text description, grant purpose, grant population group, type of support, matching support, and challenge support. The data set, which uses information provided by the foundations themselves, does not include information on each field for each grant. In practice, information about the purposes of grants and the populations served lacks both completeness and detail. Notably, this source offers no information as to the possible relationship of any individual grant to the granting foundation's larger programmatic efforts.

The Contributions of Foundations project also drew on data collected by the Center for Effective Philanthropy in February 2003 on grantee perceptions of foundations for its report *Listening to Grantees: What Nonprofits Value in Their Foundation Funders* (Center for Effective Philanthropy 2004). This survey included questions addressing foundation impact in specific fields as well as impact on individual organizations. The data set provided included anonymized data collected for the 2003 Grantee Survey. In addition, the data set included the following information on the population of foundations whose grantees were surveyed: total assets, total giving, foundation type, and state in which located.

Archives

We have consulted many written and printed sources as well as the data sets noted above. We have worked extensively in the archives of the Russell Sage Foundation in the Rockefeller Archive Center and also with records of Russell Sage-supported initiatives in the Cornell University Library, the Smith College Library, and the Social Welfare Archives at the University of Minnesota. We have also worked extensively in the papers of Merrimon Cuninggim, of the Filer Commission, and of several fundraising agencies held in the Ruth Lilly Archives in the Library of Indiana University–Purdue University at Indianapolis. At the Western Reserve Historical Society in Cleveland we have examined records of the Cleveland Foundation, the Federation for Community Planning (now the Center for Community Solutions), and other organizations. We have benefited from oral histories conducted and held by the Columbia University Library and the Bancroft Library of the University of California, Berkeley. We also owe a considerable debt both to researchers who have used the remarkable collections of sources on several foundations at the Rockefeller Archive Center, and to the consistently helpful staff of the center itself. For our purposes, publications of foundations and of their leaders are also primary sources.

Acknowledgments

We have incurred many debts in preparing this book, the second volume of the Contributions of Foundations project created and funded by the Aspen Institute's Nonprofit Sector and Philanthropy Research Program. As we worked on the project and prepared this manuscript, it became clear to us that foundations are highly flexible institutions that are profoundly shaped by institutional context. Perhaps our backgrounds, respectively as an American historian and a social scientist engaged in European as well as American affairs, led us to see context as important. Contexts—of the fields in which they work, of location, and of the larger realities of the period—have much to do with what American foundations seek to do, and with what they actually accomplish. We also became aware that no existing volume offers a concise yet comprehensive overview of foundations in the United States over the entire course of the country's history, and with an eye to current developments. Hence this book.

A book of this sort requires support of many kinds. In writing it we have drawn on financial, institutional, and intellectual resources of many kinds, and we are very glad to acknowledge and thank all who have helped us. We alone are responsible for what we have written.

The Aspen Institute's Nonprofit Sector and Philanthropy Program initiated and generously supported this project. A grant from the Packard Foundation underwrote the Aspen Institute's support for the project; we are grateful for that support—and for the fact that the Packard Foundation left supervision of the project entirely in the hands of the Aspen Institute program. We owe a special debt to Alan Abramson, that program's leader, as well as to Rachel Mosher-Williams and James A. Smith, who did much for the Contributions project. Jim Smith kindly gave the final manuscript a very close and helpful reading. This book also benefited from sustained institutional support from Case Western Reserve University's Department of History and Mandel Center for Nonprofit Organizations, and from the Luskin School of Public Affairs at the University of California at Los Angeles.

We have also made extensive use of many published books and articles about foundations, including not only the standard works on individual foundations and on foundations in general, but also the increasing number of excellent studies of the varied fields that American foundations address. We note many of the best of these works in our appendix B, "On Sources," and we designed our list of references to be extensive.

Quite a number of the best studies of foundation work were written by our fellow contributors to the first volume of the Contributions of Foundations project, *American Foundations: Roles and Contributions* (2010). We wish to thank them here: Jon Agnone, Lehn Benjamin, Wolfgang Bielefeld, Elisabeth Clemens, Daniel Fox, Peter Frumkin, Joseph Galaskiewicz, Steven Heydemann, Stephen Isaacs, Gabriel Kaplan, James R. Knickman, D. Michael Lindsay, Debra Minkoff, Jennifer Mosley, Alice O'Connor, Kevin Quigley, James Allen Smith, Steven Rathgeb Smith, Stefan Toepler, Pamela Walters, Steven Wheatley, and Robert Wuthnow. We also have greatly benefited over the years from discussions with many others who have put foundations into the larger contexts of their fields of interest. Of particular note are Emmett D. Carson, Peter Dobkin Hall, the late Barry D. Karl, Stanley N. Katz, Ellen Condliffe Lagemann, Richard Magat, Kathleen D. McCarthy, Susan Ostrander, Kenneth Prewitt, William H. Schneider, Judith Sealander, Jiannbin Lee Shiao, and the late Stanton Wheeler. Our essay on sources indicates our debts to many other researchers.

While we have focused on fields rather than foundations, we do owe a substantial debt to the increasing number of individual foundations that make available extensive information about their activities, through detailed annual reports, evaluations, and websites. The data-collection and analysis work of the Foundation Center proved very valuable; we discuss in our essay on sources the extensive data set that the center made available to us (and to all authors in the Contributions of Foundations project). Also valuable were data available to all through the Urban Institute's National Center for Charitable Statistics. The Rockefeller Archive Center and several other important archival collections did much to underwrite the work reported here by preserving and making available extensive collections of relevant materials.

We want to thank the members of the Advisory Board for the Contributions of Foundation project, who have made their own notable intellectual contributions to the field: Alan Abramson, William Bowen, Craig Calhoun, Emmett Carson, Paul DiMaggio, Sara Englehardt, Virginia Esposito, Joel Fleishman, Barry Gaberman, Vartan Gregorian, Paul Grogan, Peter Hero, Warren Ilchmann, Stanley N. Katz, Leslie Lenkowsky, Sylvia Matthews, Steve Minter, Ed Pauly, George Penick, Alicia Phillip, Kenneth Prewitt, Benjamin Shute, Bruce Sievers, Adele Simmons, John G. Simon, James Allen Smith, Pamela Waters, Burton Weisbrod, Bill White, and Julian Wolpert.

We gratefully acknowledge the following for their expertise and support: Burt Barnow, Joseph J. Cordes, Eugene Steuerle, and Burton Weisbrod for their input on methodology at the beginning of this project; Sara Englehardt, Steve Lawrence, Larry McGill, and the entire research team at the Foundation Center; Phil Buchanan and the staff at the Center for Effective Philanthropy; and for their expertise in the law relating to foundations, Paul Feinberg at Case Western Reserve, Norman I. Silber of Hofstra, and John Simon of the Yale Law School.

Several people provided excellent research and editorial support: At UCLA Jocelyn Guihama efficiently managed practical details and especially the project's finances. At Case Western Reserve University, Elise Hagesfeld provided invaluable editorial assistance, Jesse Tarbert raised important points about the American political development movement, and Corey Hazlett provided competent research. Susan Eagan gave helpful support while she led the Mandel Center for Nonprofit Organizations. This book benefited greatly from the assistance and support of Christopher Kelaher at the Brookings Institution Press, and from exceptionally helpful and careful copyediting by Gail Spilsbury and Janet Walker. Loraine Hammack's editorial skill deserves much of the credit for the book's coherence and readability.

In our writing, we have had the benefit of many conversations with researchers and foundation leaders. The Aspen Institute and the Pocantico Conference Center of the Rockefeller Brothers Fund provided facilities and funding for meetings that allowed the authors and editors to envision the project and to debate it as it moved forward. We learned much from colleagues and critics at several meetings of the Association for Research on Nonprofit Organizations and Voluntary Action and the International Society for Third Sector Research. In 2010 we discussed our work at conferences organized by the Association of Charitable Foundations and the Centre for Charitable Giving and Philanthropy and held at the Esmée Fairbairn Foundation in London; by the European Foundation Centre, held at the King Baudouin Foundation in Brussels; by the Hertie School of Governance and the Bundesverband Deutscher Stiftungen in Berlin; and by the Heidelberg University Center for Social Investment. In 2011 we benefited from discussions organized by the Foundation Center in New York, the Southern California Association of Grantmakers in Los Angeles, the Bradley Center of the Hudson Institute in Washington, D.C., the Indiana University Center on Philanthropy in Indianapolis, the Yale Law School in New Haven, and the Mandel Center for Nonprofit Organizations in Cleveland.

We have devoted a great deal of our time to this book over the past two years; for their forbearance as well as their positive help, Loraine Shils Hammack and Emilia Birlo-Anheier more than deserve our gratitude.

Notes

Preface

1. Anheier and Hammack (2010).
2.. See IRS website on "Exempt Purposes" and "Private Foundations," January 2012 (www.irs.gov/publications/p557/ch03.html; www.irs.gov/pub/irs-tege/eotopicb80.pdf).

Chapter 1

1. See appendix B, On Sources.
2. Estimated grant total from the Foundation Center (2010). Independent grant-making foundations alone gave about $31 billion; corporate and community foundations each gave a total of over $4 billion.
3. As a share of the nation's gross domestic product, data collected by the Foundation Center indicate that foundation assets amounted to just over 3 percent in 1995, rising to somewhat under 4.5 percent in 2005. American law did not require that foundations provide audited financial reports before the 1970s, so estimates of foundation assets and expenditures before the 1980s are uncertain and are almost certainly low (see Hammack 2006).
4. In several of the largest nonprofit fields (medical research, the arts, education, youth development) endowments greatly surpass annual expenditures; in others (social and employment services, religion), they are about equal, as calculated from data in Fisman and Hubbard (2003). College and university endowments alone amounted to over $340 billion in 2005 (www.nacubo.org/x2321.xml); by June, 2008, this had risen to $413 billion, as reported in the *Wall Street Journal,* January 27, 2009, p. D3;

hospitals held significantly more (see Fremont-Smith 2006). Because colleges and universities mount research programs, run hospitals, maintain libraries, and build museums, gardens, and arboreta and do many other things in addition to providing academic instruction to undergraduates, the larger university endowments resemble foundations in many ways.

5. Increasing numbers of smaller foundations do obtain professional support from such firms as the Glenmede Trust (Philadelphia), Foundation Management Services (Cleveland), Pacific Foundation Services (San Francisco), and Foundation Source (headquarters in Connecticut).

6. Data from the Foundation Center (http://foundationcenter.org/findfunders/top-funders/top100assets.html); Lawrence and Mukai (2010).

7. Business historians Leslie Hannah and Bruce Kogut note that the Emperor Caligula's reputed remark that he "wished that the Roman People had but a single neck" appeals to academics who face the impossible challenge of seeking to make sense of the large population of small- and medium-size businesses (Hannah 1999, pp. 277, 286).

8. A few of the small foundations will eventually become much larger as their founders become able and willing to transfer larger fortunes. About 17 percent of 67,543 foundations that reported on Form 990-PF to the IRS in 2002 could be classified as pass-through organizations, meaning that they made grants of 25 percent or more of the fair market value of their assets, according to the Urban Institute's National Center for Charitable Statistics.

9. Foundation Strategy Group (2003) and Bernholz, Fulton, and Kasper (2005).

10. The Foundation Center identified about 3,100 foundations with paid staff in 2009, 3,500 by a different set of definitions in 2008. In each year it found about 750 foundations that had staffs of five persons or more; see Foundation Center tables (http://foundationcenter.org/findfunders/statistics/gm_agg.html).

11. That small foundations are more likely to err is the view held not long ago by key officials of the New York State Attorney General's office in 2003 (Josephson and Goldman 2003). Boris and Steuerle (2004) summarized the agnostic view of participants in a discussion of this question, organized by the Urban Institute and the Kennedy School of Government's Hauser Center.

12. On foundations and philanthropy in the ancient world, see Veyne (1990) and Lomas and Cornell (2003).

13. "Vakf" and "Wakf" are other transliterations. This is a vast field; according to its website, VakifBank, the sixth largest "multi-specialist" financial institution in Turkey, "is controlled by over 40,000 charitable foundations" (www.vakifbank.com.tr/1240.aspx, viewed July 30, 2007). Recent introductions to the topic include Çizakça (2000) and Singer (2003).

14. Maza (2005, p. 181).

15. For a striking study of the assertion of government control over a foundation in Britain, see Garside (2000).

16. Smith and Borgmann (2001), Anheier and Daly (2006), MacDonald and Tayart de Borms (2008), and Adam (2004).

17. See appendix B, On Sources.

18. See IRS website (www.irs.gov/charities/charitable/article/0,,id=175418,00.html).

19. See IRS website (www.irs.gov/charities/charitable/article/0,,id=175418,00.html).

20. Text from www.kingjamesbibleonline.org/1-Corinthians-Chapter-13/; spelling modernized.

21. A core Christian tradition emphasized by Catholics celebrates the seven works of corporal mercy: visiting the incarcerated, feeding the hungry, clothing the naked, sheltering pilgrims, giving drink to the thirsty, tending the sick (Matthew 25:31–36), and burying the dead, as well as seven acts of spiritual mercy: instructing the ignorant, counseling the doubtful, comforting the afflicted, admonishing the sinner, forgiving offenses, bearing wrongs patiently, and praying for the living and the dead. For a recent popular discussion by a Catholic theologian, see Keenan (2007); for an art historian's excellent discussion of the relevant writings of church fathers, see Freyhan (1948). Roberts (1989) notes that several hundred European hospital foundations were devoted to the seven corporal works of mercy between 1200 and 1700.

22. The Old Testament's Job declared that he would deserve God's punishment if he "withheld the poor from their desire," "caused the eyes of the widow to fail," "saw any perish for want of clothing," or failed to share food or lifted his hand "against the fatherless." Job 31:15–22.

23. For the full Statute of Charitable Uses, see Hammack (1998, p. 68). For recent references to this statute as advancing nonreligious notions of "charity," see, for example, Hopkins (1987, p. 56) and Picarda (1977).

24. Diamond (2002, p. 116).

25. Carnegie (1889, p. 662).

26. Maier (1993, p. 54).

27. Anheier and Leat (2006) and Prewitt (2001).

28. Anheier and Hammack (2010).

29. Douglas and Wildavsky (1978), Prewitt (2001), Anheier and Leat (2006), and Fleishman (2007). Our discussion of roles is informed by Weaver (1967), Nielsen (1972), Karl and Katz (1981), Hammack (1999), Prewitt (1999), Kramer (1987), Salamon (1995), Anheier and Daly (2006), and Frumkin (2006).

30. In writing this, we acknowledge the approach to institutional analysis that emphasizes the path and context dependency of organizations and the power of routines and learned cultural repertoires in institutional life. See Powell and DiMaggio (1991), Pierson (2000), and Thelen (1999). But we also note the importance of American political institutions—protections for private property, arrangements that separate and regulate relations between religion and state, and the autonomy granted to private nonprofit corporations and trusts—that make possible the foundations that exist in the United States and that have long been studied by historians and political scientists.

31. Wolpert (2006) and Clotfelter (1992). Some researchers have argued that the redistribution effect may be less than what would have been achieved had assets and resulting revenues been taxed—though that clearly depends on who controls tax policy at a given time. See Prewitt (2001) and Anheier and Leat (2006). Many analysts argue that numerous elements of U.S. social, economic, housing, and educational policy benefit those who have higher than average incomes; see, for example, Katz (2001).

32. Notable examples include the Russell Sage Foundation and the Twentieth Century Fund's studies of foundations and the Cleveland Foundation's supply of leaders for several other early community foundations in the first half of the twentieth century; the support many foundations gave to the community chest movement in the 1930s and 1940s and beyond; continuing foundation funding for the Foundation Center; and the start-up funding for community foundations both in the United States and abroad provided by the Charles S. Mott, Ford, Lilly, and other foundations in more recent years.

33. A good general introduction to some of these issues is Fremont-Smith (2001). Wright (2001) speculates that the availability of such institutional forms as the community foundation encourages Americans to give more to charity than their British counterparts.

34. Wolpert (2006) and Prewitt and others (2006).

35. A widely read version of this complaint appeared in a series of newspaper articles in the *Philadelphia Inquirer* in 1993; these articles were published in book form as Gaul and Borowski (1993).

36. Sansing and Yetman (2006). The law counts expenditures on administrative costs together with grants to external parties as counting toward the 5 percent payout requirement and that is the standard used in the cited studies. For a thorough analysis of foundation administrative costs that concludes that higher costs are strongly associated with "international giving, direct charitable activities, and programs that make grants to individuals," see Boris and others (2008).

37. Irvin (2007), Billitteri (2005), Klausner (2003), Fremont-Smith (2001), and Deep and Frumkin (2001).

38. In a recent discussion Frederic Fransen, executive director of the Center for Excellence in Higher Education and an advocate for using foundations to influence the use of donated funds, asserted, "For too long nobody has been watching" to see whether "universities are the best possible stewards" for donors' gifts (*USA Today*, September 4, 2007, available at www.usatoday.com/news/nation/2007-09-04-2264830283_x.htm). Charles Harper, vice president of the Templeton Foundation, which joined with the Marcus Foundation and the John W. Pope Foundation to launch the center, added, "Anybody who trusts a university on a handshake is a fool" (*Wall Street Journal*, September 18, 2007, http://online.wsj.com/article/SB119007667292230616.html).

39. Hechinger (2007, p. B1). The Mandel Foundation uses the term "evergreen" to characterize continuing long-term funding commitments to nonprofit organizations; see, for example, "UJC on the Inside," March 2004 (www.ujc.org/page.html?ArticleID=59507, viewed September 18, 2007).

40. Karl and Katz (1981), Wheatley (1988), and Lagemann (1983).

41. Dahl (1971) and Prewitt (1999, 2001). Silber (2001) describe the legal changes that broadened access to nonprofit activity for African Americans and members of other racial, religious, and social minority groups during the civil rights era of the 1950s and 1960s as expanding "A Corporate Form of Freedom."

42. For a fuller development of this perspective, see Hammack (2002, 2006).

43. Of course, foundations are bound by the objectives and purposes set forth in their charters, provided these are within the limits the law permits. Typically, charters leave room for interpretation.

Chapter 2

1. Or as F. Emerson Andrews, the first director of the Foundation Center, put it in 1960, "A nonprofit, nongovernment organization having a principal fund of its own, managed by its own trustees or directors, and established to maintain or aid social, educational, charitable, religious, or other activities serving the general welfare."

2. Our effort to focus specifically on foundations and to evaluate foundation activities in the contexts of their times differentiates our work from the broader concerns of Hall (1982) with "culture" and Hall (1992) with his definition of "nonprofit," of McCarthy (2003), who emphasizes "philanthropy" and "civil society," and of Zunz (2011), who employs a broad and flexible definition of "philanthropy" and discusses a narrow range of foundations.

3. Koenig (2008, p. 144) and Roeber (2006, p. 211).

4. "Virginia turned to its Anglican vestries, and Massachusetts to its congregations, for policing morals offences and doling out poor relief" (Koenig 2008, p. 157).

5. Concern about local resistance persuaded Anglican authorities not to take this step (Roeber 2001, p. 423). For authoritative discussions of the roles of the Congregationalist establishment in New England and the aims of the Church of England throughout the colonies, see McLoughlin (1971), Doll (2000), and Woolverton (1984).

6. Koenig (2008, p. 164).

7. Witte (1991, p. 371) concludes, "Baptists, Quakers, Catholics, Jews, and other nonconformists were . . . forced to pay for the support of churches and clerics that they considered heretical or even heathen." See also Ragosta (2008) and Wilson (1990). In a thorough review of the question, Judge Michael W. McConnell (2003) lists six "elements of establishment": 1) governmental control over the doctrines, structure, and personnel of the state church; 2) mandatory attendance at religious worship services in the state church; 3) public financial support (as through land grants and religious taxes); 4) prohibition of religious worship in other religious communities; 5) use of the state church for such civil functions as social welfare, education, marriages, and public records and for the prosecution of moral offenses; and 6) limitation of political participation to members of the state church.

8. A "Society for Propagating Christian Knowledge among the Indians of North America," whose leaders included the presidents of Harvard and Dartmouth, received a charter in 1762 only to see the Privy Council revoke it as inconsistent with British policy (Davis 1917, pp. 38, 46, 48, 81).

9. A leading example was the Corporation for the Relief of Widows and Children of Clergymen in the Communion of the Church of England in America granted by the governors of Pennsylvania, New Jersey, and New York in 1769; Presbyterians and Dutch Reformed obtained similar charters in Pennsylvania and New Jersey in the last decades of British rule. Other important colonial corporations included the Contributors to the Pennsylvania Hospital "for the relief of the sick poor" (1750), the Contributors to the Relief and Employment of the Poor in the City of Philadelphia (1766), and at least one "corporate educational institution" in every colony except Delaware, North Carolina, and Georgia (Davis 1917, pp. 80–86).

10. Jones (1969, p. 38), Maier (1993), and Katz, Sullivan, and Beach (1985).

11. Quoted by Davis (1917, p. 47). When New York State passed a general incorporation act for religious congregations in 1784, the act stated, "Many of the Churches, Congregations and religious Societies in the State" had been "put to great Difficulties to support the public Worship of God, by reason of the illiberal and partial Distributions of Charters of Incorporation to religious Societies, whereby many charitable and well-disposed Persons [had] been prevented from contributing to the Support of Religion, for Want of proper Persons authorized by Law, to take charge of their pious Donations"; Act of April 6, 1784, quoted in D. G. Smith (2003).

12. The Society for the Propagation of the Gospel in Foreign Parts. Also important were two societies that represented the other religious movements that gained governmental authority in Britain, at least for a time: the Presbyterian Society in Scotland for Propagating Christian Knowledge and the New England Company.

13. Koenig (2008, pp. 158–61, 171–74).

14. Harvard, King's, Princeton, and the University of Pennsylvania raised substantial funds during the colonial period (McAnear 1952).

15. Davis (1917, p. 102).

16. Cohen (2003, p. 564).

17. Katz, Sullivan, and Beach (1985).

18. Maier (1993) and Sherwood (1900).

19. Bond and Gundersen (2007, p. 215).

20. For a classic study of the use of government regulation to protect slavery, see Wade (1964).

21. The vast literature on the religion clauses of the First Amendment continues to proliferate. Among recent contributions, see Roeber (2001), Hamburger (2002), McConnell (2003), S. D. Smith (2004), and Witte (2006).

22. Wyllie (1959, p. 218). The courts also approved trusts for a wide range of purposes and in Pennsylvania and some other states approved bequests to Quaker or Baptist associations that had not incorporated.

23. Witte (1996, p. 405). For a detailed study that dates the rapid growth in the number of voluntary societies in Massachusetts to the revolution and includes charitable corporations as well as less formal associations and excludes trusts, see Brown (1973).

24. Roeber (2001, 438). Underwood and Burke (2006) show that South Carolina changed in similar ways in the twenty years that followed the revolution.

25. *Vidal* v. *Girard's Executors*, 43 U.S. 127 (1844).

26. Witte (1996, pp. 405–06).

27. Buckley (1977).

28. Pratt (1967) and Lannie (1968).

29. Diamond (2002, p. 117).

30. For this general argument, and for some of the key documentation, see Hammack (1998); for an extensive antebellum account from a Presbyterian standpoint, see Baird (1844). A recent historical overview of private and public sponsorship of educational activity in early nineteenth-century America is Howe (2002).

31. Roeber (2001, pp. 438–40).

32. For a discussion of pre–Civil War fears that increasing numbers of nongovernment organizations would divide the nation, see Neem (2011, pp. 29–53).

33. Lamoreaux (2004, p. 34) emphasizes the small size of the great majority of business corporations through the end of the nineteenth century. An excellent introduction to key questions in the economic history of the United States, with substantial attention to the organization of economic activities, is Atack, Passell, and Lee (1994). Important articles on these points include Atack (1986), Carter and Savoca (1990), and Folbre and Wagman (1993).

34. On the placement of pauper children, see Grossberg (1985, pp. 263–68), and the references noted there. On women's roles, see, for example, Rothman (1978); on poor relief, Katz (1986); on schools, Kaestle (1983); and on hospitals, Rosner (1982). For education data, see Carter and others (2006, vol. 1).

35. For a very good general account of the development of government capabilities in the United States at all levels, including states and localities, see Campbell (1995).

36. On the regional distribution of nonprofit organizations, see Burke (2001). For striking maps of variations in economic activity, prosperity, and literacy in late nineteenth-century U.S. counties, see Bensel (2000). Among notable works on the topics touched on by this paragraph are Brown (1973), Wright (1993), Smith-Rosenberg (1971), and Rothman (1971).

37. Jones (1969, pp. 122–27, 132–33, 140–53) shows that British authorities sharply limited the charitable support of the arts and of religions other than Anglicanism.

38. For a general account of the "separation of college and state," see Whitehead (1973). Hall (1992) and Neem (2008) emphasize the undeniable elitist strain in the movement that led to the separation of Harvard and other educational corporations from state control. Neem also acknowledges Harvard leader Josiah Quincy's fear that his institution could fall "slave to the electorate," cast, as Quincy put it, "into the troughs of a politico-theological sea . . . to its injury" if not "to its destruction" (Neem 2008, p. 123).

39. Early examples include the interdenominational Magdalen Society (1800) for the care and moral education of girls in Philadelphia (later the White-Williams Foundation); the Swedenborg Foundation (1850) for the "sole purpose" of printing and distributing "the theological writings of Emanuel Swedenborg"; and the Northern Baptist Education Society (1791), the American Bible Society (1816), the Education Board of the Presbyterian Church (1820s), the American Education Society (1825), the Society for the Promotion of Collegiate and Theological Education at the West (1843), and the American Missionary Association (1846).

40. Mather (1710, pp. 58–59).

41. Beecher (1865).

42. Denominational funds include those of the Northern Baptist Education Society (1791), the Presbyterian Church (1799), the (broadly Congregationalist/Presbyterian) American Education Society (1815), the Education Board of the Presbyterian Church (1820s), and the Society for the Promotion of Collegiate and Theological Education at the West (1843). As the denominations divided over slavery and race, nineteenth-century Southern Baptists, Southern Methodists, and Southern Presbyterians created comparable funds, including the Christian Education and Ministerial Relief of the Presbyterian Church in the United States (southern) and the Student Loan Fund of the Board of Education of the Methodist Church. Naylor (1984).

43. Baird (1844). Baird added, "In almost all instances, the colleges in the United States have been founded by religious men. The common sense in establishing them is as follows.

A company is organised, a subscription list opened, and certain men of influence in the neighbourhood consent to act as trustees. A charter is then asked from the legislature of the State within which the protected institution is to be placed, and a grant in aid of the funds at the same time solicited. The charter is obtained, and with it a few thousand dollars perhaps, by way of assistance. What else is required for the purchase of a site, erecting buildings, providing a library, apparatus, &c., &c., must be made up by those interested in the project. Thus have vast sums been raised, particularly during the last twenty years, for founding colleges in all parts of the country, but particularly in the West. A great proportion of these sums have been subscribed by persons in the neighbourhood, and more directly interested in the success of the undertakings subscribed for; but in many cases, money to a large amount has been obtained from the churches along the Atlantic coast."

44. Brackenridge (1999).

45. Purcell (1918).

46. Nord (2001).

47. Important early nondenominational funds include those of the American Home Missionary Society (the oldest of several organizations that combined to form this entity, 1815), the American Bible Society (1816), the American Tract Society, and the American Sunday School Union. The best recent studies of these organizations are Boylan (1990), Wosh (1994), and Nord (2004).

48. The *American Quarterly Register* published lists of donors to the American Education Society through the 1830s and 1840s; these lists included legacies, individual gifts, funds raised through benefits and in other ways by small groups, and repayments of loans. See, for example, vol. XV (1843, p. 111).

49. For denominational fund investment and insurance activity, see, for example, Baird (1982) and Brackenridge (1999).

50. Harrison and Andrews (1946, p. 17).

51. Dalzell (1987, pp. 103–12, 115, 126, 130–33). The Massachusetts Hospital Insurance Company also invested funds for the Boston Athenaeum, the Boston Female Society, the Boston Marine Society, the Boston Dispensary, the Boys' Asylum, the Massachusetts Medical Society, the Massachusetts Charitable Eye and Ear Infirmary, Harvard College, the Handel and Haydn Society, the American Academy of Arts and Letters, the Franklin Fund, and the Greene Foundation (Dalzell 1987, p. 135). Other states exacted payments to charity from banking institutions in this period; in Connecticut, the societies that supported churches enjoyed special privileges from banks (Purcell 1918, p. 108).

52. James (1948).

53. Yenawine (2010).

54. "The Will of Stephen Girard," p. 25.

55. "The Will of Stephen Girard," p. 25.

56. See Board of Directors of City Trusts of the City of Philadelphia (1912, app. E) for a list of the several trusts under this board's care in 1912, with their dates of founding.

57. Barnard (1877, p. 623), Carpenter and Morehouse (1896, pp. 400–03), and Ebbeling (1976).

58. "A recent report of the trustees . . . shows that the trust has been most ably administered and the property largely increased so that it is now valued at more than three

times the amount of the legacy. . . . Already over seventeen thousand dollars have been given away by the trustees under the above arrangement and the prospective increase in the property and its income promises a series of gifts in the future which will many times exceed in the aggregate the original bequest" (Hill 1884, pp. 139–40). Vale (2000, p. 63) points out that Lawrence's project provided "only another twenty apartments and . . . priced itself beyond the means of the most needy."

59. Weeks (1966), Rossiter (1971), and Gelfand (1998).

60. Story (1980) and Harris (1970).

61. Hopkinson (1810), Dunlap (1834, pp. 420–24), Henderson (1911), Norton (1852, p. 34), and Harris (1966).

62. Supported entirely through private subscriptions and gifts because a library was one of the institutions that "our government from its nature does not comprise within its cares," the Boston Athenaeum initially denied access to any "inhabitant of Boston who is not a subscriber." But as early as 1811 its trustees "or their committee" were admitting non-subscribers, and in 1814 it was deploring the "dilapidations resulting from the free access of boys to the reading rooms." See Harris (1962, p. 58) and Quincy (1851, pp. 9, 15, 50, 58).

63. Unlike European universities, American colleges had provided many of their students with dormitories and dining halls. See Rudolph (1962) and Hofstadter (1961).

64. Burke (1982, p. 38).

65. Burke (1982, p. 38) and Geiger (2000, pp. 127–52). Initially, college "libraries" consisted of reading rooms and small reference collections; by 1849 eight colleges had library collections of more than 15,000 books: Harvard, Yale, Brown, Georgetown, Bowdoin, South Carolina, Virginia, and Princeton (Atkins 1991, p. 11). For the other facilities, consider, for example, Yale's Trumbull Picture Gallery (1832), Sheffield Scientific School (1861), the Peabody Museum, (1866), and Dwight Hall for the social service activities of undergraduates (1886); the Abbott Lawrence gift for Harvard's Lawrence School of Science (1847), gymnasium (1850), and Bussey and Arnold gifts (1860s–70s) for what became known as the Arnold Arboretum; Columbia's School of Mines (1864); Oberlin's Music Conservatory (1865); and the Hospital of the University of Pennsylvania (1874). And see Kohlstedt (1988). For an account of developments at the University of Pennsylvania in this period, see Thorpe (1904, part II).

66. Wren (1983).

67. The best study of the Presbyterian conflicts of 1837 is Borchert (2009); see also Dorsey (1998).

68. Rossiter (1984, pp. 46–47).

69. *Edmund Jackson* v. *Wendell Phillips & others*, 14 Allen 539, 96 Mass. 539 (1867) at http://masscases.com/cases/sjc/96/96mass539.html.

70. Burke (1982, chapter 3).

71. Kimball and Johnson (2012, p. 250).

72. Anderson (1988).

73. McPherson (1975, pp. 145–48).

74. Kimball and Johnson (2012, p. 250).

75. American Jewish Historical Society Manuscript Catalog at http://data.jewishgen.org/wconnect/wc.dll?jg-jgsys-ajhs_pb-r!!277.

76. Bobinski (1969).

77. Van Slyck (1995).

78. Waterman, Holmes, and Williams (1905, pp. 378–91).

79. Katz, Sullivan, and Beach (1985).

80. See Charles A. Collin, ed. *Revised Statutes of the State of New York*, together with all the other general statutes (except the Civil, Criminal, and Penal codes), as amended and in force on January 1, 1896, vol. 3 (Banks & Brothers, 1896).

81. Katz, Sullivan, and Beach (1985, p. 80).

82. The best account is Clemens (2000).

83. State Board of Charity of Massachusetts (1894, vol. 16, app., p. 2).

84. See, for example, the 524-page third edition of *The New York Charities Directory* (Charity Organization Society of the City of New York 1885).

85. Ginzberg (1990). Historians have also debated the use of endowments to advantage family dynasties and otherwise increase inequality. Story (1980) argued that endowment managers put considerable emphasis on dynastic interests, but Lamoreaux (1994) counters that the investment policies of the Massachusetts Hospital Life Insurance Company and other endowments intelligently promoted New England's general economic development.

86. Anderson (1988).

87. Anderson and Moss (1999, p. 11).

88. In 1831 Mississippi politician and future governor John A. Quitman denounced the "robbery and roguery" of the "stupendous organization of religious societies," with their imposing, well-staffed headquarters in New York City (Claiborne 1860, p. 109). For a characteristic evangelical denunciation of Boston rationalism, see Charles Hodge's complaint that Unitarianism's "coldness" led that city's "pulpits to resound with harangues on Slavery, Spirituous liquors, Capital punishment, Texas, Aesthetics, any thing but Christ," rather than with orthodox Calvinist Christianity (Hodge 1845b, p. 39).

89. On the general question of comparing charitable and religious giving across American regions, see the interesting observations of Burke (2001).

90. See, for example, the essays in Adam (2004) or Pullan (1971).

91. Snyder (2010, p. 153).

Chapter 3

1. One of the earliest influential discussions of the new, large, secular foundations is Ayres (1911).

2. See www.bftx.org/who, viewed May 18, 2012, and Smart (1970).

3. Surveys that discuss the activities of these and other foundations in the early twentieth century include Harrison and Andrews (1946), Andrews (1956), Cuninggim (1972), and Nielsen (1972).

4. For example, Candler (1909), Bryan (1911), and Wormser (1958).

5. Nielsen (1972) makes these critiques most forcefully, emphasizing the misuse of the foundation form for noncharitable purposes in a small number of notable cases.

Lindeman (1936) wrote the most notable earlier critique; also see Coon (1938), Goulden (1971), and Shulman, Brown, and Kahn (1972).

6. The suggestive account of federal regulation of foundations between 1914 and 1934 in Zunz (2011) ignores the wide variation in state regulation of foundations during those years, instead accepting as national the liberal approach of Massachusetts and a few other northern states.

7. Much more attention might be given to foundation consideration of state preferences. The gentle suggestions in Cuninggim (1972) are expanded by Cuninggim's correspondence, especially relating to his leadership of the Danforth Foundation in St. Louis, now in the Ruth Lilly Special Collections and Archives of the University Library at Indiana University–Purdue University in Indianapolis.

8. Kimball and Johnson (2012, p. 250).

9. Karl and Katz (1981).

10. Ayres (1911).

11. Kevles (1977), Geiger (1986), Kohler (1991), Servos (1990), Siegmund-Schultze (2001), Jonas (1989), Kay (1993), Trefil and Hazen (2001), and Cheit and Lobman (1979).

12. Kimball and Johnson (2012, p. 250).

13. Wheatley (2010, p. 3).

14. Among the key discussions of these points are Haskell (1977) and Oleson and Voss (1979).

15. For a discussion of difficulties in evaluating the early work of the Carnegie Institution of Washington, D.C., see Kohler (1991, chapter 2). Criticism of the business and labor practices of Rockefeller's businesses helped persuade Rockefeller and his aides to put their emphasis on grants rather than on direct action.

16. Walsh (1915).

17. Lagemann (2002, pp. 129–30).

18. Fosdick, Pringle, and Pringle (1962, p. 226).

19. See http://hermes.mbl.edu/about/visit/pdf/welcome_to_woods_hole.pdf.

20. Palló (2002, p. 87). As Schneider (2002, p. 4) observes, "The broadest lesson to be learned . . . is the limited ability of the funding agencies to control or predict the influence of their grants." Servos (1996) offers an unusually thorough, thoughtful, and nuanced discussion of the way university faculty and administrators and government officials often redirected corporate and foundation funds. Another case is that of the geographer Jean Gottmann, who won Rockefeller grants for studies in France early in the 1930s, then as a refugee in the United States did important work on what after World War II became the European Coal and Steel Community, predecessor to the European Union, and went on, with support from other foundations, to write the influential *Megalopolis: The Urbanized Northeastern Seaboard of the United States* (Gottmann 1961). For his early Rockefeller support, see David C. Hammack, "Jean Gottmann," an extended oral history interview, Columbia University Oral History Office, 1988.

21. These foundations raised their own questions about the ownership of intellectual capital and of knowledge about nature, about the commercialization of science, and about the relationship of research to economic growth. Berman (2008) and Servos (1996)

are excellent on these matters; among the best discussions of this group of foundations are Apple (1989) on the Wisconsin Alumni Research Foundation; Cornell (2004) and Mowery and Sampat (2001) on the Research Corporation; Metz and Viest (1991) on the Engineering Foundation; Scheiding (2011) on the Chemical Foundation. Clark (2001) describes the Textile Foundation, also created by the U.S. government from assets seized from Germany during World War I, as focused narrowly on the immediate concerns of industry, making it different from its sister Chemical Foundation.

22. Candler (1909), Bryan (1911), Laski (1930), Barzun (1959), Burtchaell (1998), and Hamerow (1987).

23. Weaver (1967, p. 299).

24. Hammack and Wheeler (1994).

25. Stocking (1985, pp. 133–42) writes of anthropology that the "Rockefeller Foundation played a critical role in a major disciplinary transformation." The museum era came to an end, and focus shifted to the "observational study of human behavior in the present."

26. Bulmer (1981, 1984). Influential critiques of Rockefeller influence on sociology and other social sciences include Ross (1991) and Fisher (1993).

27. Oswald (2009).

28. Jowett, Jarvie, and Fuller (1996) and Sproule (1997).

29. Wheatley (2010); on the notion of an "associative state," see Hawley (1974) and Hammack in Hammack and Wheeler (1994, chapter 2).

30. Hammack and Wheeler (1994). On think tanks in general, see Smith (1991).

31. FPK to Adam Leroy Jones, July 23, 1923. Carnegie Corporation of New York Archives, Columbia University, Series III.A, Box 47, Folder 17.

32. Lagemann (1983, pp. 94–121), Hollis (1938), Curti and Nash (1965), and Cheit and Lobman (1979).

33. For a Southern Methodist bishop's impassioned argument against accepting the terms of the Carnegie pensions, see Candler (1909). Watts's *College Handbook* (1975) provides detailed information on the religious affiliations of colleges and universities. Also see Bryan (1911) and Burtchaell (1998).

34. For a concise, detailed account for the colonial period, see McAnear (1952).

35. For a strong statement of the view that English university faculties enjoyed great autonomy, see Douglas and Wildavsky (1978).

36. This was the advice Exxon Educational Foundation President Robert Payton (1988, p. 21) reported he had received from David Riesman.

37. Wechsler (1977).

38. Flexner preferred the Hopkins approach over that used (also with great success) at Harvard Medical School, which did not rely on a full-time medical faculty (Wheatley 1988). For a similar analysis of the contributions of foundations to medicine in Canada, see Fedunkiw (2005).

39. Fox (2010, p. 3).

40. Ettling (1981).

41. Fetter (2006, p. 54), citing the CCMC; Fox (2010, pp. 122–33).

42. Commission on the Costs of Medical Care (1932).

43. Engel (2002, chapter 2, pp. 11–53).

44. Fox (2010, p. 8).

45. Rettig (1977) and Harden (1986).

46. A thoughtful, incisive account is Jackson (1990); also important are Anderson and Moss (1999) and Anderson (1988).

47. See generally Lagemann (1983, 1989). With funding provided by the Cleveland Foundation, Russell Sage Foundation staff conducted the *Cleveland School Survey*, whose twenty-five concise volumes did much to shape debates over big-city public education during the 1920s. See http://books.google.com/books?hl=en&id=zrsVAAAAIAAJ&dq=cleveland+school+survey&printsec=frontcover&source=web&ots=zMQrrHgDAc&sig=jXY-u9_VYSyUVbOhxSBr2QTXbt8#PPA7,M1.

48. On the persistence of Catholic opposition to foundations and endowments well into the mid-twentieth century, see Oates (1995, pp. 132–34) and Perko (1988).

49. General Education Board (1964, p. 49) and Biebel (1976).

50. For an extended discussion of structural explanations for unemployment during the Great Depression, see Bernstein (1989).

51. Walters and Bowman (2010, p. 22).

52. Sealander (1997, p. 32). The Payne Fund, which Sealander does not cite, invested creatively in efforts to understand the impact on young people's morals of movies and other forms of popular culture, as well as in effective efforts to create and enforce Hollywood's restrictive "production code" (Jowett, Jarvie, and Fuller 1996). Of greater controversy, the Pioneer Fund and other foundations supported various aspects of the eugenics movement, again as a way to advance the "social welfare" of the nation as a whole.

53. Sealander (1997, p. 242).

54. For an account of religious conflicts over social welfare in a key state, see Pratt (1967). See also Brown and McKeown (1997) and Wuthnow and Lindsay (2010). Few studies have examined the uses of foundations to support religious social service efforts, but that purpose is emphasized in the brief notes on many foundations, especially in the South, the West, and the Midwest, in such contemporary directories as Harrison and Andrews (1946).

55. For a detailed history of Catholic negotiations for federal funding during the New Deal, see Brown and McKeown (1997, chapter 5).

56. Herman (2008).

57. Sealander (1997, p. 243).

58. Magat (1999).

59. Hammack and Wheeler (1994).

60. Brown and McKeown (1997, p. 43).

61. Hammack and Wheeler (1994) and Wenocur and Reisch (2001, pp. 119–35).

62. Southern (1987), Jackson (1990), and Lagemann (1989, chapter 6).

63. Coffman (1936, p. 136): "In addition to providing grants, foundations encouraged collaboration among agencies working in the child welfare field. Their objective was to consolidate information through affiliations, consultations, and conference participation, in order to create a system that worked together on behalf of children's interests." See also Castle (1992); Hammack (1989).

64. There is no independent study of these W. K. Kellogg Foundation activities, but see the somewhat detailed official account in Powell (1956).

65. Heydemann and Kinsey (2010, p. 221).

66. Quoted by Heydemann and Kinsey (2010, p. 218).

67. On foundation support for the league, see Kuehl and Dunn (1997, p. 132); on the league's budget, see Boudreau (1944).

68. Smith (1994).

69. Sun (1986, pp. 385–86).

70. See www.neareast.org/whoweare/history.

71. Schneider (2002).

72. Bullock (1980) and Ma (1995).

73. Bulmer (1985).

74. Guzzardi (1988).

75. Wang (2007, chapter 3).

76. Pells (1997).

77. Andrew W. Mellon Educational and Charitable Trust (1980) and Cannadine (2006).

78. According to its website, the Samuel H. Kress Foundation gave its notable collection of European paintings "to scores of regional and academic art museums throughout the United States between 1929 and 1961, with the single largest donation reserved for the National Gallery of Art in Washington D.C." See www.kressfoundation.org/collection/repositorylist.aspx?id=72, viewed on January 31, 2009.

79. On its website the Kulas Foundation states that it is devoted to "the encouragement of young musicians, composers, and conductors" and to "helping handicapped children and the blind." It has supported music education at Oberlin, the Cleveland Institute of Music, Baldwin-Wallace College, the Cleveland public schools, and other institutions in northeastern Ohio. "In addition to establishing the Foundation," the website adds, "Mr. Kulas established a trust fund to perpetually support various institutions and organizations that carried highest priorities in the hearts of Mr. and Mrs. Kulas. While some of those trust legacies receive additional support from the Foundation, the trustees attempt to make grants to activities and institutions they feel Mr. and Mrs. Kulas would have found pleasure in supporting if they were still alive." See http://foundationcenter.org/grantmaker/kulas/.

80. See the influential arguments of DiMaggio (1986).

81. A classic discussion is Harris (1966).

82. Aaron (1992).

83. Wuthnow and Lindsay (2010).

84. McPherson (1975, pp. 161–63).

85. Smart (1970, p. 5).

86. For a rich account of conversations with both Jewish and gentile foundation leaders about how to respond to the threat the Nazis posed to Europe's Jews in 1933 and 1934, see Breitman, Stewart, and Hochberg (2007).

87. See www.purina.com/company/Danforth.aspx.

88. Hutchison (1989).

89. Guzzardi (1988).

90. Snow, Soule, and Kriesi (2004).

91. O'Connor (2010).

92. Among the best books on these topics are Critchlow (1996), Clarke (1998), and Gordon (2002). Kiser (1981) does note some support from the Milbank Memorial Fund for research Sanger favored. Meyer (2004) shows how the Brush Foundation, a strong supporter of Planned Parenthood, also provided critical support for a pioneering women's hospital in Cleveland.

Chapter 4

1. Ford Foundation (1950). See www.fordfoundation.org/about-us/history.

2. NASA replaced and greatly expanded the activities of the National Advisory Committee for Aeronautics, which dated from 1915, during World War I.

3. Loss (2011).

4. Yarmolinsky (1977, pp. 764, 766); Loss (2011).

5. Smith and Lipsky (1993).

6. For a vivid demonstration of the issues facing Head Start in Mississippi, see the exchange between Marian Wright and Senator John Stennis in a hearing held by a subcommittee of the U.S. Senate in Jackson, Mississippi, in April, 1967, in Hammack (1998, pp. 422–38).

7. Similar changes also increased the discretion of state and local authorities responsible for programs in fields such as job training, where funding now went for the instruction of individual workers, and substance abuse programs, now reimbursed for the costs of doctor-approved treatment for particular individuals. Other voucher programs, notably food stamps and rent subsidies, increasingly supplemented aid to families with dependent children.

8. Calculated from data in the statistical tables in Council of Economic Advisers (2007).

9. Koleda and National Planning Association (1977, p. 1680).

10. Calculated from Koleda and National Planning Association (1977, p. 1680) and Yarmolinsky (1977, pp. 762, 772).

11. The idea that government spending, or government grants, "crowd out" charitable giving, has received a good deal of attention from economists. This work universally fails to consider the great increase in the scale of the health care, educational, and other services after World War II, partly because the data on which it relies come from recent and short periods of time. The literature is heavily based on the assumption that the purposes of giving can adequately be characterized as seeking to maintain a specific organization at a certain level of income, providing a generic service as efficiently as possible, or enabling the donor to feel a "warm glow" for donating to a generalized charitable purpose. The foundations and donors we have studied are almost always seeking to accomplish quite specific religious, cultural, or social purposes—purposes that often fail to win majority

support in democratically elected legislatures. Reservations about the technical quality of much of this work expressed by Garret and Rhine (2007) are also impressive.

12. In 1951 the U.S. Court of Appeals for the Third Circuit upheld New York University's claim that profits from the Mueller Spaghetti Company, owned by the university and operated to earn income for its law school, should be exempt from taxation. The decision stated that the policy enforced by courts for thirty years had been to grant tax exemption on income earned by bona fide charities for charitable objectives "without regard to the method of procuring the funds necessary to effectuate the objective." In such cases, the rule had been "that the benefit from revenue is outweighed by the benefit to the general public welfare gained through the encouragement of charity." *C. F. Mueller Co.* v. *Commissioner of Internal Revenue*, 3d Cir. 1951, 190 F.2d 120.

13. For a contemporary discussion, see Eaton (1951).

14. On the Shubert case, see Hirsch (1998). Boys Inc. yielded $1 million for charity, but provoked criticism from Christian groups that opposed gambling; a few years later IRS disapproval prevented the addition of tracks in Illinois and Michigan (Burrough 2009, p. 242).

15. A few years later, *Time* magazine reported on a congressional investigation into the tax-exempt Americans Building Constitutionally Foundation that was, in fact, not a foundation at all. This "foundation" had—for a substantial fee—helped more than 250 people put their assets and their affairs into "foundations" designed to avoid taxes and—in part—to assure that they were not taxed to support U.S aid "to communist countries." *Time*, January 5, 2008 (www.time.com/time/magazine/article/0,9171,712079-2,00.html), and August 8, 1969 (www.time.com/time/magazine/article/0,9171,941298-1,00.html). *United States of America and Alan D. Cornue, Special Agent, Petitioners-Appellees* v. *Robert D. Hayes et al., Respondents-Appellants,* no. 16878, U.S. Court of Appeals (7th Cir., February 19, 1969) (http://bulk.resource.org/courts.gov/c/F2/408/408.F2d.932.16878.html).

16. *Business Week,* May 7, 1960, p. 153, quoted in Troyer (2000, p. 52). The controversy turned in part on a critical ambiguity: while some donors intended to use their foundations to avoid taxes and retain control for personal family or business purposes, others sought to control the legitimately charitable use of their gifts. Using a foundation to avoid taxes was illegal; an IRS investigation put the organization out of business, and those who had followed its advice had to pay back taxes and fines. See Shorter (2000) for an interesting discussion of the uses to which Joseph P. Kennedy put his foundation in the 1940s and 1950s.

17. Davis (2007).

18. *New York Times,* July 23, 1964.

19. Treasury found this fault in just over 100 foundations, less than 10 percent of all included in this study. Troyer (2000), citing U.S. Senate, Committee on Finance, 89 Cong. 1 sess. (1965). See also Troyer (1966).

20. Nielsen (1972, pp. 168, 143, 149, 319). Similarly, Marcus and Hall (1992) found very few cases of "dynastic" families who made abusive use of foundations. For cases that seem to have crossed the line, see Shorter (2000) on the Kennedy family's foundation and the discussions in Nielsen (1972) of the Moody and Irvine foundations. For general

discussions of the impact of the 1969 Tax Reform Act, see Clotfelter (1985), Margo (1992), and Simon (2000).

21. In urging an investigation of foundations in 1953, Congressman Reece asserted of foundations, "Here lies the story of how communism and socialism are financed in the United States" (U.S. House of Representatives 1954). His research aide had cited Gunnar Myrdal's *American Dilemma* as objectionable; see Dodd (1954).

22. Davidson (1998, p. 19).

23. Johnson's statement quoted from the *Congressional Record* in Davidson (1998); Davidson's essay offers a detailed study of Johnson's reasoning. Texas governor W. Lee O'Daniel's use of a tax-exempt organization to fund his election materials attracted critical attention from a U.S. Senate committee in 1944; he had defeated Johnson for the Senate in 1941 (see U.S. Senate, Special Committee on Campaign Expenditures 1945). On the Kennedy administration's concern about right-wing extremism, see Andrew (2002, chapters 1, 6); on the response of mainstream foundations, see Brilliant (2000, chapters 3, 4).

24. Moynihan (1969, pp. 102–05) and Koebel (1998, p. 100).

25. Quotations from Patman's 1962 "Chairman's Report" in Walsh (1963, p. 371).

26. For well-informed contemporary accounts, see Walsh (1963), Lankford (1964), and Andrews (1969).

27. Magat (1999, p. 51).

28. Fremont-Smith (2004, pp. 47–80) provides an excellent overview of these investigations and regulations.

29. Community foundations grew on average at a rate of almost 15 percent per year in the 1980s, 19 percent in the 1990s, and 10 percent since 2001; independent foundations grew at just under 13 percent annually between 1981 and 2001, and just over 2 percent since 2001. Calculated by the authors from the Foundation Center; see http://foundationcenter.org/findfunders/statistics/.

30. For the difficulty of evaluating the impact of the 1969 act, see Clotfelter (1985) and Margo (1992). Margo shows (pp. 214–16) that new foundations appeared more rapidly than ever in the twenty years after World War II, and that the 1970s and early 1980s saw fewer new foundations and much less asset growth.

31. Merz and Frankel (1995); Lampkin and Stern (2003). Advocates of community and supporting foundations respond that funds in poor areas can and do attract donations, and—quite separately—that by persuading affluent people to continue to use public universities, public schools, and other facilities, they help maintain broad support for public services.

32. The very considerable impact of the decline in the stock market on the Ford Foundation is apparent in Merrimon Cuninggim's notes of his extensive discussions with the foundation's leaders in the early 1970s; Cuninggim Papers, Ruth Lilly Special Collections Library, Indiana University–Purdue University at Indianapolis. It was in this period that the Ford Foundation under McGeorge Bundy pushed the idea that foundations should invest their endowments more actively in search of higher returns.

33. A group of over 3,000 family foundations held a total of just 11 percent; 7,000 very small foundations held less than $50,000 each in assets for a total of less than $100

million. In 1960 just 737 foundations were known to have assets of $1 million or more, and just ten reported assets above $100 million—though fuller reporting over the next two decades suggests that four or five others belonged in that elite group. Foundation Library Center (1960, pp. x, xv, xxv). Of the 25,000 foundations reporting to the Foundation Center in 1971, more than 11,000 held assets of $50,000 or less, whereas only 450 held $10 million or more (and could thus spend on average $500,000 annually).

34. Dwight Macdonald's *Ford Foundation* (1956) remains an effective celebration. The Ford Foundation quickly reduced its own size by giving away a considerable share of its assets in very large grants to universities and other charities in the 1950s and 1960s, by underwriting substantial portions of the core expenses of more than fifty national coordinating organizations in fields ranging from education to the arts to public affairs and civil rights, and by creating and endowing the Fund for the Advancement of Education, the Fund for Adult Education, and the Fund for the Republic as entirely independent entities.

35. The most active of these included the Mellon family's Avalon and Old Dominion funds, the Houston Endowment, the Rockefeller Brothers Fund, and the Luce Foundation. In the 1960s and 1970s large bequests moved the Robert Wood Johnson, John D. and Catherine MacArthur, Andrew W. Mellon, and Charles Stewart Mott foundations into the very top group by size as well as by activity. Galveston's Moody Foundation and southern California's Irvine Foundation, though now very large, did little in these years and kept low profiles. The best surveys of 1946 and 1960 listed Moody and Irvine—along with the Houston Endowment, the John A. Hartford, and other foundations—as having modest or unspecified assets, but from the later 1960s on they were listed as having among the largest endowments in the nation. Harrison and Andrews (1946), Foundation Library Center (1960), Nielsen (1972), Cuninggim (1972), and Simon (1987, table 2).

36. The General Education Board, the International Education Board, and the Laura Spelman Rockefeller Memorial had been consolidated into the Rockefeller Foundation in the late 1920s. The Peabody Fund, the Julius Rosenwald Fund, the Children's Fund of Michigan, Pittsburgh's Maurice and Laura Falk Foundation, and the Chemical Foundation spent out their funds in the 1940s or 1950s (Dillingham 1989, Richards and Norton 1957, Ascoli 2006, and Starrett 1966). New York's large James Foundation and the substantial Leonard C. Hanna Fund of Cleveland, created in 1957, dispersed all their funds by the early 1970s. New York's Winifred Masterson Burke Relief Foundation became Burke Rehabilitation Hospital and Burke Medical Research Institute. In the wake of the passage of Medicare and Medicaid, the Murry and Leonie Guggenheim Foundation closed its notable network of New York City dental clinics for children and disbursed its assets to Mt. Sinai Hospital, New York University, and several other universities and hospitals. For the Murry and Leonie Guggenheim Foundation, see *Foundation News*, vol. 1415 (1973, p. 34). For Wilder, see Jarchow (1981).

37. Responding to the great changes the New Deal brought to social welfare and housing, the Russell Sage Foundation ended its commitments to the social work profession and the Regional Plan of New York, sold its headquarters building and its model housing communities of Sunnyside Gardens and Forest Hills in Queens, New York, and focused on grants for social science (Hammack and Wheeler 1994). The Surdna Foundation and

associated Andrus family funds of Westchester County, New York, having established an orphanage in the 1920s and a home for the aged in the 1950s, adopted a more general focus from the 1970s. Chicago's Chapin Hall (Cmiel 1995 and Brown and Garg 1997), St. Paul's Amherst H. Wilder Foundation, the McGregor Foundation near Cleveland, and other social service charities also shifted entirely, or in part, to grantmaking. The China Medical Board, the Luce Foundation, and other funds shifted their emphases to other parts of Asia and to China-related work in the United States after the Communist Party consolidated its control of mainland China in the late 1940s. For the China Medical Board, see www.chinamedicalboard.org/history.php; for Luce, see Guzzardi (1988); for others, see their organizational websites. We don't know of a comprehensive study of such changes among smaller foundations, but foundations listed in one major survey are not infrequently missing from later compilations. The Louis D. Beaumont Foundation is one example. Launched with $16 million in 1943, by the 1970s it was "the largest private foundation in Cleveland," according to the *Encyclopedia of Cleveland History*; following its donor's instructions, it spent out its assets, then over $30 million, in 1977. See http://ech.case.edu/ech-cgi/article.pl?id=LDBF. Cleveland's much smaller Dauby Charitable Fund, which held about $2.2 million in 1982, similarly disbursed its assets, in 1988.

38. Nielsen (1972) and Cuninggim (1972); see especially the exchange between Jeffrey Hart and John G. Simon in Heimann (1973).

39. Scott (2000, especially chapter 7), Stevens (1998), and Lave, Lave, and Leinhart (1974). For Hill-Burton expenditures, see U.S. Congress, Senate Committee on Labor and Public Welfare, Subcommittee on Health (1973).

40. MacDonald (1956, pp. 4–5, 167–72) and Sutton (1987, p. 83). Value in 2010 obtained from www.measuringworth.com/ppowerus/result.php, using the consumer price index, on August 20, 2010. According to the same website, a gift that amounted to the same share of the gross domestic product in 2010 would come to $16.3 billion.

41. Sutton (1987, p. 51).

42. After protracted negotiations, the IRS and the Hughes Medical Institute agreed in 1987 to a settlement under which the institute is legally classified as a "medical research organization" under the provisions of the U.S. Tax Code of 1950; in addition, the institute agreed to pay $35 million in back taxes and to spend $500 million over and above the minimum required under its status as a medical research organization; *Nature*, vol. 326 (March 19, 1987), p. 236; www.hhmi.org/about/.

43. Geiger (1993, pp. 110–16, 219) and Graham and Diamond (1997). By the late 1960s, as Geiger notes, the Ford Foundation's emphasis had shifted away from the elite universities, partly because it had achieved a remarkable proportion of its objectives, partly because it had become clear that federal funding to sustain new initiatives in elite universities would not be forthcoming, and partly because the foundation had shifted its priorities.

44. On support from the M. D. Anderson Foundation, the Houston Endowment, and others for the Texas Medical Center, see Elliott (2004).

45. Merrimon Cuninggim discusses the Danforth gifts in correspondence available in the Cuninggim Papers Philanthropy Archives of the Ruth Lilly Special Collections and Archives at Indiana University–Purdue University, Indianapolis. For other cases, we have relied on the Indiana University Center on Philanthropy's lists of very large grants and

on a list developed by the *Chronicle of Higher Education*, reprinted at http://web.mit.edu/
newsoffice/nr/2000/neurogifts.html.

46. Wheatley (2010).

47. See www.current.org/pbpb/statistics/FordExpend.html.

48. Mitgang (2000).

49. Gelfand (1998).

50. Ford Foundation (1986, p. 15).

51. Markusen and King (2003, p. 15).

52. Critchlow (1995) is an independent account.

53. Reeves (1969).

54. The work of Resources for the Future and of the Vera Institute of Justice can best
be followed through their many publications; the Population Council and the Fund for
the Republic also have produced many publications.

55. Frumkin and Kaplan (2010) and Wheatley (2010). As late as 1967 Warren
Weaver organized a celebrated book around the notion that foundations functioned
chiefly within the research university world.

56. For the remarkable story of the Gordon Conferences, see www.grc.org/support.
aspx and www.frontiersofscience.org. For the Chemical Heritage Foundation (actually
an operating nonprofit, not a foundation), see www.chemheritage.org/about/history/
index.aspx. For the American Chemical Society, see http://portal.acs.org/portal/acs/corg/
content?_nfpb=true&_pageLabel=PP_TRANSITIONMAIN&node_id=226&use_
sec=false&sec_url_var=region1&__uuid=8650faa2-8b15-4d8d-88a1-bd2e00c59eb2
and for its Chemical Abstracts Service, which generates substantial income, see http://
cas.org/aboutcas/index.html.

57. Rettig (1977), Strickland (1972), Goudsmit (1998), Sharpless (1997), and
Chambré (2006). Foundations played a role in the process described by Rettig (2004),
by which the U.S. National Institutes of Health became more and more complex: "Insis-
tent political demands from disease-oriented interest groups, coinciding with the personal interests of legislative and executive branch sponsors, have resulted in the proliferation of new institutes, centers, and program offices attached to the Office of the Director.
. . . The latter, for example, include AIDS research, women's health, disease prevention,
and social and behavioral research. Arguably, the proliferation of new entities reflects the
failure of the existing structure to respond adequately to legitimate health needs of the
public, especially in times of a growing NIH budget."

58. Castle (1992).

59. In university extension as in other fields, foundations provided a tiny fraction of
total support. In the mid-1980s, according to a careful historian, federal funds provided
about a third of the money available for extension services, and state funds accounted for
nearly half, while foundation and other private contributions amounted to just 3 percent
(Rasmussen 1989, p. 9).

60. The Macy Conferences are still inadequately documented, but the American
Society for Cybernetics provides key details at www.asc-cybernetics.org/foundations/
history2.htm#MacySum.

61. Davis (2007).

62. Link (1997 p. 374).

63. See www.hluce.org/hrluceprofship.aspx.

64. Richardson (1981, p. 13), quoted in McCarthy (1985, p. 7).

65. McCarthy (1985) and Lazerson (1998).

66. O'Connor (2001, pp. 102–03).

67. Schlossman, Sedlak, and Weschler (1987), Hammack and Wheeler (1994), O'Connor (2001), and Fox (2010).

68. Balakrishnan and Grown (1999).

69. Brilliant (1992, p. 35) and Hammack (2002)

70. Merz and Frankel (1995) and Lampkin and Stern (2003).

71. Toepler (2010).

72. Toepler (2010). In 1999 the Pew Charitable Trusts began to support the RAND Corporation and other work in this direction; the Rockefeller and Wallace foundations have underwritten some notable related work.

73. DiMaggio (1986, p. 131).

74. Smith (2010).

75. McCaughey (1984), Szanton (2004), and Wilcox (2006).

76. Martin (1981).

77. Ford Foundation (1979, p. 177) states that it gave this program $38.5 million in its first twenty-one years.

78. See the Hertz Foundation (www.hertzfoundation.org/dx/foundation/history.aspx), Thomas J. Watson Foundation (www.watsonfellowship.org/site/what/description/history.html), and the Foundation Center (http://foundationcenter.org/grantmaker/beinecke/). For an excellent discussion of postgraduate fellowships, see Ilchman, Ilchman, and Tolar (2004).

79. Extensive documentation of the Danforth Foundation's engagement with African American colleges and community organizations is contained in the Merrimon Cuniggim papers in the Philanthropy Archives of the Ruth Lilly Archives and Special Collections at the Indiana University–Purdue University Indianapolis Library.

80. For the Starr Foundation, see www.starrfoundation.org/priorities.html.

81. The University of North Carolina at Chapel Hill offers a particularly complete index of its scholarship funds, with indication of those from foundations, at https://cfx.research.unc.edu/funding/search_results.cfm.

82. O'Connor (2001, 2010).

83. Eisenmann (2006, p. 97). O'Connor (2001, p. 279) similarly argues that foundation-funded studies of poverty during the 1960s failed "to make gender and race central issues for substantive research."

84. Jacobson (1984) and Regenstreif and others (2003).

85. Wheatley (2010), Frumkin and Kaplan (2010), Bowen and Bok (2000), and Cole and Barber (2003).

86. On the Knight Commission and its impact, see Shulman and Bowen (2002, chapter 14).

87. The Edward W. Hazen Foundation's sustained engagement with religion in colleges and universities had emphasized "raising the consciousness of faculty,

administrators, and promising graduate students about the importance of religion and values" (Bass 1989, pp. 59–60). For a very good general account, see Sloan (1994); also useful is Hart (1992). The Danforth-commissioned study is Underwood (1969). Hammond (1982, pp. 113, 114) discusses flaws in this evaluation and the reaction of one Danforth trustee, who asserted that he could understand nothing in the evaluation's first volume; in future he vowed not to touch social research "with a ten-foot pole." Whatever the Danforth board thought of the evaluation, as Hammond notes, after the study it withdrew "funding from nearly all its higher education programs."

88. Smart (1970) and Elliott (2004, p. 182).

89. Indiana University Center on Philanthropy lists of large grants noted above.

90. Engerman (2009, p. 80). On area studies, also see McCaughey (1984) and Szanton (2004), as well as the works discussed in Engerman's quite comprehensive review essay (2003).

91. Biehn (2008).

92. Robinson (1984, pp. 78, 80).

93. This topic is inadequately addressed in the existing literature, but see, for example, the acknowledgments in such works as *The Authoritarian Personality* (Adorno and others 1950), *The Nature of Prejudice* (Allport 1954), *Communism, Conformity, and Civil Liberties* (Stouffer 1955), and *The New American Right* (Bell 1955), as well as Perl (1948), Svonkin (1997), Steele (1989), and Jackson (2000).

94. Rooks (2006).

95. Eisenmann (2005, pp. 153–60).

96. Isaac (2011, p. 226). Isaac's essay is an excellent introduction to this recent work.

97. Robinson (1984, p. 76) estimated that university salary and sabbatical support for faculty research amounted in 1983 to $305 million, far more than the $25 million or so provided by the ten foundations most active in the field.

98. Robinson (1984).

99. In 1980 nonpublic elementary and preschools enrolled just 12 percent of all children; nonpublic secondary schools enrolled just 9 percent.

100. Tyack and Cuban (1995).

101. Lemann (1999).

102. Nachtigal (1972); see also http://apcentral.collegeboard.com/apc/public/program/history/8019.html.

103. Lagemann (1983).

104. We have to add that by the early 2000s it was not clear whether state governments or school districts would continue the modest additional payments to the salaries of "certified" teachers. Ballou and Podgursky (2000) offer a critical appraisal of the movement for national teacher certification.

105. Conant (1963) and Ravitch (1985, p. 230).

106. Clifford and Guthrie (1990, pp. 175–86) offer a thoughtful review of the Ford Foundation's master of arts in teaching programs. Coley and Thorpe (1985) review the MAT effort from Ford's perspective; see Sykes (1984). For the Ford Foundation's own evaluation at the time, see Nachtigal (1972).

107. Lazerson and others (1985) offers a thoughtful account of the new curricula. For an unsympathetic discussion of the "new social studies" that reveals some of the sources of resistance, see Evans (2004, chapters 5 and 6).

108. Keppel (1966), Howe (1993), Sizer (1984), and Tyack (2003).

109. Bradley Commission on History in Schools (2000).

110. Domanico and others (2000) and Cervone (2007).

111. Jonathan Kozol, Colin Greer, and Ivan Illich, for example, did not acknowledge foundation support. The Ford Foundation's Center for the Study of Democratic Institutions did support John Holt, and the Carnegie Corporation of New York underwrote Charles Silberman's widely read discussion of the "open classroom" (Holt 1964 and Silberman 1970).

112. Rogers (1990, p. 150).

113. Clemens and Chyi (2010).

114. Bodwell (2006) closely studied the funding of the provoucher movement in Cleveland, Ohio, that led to the U.S. Supreme Court decision in *Zelman* v. *Simmons-Harris*, 536 US 6392002 (2002).

115. Fenton (1966), Tyack (2003), and Lazerson and Fuhrman (2005). This last point is also based partly on the observations of one of the authors: after earning a master of arts in teaching degree under David Tyack at Reed College, David Hammack worked for several years on social studies curricula projects in the Newton, Massachusetts, high schools, with the Chicago-based Anthropology Curriculum Study project, and with the National Faculty, before consulting with the Educational Testing Service and the National Assessment of Educational Progress.

116. Heifitz, Kania, and Kramer (2004).

117. Morris (2009). On the Commonwealth Fund's extensive investments in psychiatric services for children during the 1930s and 1940s, see Bain (1990). Bryson (2002) offers a critical view of the child study work supported by the Rockefeller philanthropies and the Josiah Macy Jr. Foundation.

118. Brown and Garg (1997).

119. Bielefeld and Chu (2010) and Blank and Haskins (2001).

120. O'Connor (2001, p. 132).

121. Moynihan (1969, p. 40) notes that this formulation implied that Ylvisaker had identified those who stood against his foundation's purposes and needed to be "thrown off balance."

122. O'Connor (2001, 2010).

123. Levy (2005, p. 42) asserts that "as late as 1986" just a half dozen foundations accounted for two-thirds of all international funding and that Ford, Rockefeller, and Carnegie together provided 90 percent of U.S. foundation funds for Latin America during the 1970s. For an excellent overall account of the activities of the largest foundations concerned with international affairs in the 1940s and 1950s, see Ninkovich (1982).

124. Heydemann and Kinsey (2010).

125. As Adam Yarmolinsky put it in 1977, "Private foreign aid is increasingly a process of helping the less developed countries to pursue their own courses of development.

Research and education in international affairs is increasingly a matter of mutual education and transnational study. And these developments are in addition to and interwoven with the joint pursuit of common problems across international boundaries." (Yarmolinsky 1977, p. 762).

126. Yarmolinsky (1977, pp. 761–62).

127. Critics have raised many objections to the green revolution—notably for reducing biodiversity and reinforcing inequality—but the best studies conclude that in the short and intermediate run, at least, it did increase the supply and decrease the cost of key foodstuffs in ways that benefited entire populations. For critical discussions, see Ruttan (2004) and Hazell and Ramasamy (1991). Freebairn (1995) concludes, "Studies done by Western developed-country authors, those employing an essay approach, and those looking at a multicountry region are most likely to conclude that income inequalities increased [as a result of the green revolution]. By contrast, work done by Asian-origin authors, with study areas located in India or the Philippines and using the case method are more likely to conclude that increasing inequality is not associated with the new technology." Writing as an economist, Timmer (2005) offers a very persuasive positive evaluation.

128. MacDonald (1956) and Magat (1979) provide excellent authorized discussions of Ford Foundation purposes in this period. Sutton (1987) provides an exceptionally well-informed overview. Curti and Nash (1965) included Ford in its comprehensive discussion of the history of American philanthropy abroad. Korey (2007) is an important recent addition. Levy (2005) provides a thoughtful, detailed evaluation of Ford's involvement with Latin American universities.

129. Curti (1965, p. 581).

130. Ford Foundation (1950, p. 11).

131. Levy (2005, p. 36).

132. For a detailed account of such matters at the Ford Foundation, see Sutton (1987). In addition to the Rockefeller and Ford foundations, others with substantial international programs in these decades included the Carnegie Corporation of New York, the Lilly Endowment, the W. K. Kellogg Foundation, and the Clark Foundation. Whyte (2004, p. 19), an excellent recent overview of "capacity building for development," emphasizes the general focus of foundations and governments alike, during the 1960s, on "institution building"—creating new organizations, often based on "models transplanted from [the] North" and led by people trained in "northern" universities.

133. Graddy-Gamel (2006).

134. Wilford (2008).

135. Foundations play a small role in the very comprehensive review of American philanthropy directed across borders after World War II offered by Curti (1965). On the Christian Children's Fund, see Tise (1992).

136. David Oshinsky, review of *The Liberal Conspiracy* in the *New York Times,* August 27, 1989; see www.nytimes.com/1989/08/27/books/cranky-integrity-on-the-left.html.

137. Shils (1997, p. 211).

138. Berghahn (1999) emphasizes America's international reputation as a source of foundation support for arts organizations, including the German-based émigré ensemble, Philharmonia Hungarica.

139. Yarmolinsky (1977, p. 762) and Whyte (2004, pp. 19, 49–57).

140. Yarmolinsky (1977, pp. 771–75). Foundation money for international assistance generally went "to foundation field staff and to universities and independent research institutions in the U.S. and overseas" (Yarmolinsky (1977, p. 774).

141. Ebrahim (2003) provides an exceptionally thoughtful account of interactions between donors and recipients across borders.

142. Korey (2007). While government officials far more than the foundations had insisted that America's diplomatic interests required serious advances in civil rights within the United States, the Ford Foundation, the Cleveland Foundation, and the Taconic Foundation were no doubt partly influenced by international concerns in their voter registration and other grants related to civil rights (Wasby 1995, p. 92). Dudziak (2000) cites no foundations in showing the many ways in which diplomatic considerations prompted government officials to press for civil rights in the United States.

143. Yarmolinsky noted, for example, "When AID and the World Bank went about setting up the Consultative Group on International Agricultural Research, John Hannah, the AID Administrator, and Robert McNamara, president of the World Bank, insisted that both the Ford and Rockefeller Foundations commit themselves to a continuing role in the management and guidance of the research centers, involving foundation staff as well as foundation dollars" (Yarmolinsky 1975, p. 768).

144. Heydemann and Kinsey (2010).

145. Morrow (2006); for lists of the nearly two dozen "coproduced" country-specific versions of *Sesame Street* and of the foundation, corporate, and government funders involved, see www.sesameworkshop.org.

146. Prewitt (1999).

147. Bundy (1974).

148. We have seen that then-senator Lyndon B. Johnson initiated the explicit prohibition of tax-exempt status to charities that sought to "influence legislation" as well as "those who intervene in any political campaign on behalf of any candidate for any public office." According to a well-informed member of the Treasury Department staff at the time, some of the 1969 act's more specific restrictions on policy-related foundation activity "stemmed, primarily at least, from committee questioning of Mac [McGeorge] Bundy about Ford Foundation grants. . . . A Ford grant to the Congress on Racial Equality for voter registration, used by CORE for registration in heavily African-American areas of Cleveland during Carl Stokes's closely contested campaign for Mayor, led to the special restrictions on foundation voter registration activities. Some sloppiness in the management of funds by Ford grantees in the Oceanhill-Brownsville school decentralization controversy in New York City had much to do with the expenditure responsibility rules. The Oceanhill-Brownsville grants and perhaps other Ford grants appear also to have lent impetus to the limitation on foundation influencing of legislation" (Troyer 2000).

149. For details of the current regulations, see www.irs.gov/irm/part7/irm_07-027-019.html. The regulations emphasize that tax-exempt funds are not to be used to support candidates for election or—with regard to specific legislation—to influence legislative or regulatory decisionmakers through "direct" lobbying, or to influence the general public's view of specific legislation through "grassroots" lobbying. The prohibitions do not

apply to efforts to engage decisionmakers in executive offices, or to underwrite legal work related to court cases. For leads into the details, see Maskell (2008).

150. Ford Foundation (1974b) and Rooks (2006, chapters 1, 3, 4).

151. U.S. Internal Revenue Service, Exempt Organizations Division (1984).

152. Winks (1997), Sellars (1999), Wheeler (1985), and Endicott (1993).

153. Fisk, Hesterman, and Thorburn (2000).

154. Gottlieb (1993, 2005), Winks (1997), Richard King Mellon Foundation (2002), and Delfin and Tang (2007).

155. The Carnegie Endowment for International Peace and the Peace Foundation had of course long worked in this field, but Hiroshima and Nagasaki and the rapid development of the Soviet as well as American hydrogen bomb greatly raised the stakes.

156. More accurately, in the 1980s these foundations returned to a field that the Russell Sage Foundation, often supported by the Twentieth Century Fund, had underwritten before the 1950s, work that the Carnegie Corporation had continued with key initial funding for the Foundation Center and that the Ford Foundation had expanded with grants for research on foundation economics and history, and that some of the Rockefeller funds had taken up in the 1960s (O'Neill 1998, Brilliant 2000, and Hammack 2006).

157. Hammack and Heydemann (2009).

158. For a very good review, see Rich (2004).

159. Examples of foundations that served as policy think tanks include the office Andrew Carnegie set up to promote public libraries, the Milbank Memorial Fund (1905), the Russell Sage Foundation (1907), the Carnegie Endowment for International Peace (1910), the World Peace Foundation (1910), and the Twentieth Century Fund (1911). Early think tanks supported by foundations include the Bureau of Municipal Research (1907), the Brookings Institution (1916), the Hoover Institution (1919), the Regional Plan Association of New York (1921), the Committee for Economic Development (1942), the Rand Corporation (1946), the Council on Foreign Relations (1921), the American Enterprise Institute (1943), and several others that, like the National Housing Association (1910), have fallen from view through closure or reorganization.

160. Pressman and Wildavsky (1984).

161. O'Connor (2010) and Minkoff and Agnone (2010).

162. Vinovskis (2008, pp. 26–31). Vinovskis (1999) offers a tough critique of studies of Head Start's effectiveness.

163. It would be wrong to leave the impression that foundations provided the only support for these "progressive" think tanks: some of them are closely associated with organized labor or with larger political groups and movements, and many of them receive much of their funding from individuals. For the often conflicted relations between foundations and organized labor, see Magat (1999); for the rise of "checkbook" democracy see Skocpol (1999).

164. The literature on the War on Poverty is too vast and controversial to review here. For these comments, see Pressman and Wildavsky (1984), O'Connor (2001), Magat (1979), Tittle (1992), and Carson (1995).

165. Bundy in Ford Foundation (1974a). Shiao (2005) argues that foundations had some impact on racial preferences in Cleveland and San Francisco.

166. Eisenmann (2005) and Wasby (1995).

167. U.S. Internal Revenue Service, Exempt Organizations Division (1984).

168. On the general expansion of legal rights during the civil rights era, see Silber (2001). Brilliant (2000) offers much detail on the foundation response to the Tax Reform Act of 1969. Hall (1992) proposes a critical perspective.

169. On the Local Initiatives Support Corporation, see www.lisc.org/section/aboutus/ history. In addition to its own activities, LISC has spun off several substantial entities that raise funds for community economic development and provide technical support to local community development organizations; some of these also obtain funds from foundations, as well as from various government programs and from private investors.

170. Phillips-Fein (2009, chapter 2). The Volker Foundation did not provide information to contemporary foundation directories, including the important survey of Harrison and Andrews (1946). But if its assets remained so large that it could end in the early 1950s by giving as much to the Hoover Institution as Phillips-Fein reports, it would have ranked in the top fifty.

171. Excellent studies of foundation support for conservative causes include Miller (2005) and Stefancic and Delgado (1996). Such support was by no means limited to a small group of conservative foundations. In his 1974 report Bundy emphasized the breadth of Ford's policy-related activities by noting its subsidies to the relatively conservative journal, *The Public Interest*; the Lilly Endowment made possible the Hudson Institute's move to Indianapolis.

172. O'Connor (2010). Overall, social movement philanthropy has been fraught with tension and contradictions. "Liberal" foundations have had far less influence in this field than is sometimes thought, as the visibility of a few obscures the hesitation of many to become active advocates of one cause or another. Yet through support for some of the most influential recent social movements—those for racial and gender equality, as well as for conservative, and frequently, Christian renewal—a small number of foundations did create influential templates for activist philanthropy. The result, as Alice O'Connor and other critics see it, was to subdue militant voices and to encourage moderate actions that could bring social movements into the mainstream. The neoconservative foundations—Olin, Bradley, and others—by contrast, made more direct investments designed to create the think tanks, build intellectual leadership, and develop programs for action.

173. Congleton and others (2010) offer a very able discussion of the current literature, but do not note any investigation of the possibility that support for the welfare state is enhanced by the ability to use government funds to pay for health care or education at service providers closely affiliated with, or controlled by, religious or other minority cultural groups.

174. Sutton (1987, pp. 58–59).

175. As we have noted, precedents included, for example, the Russell Sage Foundation's work in the fields of social welfare, public education, and regional planning, the Rockefeller's and other funders' support of the National Bureau of Economic Research, the Brookings Institution's work on public administration, and the Milbank and Commonwealth Fund's work on public health.

176. Cobb and Rixford (1998) provide an excellent brief overview of the social indicators movement.

177. Fox (2010).

178. Mosley and Galaskiewicz (2010).

179. In a notable case worth more attention than it has received, the Ford Foundation provided funds through community foundations to help officials in many cities develop ways to deal with the AIDS crisis of the 1970s and 1980s and to avoid politicizing the matter (Gibbons 1999 and Funders Concerned about AIDS 2003).

Chapter 5

1. Because foundations were not then required to publish audited financial information, the following list of the fifty largest in 1945 must be based on our best estimates from a variety of sources, most notably Harrison and Andrews (1946), but also including later lists and accounts that provide more information in later years, including Foundation Library Center (1960), Goulden (1971), Cuninggim (1972), Foundation Center (1981), and Keele and Kiger (1984). In order of decreasing size, by our estimates: Rockefeller Foundation (N.Y.), Carnegie Corporation of New York (N.Y.), W. K. Kellogg Foundation (Mich.), Lilly Endowment Inc. (Ind.), Kresge Foundation (Mich.), Ford Foundation (Mich.), Charles Stewart Mott Foundation (Mich.), Duke Endowment (N.C.), Board of Directors, City Trusts of Philadelphia (Pa.), Alfred P. Sloan Foundation (N.Y.), Danforth Foundation (Mo.), predecessor funds of the Andrew W. Mellon Foundation (Avalon of New York, Old Dominion of Virginia), Houston Endowment Inc. (Tex.), Carnegie Institution of Washington, Charles Hayden Foundation (N.Y.), Commonwealth Fund (N.Y.), James Irvine Foundation (Calif.), Bernice Bishop Estate (Hawaii), James Foundation of New York (N.Y.), Gannett Foundation, Inc. (N.Y.), Amherst H. Wilder (Minn.), Surdna Foundation, Inc. (N.Y.), Moody Foundation (Tex.), Northwest Area Foundation (Minn.), (Louis W. and Maud Hill Family Foundation 1960), Rockefeller Brothers Fund, Inc. (N.Y.), Charles F. Kettering Foundation (Ohio), John A. Hartford Foundation, Inc. (N.Y.), Henry Luce Foundation, Inc. (N.Y.), China Medical Board, Inc. (N.Y.), Olin Foundation, Inc. (N.Y.), Wisconsin Alumni Research Foundation (Wisc.), Clark Foundation (N.Y.), Longwood Foundation, Inc. (Del.), Mayo Properties Association (Minn.), John Simon Guggenheim Memorial Foundation (N.Y.), M. D. Anderson Foundation (Tex.), Carnegie Foundation for the Advancement of Teaching (N.Y.), Field Foundation, Inc. (Ill.), General Education Board (N.Y.), New York Community Trust (N.Y.), John and Mary R. Markle Foundation (N.Y.), Russell Sage Foundation (N.Y.), El Pomar Foundation (Col.), Nemours Foundation (Del.), A. W. Mellon Charitable Trust (Pa.), Jarvie Commonweal Service of the Board of National Missions of the Presbyterian Church in the USA (Pa.), National Foundation for Infantile Paralysis, Buhl Foundation (Pa.), Juilliard Musical Foundation (N.Y.), LeTourneau Foundation (Tex.), and American Missionary Association (N.Y.).

2. The thirteen foundations still in the top fifty in 2010 included, in order of size in 1946, Rockefeller, Carnegie Corporation, W. K. Kellogg, Lilly, Kresge, Ford, C. S.

Mott, Duke, A. P. Sloan, A. W. Mellon, The Houston Endowment, Irvine, and New York Community Trust. By 2010 more than a dozen of the largest of the new foundations that had emerged after 1945 were no longer among the top 100. Of those among the fifty largest in 1979 that were not in the top 100 in 2010, De Rance, Inc., had become a fund of the Catholic Diocese of Milwaukee in 1992, two Norton Simon funds had consolidated into the notable Pasadena museum of that name, and three Pew funds had joined into the Pew Charitable Trusts, which in 2004 converted into a nonprofit corporation. In early 2010 all but four of those located in the Northeast or Midwest were still among the larger and more active foundations nationally: Alcoa (Pa.), Amherst H. Wilder (Minn.), Clark (N.Y.), the Commonwealth Fund (N.Y.), Gannett (formerly N.Y., now Va.), Henry J. Kaiser Family (Calif.), Herbert H. and Grace A. Dow (Mich.), John A. Hartford (N.Y.), Joyce (Ill.), Northwest Area (Minn.), Robert A. Welch (Tex.), Rockefeller Brothers Fund (N.Y.), and Sherman Fairchild (Conn.).

3. The Foundation Center's database (http://foundationcenter.org/findfunders/topfunders/top100assets.html) as of June 11, 2012, listed these as the fifty largest: Bill and Melinda Gates (Wa.), Ford (N.Y.), J. Paul Getty Trust (Calif.), Robert Wood Johnson (N.J.), W. K. Kellogg (Mich.), William and Flora Hewlett (Calif.), David and Lucile Packard (Calif.), John D. and Catherine T. MacArthur (Ill.), Gordon and Betty Moore (Calif.), Andrew W. Mellon (N.Y.), Lilly (Ind.), Tulsa Community Foundation (Okla.), William Penn Foundation (Pa.), California Endowment (Calif.), Rockefeller Foundation (N.Y.), Leona M. and Harry B. Helmsley Charitable Trust (N.Y.), Kresge (Mich.), Foundation to Promote Open Society (N.Y.), Annie E. Casey Foundation (Md.), Duke (N.C.), Bloomberg Family Foundation, Inc. (N.Y.), Robert W. Woodruff (Ga.), Susan Thompson Buffett (Neb.), Carnegie Corporation of New York (N.Y.), Charles Stewart Mott (Mich.), Conrad N. Hilton (Calif.), John S. and James L. Knight (Fla.), Harry and Jeanette Weinberg (Md.), Richard King Mellon (Pa.), McKnight Foundation (Minn.), Margaret A. Cargill Foundation (Minn.), Casey Family Programs (Wa.), Kimbell Art Foundation (Tex.), Cleveland Foundation (Ohio), Ewing Marion Kauffman (Mo.), New York Community Trust (N.Y.), Simons (N.Y.), Silicon Valley Community Foundation, Annenberg Foundation (Calif., formerly Pa.), Doris Duke Charitable Foundation (N.Y.), Alfred P. Sloan (N.Y.), John Templeton (Pa.), Eli and Edythe Broad (Calif.), Chicago Community Trust (Ill.), James Irvine (Calif.), Houston Endowment (Tex.), Heinz Endowments (Pa.), Wallace (N.Y.), Starr (N.Y.), and Walton Family (Ark.).

4. The federal government created the Chemical Foundation (critical to developing the science of chemistry in American universities) from German assets confiscated during World War I; the extraordinary wealth of the Ford Foundation derived from the transformation of a family-owned firm into a public corporation. State courts have required the creation of "health conversion foundations" to preserve for the public the charitable assets of nonprofit hospitals and insurance companies that wish to become profit-seeking corporations.

The preamble to a formal statement of "Principles and Practices for Effective Grantmaking," adopted by the Council on Foundations in June 2002, emphasized the relation of foundations to their donors: "Foundations and corporate giving programs reflect philanthropic impulses to promote the public good. We recognize the wide diversity of philanthropic goals. We also strive to respect donors' charitable intentions expressed in organizational charters and core documents as we apply our philanthropic resources to contemporary social conditions. We attend to the future through prudent stewardship of financial and other resources and we recognize that accountability calls for openness, responsiveness, fairness, and trust. In short, we hold ourselves responsible to those who created us, those with whom we currently interact, and those who may look to us in the future." See www.cof.org/Council/content.cfm?ItemNumber=860. The council replaced this statement with a new "Statement of Ethical Principles" in September 2005; this statement covers much of the same ground, with an initial point regarding "mission": "Our members are committed to the public benefit *and to their philanthropic purposes* and act accordingly" (emphasis added). See Council on Foundations website (www.cof. org/Learn/content.cfm?ItemNumber=1643&navItemNumber=2664).

5. The figure for 2011 is an estimate published in June 2012; Lawrence (2012); about $2.6 billion of these totals consisted of "medicine to patients with financial hardships"; Lawrence and Mukai (2009).

6. According to a study published by the Kaiser Family Foundation, charges for a normal, uncomplicated birth in Maryland in 2006 could range from $9,000 to $13,000, with charges for somewhat complicated preterm births exceeding $100,000. See www. kff.org/womenshealth/upload/7636ES.pdf. In 2005–06 the average cost of elementary and secondary education in the United States was over $9,100. See http://nces.ed.gov/ fastfacts/display.asp?id=66.

7. Foundation grant data from http://foundationcenter.org/findfunders/statistics, GDP data from www.bea.gov/national/nipaweb/SelectTable.asp?Selected=N. From the early 2000s, gifts of drugs through foundations set up by the pharmaceutical industry accounted for about half the increased ratio.

8. The share of all income going to the wealthiest 10 percent of the population, for example, rose from about 34 percent in the mid-1970s to 50 percent in 2007. See Saez and Piketty (2003) and Saez (2009). On the increasing inequality of spending capacity, see the excellent analysis of Attanasio, Hurst, and Pistaferri (2012).

9. See http://content.healthaffairs.org/cgi/content/abstract/29/1/147. Total federal spending for health, education, and welfare (including aid to veterans), which before World War II had never risen above 3.5 percent of gross domestic product, also grew more rapidly than did foundations, reaching more than 13 percent of GDP by 1970 (Carter and others 2006, "Social Insurance and Public Assistance"). Income security spending alone (mostly Social Security, but also payments for disability, for housing and food aid, for unemployment, for veterans, and for several other income support programs) exceeded 4 percent of GDP in 1965, was 7 percent by 1990, and approached 9 percent in 2010. Medicare and Medicaid spending amounted to 1 percent of GDP in 1970, almost 3.5 percent in 2000, and 5.5 percent in 2010.

10. See www.cms.gov/NationalHealthExpendData/25_NHE_Fact_Sheet.asp.

11. Foundation assets did grow more rapidly than college and university endowments between 1975 and 2005, but endowment and foundation income both fell significantly as a share of funding for higher education (Carter and others 2006, part B, p. 2–48); see

also National Center for Educational Statistics (http://nces.ed.gov/programs/digest/d08/tables/dt08_349.asp).

12. Lindemann (1936) traced the religious affiliations of members of the boards of many of the largest foundations in the 1920s.

13. Finke and Stark (1992).

14. J. A. Smith (2010) and O'Connor (2010).

15. See www.americansforthearts.org/pdf/information_services/art_index/NAI_full_report_print_quality.pdf.

16. Cherbo and Wyszomirski (2000, pp. 5–6) and Toepler (2010).

17. Wichterman (1998).

18. See www.americansforthearts.org/pdf/information_services/art_index/NAI_full_report_print_quality.pdf.

19. Some 701 independent and community or other public foundations pledged $360.1 million for New York City victims (Schoff 2004). Large as it was, this sum covered a very small part of the total cost of responding to the attack on the World Trade Center. The city of New York and a group of contractors agreed to pay nearly twice as much, $657 million, just to deal with dust and smoke injuries suffered by 10,000 firefighters, police officers, demolition and construction workers, and volunteers in the collapse and subsequent cleanup of the center's towers. *Wall Street Journal*, March 11, 2010 (http://online.wsj.com/article/SB10001424052748703625304575116431376090518.html?mod=WSJ_hps_MIDDLEForthNews).

20. Foundations responded to Hurricane Katrina in widely varied ways: the Walton Family Foundation gave $8 million for relief; the Packard Foundation sent a private plane to evacuate animals from the New Orleans zoo; the Knight Foundation, the Foundation for the Mid South, and the Baton Rouge Area Foundation also responded. See Brinkley (2006, pp. 252, 521), Birch and Wachter (2006, p. 146), and http://foundationcenter.org/pnd/hurricane/hurricane_newsmakers.jhtml;jsessionid=JYGYKXPOTDBOJLAQBQ4CGW15AAAACI2F.

21. See http://desmoinesfoundation.org/lu.cfm?lu=420.

22. Otto (2010, p. 144). The *Chronicle of Philanthropy* reported in July 2008 that private gifts in response to flooding in all Midwestern states had come to less than $30 million.

23. Brown and Rooney (2010).

24. Notable examples since 1990 include very large grants to civic and educational affairs in Tulsa, to the High Museum, the Georgia Aquarium, Emory University, and Grady Memorial Hospital in Atlanta, to the Smith Center for the performing arts in Las Vegas, to community foundations and colleges across the state of Indiana, and to colleges in the Los Angeles region (Indiana University Center on Philanthropy list of the largest gifts).

25. The Indiana University Center on Philanthropy maintains a list of charitable and philanthropic gifts of $50 million or more; reference here is to the 100 largest foundation grants included on this list. The 100 largest grants by themselves accounted for about 5 percent of all foundation grants made since 1990.

26. The Ford Foundation's Local Initiatives Support Corporation (LISC) is the leading example in the community development field. The Lilly Endowment made three of the largest foundation gifts of the 1990s and 2000s to new or growing community foundations in Indiana (amounting to $85 million, $189 million, and $191 million; Indiana University Center on Philanthropy list of the largest gifts). Paul Brest and Hal Harvey, *Money Well Spent* website (www.smartphilanthropy.org/Ch15_CommunityFoundations. html), www.irvine.org/evaluation/program-evaluations/community_foundations_initiative, and Sacks (2005, part II, p. 33).

27. Foundation Center (2009).

28. In very recent decades Catholics have created foundations to support diocesan activities and the retirement of religious workers; Jews have created foundations and supporting funds for Jewish federations. Catholics and Jews have both created community foundations for their communities in several areas. And increasing numbers of individuals have created foundations that direct much or even all of their giving to their religious community. The Shimon Ben Joseph Foundation, established in California in 2006 and one of the nation's 100 largest in 2010, for example, "is devoted exclusively to supporting education of Jewish youth"; in 1912 the Koch Foundation, Inc., described itself as "one of the largest Catholic foundations in the United States." See www.thekochfoundation. org. For an overview of Jewish foundations, see Tobin and Weinberg (2007); for a thoughtful and well-informed recent discussion of philanthropy among Orthodox Jews, see Davis and Davis (2010, pp. 31–51).

29. Smart (1970) and Stetzer (2006). Although the majority of foundation support for religion is concentrated among a relatively small group of funders, taken altogether small foundations also play an important role. Many of these foundations are founded locally by families or congregations without professional staffs or formal boards. Many, too, operate as funders but incorporate as nonprofit organizations that also rely on donations. Examples include the Twelve Women Foundation of Nashville, the Ah Lul Bayt Foundation of Houston, the Afikim Foundation of New York, and the Christus Foundation of Lincoln, Nebraska. Clearly, there is a large world of religious foundations and related organizations that researchers have yet to explore. Among the questions to be asked are whether these organizations mobilize exceptional contributions of enthusiasm, time, and money or whether they are dominated by inexperienced staff and volunteers, a lack of resources, and low levels of accountability.

30. A careful analysis of Jewish-funded foundations found that while some focus strongly on religious activities, others "give nothing (less than 1 percent) to the Jewish community" (Tobin and Weinberg 2007).

31. Notable in this connection was the support of the Lilly Endowment for serious studies on how religious congregations might build "social capital" as well as provide valuable social services in their communities. In 2002 Lilly also funded the Salvation Army's Natural Disaster Training Program.

32. The Foundation for a Better Life and the Acts of Kindness Foundation, both funded by Philip Anschutz, also mount media campaigns intended to encourage good behavior. See Michael Roberts, http://blogs.westword.com/latestword/2010/02/phil_ anschutz_brings_us_random.php, February 17, 2010, viewed on March 9, 2010.

33. Wuthnow and Lindsay (2010). Jewish foundations also often supported Jewish concerns relating to social welfare (Tobin and Weinberg 2007).

34. Reinforcing the point that foundations did not seek to compete with, or substitute for, government action in the field of social welfare, not one of the 100 largest foundation grants in the past three decades focused on the social welfare field—unless we count the Eugene B. Casey, George Kaiser, and Bloomberg foundation grants for the coordination of government services in Washington, D.C., Tulsa, and New York. The William Penn Foundation also supported a government-initiated network of Philadelphia organizations offering neighborhood-based prevention services to welfare recipients and immigrants.

35. Mosley and Galaskiewicz (2010).

36. Bielefeld and Chu (2010).

37. The Indiana University Center on Philanthropy list of the largest gifts includes contributions from the Bernie Marcus Foundation, the Andy Warhol Foundation, the Catherine B. Reynolds Foundation, and the Donald W. Reynolds Foundation to arts institutions in Atlanta, Pittsburgh, Washington, and Las Vegas; much press attention has gone to the Walton Family Foundation's creation of an important museum in Bentonville, Arkansas; websites of the Art Institute of Chicago, the Cleveland Museum of Art, the Metropolitan Museum of Art, the Whitney Museum of Art, the Guggenheim Museum of Art, and the Boston Museum of Fine Arts all note recent foundation support for major expansions.

38. Toepler (2010).

39. Benjamin and Quigley (2010) note that in the 1989–90 period Carnegie, Ford, and other foundations convened important meetings of private and corporate donors as well as representatives of the World Bank and the U.S. government to encourage engagement with transitioning societies. In their view these gatherings speeded action and "leverage[d] the foundations' investments by attracting significant other resources." Similarly, the Rockefeller Brothers Fund and the Mott Foundation brought together local NGOs in various countries which helped to identify "salient issues" as well as the potential partners and institutional resources that might be recruited to address them. By developing a consortium of regional higher education institutions from then Czechoslovakia, Hungary, and Poland, the Mellon Foundation helped build consensus around university library issues in Eastern Europe. Benjamin and Quigley (2010), Slocum (2009), and Aksartova (2009.)

40. VanAntwerpen (2009).

41. Wheatley (2010).

42. The beneficiaries were Ave Maria University and the new Olin engineering college in Massachusetts, launched in the late 1990s with a gift of more than $450 million.

43. See http://foundationcenter.org/pnd/news/story.jhtml?id=212300009.

44. Frumkin and Kaplan (2010).

45. The foundation-school pairs listed here involved at least two of the 100 largest grants of the past three decades listed by the Indiana University Center on Philanthropy. For a detailed account of Mellon's major, sustainable initiative in support of research in a wide range of fields, see Schonfeld (2003).

46. See www.moreheadcain.org/what-is-morehead-cain.html; see also www.more-headcain.org/gordon-cain.html. Compare the similar language for the Gates Millennium Scholars, a program of the United Negro College Fund launched with a $1 billion gift from the Bill and Melinda Gates Foundation: "Developing a diversified cadre of future leaders for America by facilitating successful completion of bachelor's, master's and doctoral degrees" in part by combining "leadership development programs with distinctive personal, academic, and professional growth opportunities." See www.gmsp.org/public web/aboutus.aspx.

47. The Indiana University Center on Philanthropy list of the largest private gifts includes scholarship-fund grants of $50 million or more from the Weingart Fund for students attending schools in Southern California, several Lilly Endowment grants for students attending schools in Indiana, the Gates Millennium Scholars program, and several others.

48. In the past, such support occasionally went to public schools for administrative activities such as retreats, to public school teachers for materials or special projects (often held during the summer), or to pupils for the costs of field trips or scholarships for special programs (Clemens and Lee 2010).

49. *Cleveland Plain Dealer,* March 19, 2010 (http://blog.cleveland.com/architecture/2010/03/the_maltz_family_foundation_do.html).

50. See www.case.edu/announcement/.

51. For an excellent recent overview, see Singer (2008).

52. See www.emcf.org.

53. Wuthnow and Lindsay (2010).

54. Foundation Center (2011). Community foundations had provided 6 percent of the value of all foundation gifts in 1990, 10 percent in 2008, and 9 percent in 2009. For the 1990 and 2008 years, see Lawrence and Mukai (2009).

55. In April 2009, the three funds named here held between $1.6 billion and $3.7 billion (http://online.wsj.com/article/SB124036165997141685.html). For the rules enforced by the Internal Revenue Service, see the "Donor-Advised Funds Guide Sheet Explanation," July 31, 2008 (www.irs.gov/pub/irs-tege/donor_advised_explanation_073108.pdf); on some of the issues, see Walsh (1999).

56. The Internal Revenue Service distinguishes three types of supporting organizations; see www.irs.gov/Charities-&-Non-Profits/Section-509%28a%29%283%29-Supporting-Organizations, viewed September 22, 2012, and Arenson (2008). The University of California ranks eight on the list of top 120 university endowments with $5.7 billion in 2006, an increase of about 10 percent from 2005 (U.S. Department of Education 2007, table 355). The popularity of the supporting organization device has prompted the careful redrawing of Internal Revenue Service regulations; see www.irs.gov/irb/2009-28_IRB/ar10.html.

57. See www.irs.gov/charities/article/0,,id=137609,00.html and the Council on Foundations discussion of the ongoing development of regulations under this act at www.cof.org/templates/41.cfm?ItemNumber=16983&navItemNumber=14859.

58. For a thoughtful discussion of philanthropic investment in housing in the United States before the New Deal, see Rodgers (1998).

59. Ford Foundation (1991), Foundation Center (2003), and Rockefeller Philanthropy Advisors (2008). For an example of a consulting firm that specializes in this field, see http://socialphilanthropy.org/about.php, viewed March 31, 2010.

60. Press release, "LISC celebrates 30th anniversary with nat'l symposium examining economic outlook, strategies for revitalizing distressed communities," March, 21 2011. LISC's Living Cities claims to have "brought together foundations and financial institutions—some of the biggest in the world—to launch a new approach to aggregating capital for philanthropic use," investing "more than $600 million" between 1991 and 2010. From 1993 it obtained a 3-1 match of federal funds from the U.S. Department of Housing and Urban Development, an endorsement of the quality of the project-evaluation skill it had developed. See www.livingcities.org/about.

61. The Ford Foundation started, then persuaded a total of thirty other funders to support the Urban Institute in pursuing additional research on this topic. The creation of Creative Capital and United States Artists accompanied the research, which was followed up in 2003 when a number of foundations launched a ten-year initiative, Leveraging Investments in Creativity (LINC), to support the work of individual artists (by, for example, expanding financial resources, building networks, and influencing policy). See www.unitedstatesartists.org/Public2/Home/index.cfm. To date, Creative Capital has operated more as a fundraiser and grantmaker than as an endowed foundation; see http://creative-capital.org/aboutus/story. Both sites viewed March 15, 2010.

62. J. A. Smith (2010).

63. McGray (2007). See also www.omidyar.net.

64. Strom (2006).

65. Light (2008); also see www.skollfoundation.org/approach/partners, viewed April 2, 2011.

66. As of August 2008 Google.org had committed over $95 million in grants and investments to funding coalitions of civil society organizations in these initiatives. Google reinforced this work by hosting the fifth annual Global Philanthropy Forum in 2007 (see Ostrom 2007). For its charitable activity as of early 2011, see Strom (2011). A related effort is the World Wide Web Foundation, launched in 2008 with a $5 million grant from the John S. and James L. Knight Foundation. It is not clear whether this will become a grantmaking foundation or take another form. The stated vision of its promoter, Sir Tim Berners-Lee, director of the World Wide Web Consortium, is to give the web a humanitarian focus that will allow access to and benefit underserved, economically deprived communities (www.webfoundation.org/about/community/knight-2008-tbl-speech, viewed July 24, 2012).

67. Yunus (2010, p. 127).

68. See www.bcorporation.net and *Chronicle of Philanthropy*, October 3, 2010 (http://blog.pappastax.com/index.php/2010/06/26/whats-a-b-corporation); both sites viewed on October 3, 2012. See also Doeringer (2010) and Kleinberger (2010).

69. Particularly important have been the "anti-kickback" terms of the Medicare and Medicaid Patient Protection Act of 1987 and the rulings of the Office of the Inspector General in the federal Department of Health and Human Services. As the Foundation Center observed, "Nothing in the prior history of the nation's foundation community

approaches the scale of product giving seen with this handful of recently established foundations" (Foundation Center 2007, p. 5). As Shah (2008) notes, the large pharmaceutical companies also provide the great bulk of funding to several large, independent "copayment foundations" that by 2007 were helping more than 10,000 patients meet costs of expensive drugs that were not fully covered by health insurance.

70. S. R. Smith (2010). See also www.physiciansfoundations.org/; www.legacy forhealth.org/25.aspx, www.circleid.com/posts/a_look_at_the_facebook_privacy_class_ action_beacon_settlement, and www.bmtfoundation.com/bfa/about-overview.html), viewed September 22, 2012. The Northern Coastal California Restoration Fund, for example, was established by the U.S. Fish and Wildlife Service and the National Fish and Wildlife Foundation with community service payments from settlement agreements entered into by the owners of marine vessels charged with violating federal maritime pollution laws. For detailed information, see http://foundationcenter.org/pnd/rfp/rfp_item. jhtml?id=253300030, viewed September 22, 2012.

71. "The Rockefeller Foundation Social Investing Guidelines" (www.rosefdn.org/ article.php?id=201) and the Investor Environmental Health Network (www.iehn.org/ home.php; www.uua.org/leaders/finance/sri/shareholderadvocacy/index.shtml), both sites viewed March 31, 2010.

72. The Foundation Center, created in the late 1950s, continued work begun by the Russell Sage Foundation in the first decades of the twentieth century. The Tax Reform Act of 1969 required that foundations produce audited financial reports; using these, the Foundation Center has assembled much more complete and accurate summaries of foundation activity.

73. Foundations created the Foundation Center in the late 1950s. Independent Sector created the National Center for Charitable Statistics (NCCS) in 1982. In the 1980s, the National Center developed the National Taxonomy of Exempt Entities (NTEE) to classify nonprofit organizations; in the 1990s, it worked with the Internal Revenue Service to align the NTEE with the federal government's more general North American Industry Classification System. The IRS, the NCCS, and the Foundation Center all use the NTEE in analyzing foundation activity (see http://nccs.urban.org/classification/ NTEE.cfm, viewed September 22, 2012). Foundation grants also launched the Guide Star website, which cooperates with the Internal Revenue Service to put all 990 forms filed by foundations and other nonprofits on the web. (GuideStar, like the Foundation Center, increasingly pays its own way by charging for the special search services it offers to fundraisers.) For a major effort to improve foundation reporting, see www2. guidestar.org and http://efile.form990.org, both viewed September 22, 2012. To these efforts we might add the continuing development of professional education for fundraisers through the Association of Fundraising Professionals. Also significant was the development of the academic side of the research enterprise, including, in addition to the major effort at Indiana University's Center on Philanthropy (www.philanthropy.iupui. edu/research, viewed September 22, 2012), the creation of the Association for Research on Nonprofit Organizations and Voluntary Action, and groups of academic researchers who focus on foundations, philanthropy, and the nonprofit sector at Yale, Harvard, Princeton, Boston College, Case Western Reserve University, Stanford, the University of

Southern California, and other universities. Collectively, these and other developments have achieved most of the steps toward the formal reporting of foundation activities recommended by observers such as McIlnay (1995, pp. 117–41). It is still true that many foundations do not issue detailed annual reports or maintain websites.

74. The James Irvine Foundation provides a very good example; see www.irvine.org/publications, viewed April 9, 2010.

75. See www.commonfund.org/AboutUs/Governance/Pages/default.aspx, viewed April 5, 2010.

76. See www.cfinsights.org/home, viewed April 5, 2010. The Foundation Study Group has also done substantial, though confidential, analyses of community foundation operating practices.

77. See www.effectivephilanthropy.org/index.php?page=gpr-reports, viewed April 5, 2010.

78. See www.mcknight.org/arts/arts_eval.aspx and www.wallacefoundation.org/KNOWLEDGECENTER/Pages/default.aspx. For briefer reports, see www.irvine.org/evaluation/our-approach. Sites viewed April 5, 2010. For an example of Robert Wood Johnson Foundation analysis, see Knickman and Isaacs (2010).

79. Fox (2005).

80. See www.rwjf.org/en/blogs/pioneering-ideas.html, viewed September 22, 2012; Wuthnow and Lindsay (2010).

81. Clemens and Lee (2010); see www.wallacefoundation.org and www.edexcellence.net/template/index.cfm, both sites viewed April 9, 2010. Several Fordham people have promoted charter schools, but Diane Ravitch, long associated with Fordham, published a strong critique of that movement in March 2010 (see http://online.wsj.com/article/SB10001424052748704869304575109443305343962.html?KEYWORDS=Diane+Ravitch, viewed March 14, 2010).

82. See www.emcf.org/results/index.htm, viewed April 9, 2010.

83. Mosley and Galaskiewicz (2010). Other foundations that invest in research on persistent poverty include Rockefeller, Smith Richardson, William T. Grant, John D. and Catherine T. MacArthur, and the Foundation for Child Development.

84. Toepler (2010).

85. See www.dupontfund.org/learning/research-reports.asp, viewed April 9, 2010.

86. Freund (1996) and Lazerson (1998).

87. Toepler (2010) and Minkoff and Agnone (2010). Even the relatively adventurous Andy Warhol Foundation has recently sought to support the arts through modest grants to writers willing to celebrate the arts and to curators needing time to plan exhibitions (www.warholfoundation.org, viewed September 22, 2012).

88. Knickman and Isaacs (2010).

89. See www.packard.org, viewed September 22, 2012.

90. Benjamin and Quigley (2010).

91. Benjamin and Quigley (2010).

92. For an enthusiastic overview of initiatives, see Sacks (2000). On some of the challenges, see Hammack and Heydemann (2009, pp. 137–59).

93. Clemens and Lee (2010).

94. The Hewlett Foundation purposefully directs its school giving to nonprofits that can become continuing "tools" for addressing education at the local level. On the Annenberg Challenge, see Goldberg (1996, pp. 685–87) and Domanico and others (2000, p. 17).

95. The Walton Family Foundation has been notably broad in its work for charter and private schools. Its fellowship programs, for example, seek to recruit and train new public charter school leaders through three organizations to which it has been giving substantial subsidies: Building Excellent Schools (BES), the Knowledge Is Power Program (KIPP) and New Leaders for New Schools (NLNS). In 2007 the foundation supported forty fellows it hoped would open new public charter schools in 2008 or 2009. See www.waltonfamilyfoundation.org, viewed September 22, 2012. For her critique, see Ravitch (2010). The topic is too complex for full discussion here, but we note the importance of political factors left out of most studies that credit foundations with excessive influence over elementary and secondary education: the collapse of the Republican-liberal Democratic coalition that long supported public education; the continuing desire of many Catholics for public funding for their schools; the desire of evangelical Protestants and many African Americans for more direct influence over the schools attended by their children; and local conflicts over busing and taxation. We think it is fair to suggest that after the brief burst of enthusiasm for public education in the 1960s and the Annenberg Challenge programs of the 1990s, more foundations have sought to reduce than to enhance support for public education.

96. Mosley and Galaskiewicz (2010).

97. Toepler (2010).

98. Frumkin (2006), ch. 6.

99. See, for example, the W. K. Kellogg Foundation's "Logic Model Development Guide" (www.wkkf.org/~/media/475A9C21974D416C90877A268DF38A15.ashx) and the discussion on the Consumer Health Foundation website at www.consumerhealthfdn.org/~conshfdn/images/uploads/files/chf_logic_model.pdf, or the Bruner Foundation's discussion of its "effectiveness initiatives" in the Rochester, New York, area (www.bruner foundation.org/ei), websites viewed March 18, 2010. For a positive discussion, see Cheadle (2003). For a general discussion of strategic philanthropy, see website of the International Network of Strategic Philanthropy, a virtual think tank project that operated from 2001 to 2005 (www.insp.efc.be).

100. Sievers (2001, p. 3).

101. For the difficulties that prevailed before the 1950s, see, for example, Sealander (1997).

102. For example, Walker and others (2008), Sullivan and Rosin (2008), Bacchetti and Ehrlich (2006), and Colby and others (2007). The Carnegie Foundation website posts abstracts and more information (www.carnegiefoundation.org)

103. Huggins and others (2007) and Cochrane and others (2008).

104. Knickman and Isaacs (2010).

105. For example, the California Endowment was created in 1996 following Blue Cross of California's conversion to a profit-seeking entity; it employs a "multicultural approach to health" that takes into account not only prevention, but also a person's cultural beliefs, financial status, and location, among other things. See www.calendow.org.

106. Weaver (2000) notes the roles of the Heritage Foundation, the American Enterprise Institute, and the Cato Institute in the years preceding the 1996 welfare reform legislation; two important conservative foundations, Olin and Scaife, joined many other donors in supporting these think tanks, while the Smith Richardson Foundation and the Bradley Foundation similarly contributed to the many streams that financed the American Enterprise Institute (Mosley and Galaskiewicz 2010).

107. Mosely and Galaskiewicz (2010) and Miller (2006).

108. O'Connor (2010).

109. J. A. Smith (2010).

110. Scrivener and others (2008) and www.mdrc.org/publications/473/full.pdf, viewed September 22, 2012.

111. Benjamin and Quigley (2010). The institutions established through their efforts are Gdansk Institute in Poland, the Central European University, the Institute for Economics in Hungary, the Center for Economic Development in Slovakia, and the Market Institute in Lithuania.

112. Jantz and others (2002).

113. It can be as difficult to define "particularism" as to define "quality" in the arts. Was it particularism that led foundations to direct 68 percent of arts grant dollars toward the performing arts and museums in 2009? To give the largest share of this, 38 percent, to museums and music, compared to 31 percent to the performing arts, 11 percent to media, 22 percent to other arts purposes? Or to make the other allocations detailed by Grantmakers in the Arts (2011)?

114. Indiana University Center on Philanthropy list of largest gifts.

115. Every religious community contains within it a variety of impulses and initiatives; supporters of a particular impulse can assure continued support for their approach by establishing a foundation and persuading their larger religious community to accept it. On occasion, foundation leaders have found it impossible not to choose among contending impulses within the religious communities they support, knowing that they must then deal with the resulting complaints.

116. Tobin and Weinberg (2007).

117. Clemens and Lee (2010).

118. Heifitz, Kania, and Kramer (2004).

119. Too often, foundations failed to understand local contexts. Benjamin and Quigley note, "Each country in Eastern Europe had vastly different experiences with democracy. Poland, Czechoslovakia, and Hungary had a brief experience between the two World Wars, while other countries like Ukraine, Yugoslavia, Bulgaria, and Romania had no prior experience. At the same time, each country had very different experiences with mass movements, often the precursors of civil society" (Benjamin and Quigley 2010, p. 257).

120. Clemens and Lee (1910, p. 58).

121. Salamon (1995) and S. R. Smith (2010).

122. For a thoughtful discussion of some of the issues relating to these matters, see Simon (1987).

123. See Simon (1987) as well as discussion on the history of the law and regulation of foundations in the previous chapters.

124. Nielsen (1972).

Appendix A

1. Andrews (1956, p. 11; 1960, p. ix).

2. See www.irs.gov/charities/charitable/article/0,,id=136459,00.html, viewed March 26, 2012. Almost identical language is at www.irs.gov/charities/charitable/article/0,,id=96114,00.html: "Every organization that qualifies for tax exemption as an organization described in section 501(c)(3) is a private foundation unless it falls into one of the categories specifically excluded from the definition of that term (referred to in section 509(a))."

3. The Foundation Center identified about 3,100 foundations with paid staff in 2009, 3,500 by a different set of definitions in 2008. In each year it found about 750 foundations that had staffs of five persons or more; see tables at http://foundationcenter.org/findfunders/statistics/gm_agg.html.

4. The precise rules, available on the IRS website for U.S. revenue code sections 509(a)(1) and 170(b)(1)(A)(6), are somewhat technical and complex.

5. Seehttp://nccsdataweb.urban.org/knowledgebase/detail.php?linkID=56&category=7&xrefID=3265.

Appendix B

1. See www.irs.gov/charities/charitable/article/0,,id=175418,00.html.

2. See the Rockefeller report at www.rockefellerfoundation.org/about-us/annual-reports.

References

Aaron, Henry J. 1992. "Commentary." In *Who Benefits from the Nonprofit Sector?* edited by Charles T. Clotfelter. University of Chicago Press.

Achenbaum, W. Andrew. 1995. *Crossing Frontiers: Gerontology Emerges as a Science.* Cambridge University Press.

Adam, Thomas. 2004. *Philanthropy, Patronage, and Civil Society: Experiences from Germany, Great Britain, and North America.* Indiana University Press.

Adorno, Theodor W., Else Frenkel-Brunswik, Daniel Levinson, and Nevitt Sanford. 1950. *The Authoritarian Personality.* Studies in Prejudice Series vol. 1. Harper and Row.

Aksartova, Sada. 2009. "Promoting Civil Society or Diffusing NGO's? U.S. Donors in the Former Soviet Union." In *Globalization, Philanthropy, and Civil Society: Projecting Institutional Logics Abroad,* edited by David C. Hammack and Steven Heydemann. Indiana University Press.

Alchon, Guy. 1985. *The Invisible Hand of Planning: Capitalism, Social Science, and the State in the 1920s.* Princeton University Press.

Allport, Gordon W. 1954. *The Nature of Prejudice.* Addison-Wesley.

Anderson, Eric, and Alfred A. Moss. 1999. *Dangerous Donations: Northern Philanthropy and Southern Black Education, 1902–1930.* University of Missouri Press.

Anderson, James D. 1988. *The Education of Blacks in the South, 1860–1935.* University of North Carolina Press.

Andrew, John A. 2002. *Power to Destroy: The Political Uses of the IRS from Kennedy to Nixon.* I. R. Dee.

Andrew W. Mellon Educational and Charitable Trust. 1980. *A Report of Its Work for the Fifty Years 1930–1980.* Andrew W. Mellon Educational and Charitable Trust.

Andrews, Frank Emerson. 1956. *Philanthropic Foundations.* Russell Sage Foundation.

————. 1961. "Growth and Present Status of American Foundations." *Proceedings of the American Philosophical Association* 105: 157–161.

————. 1969. *Patman and Foundations: Review and Assessment.* Foundation Center.

————. 1973. *Foundation Watcher.* Franklin and Marshall College.

Anheier, Helmut K., and Siobhan Daly. 2007. *The Politics of Foundations: A Comparative Analysis.* Routledge.

Anheier, Helmut K., and David C. Hammack, eds. 2010. *American Foundations: Roles and Contributions.* Brookings.

Anheier, Helmut K., and Diana Leat. 2006. *Creative Philanthropy: Toward a New Philanthropy for the Twenty-first Century.* Routledge.

Anheier, Helmut K., and Stefan Toepler. 1999. *Private Funds, Public Purpose: Philanthropic Foundations in International Perspective.* Springer.

Apple, Rima D. 1989. "Patenting University Research: Harry Steenbock and the Wisconsin Alumni Research Foundation." *Isis* 80: 374–94.

Arenson, Karen W. 2008. "Endowments Widen a Higher Education Gap." *New York Times,* February 4 (www.nytimes.com/2008/02/04/education/04endowment.html?pagewanted=all, viewed September 22, 2012).

Arnove, Robert F., ed. 1980. *Philanthropy and Cultural Imperialism: The Foundations at Home and Abroad.* G. K. Hall.

Ascoli, Peter Max. 2006. *Julius Rosenwald: The Man Who Built Sears, Roebuck and Advanced the Cause of Black Education in the American South.* Indiana University Press.

Atack, Jeremy. 1986. "Firm Size and Industrial Structure in the United States during the Nineteenth Century." *Journal of Economic History* 46: 463–75.

Atack, Jeremy, Peter Passell, and Susan Lee. 1994. *A New Economic View of American History: From Colonial Times to 1940.* 2nd ed. Norton.

Atkins, Stephen E. 1991. *The Academic Library in the American University.* American Library Association.

Attanasio, Orazio, Erik Hurst, and Luigi Pistaferri. 2012. "The Evolution of Income, Consumption, and Leisure Inequality in the U.S., 1980–2010." Working Paper 17982. Cambridge, Mass.: National Bureau of Economic Research (April).

Ayres, Leonard Porter. 1911. *Seven Great Foundations.* Russell Sage Foundation. Philanthropy Classics ed., Harvard University, Hauser Center for Nonprofit Organizations, 2007 (www.ksghauser.harvard.edu/philanthropyclassics).

Bacchetti, Ray. 2006. "Many Motives, Mixed Reviews: Foundations and Higher Education as a Relationship Richer in Possibilities Than Results." In *Reconnecting Education and Foundations: Turning Good Intentions into Educational Capital,* edited by Ray Bacchetti and Thomas Ehrlich. Jossey-Bass.

Bacchetti, Ray, and Thomas Ehrlich, eds. 2006. *Reconnecting Education and Foundations: Turning Good Intentions into Educational Capital.* Jossey-Bass.

Bain, Robert Bruce. 1990. "'Our Greatest Social Welfare Agency': Cleveland's Public School Policies for Educating Problem Boys, 1917–1938." Ph.D. dissertation, Case Western Reserve University.

Baird, John A. 1982. *Horn of Plenty: The Story of the Presbyterian Ministers' Fund.* Tyndale House Publisher.

Baird, Robert. 1844. *Religion In America, Or, An Account of The Origin, Progress, Relation to the State, And Present Condition of the Evangelical Churches in the United States: With Notices of the Unevangelical Denominations.* Harper: Blackie and Son. Selection reprinted in *Making the Nonprofit Sector in the United States: A Reader,* edited by David C. Hammack. Indiana University Press, 1998.

Balakrishnan, Radhika, and Caren Grown. 1999. "Foundations and Economic Knowledge." In *What Do Economists Know? New Economics of Knowledge,* edited by Robert F. Garnett. Routledge.

Ballou, Dale, and Michael Podgursky. 2000. "Reforming Teacher Preparation and Licensing: What Is the Evidence?" *Teachers College Record* 102: 5–27.

Balogh, Brian. 1991. *Chain Reaction: Expert Debate and Public Participation in American Commercial Nuclear Power, 1945–1975.* Cambridge University Press.

Barnard, Henry. 1877. "Oliver Smith and the Smith Charities." *Barnard's American Journal of Education* 27 (January): 623.

Barzun, Jacques. 1959. "The Folklore of Philanthropy." In *The House of Intellect,* by Jacques Barzun. Harper and Row.

Bass, Dorothy C. 1989. "Ministry on the Margin: Protestants and Education." In *Between the Times: The Travail of the Protestant Establishment in America, 1900–1960,* edited by William R. Hutchison. Cambridge University Press.

Beecher, Lyman. 1865. *Autobiography.* Harper. Excerpts in *Making the Nonprofit Sector in the United States: A Reader,* edited by David C. Hammack. Indiana University Press, 1998.

Bell, Daniel, ed. 1955. *The New American Right.* Criterion Books.

Benjamin, Lehn M., and Kevin F. F. Quigley. 2010. "For the World's Sake: U.S. Foundations and International Grant Making, 1990–2002." In *American Foundations,* edited by Helmut K. Anheier and David C. Hammack. Brookings.

Bensel, Richard Franklin. 1984. *Sectionalism and American Political Development, 1880–1980.* University of Wisconsin Press.

———. 2000. *The Political Economy of American Industrialization, 1877–1900.* Cambridge University Press.

Berghahn, Volker. 1999. "Philanthropy and Diplomacy in the 'American Century.'" *Diplomatic History* 23: 393–419.

Berle, Adolf Augustus. 1969. *Leaning against the Dawn: An Appreciation of the Twentieth Century Fund and Its Fifty Years of Adventure in Seeking to Influence American Development toward a More Effectively Just Civilization, 1919–1969.* Twentieth Century Fund.

Berman, Edward H. 1983. *The Ideology of Philanthropy: The Influence of the Carnegie, Ford, and Rockefeller Foundations on American Foreign Policy.* State University of New York Press.

Berman, Elizabeth Popp. 2008. "Why Did Universities Start Patenting? Institution-Building and the Road to the Bayh-Dole Act." *Social Studies of Science* 38: 835–71.

Bernholz, Lucy, Katherine Fulton, and Gabriel Kasper. 2005. *On the Brink of New Promise: The Future of U.S. Community Foundations.* Monitor Institute.

Bernstein, Michael A. 1989. *The Great Depression: Delayed Recovery and Economic Change in America, 1929–1939.* Cambridge University Press.

Biebel, Charles D. 1976. "Private Foundations and Public Policy: The Case of Secondary Education during the Great Depression." *History of Education Quarterly* 16: 3–33.

Biehn, Kersten Jacobson. 2008. "Psychobiology, Sex Research, and Chimpanzees: Philanthropic Foundation Support for the Behavioral Sciences at Yale University, 1923–41." *History of the Human Sciences* 21, no. 2: 21–43.

Bielefeld, Wolfgang, and Jane Chu. 2010. "Foundations and Social Welfare in the Twentieth Century." In *American Foundations*, edited by Helmut K. Anheier and David C. Hammack. Brookings.

Billitteri, Thomas J. 2005. *Money, Mission, and the Payout Rule: In Search of a Strategic Approach to Foundation Spending*. Nonprofit Sector Research Fund.

Birch, Eugenie Ladner, and Susan M. Wachter. 2006. *Rebuilding Urban Places after Disaster: Lessons from Hurricane Katrina*. University of Pennsylvania Press.

Blank, Rebecca M., and Ron Haskins. 2001. *The New World of Welfare*. Brookings.

Board of Directors of City Trusts of the City of Philadelphia. 1912. *Forty-Second Annual Report, for the Year 1912*. Philadelphia.

Bobinski, George Sylvan. 1969. *Carnegie Libraries: Their History and Impact on American Public Library Development*. American Library Association.

Bodwell, Gregory B. 2006. "Grassroots, Inc.: A Sociopolitical History of the Cleveland School Voucher Battle, 1992–2002." Ph.D. dissertation, Case Western Reserve University.

Bond, Edward L., and Joan R. Gundersen. 2007. "The Episcopal Church in Virginia, 1607–2007." *Virginia Magazine of History and Biography*, 115: 163–344.

Borchert, Catherine G. 2009. "Exscinded! The Presbyterian Church in the United States of America and the Role of Slavery." Ph.D. dissertation, Case Western Reserve University.

Boris, Elizabeth T., Loren Renz, Mark A. Hager, Rachel Elias, and Mahesh Somashenkhar. 2008. *What Drives Foundation Expenses and Compensation?* Urban Institute.

Boris, Elizabeth T., and Eugene Steuerle. 2004. "Philanthropic Foundations: Payout and Related Public Policy Issues." Urban Institute.

Boudreau, Frank G. 1944. "International Civil Service." In *Pioneers in World Order: An American Appraisal of the League of Nations*, edited by Harriet E. Davis. Columbia University Press.

Bowen, William G., and Derek Curtis Bok. 2000. *The Shape of the River: Long-Term Consequences of Considering Race in College and University Admissions*. Princeton University Press.

Boylan, Anne M. 1990. *Sunday School: The Formation of an American Institution, 1790–1880*. Yale University Press.

Brackenridge, R. Douglas. 1999. *The Presbyterian Church (U.S.A.) Foundation: A Bicentennial History, 1799–1999*. Geneva Press.

Bradley Commission on History in Schools. 2000. *Building a History Curriculum: Guidelines for Teaching History in Schools*. National Council for History Education.

Braudel, Fernand. 1995. *A History of Civilizations*. Penguin.

Breitman, Richard, Barbara McDonald Stewart, and Severin Hochberg, eds. 2007. *Advocate for the Doomed: The Diaries and Papers of James G. McDonald*. Indiana University Press.

Brest, Paul, and Hal Harvey. 2008. *Money Well Spent: A Strategic Plan for Smart Philanthropy*. John Wiley and Sons.

Brilliant, Eleanor L. 2000. *Private Charity and Public Inquiry: A History of the Filer and Peterson Commissions*. Indiana University Press.

———. 1992. *The United Way: Dilemmas of Organized Charity*. Columbia University Press.

Brinkley, Douglas. 2006. *The Great Deluge: Hurricane Katrina, New Orleans, and the Mississippi Gulf Coast*. William Morrow.

Brown, Dorothy M., and Elizabeth McKeown. 1997. *The Poor Belong to Us: Catholic Charities and American Welfare*. Harvard University Press.

Brown, Melissa S., and Patrick M. Rooney. 2010. *Giving Following a Crisis: An Historical Analysis*. Indiana University Center on Philanthropy.

Brown, Prudence, and Sunil Garg. 1997. *Foundations and Comprehensive Community Initiatives: The Challenges of Partnership*. Chapin Hall Center for Children.

Brown, Prudence, Robert J. Chaskin, Ralph Hamilton, and Harold Richman. 2003. *Toward Greater Effectiveness in Community Change: Challenges and Responses for Philanthropy*. Chapin Hall.

Brown, Richard D. 1973. "The Emergence of Voluntary Associations in Massachusetts, 1760–1830." *Journal of Voluntary Action Research* 2: 64–73.

Bryan, W. S. Plummer. 1911. *The Church, Her Colleges, and the Carnegie Foundation*. Princeton University Press.

Bryson, Dennis Raymond. 2002. *Socializing the Young: The Role of Foundations, 1923–1941*. New York: Bergin and Garvey.

Buckley, Thomas J. 1977. *Church and State in Revolutionary Virginia, 1776–1787*. University Press of Virginia.

Bullock, Mary Brown. 1980. *An American Transplant: The Rockefeller Foundation and Peking Union Medical College*. University of California Press.

Bulmer, Martin. 1981. "Philanthropy and Social Science in the 1920s: Beardsley Ruml and the Laura Spellman Rockefeller Memorial, 1922–29." *Minerva* 19: 347–407.

———. 1984. *The Chicago School of Sociology: Institutionalization, Diversity, and the Rise of Sociological Research*. University of Chicago Press.

———. 1985. *Essays on the History of British Sociological Research*. Cambridge University Press.

Bundy, McGeorge. 1974. "Public Policy and the Private Foundation." In *Ford Foundation Annual Report for 1973*. New York (www.fordfound.org/archives/item/1973/text/14).

Burke, Colin B. 1982. *American Collegiate Populations: A Test of the Traditional View*. New York University Press.

———. 2001. "Nonprofit History's New Numbers (and the Need for More)." *Nonprofit and Voluntary Sector Quarterly* 30: 174–203.

Burrough, Bryan. 2009. *The Big Rich: The Rise and Fall of the Greatest Texas Oil Fortunes*. Penguin.

Burtchaell, James Tunstead. 1998. *The Dying of the Light: The Disengagement of Colleges and Universities from Their Christian Churches*. W. B. Eerdmans Publishing Company.

Campbell, Ballard C. 1995. *The Growth of American Government: Governance from the Cleveland Era to the Present*. Indiana University Press.

Candler, Warren Akin. 1909. *Dangerous Donations and Degrading Doles: Or, A Vast Scheme for Capturing and Controlling the Colleges and Universities of the Country.* Privately printed.

Cannadine, David. 2006. *Mellon: An American Life.* Knopf.

Carnegie, Andrew. 1889. "Wealth." *North American Review* 148, no. 391: 653–64.

Carpenter, Daniel P. 2001. *The Forging of Bureaucratic Autonomy: Reputations, Networks, and Policy Innovation in Executive Agencies, 1862–1928.* Princeton University Press.

Carpenter, Edward Wilton, and Charles Frederick Morehouse. 1896. *The History of the Town of Amherst, Massachusetts.* Press of Carpenter and Morehouse.

Carson, Clayborne. 1995. *In Struggle: SNCC and the Black Awakening of the 1960s.* Harvard University Press.

Carson, Emmett Devon. 1993. *A Hand Up: Black Philanthropy and Self-Help in America.* Joint Center for Political and Economic Studies Press.

Carter, Susan B., Scott Sigmund Gartner, Michael R. Haines, Alan L. Olmstead, Richard Sutch, and Gavin Wright, eds. 2006. *Historical Statistics of the United States.* Millenium ed. Cambridge University Press.

Castle, Alfred L. 1992. *A Century of Philanthropy: A History of the Samuel N. and Mary Castle Foundation.* Honolulu: Hawaiian Historical Society.

Cervone, Barbara. 2007. "When Reach Exceeds Grasp: Taking the Annenberg Challenge to Scale." In *Reconnecting Education and Foundations: Turning Good Intentions into Educational Capital*, edited by Ray Bacchetti and Thomas Ehrlich. Jossey-Bass.

Chambers, Merritt Madison. 1948. *Charters of Philanthropies: A Study of Selected Trust Instruments, Charters, By-laws, and Court Decisions.* Carnegie Foundation for the Advancement of Teaching.

Chambré, Susan Maizel. 2006. *Fighting for Our Lives: New York's AIDS Community and the Politics of Disease.* New Brunswick: Rutgers University Press.

Charity Organization Society of the City of New York. 1885. *The New York Charities Directory.* 3rd ed. New York.

Cheadle, Allen. 2003. "Evaluating the California Wellness Foundation's Health Improvement Initiative: A Logic Model Approach." *Health Promotion Practice* 4: 146–56.

Cheit, Earl F., and Theodore Lobman. 1979. *Foundations and Higher Education: Grant Making from Golden Years through Steady State.* Carnegie Council on Policy Studies in Higher Education.

Cherbo, Joni, and Margaret Wyszomirski. 2000. "Mapping the Public Life of the Arts in America." In *The Public Life of the Arts in America*, edited by Joni Cherbo and Margaret Wyszomirski. Rutgers University Press.

CIBA. 1973. *The Future of Foundations.* CIBA Foundation.

Çizakça, Murat. 2000. *A History of Philanthropic Foundations: The Islamic World from the Seventh Century to the Present.* Bosphorus University Press.

Claiborne, John Francis Hamtramck. 1860. *Life and Correspondence of John A. Quitman, Major-General, U.S.A., and Governor of the State of Mississippi.* Harper and Brothers.

Clark, Mark. 2001. *Dyeing for a Living: A History of the American Association of Textile Chemists and Colorists.* American Association of Textile Chemists and Colorists.

Clarke, Adele. 1998. *Disciplining Reproduction: Modernity, American Life Sciences, and "the Problems of Sex."* University of California Press.

Clemens, Elisabeth S. 2000. "The Encounter of Civil Society and the States: Legislation, Law, and Association, 1900–1920." Paper presented at the Social Science History Association (http://users.polisci.wisc.edu/apw/archives/clemens.pdf).

Clemens, Elisabeth S., and Linda Lee. 2010. "Catalysts for Change? Foundations and School Reform, 1950–2005." In *American Foundations*, edited by Helmut K. Anheier and David C. Hammack. Brookings.

Clifford, Geraldine Jonçich, and James W. Guthrie. 1990. *Ed School: A Brief for Professional Education*. University of Chicago Press.

Clotfelter, Charles T. 1985. *Federal Tax Policy and Charitable Giving*. University of Chicago Press.

———. 1992. *Who Benefits from the Nonprofit Sector?* University of Chicago Press.

Clotfelter, Charles T., and Thomas Ehrlich. 1999. *Philanthropy and the Nonprofit Sector in a Changing America*. Indiana University Press.

Cmiel, Kenneth. 1995. *A Home of Another Kind: One Chicago Orphanage and the Tangle of Child Welfare*. University of Chicago Press.

Cobb, Clifford W., and Craig Rixford. 1998. *Lessons Learned from the History of Social Indicators*. Redefining Progress.

Coben, Stanley. 1976. "Foundation Officials and Fellowships: Innovation in the Patronage of Science." *Minerva* 14: 225–40.

Cochrane, D. F., and others. 2008. "Denied: Community College Students Lack Access to Affordable Loans." Pew Charitable Trusts (www.pewtrusts.org/uploadedFiles/wwwpewtrustsorg/Reports/Student_debt/denied.pdf).

Coffman, Harold Coe. 1936. *American Foundations: A Study of Their Role in the Child Welfare Movement*. General Board of the Young Men's Christian Association.

Cohen, Charles L. 2003. "The Colonization of British North America as an Episode in the History of Christianity." *Church History* 72: 553–68.

Colby, Anne, Elizabeth Beaumont, Thomas Ehrlich, and Josh Corngold. 2007. *Educating for Democracy: Preparing Undergraduates for Responsible Political Engagement*. Wiley.

Cole, Stephen, and Elinor G. Barber. 2003. *Increasing Faculty Diversity: The Occupational Choices of High-Achieving Minority Students*. Harvard University Press.

Coley, Richard J., and Margaret E. Thorpe. 1985. *A Look at the MAT Model of Teacher Education and Its Graduates: Lessons for Today*. Educational Testing Service.

Colwell, Mary Anna Culleton. 1993. *Private Foundations and Public Policy: The Political Role of Philanthropy*. Garland.

Commission on the Costs of Medical Care. 1932. *Medical Care for the American People*. University of Chicago Press.

Commission on Foundations and Private Philanthropy. 1971. *Foundations, Private Giving, and Public Policy: Report and Recommendations*. University of Chicago Press.

Commission on Private Philanthropy and Public Needs. 1975. *Giving in America: Toward a Stronger Voluntary Sector*. Commission on Private Philanthropy and Public Needs.

Conant, James B. 1963. *The Education of American Teachers*. McGraw-Hill.

Congleton, Roger D., Alberto Batinti, Feler Bose, Youngshin Kim, and Rinaldo Pietrantonio. 2010. "Public Choice and the Modern Welfare State: On the Growth of Government in the Twentieth Century." George Mason University, Center for Study of Public Choice (www.rdc1.net/forthcoming/Welfare%20state%20_with%20 Youngshin,%20Alberto,%20Feler,%20and%20Rinaldo,%20for%20Public%20 Choice%20Companion,3_.pdf).

Congressional Research Service. 1983. *Development of the Law and Continuing Legal Issues in the Tax Treatment of Private Foundations.* Report prepared for the Subcommittee on Oversight of the House Ways and Means Committee, 98 Cong. 1 sess. WMCP 98-9 1983. Washington.

Coon, Horace. 1938. *Money to Burn: What the Great American Philanthropic Foundations Do with Their Money.* Longmans, Green.

Cornell, Thomas D. 2004. *Establishing Research Corporation: A Case Study of Patents, Philanthropy, and Organized Research in Early Twentieth-Century America.* Research Corporation.

Council of Economic Advisers. 2007. *Economic Report of the President: 2007,* app. B: "Statistical Tables Relating to Income, Employment, and Production." Government Printing Office (www.gpoaccess.gov/eop/tables07.html).

Critchlow, Donald T. 1995. "Birth Control, Population Control, and Family Planning: An Overview." In *The Politics of Abortion and Birth Control in Historical Perspective,* edited by Donald T. Critchlow. Pennsylvania State University Press.

Cuninggim, Merrimon. 1972. *Private Money and Public Service: The Role of Foundations in American Society.* McGraw-Hill.

Curti, Merle, Judith Green, and Roderick Nash. 1963. "Anatomy of Giving: Millionaires in the Late 19th Century." *American Quarterly* 15: 416–35.

Curti, Merle, and Roderick Nash. 1965. *Philanthropy in the Shaping of American Higher Education.* Rutgers University Press.

Dahl, Robert A. 1971. *Polyarchy: Participation and Opposition.* Yale University Press.

Dalzell, Robert F. 1987. *Enterprising Elite: The Boston Associates and the World They Made.* Harvard University Press.

Davidson, James D. 1998. "Why Churches Cannot Endorse or Oppose Political Candidates." *Review of Religious Research* 40: 16–34.

Davidson, James D., C. Lincoln Johnson, and Alan K. Mock. 1990. *Faith and Social Ministry: Ten Christian Perspectives.* Loyola University Press.

Davis, Joseph Stancliffe. 1917. *Essays in the Earlier History of American Corporations.* Vol. 1. Harvard University Press.

Davis, Margaret L. 2007. *The Culture Broker: Franklin D. Murphy and the Transformation of Los Angeles.* University of California Press.

Davis, Margy-Ruth, and Perry Davis. 2010. "For the Poor and the Stranger: Fundraisers' Perspectives on Orthodox Philanthropy." In *Toward a Renewed Ethic of Jewish Philanthropy,* edited by Yossi Prager. Yeshiva University Press.

Deep, Akash, and Peter Frumkin. 2001. *The Foundation Payout Puzzle.* Working Paper 9. Harvard University, Hauser Center for Nonprofit Organizations.

Delfin, F. G., Jr., and S. Y. Tang. 2007. "Elitism, Pluralism, or Resource Dependency: Patterns of Environmental Philanthropy among Private Foundations in California." *Environmental Planning* 39: 2167–86.

Diamond, Sara. 1995. *Roads to Dominion: Right-Wing Movements and Political Power in the United States.* Guilford Press.

Diamond, Stephen. 2002. "Efficiency and Benevolence: Philanthropic Tax Exemptions in 19th-Century America." In *Property-Tax Exemption for Charities: Mapping the Battlefield*, edited by Evelyn Brody. Urban Institute.

Dickinson, Frank G. 1962. *Philanthropy and Public Policy*. Columbia University Press.

Dillingham, George A. 1989. *The Foundation of the Peabody Tradition*. University Press of America.

DiLorenzo, Thomas J., William T. Poole, Daniel T. Oliver, and Robert E. Winters. 1990. *Patterns of Corporate Philanthropy: The "Suicidal Impulse."* Capital Research Center.

DiMaggio, Paul. 1986. "Support for the Arts from Independent Foundations." In *Nonprofit Enterprise in the Arts: Studies in Mission and Constraint*, edited by Paul DiMaggio. Oxford University Press.

Dodd, Norman. 1954. *Report to the Special Committee of the House of Representatives to Investigate Tax Exempt Foundations*. Long House.

Doeringer, Matt. 2010. "Reevaluating the L3C: Mistaken Assumptions and Potential Solutions." Philanthropy, Voluntarism, and Not-for-Profit Management Paper Series. Duke University (http://ssrn.com/abstract=1696267).

Doll, Peter M. 2000. *Revolution, Religion, and National Identity: Imperial Anglicanism in British North America, 1745–1795*. Fairleigh Dickinson University Press.

Domanico, Raymond, Carol Innerst, Marci Kanstoroom, and Alexander W. W. Russo. 2000. *Can Philanthropy Fix Our Schools? Appraising Walter Annenberg's $500 Million Gift to Public Education*. Diane Publishing Company.

Dorsey, Bruce. 1998. "Friends Becoming Enemies: Philadelphia Benevolence and the Neglected Era of American Quaker History." *Journal of the Early Republic* 18: 395–428.

Douglas, James, and Aaron B. Wildavsky. 1978. "The Knowledgeable Foundations." In *The Future of Foundations: Some Reconsiderations*, edited by Landrum Rymer Bolling. Change Magazine Press.

Dowie, Mark. 2001. *American Foundations: An Investigative History*. MIT Press.

Dudziak, Mary L. 2000. *Cold War Civil Rights: Race and the Image of American Democracy*. Princeton University Press.

Dunlap, William. 1834. *History of the Rise and Progress of the Arts of Design in the United States*. George P. Scott, Printers.

Eaton, Berrien C. 1951. "Charitable Foundations and Related Matters under the 1950 Revenue Act: Part I." *Virginia Law Review* 37: 1–54.

Ebbeling, Donald C. 1976. *Courtroom Crucible: The Smith Charities*. Trustees of the Smith Charities.

Ebrahim, Alnoor. 2003. *NGOs and Organizational Change: Discourse, Reporting, and Learning*. Cambridge University Press.

Eisenmann, Linda. 2005a. "Brokering Old and New Philanthropic Traditions: Women's Continuing Education in the Cold War Era." In *Women and Philanthropy in Education*, edited by Andrea Walton. Indiana University Press.

———. 2005b. "A Time of Quiet Activism: Research, Practice, and Policy in American Women's Higher Education, 1945–65." *History of Education Quarterly* 45: 1–17.

———. 2006. *Higher Education for Women in Postwar America, 1945–1965*. Johns Hopkins University Press.

Elliott, Frederick C. 2004. *The Birth of the Texas Medical Center: A Personal Account.* Texas A&M University Press.

Embree, Edwin R. 1949. *Investment in People: The Story of the Julius Rosenwald Fund.* Harper and Brothers.

Endicott, Eve. 1993. *Land Conservation through Public/Private Partnerships.* Island Press.

Engel, Jonathan. 2002. *Doctors and Reformers: Discussion and Debate over Health Policy, 1925–1950.* University of South Carolina Press.

Engerman, David. 2003. "Rethinking Cold War Universities: Some Recent Histories." *Journal of Cold War Studies* 5, no. 3: 80–95.

———. 2009. *Know Your Enemy: The Rise and Fall of America's Soviet Experts.* Oxford University Press.

English, James F. 2005. *The Economy of Prestige: Prizes, Awards, and the Circulation of Cultural Value.* Harvard University Press.

Ettling, John. 1981. *The Germ of Laziness: Rockefeller Philanthropy and Public Health in the New South.* Harvard University Press.

Evans, Ronald W. 2004. *The Social Studies Wars: What Should We Teach Our Children?* Teachers College Press.

Fedunkiw, Marianne. 2005. *Rockefeller Foundation Funding and Medical Education in Toronto, Montreal, and Halifax.* McGill-Queen's University Press.

Fenton, Edwin. 1966. *Teaching the New Social Studies in Secondary Schools: An Inductive Approach.* Holt, Rinehart, and Winston.

Fetter, Bruce. 2006. "Origins and Elaboration of the National Health Accounts, 1926 –2006." *Health Care Financing Review* 28: 53–67.

Finke, Roger, and Rodney Stark. 1992. *The Churching of America, 1776–1990: Winners and Losers in Our Religious Economy.* Rutgers University Press.

Fisher, Donald. 1993. *Fundamental Development of the Social Sciences: Rockefeller Philanthropy and the United States Social Science Research Council.* University of Michigan Press.

Fisk, John W., Oran Hesterman, and Thomas L. Thorburn. 2000 "Integrated Farming Systems: A Sustainable Agriculture Learning Community in the USA." In *Facilitating Sustainable Agriculture: Participatory Learning and Adaptive Management in Times of Environmental Uncertainty*, edited by Niels G. Röling and M. A. E. Wagemakers. Cambridge University Press.

Fisman, Raymond R., and R. Glenn Hubbard. 2003. "The Role of Nonprofit Endowments." In *The Governance of Not-for-Profit Organizations*, edited by Edward L. Glaeser. University of Chicago Press.

Fleishman, Joel L. 2007. *The Foundation: A Great American Secret: How Private Wealth Is Changing the World.* PublicAffairs.

Flexner, Abraham. 1952. *Funds and Foundations; Their Policies, Past and Present.* Harper and Brothers.

Folbre, Nancy, and Barnet Wagman. 1993. "Counting Housework: New Estimates of Real Product in the United States, 1800–1860." *Journal of Economic History* 53: 275–88.

Ford Foundation. 1949. *Report of the Study for the Ford Foundation on Policy and Program.* Gaither Report. New York.

———. 1950. "Report of the Trustees of the Ford Foundation." New York (September 27).

———. 1974a. *Ford Foundation Annual Report for 1973*. New York (www.fordfound. org/archives/item/1973/text/14).

———. 1974b. "The President's Review: Public Policy and the Private Foundation." New York.

———. 1979. *Ford Foundation International Programs*. New York.

———. 1986. *Ford Foundation Support for the Arts in the United States: A Discussion of New Emphases in the Foundation's Arts Program*. New York.

———. 1991. "Investing for Social Gain; Reflections on Two Decades of Social Investments." New York (www.fordfoundation.org/pdfs/library/Investing_For_Social_Gain.pdf, viewed September 22, 2012).

Fosdick, Raymond B. 1952. *The Story of the Rockefeller Foundation*. Harper and Brothers.

Fosdick, Raymond B., with Henry Pringle and Katherine Douglas Pringle. 1962. *Adventure in Giving: The Story of the General Education Board, a Foundation Established by John D. Rockefeller*. Harper and Row.

Foundation Center. 1981. *The Foundation Directory*. 8th ed. New York.

———. 2007. *Foundation Growth and Giving Estimates: Current Outlook*. New York (www.lgbtfunders.org/files/fgge07.pdf).

———. 2009. *Key Facts on Community Foundations*. New York.

———. 2010. *Foundation Growth and Giving Estimates*. New York (http://foundation center.org/gainknowledge/research/pdf/fgge12.pdf).

———. 2011. "Highlights of Foundation Yearbook." New York (December). (http:// foundationcenter.org/gainknowledge/research/pdf/fy2011_highlights.pdf).

———. 2003. *The PRI Directory: Charitable Loans and Other Program-Related Investments by Foundations*. New York (August).

Foundation Library Center. 1960. *The Foundation Directory*. 1st ed. Russell Sage Foundation.

Foundation Strategy Group. 2003. *Strengthening Community Foundations: Redefining the Opportunities*. Foundation Strategy Group commissioned by the Council on Foundations.

Fox, Daniel M. 1963. *Engines of Culture: Philanthropy and Art Museums*. State Historical Society of Wisconsin.

———. 2005. "Evidence of Evidence-Based Health Policy: The Politics of Systematic Reviews in Coverage Decisions." *Health Affairs* 24: 114–22.

———. 2010. "Foundations and Health: Innovation, Marginalization, and Relevance since 1900." In *American Foundations*, edited by Helmut Anheier and David C. Hammack. Brookings.

Freebairn, Donald K. 1995 "Did the Green Revolution Concentrate Incomes? A Quantitative Study of Research Reports." *World Development* 23: 265–79.

Fremont-Smith, Marion R. 1965. *Foundations and Government*. Russell Sage Foundation.

———. 2001. *Accumulations of Wealth by Nonprofits*. Emerging Issues in Philanthropy Seminar Series. Urban Institute and Hauser Center for Nonprofit Organizations.

———. 2004. *Governing Nonprofit Organizations: Federal and State Law and Regulation*. Harvard University Press.

————. 2006. "Is It Time to Treat Private Foundations and Public Charities Alike?" *Exempt Organization Tax Review* 52: 257.

Freund, Gerald. 1996. *Narcissism and Philanthropy: Ideas and Talent Denied.* Viking.

Freyhan, R. 1948. "The Evolution of the Caritas Figure in the Thirteenth and Fourteenth Centuries." *Journal of the Warburg and Courtauld Institutes* 11: 68–86.

Frumkin, Peter. 2006. *Strategic Giving: The Art and Science of Philanthropy.* University of Chicago Press.

Frumkin, Peter, and Gabriel Kaplan. 2010. "Foundations and Higher Education." In *American Foundations*, edited by Helmut Anheier and David C. Hammack. Brookings.

Fuhrman, Susan, and Marvin Lazerson, eds. 2005. *The Public Schools.* Oxford University Press.

Funders Concerned about AIDS. 2003. "HIV/AIDS Philanthropy: History and Current Parameters, 1980–2000." Washington (www.fcaaids.org/Portals/0/Uploads/Documents/Public/Kaiser.pdf).

Garrett, Thomas A., and Russell M. Rhine. 2007. "Does Government Spending Really Crowd out Charitable Contributions?" New Time Series Evidence Working Paper 2007-012A. Federal Reserve Bank of St. Louis (http://research.stlouisfed.org/wp/2007/2007-012.pdf).

Garside, Patricia L. 2000. *The Conduct of Philanthropy: William Sutton Trust, 1900–2000.* Athlone Press.

Gaul, Gilbert M., and Neill A. Borowski. 1993. *Free Ride: The Tax-Exempt Economy.* Andrews and McMeel.

Geiger, Roger L. 1986. *To Advance Knowledge: The Growth of American Research Universities, 1900–1940.* Oxford University Press.

————. 1993. *Research and Relevant Knowledge: American Research Universities since World War II.* Oxford University Press.

————. 2000. "The Era of Multipurpose Colleges in American Higher Education, 1850–1890." In *The American College in the Nineteenth Century*, edited by Roger L. Geiger. Vanderbilt University Press.

Gelfand, Mark I. 1998. *Trustee for a City: Ralph Lowell of Boston.* Northeastern University Press.

General Education Board. 1964. *The General Education Board: Review and Final Report, 1902–1964.* New York.

Gibbons, Martha. 1999. "Who Funded AIDS?" Aspen Institute Nonprofit Sector Research Fund.

Ginzberg, Lori D. 1990. *Women and the Work of Benevolence: Morality, Politics, and Class in the Nineteenth-Century United States.* Yale University Press.

Girard, Stephen. 1840. "The Will of Stephen Girard." In *The United States of North America as They Are*, edited by Thomas Brothers. Longman, Orme, Brown, Green, and Longmans.

Glenn, John M., Lillian Brandt, and F. Emerson Andrews. 1947. *Russell Sage Foundation, 1907–1947.* Russell Sage Foundation.

Goldberg, Mark F. 1996. "Here for the Long Haul: An Interview with Theodore Sizer." *Phi Delta Kappan* 77: 685–87.

Gordon, Linda. 2002. *The Moral Property of Women: A History of Birth Control Politics in America*. University of Illinois Press.

Gottlieb, Robert. 1993. "Reconstructing Environmentalism: Complex Movements, Diverse Roots." *Environmental History Review* 17, no. 4: 1–19.

———. 2005. *Forcing the Spring: The Transformation of the American Environmental Movement*. Island Press.

Gottmann, Jean. 1961. *Megalopolis: The Urbanized Northeastern Seaboard of the United States*. Twentieth Century Fund.

Goudsmit, Jaap. 1998. *Viral Sex: The Nature of AIDS*. Oxford University Press.

Goulden, Joseph C. 1971. *The Money Givers*. Random House.

Graddy-Gamel, Acacia. 2006. "Off the Shelf: Review of *Philanthropy and Reconciliation: Rebuilding Postwar U.S.-Japanese Relations* by Tadashi Yamamoto, Akira Iriye, and Makoto Iokibe, Eds." Foundation Center, Philanthropy News Digest (http://foundation center.org/pnd/offtheshelf/ots.jhtml?id=158400002).

Graham, Hugh Davis, and Nancy Diamond. 1997. *The Rise of American Research Universities: Elites and Challengers in the Postwar Era*. Johns Hopkins University Press.

Grantmakers in the Arts. 2011. "Arts Funding Snapshot: GIA's Annual Research on Support for Arts and Culture." *GIA Reader* 22, no. 3: 3–8.

Grossberg, Michael. 1985. *Governing the Hearth: Law and the Family in Nineteenth-Century America*. University of North Carolina Press.

Guzzardi, Walter. 1988. *The Henry Luce Foundation: A History: 1936–1986*. University of North Carolina Press.

Hacker, Jacob S. 2002. *The Divided Welfare State: The Battle over Public and Private Social Benefits in the United States*. Cambridge University Press.

Hall, Peter Dobkin. 1982. *The Organization of American Culture, 1700–1900: Private Institutions, Elites, and the Origins of American Nationality*. New York University Press.

———. 1992. *Inventing the Nonprofit Sector and Other Essays on Philanthropy, Voluntarism, and Nonprofit Organizations*. Johns Hopkins University Press.

Hall, Peter Dobkin, and Colin B. Burke. 2006. "Voluntary, Nonprofit, and Religious Entities and Activities: Underlying Concepts, Concerns, and Opportunities." In *Historical Statistics of the United States*. Vol. 4. Cambridge University Press.

Hamburger, Philip. 2002. *Separation of Church and State*. Harvard University Press.

Hamerow, Theodore S. 1987. "The Philanthropic Foundations and Historical Scholarship in the Endowment for the Humanities, the Rockefeller Foundation, and the Social Science Research Council." In *Reflections on History and Historians*. University of Wisconsin Press.

Hammack, David C. 1978. "Problems in the Historical Study of Power in the Cities and Towns of the United States, 1800–1960." *American Historical Review* 83: 323–49.

———. 1982. *Power and Society: Greater New York at the Turn of the Century*. Russell Sage Foundation.

———. 1983. "The Development of Urban Schooling in America." *History of Education Quarterly* 23: 69–76.

———. 1988. *The Russell Sage Foundation: Social Research and Social Action in America, 1907–1947: Guide to the Microfiche Collection*. UPA Academic Editions.

———. 1989. "Community Foundations: The Delicate Question of Purpose." In *An Agile Servant*, edited by Richard Magat. Foundation Center.

———. 1999. "Foundations in the American Polity." In *Philanthropic Foundations*, edited by Ellen Condliffe Lagemann. Indiana University Press.

———. 2002. "Nonprofit Organizations in American History: Research Opportunities and Sources." *American Behavioral Scientist* 45, no. 11: 1638–74.

———. 2003. "Failure and Resilience: Pushing the Limits in Depression and Wartime." In *Charity, Philanthropy, and Civility in American History*, edited by Lawrence Friedman and Mark D. McGarvie. Cambridge University Press.

———. 2006. "American Debates on the Legitimacy of Foundations." In *The Legitimacy of Philanthropic Foundations: United States and European Perspectives*, edited by Kenneth Prewitt, Mattei Dogan, Steven Heydemann, and Stefan Toepler. Russell Sage Foundation.

———. 2012. "F. Emerson Andrews: A Biographical Note."

———, ed. 1998. *Making the Nonprofit Sector in the United States: A Reader*. Indiana University Press.

Hammack, David C., Diane L. Grabowski, and John J. Grabowski, eds. 2002. *Identity, Conflict, and Cooperation: Central Europeans in Cleveland, 1850–1930*. Western Reserve Historical Society.

Hammack, David C, and Steven Heydemann, eds. 2009. *Globalization, Philanthropy, and Civil Society: Projecting Institutional Logics Abroad*. Indiana University Press.

Hammack, David C., and Stanton Wheeler. 1994. *Social Science in the Making: Essays on the Russell Sage Foundation, 1907–1972*. Russell Sage Foundation.

Hammond, Phillip E. 1982. "Vision and Research: The Social Policy Perspective of Kenneth W. Underwood." *Review of Religious Research* 24: 104–15.

Hanle, Paul A. 1982. *Bringing Aerodynamics to America*. MIT Press.

Hannah, Leslie. 1999. "Marshall's 'Trees' and the Global 'Forest': Were 'Giant Redwoods' Different?" In *Learning by Doing in Markets, Firms, and Countries*, edited by Naomi R. Lamoreaux, Daniel M. G. Raff, and Peter Temin. University of Chicago Press.

Harden, Victoria A. 1986. *Inventing the N.I.H.: Federal Biomedical Research Policy, 1887–1937*. Johns Hopkins University Press.

Harlan, Louis R. 1958. *Separate and Unequal: Public School Campaigns and Racism in the Southern Seaboard States, 1901–1915*. Athenaeum.

Harris, Neil. 1962. "The Gilded Age Revisited: Boston and the Museum Movement." *American Quarterly* 14: 545–66.

———. 1966. *The Artist in American Society; the Formative Years, 1790–1860*. G. Braziller.

Harris, Seymour Edwin. 1970. *Economics of Harvard*. McGraw-Hill.

Harrison, Shelby M., and F. Emerson Andrews. 1946. *American Foundations for Social Welfare*. Russell Sage Foundation.

Hart, D. G. 1992. "The Troubled Soul of the Academy: American Learning and the Problem of Religious Studies." *Religion and American Culture: A Journal of Interpretation* (Winter): 49–77.

Hart, Jeffrey. 1973. "Foundations and Social Activism." In *The Future of Foundations*, edited by Fritz F. Heimann. Prentice-Hall.

Haskell, Thomas L. 1977. *The Emergence of Professional Social Science: The American Social Science Association and the Nineteenth-Century Crisis of Authority.* University of Illinois Press.

Hawley, Ellis W. 1974. "Herbert Hoover, the Commerce Secretariat, and the Vision of an Associative State, 1921–1928." *Journal of American History* 61, no. 1: 16–40.

Hazell, P. B. R., C. Ramsamy, and P. K. Aiyasamy. 1991. *The Green Revolution Reconsidered: The Impact of High-Yielding Rice Varieties in South India.* Johns Hopkins University Press.

Hechinger, John. 2007. "Big-Money Donors Move to Curb Colleges' Discretion to Spend Gifts." *Wall Street Journal*, September 18, p. B1 (http://online.wsj.com/article/SB119007667292230616.html, viewed September 18, 2007).

Heifitz, Ronald A., John V. Kania, and Mark R. Kramer. 2004. "Leading Boldly: Foundations Can Move Past Traditional Approaches to Create Social Change through Imaginative—and Even Controversial—Leadership." *Stanford Social Innovation Review* (Winter): 21–31 (www.ssireview.com/pdf/2004WI_feature_heifetz.pdf, viewed September 22, 2012).

Heimann, Fritz F., ed. 1973. *The Future of Foundations.* Prentice-Hall.

Henderson, Helen Weston. 1911. *The Pennsylvania Academy of the Fine Arts and Other Collections of Philadelphia, Including the Pennsylvania Museum, the Wilstach Collection, and the Collections of Independence Hall and the Historical Society of Pennsylvania.* L. C. Page and Company.

Herman, Ellen. 2008. *Kinship by Design: A History of Adoption in the Modern United States.* University of Chicago Press.

Hess, Frederick M. 2005. *With the Best of Intentions: How Philanthropy Is Reshaping K–12 Education.* Harvard Education Press.

Heydemann, Steven, and Rebecca Kinsey. 2010. "The State and International Philanthropy: The Contribution of American Foundations, 1919–1991." In *American Foundations*, edited by Helmut K. Anheier and David C. Hammack. Brookings.

Hill, Hamilton Andrews. 1884. *Memoir of Abbott Lawrence.* Little, Brown, and Company.

Hirsch, Foster. 1998. *The Boys from Syracuse: The Shuberts' Theatrical Empire.* Southern Illinois University Press.

Hodge, Charles. 1845a. "Review of *Christ, The Only Sacrifice: or the Atonement in Its Relations to God and Man*, by Nathan S. S. Beman." *Princeton Review* 17, no. 1 (January): 84–138.

———. 1845b. "Review of *Religion in America*, by Robert Baird," *Biblical Repertory and Princeton Review*, vol. 17: 17–43.

Hofstadter, Richard. 1961. *Academic Freedom in the Age of the College.* Columbia University Press.

Holcombe, Randall G. 2000. *Writing Off Ideas: Taxation, Foundations, and Philanthropy in America.* Transaction Publishers.

Hollis, Ernest V. 1938. *Philanthropic Foundations and Higher Education.* Columbia University Press.

Holt, John C. 1964. *How Children Fail.* Pitman.

Hopkins, Bruce R. 1987. *The Law of Tax-Exempt Organizations.* 5th ed. Wiley.

Hopkinson, Joseph. 1810. "Annual Discourse to the Pennsylvania Academy of the Fine Arts." May 13. Published in *The Port Folio* (supplement): 632.

Howard, Nathaniel R. 1963. *Trust for All Time: The Story of the Cleveland Foundation and the Community Trust Movement.* Cleveland Foundation.

Howe, Daniel Walker. 2002. "Church, State, and Education in the Young American Republic." *Journal of the Early Republic* 22: 1–24.

Howe, Harold II. 1993. *Thinking about Our Kids.* Free Press.

Huggins, N., and others. 2007. "Inclusive Scholarship: Developing Black Studies in the United States." Ford Foundation (www.fordfound.org/pdfs/impact/inclusive_scholarship.pdf).

Hutchins, Robert Maynard. 1956. *Freedom, Education, and the Fund: Essays and Addresses, 1946–1956.* Meridian Books.

Hutchison, William R. 1989. *Between the Times: The Travail of the Protestant Establishment in America, 1900–1960.* Cambridge University Press.

Ilchman, Alice Stone, Warren F. Ilchman, and Mary Hale Tolar, eds. 2004. *The Lucky Few and the Worthy Many: Scholarship Competitions and the World's Future Leaders.* Indiana University Press.

Irvin, Renee A. 2007. "Endowments: Stable Largesse or Distortion of the Polity?" *Public Administration Review* 67: 445–57.

Isaac, Joel. 2011. "The Human Sciences and Cold War America." *Journal of the History of the Behavioral Sciences* 47: 225–31.

Jackson, John P., Jr. 2000. "Blind Law and Powerless Science: The American Jewish Congress, the NAACP, and the Scientific Case against Discrimination, 1945–1950." *Isis* 91, no. 1: 89–116.

Jackson, Walter A. 1990. *Gunnar Myrdal and America's Conscience: Social Engineering and Racial Liberalism, 1938–1987.* University of North Carolina Press.

Jacobson, Judith S. 1984. *The Greatest Good: A History of the John A. Hartford Foundation.* John A. Hartford Foundation.

James, Francis Godwin. 1948. "Charity Endowments as Sources of Local Credit in Seventeenth- and Eighteenth-Century England." *Journal of Economic History* 8: 153–70.

Jantz, Amy, Rob Geen, Roseana Bess, Cynthia Andrews, and Victoria Russell. 2002. "The Continuing Evolution of State Kinship Care Policies." Assessing the New Federalism Discussion Paper 02-11. Urban Institute (www.urban.org/Uploaded PDF/310597_state_kinship_care.pdf, viewed September 22, 2012).

Jarchow, Merrill E. 1981. *Amherst H. Wilder and His Enduring Legacy to Saint Paul.* Amherst H. Wilder Foundation.

Jenkins, Edward Corbin. 1950. *Philanthropy in America: An Introduction to the Practices and Prospects of Organizations Supported by Gifts and Endowments, 1924–1948.* Association Press.

Jenkins, J. Craig. 1985. *The Politics of Insurgency: The Farm Worker Movement in the 1960s.* Columbia University Press.

Johnson, Gerald W. 1948. *Liberal's Progress.* Coward-McCann.

Jonas, Gerald. 1989. *The Circuit Riders: Rockefeller Money and the Rise of Modern Science.* Norton.

Jones, Gareth. 1969. *History of the Law of Charity 1532–1827.* Cambridge University Press.

Josephson, Emanuel Mann. 1952. *Rockefeller, "Internationalist," the Man Who Misrules the World.* Chedney Press.

Josephson, William, and Karin Kunstler Goldman. 2003. "Written Comments on Taxpayer Rights Proposals to the Subcommittee on Oversight of the Committee on Ways and Means, U.S. House of Representatives." Government Printing Office.

Jowett, Garth S., Ian C. Jarvie, and Kathryn H. Fuller. 1996. *Children and the Movies: Media Influence and the Payne Fund Controversy.* Cambridge University Press.

Kaestle, Carl F. 1983. *Pillars of the Republic: Common Schools and American Society, 1780–1860.* Hill and Wang.

Karl, Barry D. 1968. "The Power of Intellect and the Politics of Ideas." *Daedalus* 97: 1002–35.

———. 1974. *Charles E. Merriam and the Study of Politics.* University of Chicago Press.

Karl, Barry D., and Stanley N. Katz. 1981. "The American Private Philanthropic Foundation and the Public Sphere 1890–1930." *Minerva: A Review of Science, Learning, and Policy* 19: 236–70.

Katz, Michael B. 1986. "Review: Child-Saving." *History of Education Quarterly* 26: 413–24.

———. 1996. *In the Shadow of the Poorhouse: A Social History of Welfare in America.* 10th anniversary ed. Basic Books.

———. 2001. *The Price of Citizenship: Redefining the American Welfare State.* Metropolitan Books.

Katz, Stanley N., Barry Sullivan, and C. Paul Beach. 1985. "Legal Change and Legal Autonomy: Charitable Trusts in New York, 1777–1893." *Law and History Review* 3: 51–89.

Kay, Lily E. 1993. *The Molecular Vision of Life: Caltech, the Rockefeller Foundation, and the Rise of the New Biology.* Oxford University Press.

Keele, Harold M., and Joseph C. Kiger, eds. 1984. *Foundations.* Greenwood Press.

Keenan, James F. 2007. *The Works of Mercy: The Heart of Catholicism.* Rowman and Littlefield.

Keppel, Francis. 1966. *The Necessary Revolution in American Education.* Harper and Row.

Keppel, Frederick P. 1930. *The Foundation: Its Place in American Life.* Macmillan.

Kevles, Daniel J. 1977. *The Physicists: The History of a Scientific Community in Modern America.* Vintage Books.

Kimball, Bruce A., and Benjamin Ashby Johnson. 2012. "The Beginning of 'Free Money' Ideology in American Universities: Charles W. Eliot at Harvard, 1869–1909." *History of Education Quarterly* 52: 222–50.

Kiser, Clyde. 1981. "The Role of the Milbank Memorial Fund in the Early History of the Association." *Population Index* 47: 490–94.

Klausner, Michael. 2003. "When Time Isn't Money: Foundation Payouts and the Time Value of Money." *Stanford Social Innovation Review* 1: 51–59.

Kleinberger, Daniel. 2010. "A Myth Deconstructed: The 'Emperor's New Clothes' on the Low-Profit Limited Liability Company." Formerly titled "The Snare and Delusion of the L3C." (http://papers.ssrn.com/sol3/papers.cfm?abstract_id=1554045).

Knickman, James R., and Stephen L. Isaacs. 2010. "The Robert Wood Johnson Foundation's Efforts to Improve Health and Health Care for All Americans." In *American Foundations*, edited by Helmut K. Anheier and David C. Hammack. Brookings.

Koebel, C. Theodore, ed. 1998. *Shelter and Society: Theory, Research, and Policy for Nonprofit Housing*. State University of New York Press.

Koenig, David Thomas. 2008. "Regionalism in Early American Law." In *The Cambridge History of Law in America: Early America (1580–1815)*, edited by Michael Grossberg and Christopher L. Tomlins. Cambridge University Press.

Kohler, Robert E. 1991. *Partners in Science: Foundations and Natural Scientists, 1900 –1945*. University of Chicago Press.

Kohlstedt, Sally Gregory. 1988. "Curiosities and Cabinets: Natural History Museums and Education on the Antebellum Campus." *Isis* 79: 405–26.

Koleda, Michael S., and National Planning Association. 1977. *The Federal Health Dollar, 1969–1976: A Chartbook Analysis of Activities Supported and Strategies Pursued in Federal Expenditures for Health*. National Planning Association.

Korey, William. 2007. *Taking on the World's Repressive Regimes: The Ford Foundation's International Human Rights Policies and Practices*. Palgrave Macmillan.

Kramer, Ralph M. 1987. "Voluntary Agencies and the Personal Social Services." In *The Nonprofit Sector: A Research Handbook*. Yale University Press.

Kristol, Irving, Paul Johnson, and Michael Novak. 1980. *The Moral Basis of Democratic Capitalism: Three Essays*. American Enterprise Institute for Public Policy Research.

Kuehl, Warren F., and Lynne K. Dunn. 1997. *Keeping the Covenant: American Internationalists and the League of Nations, 1920–1939*. Kent State University Press.

Lagemann, Ellen Condliffe. 1983. *Private Power for the Public Good: A History of the Carnegie Foundation for the Advancement of Teaching*. Wesleyan University Press.

———. 1989. *The Politics of Knowledge: The Carnegie Corporation, Philanthropy, and Public Policy*. Wesleyan University Press.

———. 1999. *Philanthropic Foundations: New Scholarship, New Possibilities*. Indiana University Press.

———. 2002. *An Elusive Science: The Troubling History of Education Research*. University of Chicago Press.

Lamoreaux, Naomi R. 1994. *Insider Lending: Banks, Personal Connections, and Economic Development in Industrial New England*. Cambridge University Press.

———. 2004. "Partnerships, Corporations, and the Limits on Contractual Freedom in U.S. History: An Essay in Economics, Law, and Culture." In *Constructing Corporate America: History, Politics, Culture*, edited by Kenneth Lipartito and David B. Sicilia. Oxford University Press.

Lampkin, Linda M., and David D. Stern. 2003. *Who Helps Public Schools? A Portrait of Local Education Funds, 1991–2001*. Urban Institute, Center on Nonprofits and Philanthropy (www.urban.org/UploadedPDF/410915_PENReport.pdf).

Lankford, John. 1964. *Congress and the Foundations in the Twentieth Century*. Wisconsin State University.

Lannie, Vincent P. 1968. *Public Money and Parochial Education: Bishop Hughes, Governor Seward, and the New York School Controversy*. Case Western Reserve University Press.

Laski, Harold Joseph. 1930. "Foundations, Universities, and Research." In *The Dangers of Obedience and Other Essays*. Harper and Brothers.

Lave, Judith, Lester B. Lave, and Samuel Leinhart. 1974. *Medical Manpower Models*. Rand Corporation (www.rand.org/pubs/reports/R1481.html).

Lawrence, Steven. 2012. *Foundation Growth and Giving Estimates*. Foundation Center.

Lawrence, Steven, and Reina Mukai. 2009. *Foundation Growth and Giving Estimates: Current Outlook*. Foundation Center.

———. 2010. *Foundation Growth and Giving Estimates 2010*. Foundations Today Series. Foundation Center.

Lazerson, Marvin. 1998. "Whither America's Fellowships?" *Change* 30, no. 3: 26.

Lazerson, Marvin, and Susan Fuhrman, eds. 2005. *The Public Schools*. Oxford University Press.

Lazerson, Marvin, Judith Block McLaughlin, Bruce McPherson, and Stephen K. Bailey. 1985. *An Education of Value: The Purposes and Practices of Schools*. Cambridge University Press.

Lemann, Nicholas. 1999. *The Big Test: The Secret History of the American Meritocracy*. Farrar, Straus, and Giroux.

Levy, Daniel C. 2005. *To Export Progress: The Golden Age of University Assistance in the Americas*. Indiana University Press.

Levy, Reynold. 1999. *Give and Take: A Candid Account of Corporate Philanthropy*. Harvard Business Press.

Light, Paul Charles. 2008. *The Search for Social Entrepreneurship*. Brookings.

Lindeman, Eduard. 1936. *Wealth and Culture: A Study of One Hundred Foundations and Community Trusts and Their Operations during the Decades 1921–1930*. Harcourt Brace.

Link, William A. 1997. *William Friday: Power, Purpose, and American Higher Education*. University of North Carolina Press.

Lomas, Kathryn, and Tim Cornell, eds. 2003. *"Bread and Circuses": Euergetism and Municipal Patronage in Roman Italy*. Routledge.

Lomask, Milton. 1964. *Seed Money: The Guggenheim Story*. New York: Farrar, Straus.

Loomis, Frank Denman. 1962. *The Chicago Community Trust: A History of Its Development, 1915–62*. Chicago Community Trust.

Lundberg, Ferdinand. 1937. *America's 60 Families*. Vanguard Press.

Ma, Qiusha. 1995. "The Rockefeller Foundation and Modern Medical Education in China, 1915–1951." Ph.D. dissertation, Case Western Reserve University.

MacDonald, Dwight. 1956. *The Ford Foundation: The Men and the Millions*. Reynal.

MacDonald, Norine, and Luc Tayart de Borms, eds. 2008. *Philanthropy in Europe: A Rich Past, a Promising Future*. Alliance Publishing Trust.

Magat, Richard. 1979. *The Ford Foundation at Work, Philanthropic Choices, Methods, and Styles*. Plenum Press.

———. 1999. *Unlikely Partners: Philanthropic Foundations and the Labor Movement*. ILR Press.

Maier, Pauline. 1993. "The Revolutionary Origins of the American Corporation." *William and Mary Quarterly* 50: 51–84.

Marcus, George, and Peter Dobkin Hall. 1992. *Lives in Trust: The Fortunes of Dynastic Families in Late Twentieth-Century America.* Westview Press.

Margo, Richard. 1992. "Foundations." In *Who Benefits from the Nonprofit Sector?* edited by Charles T. Clotfelter. University of Chicago Press.

Markusen, Ann, and David King. 2003. *The Artistic Dividend: The Arts' Hidden Contributions to Regional Development.* University of Minnesota, Humphrey Institute of Public Affairs (July).

Marris, Peter, and Martin Rein. 1973. *Dilemmas of Social Reform: Poverty and Community Action in the United States.* Transaction Publishers.

Martin, Warren Bryan. 1981. "The Narrow End of the Cornucopia: Lessons on Equity from the Danforth Fellowship Program." *Change* 13: 35–37.

Maskell, Jack H. 2008. "Lobbying Regulations on Non-Profit Organizations." Congressional Research Service Report for Congress.

Mather, Cotton. 1710. *Bonifacius: Essays to Do Good.* Chalmers and Collins. Excerpt in *Making the Nonprofit Sector in the United States,* edited by David C. Hammack. Indiana University Press, 1998.

Maza, Sarah C. 2005. *The Myth of the French Bourgeoisie: An Essay on the Social Imaginary, 1750–1850.* Harvard University Press.

McAnear, Beverly. 1952. "The Raising of Funds by the Colonial Colleges." *Mississippi Valley Historical Review* 38: 591–612.

McCarthy, Kathleen D. 1982. *Noblesse Oblige: Charity and Cultural Philanthropy in Chicago, 1849–1929.* University of Chicago Press.

———. 1985. "The Short and Simple Annals of the Poor: Foundation Funding for the Humanities, 1900–1983." *Proceedings of the American Philosophical Society* 129, no. 1: 3–8.

———. 2003. *American Creed: Philanthropy and the Rise of Civil Society, 1700–1865.* University of Chicago Press.

McCaughey, Robert A. 1984. *International Studies and Academic Enterprise: A Chapter in the Enclosure of American Learning.* Columbia University Press.

McConnell, Michael W. 2003. "Establishment and Disestablishment at the Founding, Part I: Establishment of Religion." *William and Mary Law Review* 44: 2105–06.

McGray, Douglas. 2007. "Network Philanthropy." *Los Angeles Times,* January 21.

McIlnay, Dennis P. 1995. "The Privilege of Privacy: Twenty-Five Years in the Public-Accountability Record of Foundations." *Nonprofit and Voluntary Sector Quarterly* 24: 117–41.

McLoughlin, William Gerald. 1971. *New England Dissent, 1630–1833: The Baptists and the Separation of Church and State.* Harvard University Press.

McPherson, James M. 1975. *The Abolitionist Legacy: From Reconstruction to the NAACP.* Princeton University Press.

Merz, Carol, and Sheldon S. Frankel. 1995. *Private Funds for Public Schools: A Study of School Foundations.* University of Puget Sound.

Metz, Lance E., and Ivan Miroslav Viest. 1991. *The First 75 Years: A History of the Engineering Foundation.* Engineering Foundation.

Meyer, Jimmy Elaine Wilkinson. 2004. *Any Friend of the Movement: Networking for Birth Control, 1920–1940.* Ohio State University Press.

Miller, Howard Smith. 1961. *The Legal Foundations of American Philanthropy, 1776–1844*. State Historical Society of Wisconsin.

Miller, John J. 2006. *A Gift of Freedom: How the John M. Olin Foundation Changed America*. Encounter Books.

Minkoff, Debra C., and Jon Agnone. 2010. "Consolidating Social Change: The Consequences of Foundation Funding for Developing Social Movement Infrastructures." In *American Foundations*, edited by Helmut K. Anheier and David C. Hammack. Brookings.

Mitgang, Lee D. 2000. *Big Bird and Beyond: The New Media and the Markle Foundation*. Fordham University Press.

Morris, Andrew J. F. 2009. *The Limits of Voluntarism: Charity and Welfare from the New Deal through the Great Society*. Cambridge University Press.

Morrow, Robert W. 2006. *Sesame Street and the Reform of Children's Television*. Johns Hopkins University Press.

Mosley, Jennifer E., and Joseph Galaskiewicz. 2010. "The Role of Foundations in Shaping Social Welfare Policy and Services: The Case of Welfare Reform." In *American Foundations*, edited by Helmut K. Anheier and David C. Hammack. Brookings.

Mowery, David C., and Bhaven N. Sampat. 2001. "Patenting and Licensing University Inventions: Lessons from the History of the Research Corporation." *Industrial and Corporate Change* 10: 317–55.

Moynihan, Daniel Patrick. 1969. *Maximum Feasible Misunderstanding: Community Action in the War on Poverty*. Free Press.

Munnell, Alicia Haydock, and Annika E Sunden. 2003. *Death and Dollars: The Role of Gifts and Bequests in America*. Brookings.

Nachtigal, Paul M. 1972. *A Foundation Goes to School: The Ford Foundation Comprehensive School Improvement Program*. Ford Foundation.

National Commission on Philanthropy and Civic Renewal. 1997. *Giving Better, Giving Smarter: The Report of the National Commission on Philanthropy and Civic Renewal*. National Commission on Philanthropy and Civic Renewal.

Naylor, Natalie A. 1984. "'Holding High the Standard': The Influence of the American Education Society in Ante-Bellum Education." *History of Education Quarterly* 24: 479–97.

Neem, Johann N. 2008. *Creating a Nation of Joiners: Democracy and Civil Society in Early National Massachusetts*. Harvard University Press.

———. 2011. "Civil Society and American Nationalism, 1776–1865." In *Politics and Partnerships: The Role of Voluntary Associations in America's Political Past and Present*, edited by Elisabeth S. Clemens and Doug Guthrie. University of Chicago Press.

Nielsen, Waldemar A. 1972. *The Big Foundations*. Columbia University Press.

———. 1985. *The Golden Donors: A New Anatomy of the Great Foundations*. Truman Talley Books.

Ninkovich, Frank A. 1982. "Ideology, the Open Door, and Foreign Policy." *Foreign Policy* 6: 185–208.

Nord, David Paul. 2001. "Benevolent Capital: Financing Evangelical Book Publishing in Early Nineteenth-Century America." In *God and Mammon: Protestants, Money, and the Market, 1790–1860*, edited by Mark A. Noll. Oxford University Press.

———. 2004. *Faith in Reading: Religious Publishing and the Birth of Mass Media in America*. Oxford University Press.

Norton, Charles Benjamin. 1852. *Norton's Literary Register*. C. B. Norton.

Oates, Mary J. 1995. *The Catholic Philanthropic Tradition in America*. Indiana University Press.

O'Connor, Alice. 2001. *Poverty Knowledge: Social Science, Social Policy, and the Poor in Twentieth-Century U.S. History*. Princeton University Press.

———. 2010. "Foundations, Social Movements, and the Contradictions of Liberal Philanthropy." In *American Foundations*, edited by Helmut K. Anheier and David C. Hammack. Brookings.

Ogg, Frederic Austin. 1928. *Research in the Humanistic and Social Sciences: Report of a Survey Conducted for the American Council of Learned Societies*. Century Company.

Olasky, Marvin N., Daniel T. Oliver, William T. Poole, and Robert V. Pambianco. 1991. *Patterns of Corporate Philanthropy: Funding False Compassion*. Capital Research Center.

Oleson, Alexandra, and John Voss. 1979. *The Organization of Knowledge in Modern America, 1860–1920*. Johns Hopkins University Press.

O'Neill, Michael, and Kathleen Fletcher. 1998. *Nonprofit Management Education: U.S. and World Perspectives*. Praeger.

Ostrander, Susan A. 1995. *Money for Change: Social Movement Philanthropy at Haymarket People's Fund*. Temple University Press.

Ostrom, Mary Ann. 2007. "Global Philanthropy Forum Explores New Way of Giving." *San Jose Mercury News*, April 12.

Oswald, Andrew J. 2009. "World-Leading Research and Its Measurement." Economic Research Paper. University of Warwick.

Otto, Daniel. 2010. "Economic Losses from the Floods." In *A Watershed Year: Anatomy of the Iowa Floods of 2008*, edited by Cornelia F. Mutel. University of Iowa Press.

Palló, Gábor. 2002. "Make a Peak on the Plain: The Rockefeller Foundation's Szeged Project." In *Rockefeller Philanthropy and Modern Biomedicine: International Initiatives from World War I to the Cold War*, edited by William H. Schneider. Indiana University Press.

Payton, Robert L. 1988. *Philanthropy: Voluntary Action for the Public Good*. American Council on Education and Macmillan.

Pells, Richard H. 1997. *Not Like Us: How Europeans Have Loved, Hated, and Transformed American Culture since World War II*. Basic Books.

Perko, F. Michael. 1988. *Enlightening the Next Generation: Catholics and Their Schools, 1830–1980*. Garland.

Perl, Arnold. 1948. "To Secure These Rights." *Hollywood Quarterly* 3, no. 3: 267–77.

Phillips-Fein, Kim. 2009. *Invisible Hands: The Making of the Conservative Movement from the New Deal to Reagan*. W. W. Norton.

Picarda, Hubert. 1977. *The Law and Practice Relating to Charities*. Butterworths.

Pierson, P. 2000. "Increasing Returns, Path Dependence, and the Study of Politics." *American Political Science Review* 94: 251–67.

Powell, Horace B. 1956. *The Original Has This Signature: W. K. Kellogg*. Prentice-Hall.

Powell, Walter, and Paul DiMaggio. 1991. *The New Institutionalism in Organizational Analysis*. University of Chicago Press.

Pratt, John Webb. 1967. *Religion, Politics, and Diversity: The Church-State Theme in New York History.* Cornell University Press.

Pressman, Jeffrey L., and Aaron B. Wildavsky. 1984. *Implementation: How Great Expectations in Washington Are Dashed in Oakland.* University of California Press.

Prewitt, Kenneth. 1999. "The Importance of Foundations in an Open Society." In *The Future of Foundations in a Free Society.* Bertelsmann Foundation.

———. 2001. "The Foundation Mission: Purpose, Practice, Public Pressures." In *Foundations in Europe: Society, Management, and Law*, edited by Andreas Schlüter, Volker Then, and Peter Walkenhorst. Directory of Social Change.

Prewitt, Kenneth, Mattei Dogan, Steven Heydemann, and Stefan Toepler. 2006. *The Legitimacy of Philanthropic Foundations: United States and European Perspectives.* Russell Sage Foundation.

Pullan, Brian. 1971. *Rich and Poor in Renaissance Venice: The Social Institutions of a Catholic State.* Oxford University Press.

Purcell, Richard J. 1918. *Connecticut in Transition, 1775–1818.* American Historical Association.

Quadagno, Jill. 2005. *One Nation, Uninsured: Why the U.S. Has No National Health Insurance.* Oxford University Press.

Quigley, Kevin F. F. 1997. *For Democracy's Sake: Foundations and Democracy Assistance in Central Europe.* Johns Hopkins University Press.

Quincy, Josiah. 1851. *History of the Boston Athenæum.* Metcalf and Company.

Rabinowitz, Alan. 1990. *Social Change Philanthropy in America.* Quorum Books.

Ragosta, John A. 2008. "Fighting for Freedom: Virginia Dissenters' Struggle for Religious Liberty during the American Revolution." *Virginia Magazine of History and Biography* 116, no. 3: 226–61.

Rasmussen, Wayne D. 1989. *Taking the University to the People: Seventy-Five Years of Cooperative Extension.* Iowa State University Press.

Ravitch, Diane. 1985. *The Troubled Crusade: American Education, 1945–1980.* Basic Books.

———. 2010. *The Death and Life of the Great American School System: How Testing and Choice Are Undermining Education.* Basic Books.

Reeves, Thomas C. 1969. *Freedom and the Foundation: The Fund for the Republic in the Era of McCarthyism.* Knopf.

Regenstreif, Donna I., Sarajane Brittis, Claire M. Fagin, and Corinne H. Rieder. 2003. "Strategies to Advance Geriatric Nursing: The John A. Hartford Foundation Initiatives." *Journal of the American Geriatrics Society* 51: 1479–83.

Rettig, Richard A. 1977. *Cancer Crusade: The Story of the National Cancer Act of 1971.* Princeton University Press.

———. 2004. "Reorganizing the National Institutes of Health." *Health Affairs* 23: 257–62.

Rich, Andrew. 2004. *Think Tanks, Public Policy, and the Politics of Expertise.* Cambridge University Press.

Richard King Mellon Foundation. 2002. *From Sea to Shining Sea: Richard King Mellon Foundation, American Land Conservation Program, 1988–2002.* Pittsburgh.

Richards, William C., and William J. Norton. 1957. *Biography of a Foundation: The Story of the Children's Fund of Michigan, 1929–1954. A Terminal Philanthropic Foundation.* Children's Fund of Michigan.

Richardson, Malcolm L. 1981. "The Humanities and International Understanding: Some Reflections on the Experience at the Rockefeller Foundation." Paper delivered at the International Philanthropy and the Humanities conference, Bellagio, Italy, November 16–20.

Roberts, Perri Lee. 1989. "Comelis Buys the Elder's Seven Works of Mercy: An Exemplar of Confratemal Art from Early Sixteenth-Century Northern Europe." *Renaissance and Reformation/Renaissance et Reforme* 25: 135–49.

Robinson, Marshall. 1984. "Private Foundations and Social Science Research." *Society* 9: 76–80.

Rockefeller Philanthropy Advisors. 2008. *Philanthropy's New Passing Gear: Mission-Related Investing; a Policy and Implementation Guide for Foundation Trustees.* New York (February).

Rodgers, Daniel T. 1998. *Atlantic Crossings: Social Politics in a Progressive Age.* Harvard University Press.

Roeber, Anthony G. 2001. "The Long Road to Vidal: Charity Law and State Formation in Early America." In *The Many Legalities of Early America*, edited by Christopher L. Tomlins and Bruce H. Mann. University of North Carolina Press.

———. 2006. "The Law, Religion, and State Making in the Early Modern World: Protestant Revolutions in the Works of Berman, Gorski, and Witte." *Law and Social Inquiry* 31: 199–227.

Roelofs, Joan. 2003. *Foundations and Public Policy: The Mask of Pluralism.* State University of New York Press.

Rogers, David. 1990. "Community Control and Decentralization." In *Urban Politics, New York Style*, edited by Jewel Bellush and Dick Netzer. M. E. Sharpe.

Rooks, Noliwe M., 2006. *White Money Black Power: The Surprising History of African American Studies and the Crisis of Race in Higher Education.* Beacon Press.

Rosner, David. 1982. *A Once Charitable Enterprise: Hospitals and Health Care in Brooklyn and New York, 1885–1915.* Cambridge University Press.

Ross, Dorothy. 1991. *The Origins of American Social Science.* Cambridge University Press.

Rossiter, Margaret W. 1971. "Benjamin Silliman and the Lowell Institute: The Popularization of Science in Nineteenth-Century America." *New England Quarterly* 44: 602–26.

———. 1984. *Women Scientists in America: Struggles and Strategies to 1940.* Johns Hopkins University Press.

Rothman, David J. 1971. *The Discovery of the Asylum : Social Order and Disorder in the New Republic.* Little, Brown and Company.

Rothman, Sheila M. 1978. *Woman's Proper Place: A History of Changing Ideals and Practices, 1870 to the Present.* Basic Books.

Rudolph, Frederick. 1962. *The American College and University: A History.* Knopf.

Rusk, Dean. 1961. *The Role of the Foundation in American Life.* Claremont University College.

Ruttan, Vernon W. 2004. "Controversy about Agricultural Technology Lessons from the Green Revolution." *International Journal of Biotechnology* 6: 43–54.

Sacks, Albert M. 1960. "The Role of Philanthropy: An Institutional View." *Virginia Law Review* 46: 516–38.

Sacks, Eleanor W. 2000. *The Growth of Community Foundations around the World: An Examination of the Vitality of the Community Foundation Movement.* Council on Foundations.

———. 2005. *Community Foundation Global Status Report.* Worldwide Initiatives for Grantmaker Support.

Saez, Emmanuel. 2009. "Tables and Figures Updated to 2007 in Excel Format." (http://elsa.berkeley.edu/~saez).

Saez, Emmanuel, and Thomas Piketty. 2003. "Income Inequality in the United States, 1913–1998." *Quarterly Journal of Economics* 118, no. 1: 1–39.

Salamon, Lester M. 1995. *Partners in Public Service: Government-Nonprofit Relations in the Modern Welfare State.* Johns Hopkins University Press.

———. 2002. "The Resilient Sector: The State of Nonprofit America." In *The State of Nonprofit America*, edited by Lester M. Salamon. Brookings.

Salamon, Lester M., and Michael S. Lund. 1989. *Beyond Privatization: The Tools of Government Action.* Urban Institute.

Sansing, R., and R. Yetman. 2006. "Governing Private Foundations Using the Tax Law." *Journal of Accounting and Economics* 41: 363–84.

Scheiding, Tom. 2011. "Boundary Institutions for Reconciliation of Academic Chemistry to Industry: Germany vs. the United States." Social Science Research Network, posted August 19 (http://papers.ssrn.com/sol3/papers.cfm?abstract_id=1912161).

Schlossman, Steven L., Michael W. Sedlak, and Harold Wechsler. 1987. *The "New Look": The Ford Foundation and the Revolution in Business Education.* Graduate Management Admission Council.

Schneider, William H. 2002. *Rockefeller Philanthropy and Modern Biomedicine: International Initiatives from World War I to the Cold War.* Indiana University Press.

Schoff, Rick, ed. 2004. "September 11: The Philanthropic Response." Foundation Center (http://foundationcenter.org/gainknowledge/research/pdf/911book3.pdf).

Schonfeld, Roger C. 2003. *JSTOR: A History.* Princeton University Press.

Schramm, Carl J. 2006. *The Entrepreneurial Imperative: How America's Economic Miracle Will Reshape the World and Change Your Life.* HarperCollins.

Schwartz, John J. 1994. *Modern American Philanthropy: A Personal Account.* Wiley.

Scott, W. Richard. 2000. *Institutional Change and Healthcare Organizations: From Professional Dominance to Managed Care.* University of Chicago Press.

Scrivener, Susan, and others. 2008. *A Good Start: Two-Year Effects of a Freshmen Learning Community Program at Kingsborough Community College.* John D. and Catherine T. MacArthur Foundation.

Sealander, Judith. 1997. *Private Wealth and Public Life: Foundation Philanthropy and the Reshaping of American Social Policy from the Progressive Era to the New Deal.* Johns Hopkins University Press.

Sears, J. B. 1922. *Philanthropy in the Shaping of American Higher Education.* U.S. Bureau of Education.

Sellars, Richard West. 1999. *Preserving Nature in the National Parks: A History*. Yale University Press.

Servos, John W. 1990. *Physical Chemistry from Ostwald to Pauling: The Making of a Science in America*. Princeton University Press.

————. 1996. "Engineers, Businessmen, and the Academy: The Beginnings of Sponsored Research at the University of Michigan." *Technology and Culture* 37: 721–62.

Shah, Tina. 2008. "Copayment Foundations: Help for the Underinsured." *Biotechnology Healthcare* 5, no. 4: 41–43 (www.ncbi.nlm.nih.gov/pmc/articles/PMC2702190).

Sharpless, John. 1997. "Population Science, Private Foundations, and Development Aid: The Transformation of Demographic Knowledge in the United States, 1945–1965." In *International Development and the Social Sciences: Essays on the History and Politics of Knowledge*, edited by Frederick Cooper and Randall Packard. University of California Press.

Sherwood, Sidney. 1900. *The University of the State of New York: History of Higher Education in the State of New York*. U.S. Bureau of Education.

Shiao, Jiannbin Lee. 2005. *Identifying Talent, Institutionalizing Diversity: Race and Philanthropy in Post–Civil Rights America*. Duke University Press.

Shils, Edward. 1997. *Portraits: A Gallery of Intellectuals*. University of Chicago Press.

Shorter, Edward. 2000. *The Kennedy Family and the Story of Mental Retardation*. Temple University Press.

Shulman, James L., and William G. Bowen. 2002. *The Game of Life: College Sports and Educational Values*. Princeton University Press.

Shulman, Jay, Carol Brown, and Roger Kahn. 1972. "Report on the Russell Sage Foundation." *Insurgent Sociologist* 2, no. 4: 6–34.

Siegmund-Schultze, R. 2001. *Rockefeller and the Internationalization of Mathematics between the Two World Wars: Documents and Studies for the Social History of Mathematics in the 20th Century*. Science Networks Historical Studies vol. 25. Birkhäuser Verlag.

Sievers, Bruce. 2001. "If Pigs Had Wings: The Appeals and Limits of Venture Philanthropy." Waldemar A. Nielsen Issues in Philanthropy Seminar Series. Georgetown University.

————. 2010. *Civil Society, Philanthropy, and the Fate of the Commons*. Tufts University Press.

Silber, Norman Isaac. 2001. *A Corporate Form of Freedom: The Emergence of the Nonprofit Sector*. Westview Press.

Silberman, Charles E. 1970. *Crisis in the Classroom: The Remaking of American Education*. Random House.

Simon, John G. 1965. "Written Statement on Treasury Department Report on Private Foundations." House Committee on Ways and Means, 89 Cong. 1 sess. Report on Private Foundations, vol. I, p. 446.

————. 1973. "Foundations and Public Controversy: An Affirmative View." In *The Future of Foundations*, edited by Fritz F. Heimann. Prentice-Hall.

————. 1987a. "American Philanthropy and the Buck Trust." Faculty Scholarship Series Paper 1940 (http://digitalcommons.law.yale.edu/fss_papers/1940).

————. 1987b. "The Tax Treatment of Nonprofit Organizations: A Review of Federal and State Policies." In *The Nonprofit Sector: A Research Handbook*, edited by Walter W. Powell. Yale University Press.

————. 2000. "Private Foundations as a Federally Regulated Industry: Time for a Fresh Look?" *Exempt Organization Tax Review* 27: 66–80.

Singer, Amy. 2003. "Charity's Legacies: Reconsideration of Ottoman Imperial Endowment-Making." In *Poverty and Charity in Middle Eastern Contexts*, edited by Michael Bonner, Mine Ener, and Amy Singer. State University of New York Press.

————. 2008. *Charity in Islamic Societies*. Cambridge University Press.

Sizer, Theodore R. 1984. *Horace's Compromise: The Dilemmas of the American High School*. Houghton, Mifflin.

Skocpol, Theda. 1992. *Protecting Soldiers and Mothers: The Political Origins of Social Policy in the United States*. Harvard University Press.

Skocpol, Theda, and Morris P. Fiorina. 1999. *Civic Engagement in American Democracy*. Brookings.

Sloan, Douglas. 1994. *Faith and Knowledge: Mainline Protestantism and American Higher Education*. Westminster/John Knox Press.

Slocum, John W. 2009. "Philanthropic Foundations in Russia: Western Projection and Local Legitimacy." In *Globalization, Philanthropy, and Civil Society: Projecting Institutional Logics Abroad*, edited by David C. Hammack and Steven Heydemann. Indiana University Press.

Smart, Kenneth. 1970. *A Sacred Trust: The Story of the Baptist Foundation of Texas*. Baptist Foundation of Texas.

Smith, Douglas G. 2003. "The Establishment Clause: Corollary of Eighteenth-Century Corporate Law?" *Northwestern University Law Review* 98: 239–69.

Smith, James A. 1991. *The Idea Brokers: Think Tanks and the Rise of the New Policy Elite*. Free Press.

————. 2010. "Foundations as Cultural Actors." In *American Foundations*, edited by Helmut K. Anheier and David C. Hammack. Brookings.

Smith, James A., and Karsten Borgmann. 2001. "Foundations in Europe: The Historical Context." In *Foundations in Europe: Society, Management, and Law*, edited by Andreas Schluter. Directory of Social Change.

Smith, Steven Douglas. 2004. "The Pluralist Predicament: Contemporary Theorizing in the Law of Religious Freedom." Public Law and Legal Theory Research Paper Series. University of San Diego School of Law.

Smith, Steven Rathgeb. 2010. "Foundations and Public Policy." In *American Foundations*, edited by Helmut K. Anheier and David C. Hammack. Brookings.

Smith, Steven Rathgeb, and Michael Lipsky. 1993. *Nonprofits for Hire: The Welfare State in the Age of Contracting*. Harvard University Press.

Smith, Tony. 1994. *America's Mission: The United States and the Worldwide Struggle for Democracy in the Twentieth Century*. Princeton University Press.

Smith-Rosenberg, Carroll. 1971. *Religion and the Rise of the American City: The New York City Mission Movement, 1812–1870*. Cornell University Press.

Snow, David A., Sarah Anne Soule, and Hanspeter Kriesi, eds. 2004. *The Blackwell Companion to Social Movements*. Blackwell.

Snyder, Timothy. 2010. *Bloodlands: Europe between Hitler and Stalin*. Basic Books.

Sontz, Ann H. L. 1989. *Philanthropy and Gerontology: The Role of American Foundations*. Greenwood Press.

Southern, David W. 1987. *Gunnar Myrdal and Black-White Relations: The Use and Abuse of an American Dilemma, 1944–1969*. Louisiana State University Press.

Sproule, J. Michael. 1997. *Propaganda and Democracy: The American Experience of Media and Mass Persuasion*. Cambridge University Press.

Stanfield, John H. 1985. *Philanthropy and Jim Crow in American Social Science*. Greenwood Press.

Starrett, Agnes Lynch. 1966. *The Maurice and Laura Falk Foundation: A Private Fortune, a Public Trust*. Historical Society of Western Pennsylvania.

State Board of Charity of Massachusetts. 1894. *Annual Report*. Vol. 16. Boston.

Steele, Richard W. 1989. "The War on Intolerance: The Reformulation of American Nationalism, 1939–1941." *Journal of American Ethnic History* 9, no. 1: 9–35.

Stefancic, Jean, and Richard Delgado. 1996. *No Mercy: How Conservative Think Tanks and Foundations Changed America's Social Agenda*. Temple University Press.

Stetzer, Ed. 2006. *Planting Missional Churches*. B&H Publishing Group.

Stevens, Rosemary. 1998. *American Medicine and the Public Interest*. University of California Press.

Stocking, George W., Jr. 1985. "Philanthropoids and Vanishing Cultures: Rockefeller and the End of the Museum Era in Anglo-American Anthropology." In *Objects and Others: Essays on Museums and Material Culture*, edited by George W. Stocking Jr. University of Wisconsin Press.

Story, Ronald. 1980. *The Forging of an Aristocracy: Harvard and the Boston Upper Class, 1800–1870*. Wesleyan University Press.

Stouffer, Samuel A. 1955. *Communism, Conformity, and Civil Liberties: A Cross-Section of the Nation Speaks Its Mind*. Doubleday.

Strickland, Stephen P. 1972. *Politics, Science, and Dread Disease: A Short History of United States Medical Research Policy*. Harvard University Press.

Strom, Stephanie. 2006. "What's Wrong with Profit?" *New York Times,* November 13 (www.nytimes.com/2006/11/13/us/13strom.html?pagewanted=print, viewed on September 23, 2012).

———. 2011. "Google Finds It Hard to Reinvent Philanthropy." *New York Times,* January 29. (www.nytimes.com/2011/01/30/business/30charity.html?pagewanted=all, viewed July 24, 2012).

Sullivan, William M., and Matthew S. Rosin. 2008. *A New Agenda for Higher Education: Shaping a Life of the Mind for Practice*. Jossey-Bass.

Sun, E-Tu Zen. 1986. "The Growth of the Academic Community." In *Republican China, 1912–1919*, edited by Denis Twitchett, John King Fairbank, and Albert Feuerwerker. Cambridge University Press.

Sutton, Frances X. 1987. "The Ford Foundation: The Early Years." *Daedalus* 116: 41–91.

Svonkin, Stuart. 1997. *Jews against Prejudice: American Jews and the Fight for Civil Liberties*. Columbia University Press.

Sykes, Gary. 1984. "Teacher Education and the Predicament of Reform." In *Against Mediocrity: The Humanities in America's High Schools*, edited by C. E. J. Finn, Diane Ravitch, and R. T. Fancher. Holmes and Meier.

Szanton, David L. 2004. *The Politics of Knowledge: Area Studies and the Disciplines*. University of California Press.

Teles, Steven Michael. 2008. *The Rise of the Conservative Legal Movement: The Battle for Control of the Law*. Princeton University Press.

Thelen, Kathleen Ann. 1999. "Historical Institutionalism in Comparative Politics." *Annual Review of Political Science* 2: 369–404.

Thorpe, Francis Newton. 1904. *William Pepper, M.D., LL.D. (1843–1898), Provost of the University of Pennsylvania*. J. B. Lippincott.

Timmer, Peter. 2005. "Agriculture and Pro-Poor Growth: An Asian Perspective." SSRN eLibrary (http://papers.ssrn.com/sol3/papers.cfm?abstract_id=984256).

Tise, Larry E. 1992. *A Book about Children: Christian Children's Fund, 1938–1991*. Hartland Publishing for the Christian Children's Fund.

Tittle, Diana. 1992. *Rebuilding Cleveland: The Cleveland Foundation and Its Evolving Urban Strategy*. Ohio State University Press.

Tobin, Gary A., and Aryeh Weinberg. 2007. *A Study of Jewish Foundations*. Institute for Jewish and Community Research.

Toepler, Stefan. 2010. "Roles of Foundations and Their Impact in the Arts." In *American Foundations*, edited by Helmut K. Anheier and David C. Hammack. Brookings.

Trefil, James S. 2002. *Good Seeing: A Century of Science at the Carnegie Institution of Washington, 1902–2002*. Joseph Henry Press.

Trefil, James, and Robert Hazen. 2001. *The Sciences: An Integrated Approach*. 3rd ed. John Wiley and Sons.

Troyer, Thomas. 1966. "The Treasury Department Report on Private Foundations: A Response to Some Criticisms." *UCLA Law Review* 13, no. 965: 983–85.

———. 2000. "The 1969 Private Foundation Law: Historical Perspective on Its Origins and Underpinnings." *Exempt Organization Tax Review* 27: 52–53.

Tyack, David B. 2003. *Seeking Common Ground: Public Schools in a Diverse Society*. Harvard University Press.

Tyack, David B., and Larry Cuban. 1995. *Tinkering toward Utopia: A Century of Public School Reform*. Harvard University Press.

Underwood, James L., and William Lewis Burke. 2006. *The Dawn of Religious Freedom in South Carolina*. University of South Carolina Press.

Underwood, Kenneth W. 1969. *The Church, the University, and Social Policy*. Wesleyan University Press.

U.S. Congress, Senate Committee on Labor and Public Welfare, Subcommittee on Health. 1973. "Hill-Burton Hospital Survey and Construction Act: History of the Program and Current Problems and Issues." Washington, D.C.

U.S. Department of Education. 2007. *Digest of Educational Statistics 2007*. National Center for Education Statistics (http://nces.ed.gov/programs/digest/d07/tables/dt07_355.asp?referrer=report).

U.S. House of Representatives. 1954. "Hearings before the Special Committee to Investigate Tax-Exempt Foundations and Comparable Organizations." 83 Cong. 2 sess. Washington, D.C.

U.S. Internal Revenue Service, Exempt Organizations Division. 1984. "Litigation by IRC 501(c)(3) Organizations." 1984 EO CPE Text. Washington, D.C. (www.irs.gov/pub/irs-tege/eotopicd84.pdf).

U.S. Office of Management and the Budget. 2009. *A New Era of Responsibility: Renewing America's Promise.* Government Printing Office (www.whitehouse.gov/.../A_New_Era_of_Responsibility2.pdf).

U.S. Senate, Special Committee on Campaign Expenditures. 1945. *Investigation of Presidential, Vice Presidential, and Senatorial Campaign Expenditures in 1944.* Government Printing Office.

Vale, Lawrence J. 2000. *From the Puritans to the Projects: Public Housing and Public Neighbors.* Harvard University Press.

Van Slyck, Abigail A. 1995. *Free to All: Carnegie Libraries and American Culture, 1890–1920.* University of Chicago Press.

VanAntwerpen, Jonathan. 2009. "Moral Globalization and Discursive Struggle: Reconciliation, Transitional Justice, and Cosmopolitan Discourse." In *Globalization, Philanthropy, and Civil Society: Projecting Institutional Logics Abroad*, edited by David C. Hammack and Steven Heydemann. Indiana University Press.

Veyne, Paul. 1990. *Bread and Circuses: Historical Sociology and Political Pluralism.* Penguin.

Vinovskis, Maris A. 1999. *History and Educational Policymaking.* Yale University Press.

———. 2008. *The Birth of Head Start: Preschool Education Policies in the Kennedy and Johnson Administrations.* University of Chicago Press.

Wade, Richard C. 1964. *Slavery in the Cities: The South, 1820–1860.* Oxford University Press.

Walker, George E., Chris M. Golde, Laura Jones, Andrea Conklin Bueschel, and Pat Hutchings. 2008. *The Formation of Scholars: Rethinking Doctoral Education for the Twenty-First Century.* Jossey-Bass.

Walsh, Frank P. 1915. "Perilous Philanthropy." *Independent* 83 (August 23): 262–64.

Walsh, John. 1963. "Foundations: Patman Plugs Away at Theme That Growth, Operations of Tax Exempts Call for Scrutiny." *Science* 142: 370–72.

Walsh, Mary Williams. 1999. "The Charitable Gift Fund Phenomenon." *Los Angeles Times,* reprinted by the Grantsmanship Center (www.tgci.com/.../The percent20Charitable percent20Gift percent20Fund percent20Phenomenon.pdf).

Walters, Pamela Barnhouse, and Emily A. Bowman. 2010. "Foundations and the Making of Public Education in the United States, 1867–1950." In *American Foundations*, edited by Helmut K. Anheier and David C. Hammack. Brookings.

Walton, Andrea, ed. 2005. *Women and Philanthropy in Education.* Indiana University Press.

Wang, Dong. 2007. *Managing God's Higher Learning: U.S.-China Cultural Encounter and Canton Christian College Lingnan University 1888–1952.* Lexington Books.

Wasby, Stephen L. 1995. *Race Relations Litigation in an Age of Complexity.* University of Virginia Press.

Waterman, Thomas Hewett, Frank R Holmes, and Lewis A. Williams Jr. 1905. *Cornell University, a History.* University Publishing Society.

Watts, Susan, ed. 1975. *The College Handbook.* College Entrance Examination Board.

Weaver, R. Kent. 2000. *Ending Welfare as We Know It.* Brookings.

Weaver, Warren, and George Wells Beadle. 1967. *U.S. Philanthropic Foundations: Their History, Structure, Management, and Record.* Harper and Row.

Wechsler, Harold. 1977. *The Qualified Student: A History of Selective College Admission in America*. Wiley.

Weeks, Edward. 1966. *The Lowells and Their Institute*. Atlantic Monthly Press.

Weindling, Paul. 1995. *International Health Organisations and Movements, 1918–1939*. Cambridge University Press.

Wenocur, Stanley, and Michael Reisch. 2001. *From Charity to Enterprise: The Development of American Social Work in a Market Economy*. University of Illinois Press.

Wheatley, Steven C. 1988. *The Politics of Philanthropy: Abraham Flexner and Medical Education*. University of Wisconsin Press.

———. 2010. "The Partnerships of Foundations and Research Universities." In *American Foundations*, edited by Helmut K. Anheier and David C. Hammack. Brookings.

Wheeler, Sessions A. 1985. *Gentleman in the Outdoors: A Portrait of Max C. Fleischmann*. University of Nevada Press.

Whitehead, John S. 1973. *The Separation of College and State: Columbia, Dartmouth, Harvard, and Yale, 1776–1876*. Yale University Press.

Whyte, Anne. 2004. *Human and Institutional Capacity Building: Landscape Analysis of Donor Trends in International Development*. Rockefeller Foundation.

Wichterman, Catherine. 1998. "The Orchestra Forum: A Discussion of Symphony Orchestras in the US." In *Andrew W. Mellon Foundation Annual Report, 1998*. New York (www.mellon.org/news_publications/annual-reports-essays/presidents-essays/the-orchestra-forum-the-orchestra-forum-a-discussion-of-symphony-orchestras-in-the-us).

Wilcox, Clifford. 2006. *Robert Redfield and the Development of American Anthropology*. Lexington Books.

Wilford, Hugh. 2008. *The Mighty Wurlitzer: How the CIA Played America*. Harvard University Press.

Wilhelm, Mark O., Patrick M. Rooney, and Eugene R. Tempel. 2007. "Changes in Religious Giving Reflect Changes in Involvement: Age and Cohort Effects in Religious Giving, Secular Giving, and Attendance." *Journal of the Scientific Study of Religion* 46: 217–32.

Wilson, John K. 1990. "Religion under the State Constitutions, 1776–1800." *Journal of Church and State* 32: 753–74.

Winks, Robin W. 1997. *Laurance S. Rockefeller: Catalyst for Conservation*. Island Press.

Witte, John, Jr. 1991. "Tax Exemption of Church Property: Historical Anomaly or Valid Constitutional Practice?" *Southern California Law Review* 64: 363.

———. 1996. "The Essential Rights and Liberties of Religion in the American Constitutional Experiment." *Notre Dame Law Review* 71: 371.

———. 2006. "Facts and Fictions about the History of Separation of Church and State." *Journal of Church and State* 48: 15.

Wolpert, Julian. 2006. "Redistributional Effects of America's Private Foundations." In *The Legitimacy of Philanthropic Foundations: United States and European Perspectives*, edited by Kenneth Prewitt and others. Russell Sage Foundation.

Woolverton, John Frederick. 1984. *Colonial Anglicanism in North America*. Wayne State University Press.

Wormser, René Albert. 1958. *Foundations, Their Power and Influence.* Devin-Adair.

Wosh, Peter J. 1994. *Spreading the Word: The Bible Business in Nineteenth-Century America.* Cornell University Press.

Wren, Daniel A. 1983. "American Business Philanthropy and Higher Education in the Nineteenth Century." *Business History Review* 57: 321–46.

Wright, Conrad Edick. 1993. *The Transformation of Charity in Postrevolutionary New England.* Northeastern University Press.

Wright, Karen. 2001. "Generosity vs. Altruism: Philanthropy and Charity in the United States and United Kingdom." *Voluntas* 12: 399–416.

Wuthnow, Robert, and D. Michael Lindsay. 2010. "The Role of Foundations in American Religion." In *American Foundations*, edited by Helmut K. Anheier and David C. Hammack. Brookings.

Wyllie, Irvin G. 1959. "The Search for an American Law of Charity, 1776–1844." *Mississippi Valley Historical Review* 46: 203–21.

Yarmolinksy, Adam. 1975. "Philanthropic Activity in International Affairs." In *Research Papers Sponsored by the Commission on Private Philanthropy and Public Needs.* Vol. 2. U.S. Department of Treasury, 1977.

Yarmolinksy, Adam, and Marion R. Fremont-Smith. 1976. "Preserving the Private Voluntary Sector: A Proposal for a Public Advisory Commission on Philanthropy." *Research Papers Sponsored by The Commission on Private Philanthropy and Public Needs.* Vol. 5. U.S. Department of Treasury, 1977.

Yenawine, Bruce. 2010. *Benjamin Franklin and the Invention of Microfinance.* Ashgate.

Ylvisaker, Paul N. 2008. "The Spirit of Philanthropy and the Soul of Those Who Manage It." In *Giving Well, Doing Good: Readings for Thoughtful Philanthropists*, edited by Amy A. Kass. Indiana University Press.

Yunus, Muhammad. 2010. *Building Social Business: The New Kind of Capitalism That Serves Humanity's Most Pressing Needs.* PublicAffairs.

Zelizer, Julian E. 2004. *The American Congress: The Building of Democracy.* Houghton Mifflin Harcourt.

———. 2010. *The Presidency of George W. Bush: A First Historical Assessment.* Princeton University Press.

Zunz, Olivier. 2011. *Philanthropy in America: A History.* Princeton University Press.

Index of Foundation Names

Index of Subjects